Proportionality

Proportionality

A Guiding Principle in Public Health Law, Ethics, and Policy

Edited by

NIKOLA BILLER-ANDORNO
JULIAN W. MÄRZ
CORINE MOUTON-DOREY
STÉPHANIE DAGRON

OXFORD
UNIVERSITY PRESS

OXFORD
UNIVERSITY PRESS

Oxford University Press is a department of the University of Oxford.
It furthers the University's objective of excellence in research, scholarship,
and education by publishing worldwide. Oxford is a registered trade mark of
Oxford University Press in the UK and in certain other countries.

Published in the United States of America by Oxford University Press
198 Madison Avenue, New York, NY 10016, United States of America.

CIP data is on file at the Library of Congress.

ISBN 9780197759349

DOI: 10.1093/9780197759370.001.0001

The manufacturer's authorized representative in the EU for product safety is
Oxford University Press España S.A. of Parque Empresarial San Fernando de Henares,
Avenida de Castilla, 2 – 28830 Madrid (www.oup.es/en or product.safety@oup.com).
OUP España S.A. also acts as importer into Spain of products made by the manufacturer.

Foreword

Jerome Amir Singh

As someone who works deeply at the global level of health, ethics, law, and governance, I am struck by what a prescient publication this book has turned out to be. The World Health Organization (WHO) declares a Public Health Emergency of International Concern (PHEIC) for "an extraordinary event which is determined to constitute a public health risk to other States through the international spread of disease and to potentially require a coordinated international response." Such a designation denotes a situation that "carries implications for public health beyond the affected state's national border" and requires "immediate international action." In recent years, WHO has declared a PHEIC for the 2018–2020 Kivu Ebola epidemic, the 2020–2023 COVID-19 pandemic, and the 2022–2023 and 2024 mpox outbreaks.

As I pen this foreword, other major public health threats have appeared on the global radar: A Marburg virus outbreak in Rwanda has claimed more than a dozen lives, and sporadic but alarming strains of avian flu (H5N1 and H5N2) have been detected in different parts of the world. Meanwhile, SARS-CoV-2, the causative agent of the COVID-19 pandemic, has continued to evolve and claim lives. Our response to such emerging and resurgent public health threats will determine not just their trajectories but their impact on society, too. What type of countermeasures ought we to adopt against novel, emerging, or resurgent public health threats? What type of resources ought we to dedicate to such threats? What constitutes adequate justificatory countermeasures? How should society determine whether the response of authorities is proportionate to the threat posed? To answer such questions, the benefit of hindsight allows us to critically appraise the lessons learned from the COVID-19 pandemic, which had an unprecedented disruptive impact on the world.

Governments at all levels, globally, adopted an extraordinarily heterogeneous approach to the COVID-19 pandemic—including to the perceived severity of the crisis, surveillance, the need for mask wearing, social distancing, mobility restrictions, home and institutional isolation, monitoring, contact tracing, school attendance, workplace attendance, and vaccination—and most of their decisions and challenges boiled down to the proportionality of the measure in question. Looming public health threats on the horizon make *Proportionality:*

A Guiding Principle in Public Health Law, Ethics and Policy a prescient publication. The contributors to this comprehensive body of work count among the leading scholars and practitioners globally on public health and the principle of proportionality. Armed with diverse geographic settings and illustrative real-world examples, this impressive multidisciplinary body of work offers a thorough, accessible, and engaging overview of how the principle of proportionality shaped, or failed to shape, decision-making processes and measures to counter the COVID-19 pandemic in settings across the globe. In so doing, this work serves as an invaluable resource for the management of future public health threats. More specifically, this solid body of work will undoubtedly improve our understanding of how the principle of proportionality can, and should, inform our response to future public health threats. In so doing, this work will help shape the ongoing evolution of international and local norms on the principle of proportionality and enhance our resilience to future public health threats.

Preface

Nikola Biller-Andorno, Julian W. März, Corine Mouton-Dorey, and Stéphanie Dagron

> The important thing is not to stop questioning. Curiosity has its own reason for existing.
>
> Albert Einstein

Democratic societies are guided by the principles of liberty and equality while aiming to protect and promote the welfare of their citizens. As the first COVID-19 response measures were introduced across Europe, we began to reflect on how effective pandemic management could be reconciled with upholding fundamental human rights, including the right to the enjoyment of the highest attainable standard of health. This reflection led us to explore pandemic-related policies in various countries, their legitimacy, and the public's acceptance of them. From this exploration, a central research question emerged that guided our work: *What defines a proportionate response to a public health crisis such as a pandemic?*

Now, over five years after the first reported COVID-19 cases, we are both humbled and proud to present this book, which provides an unprecedented international and interdisciplinary perspective on proportionality as a guiding principle in public health law, ethics, and policy. Reflecting on the lessons of the COVID-19 pandemic, we intend this book to offer a thorough and balanced analysis that can provide public health responses to future crises. It emphasizes the urgent need to protect vulnerable and underserved populations while critically assessing the actions taken by policymakers and healthcare systems around the globe.

The chapters in this book tackle the intricate challenge of applying proportionality in public health through an analysis of ethical, legal, and social implications in a variety of contexts. Each chapter was rigorously reviewed by two independent experts, whose insightful critiques and constructive feedback were crucial to shaping the final outcome of this work. In particular, we would like to thank Fayez Abdulrazeq, Roberto Andorno, Richmond Aryeetey, Steffen Augsberg, Yaniv Benamou, Michael Birnhack, Iris Canor, Sara Meg Davis, Lena Gloeckler, Sophie Gloeckler, Joelle Grogan, Dirk Hanschel, Tsung-Ling Lee, Ken Laidlaw, Valerie Luyckx, Els Maeckelberghe, Stephen Molldrem, Maria del Rocio Franch, Alicia Navarro de Souza, Inge van Nistelrooij, Rouven Porz, Bernhard Rütsche, Owen Schaefer, Jana Sedlakova, Emilio J. Sanz, José Maria Serna de la Garza, Jan Schwarz, Sharifa Sekalala, Lorraine Smith, Vitalii Stetsyk, Paulina Tindana, Pedro A. Villarreal, and Nesa Zimmermann for their contributions.

Our sincere thanks go to Leticia Andorno for her invaluable work on formal editing and to Sophie Gloeckler and April Ball for their careful language editing. Their contributions have been crucial in shaping this manuscript.

This project owes much to the workshop and symposium organized by Tania Manríquez Roa and Jennifer Hasselgard-Rowe, where many key ideas first emerged. We extend our sincere thanks to them.

We also wish to acknowledge Emily Benitez, Sarah Humphreville, and Andrea Smith of Oxford University Press as well as Abishayareddy Vijaybabu and her colleagues, for their guidance and support throughout this process.

We gratefully acknowledge the financial support from the Universities of Geneva and Zurich, provided through the UNIGE-UZH Joint Funding for Collaboration in Research and Teaching under the Call 2021—"Shaping Resilient and Responsive Societies and Ecosystems in View of Global Crises." This funding was essential in enabling the research and collaboration that form the foundation of this book.

Finally, we thank all those who shared their knowledge, time, and encouragement. This book is a result of collective effort, and we are profoundly grateful for all the contributions that have made it possible.

Contents

List of Editors xii
List of Contributors xiv

Introduction 1
Nikola Biller-Andorno, Julian W. März, Corine Mouton-Dorey, and Stéphanie Dagron

1. Proportionality and Uncertainty in Physical Distancing Policies in US States 10
Justin Bernstein, Athmeya Jayaram, Brian Hutler, Jeff Jones, Travis Rieder, and Anne Barnhill

2. Proportionality and Resource Allocation in a Pandemic: The Example of Chile 20
Rodrigo López Barreda and Luca Valera

3. Proportionality in Public Health Ethics, Fear, and State of Exception: A Critical Narrative Approach 28
Silvia Camporesi

4. Perceptions of Proportionality: An Empirical Study of Swiss Residents' Moral Considerations about COVID-19 Containment Measures 44
Corine Mouton-Dorey, Bettina Schwind, Giovanni Spitale, Kristen Jafflin, and Nikola Biller-Andorno

5. Proportionality and the Need for Evidence: A Case Study of Outdoor Public Health Interventions for Respiratory Viruses in Australia 79
Euzebiusz Jamrozik

6. Inaction and the Proportionality Principle: A Review of the Management of the COVID-19 Pandemic in Mexico 88
Felicitas Holzer, Ivette María Ortiz Alcántara, Tobias Eichinger, Nikola Biller-Andorno, and Julian W. März

7. Public Health Proportionality for Sexual and Gender Minority Youth 107
Stewart Adelson, Alice Miller, Daniel Newton, and Graeme Reid

8. Responding Proportionately to the COVID-19 Pandemic in UK Long-Stay Inpatient Pediatric Wards 122
Heather Draper, Caroline Redhead, Anna Chiumento, Sara Fovargue, and Lucy Frith

9. Proportionality in Public Health Law: A Case Study of Singapore's Travel Restrictions for Migrant Healthcare Workers 142
Hui Yun Chan

10. COVID-19 Restrictions in Long-Term Care Facilities in the United States: Unintended Consequences and Possible Lessons 155
Jakub P. Hlávka, Yimin Ge, Shengjia Xu, and Alexander M. Capron

11. Proportionality Behind Locked Doors: Nursing Homes, Fundamental Rights, and Visit Restrictions During the Coronavirus Pandemic 184
Settimio Monteverde

12. Mobile Vaccination Teams in Long-Term Care Homes for the Elderly in Germany During the COVID-19 Pandemic 205
Jonathan Hunger and Eva Kuhn

13. Proportionality of the COVID-19 Measures: The European Court of Human Rights' Approach 222
Helen Keller and Viktoriya Gurash

14. Proportionality and the Swiss Courts 237
Helen Keller and Violetta Sefkow-Werner

15. The Right to Privacy, Contact Tracing, and Public Health During the COVID-19 Pandemic: The Israeli Case 255
Maya Peled-Raz, Shelly Kamin-Friedman, and Nadav Davidovitch

16. The Principle of Proportionality and the Digitalization of Epidemic Countermeasures in Hong Kong Special Administrative Regions 267
Calvin Wai-Loon Ho

17. Proportionality, Epidemiological Research, and Data Protection in a Pandemic 285
Fruzsina Molnár-Gábor

18. (Dis)proportionate Abortion Care Regulation and the COVID-19 Pandemic in Great Britain 300
Jordan A. Parsons and Elizabeth Chloe Romanis

19. A Proportional Response?: Abortion Exceptionalism, Telemedicine, and the COVID-19 Pandemic in Great Britain 320
Lucía Berro Pizzarossa and Rishita Nandagiri

Index 336

List of Editors

Nikola Biller-Andorno directs the Institute for Biomedical Ethics and History of Medicine at the University of Zurich (Switzerland). Having trained as a physician and philosopher, she specializes in biomedical ethics and has held positions at University of Göttingen (DE), the WHO, and the Charité in Berlin. Between 2012 and 2014, she was a Visiting Professor and Commonwealth Fund Harkness Fellow at Harvard, exploring ethical issues at the interface of healthcare management and economics; from 2016 to 2020, she held a fellowship at the Collegium Helveticum, a Swiss Institute of Advanced Studies, that focused on the digital transformation of medicine. As a Past-President of the International Association of Bioethics and as Chair of the WHO Collaborating Centre Network for Bioethics, she has a keen interest in the global dimension of the key bioethical challenges our societies face.

Julian W. März is a physician, lawyer, and bioethicist currently working as a research fellow at the Institute of Biomedical Ethics and History of Medicine at the Medical Faculty of the University of Zurich. In addition, he is currently leading a WHO curriculum development project on Integrating Ethics and Governance into the Design of Artificial Intelligence Technologies for Health. He is also acting as lead scientific adviser for the review and reform process of the Federal Law on the Genetic Testing of Humans by the Swiss federal government. Before joining the University of Zurich, he worked for the Division of Health Economics at the German Cancer Research Center in Heidelberg for three years, where he wrote his doctoral thesis in medicine. In parallel, he has worked as a research affiliate in pharmaceutical law for the University of Cambridge's Centre for Law, Medicine, and Life Sciences and as a lecturer in public health law at Sciences Po Paris.

Corine Mouton-Dorey is a physician and ethicist. After working as a Cardiology Specialist and Researcher on myocardial metabolism in France (MD, postgraduate diploma in cardiology, DEA in cellular and molecular biology), Corine pursued research in the pharmaceutical industry in Paris, Frankfurt, and London (MBA at London Business School). She returned to the academic world first at the Swiss Federal Institute of Technology in Zurich (Institute of Clinical Nutrition), then at the University of Neuchâtel (LLM in health law) and at the University of Zurich (UZH) at the Institute of Biomedical Ethics and History of Medicine (IBME), where she obtained her doctorate in biomedical ethics and law, specifically in the development of a new ethical framework for managing patient data. She coordinated a multidisciplinary approach to digital health as part of UZH's Digital Society Initiative. She is an affiliated researcher at IBME. Her interests include qualitative research, social ethics, and the application of care ethics to ecology.

Stéphanie Dagron is Professor of Law at the University of Geneva with a special expertise in international social security law and global health law. She has a double appointment at the Faculty of Law and the Faculty of Medicine and is affiliated with the Global Studies Institute. Since 2013, Stéphanie has practiced international law in her work as a consultant for the WHO in the fields of tuberculosis, human rights, research ethics, and infectious diseases.

List of Contributors

Stewart L. Adelson , MD, is Clinical Associate Professor at Weill Cornell Medical College and an Adjunct Associate Clinical Professor at Columbia Vagelos College of Physicians and Surgeons. He received his undergraduate degree from Yale College and medical degree from New York University; completed residency and fellowship trainings in adult, child, and adolescent psychiatry at Cornell University's medical school and in public psychiatry at Columbia University's medical school; and is a graduate of the Harvard Medical School Global Clinical Research Scholars Training Program. He is also a Senior Visiting Fellow and the Founding Director of the Youth Equity Science / YES Project of Yale Public Health and Law Schools, a collaboration of youth mental health researchers and legal scholars to support policy and law that support LGBTQ youth mental health.

Anne Barnhill is Associate Research Professor at the Berman Institute of Bioethics at Johns Hopkins University. She has a PhD in philosophy from New York University and is a philosopher and bioethicist whose research centers on public health ethics and food ethics.

Justin Bernstein is an Assistant Professor of Philosophy at The University of Virginia. He holds a PhD in philosophy from the University of Pennsylvania. Bernstein's research focuses primarily on political philosophy and public health ethics, especially the ethics and politics of infectious disease.

Lucía Berro Pizzarossa is a British Academy International Fellow at the University of Birmingham and an affiliated researcher of the Global Health and Rights Project at the Petrie-Flom Center for Health Law Policy, Biotechnology, and Bioethics at Harvard Law School. Berro Pizzarossa was a Visiting Fellow at the London School of Economics and held postdoctoral positions at the O'Neill Institute for National and Global Health Law at the University of Georgetown and the Faculty of Law at the University of Groningen. She holds a PhD in international law from the University of Groningen, an MJur from the University of Oxford, and an LLB from the Universidad de la República in Uruguay. She has consulted for UNICEF, the WHO, the International Commission of Jurists, and others. Her academic work has been published in renowned peer-reviewed journals such *as Reproductive Health Matters, Harvard Health and Human Rights, and BMC International Health and Human Rights.*

Silvia Camporesi is a bioethicist with a long-standing interest in technologies and health and interdisciplinary training in biotechnology and philosophy of medicine. She is Professor of bioethics and sports integrity and ethics in the Centre for Biomedical Ethics and Law, Department of Public Health and Primary Care at KU Leuven University (Belgium). She was formerly a Reader in bioethics and society in the Department of Global Health and Social Medicine at King's College London. In addition to her academic research outputs, Silvia writes for a variety of media outlets, including AEON, the International Public Policy Observatory, and the Conversation.

Alexander Capron is University Professor Emeritus, Scott H. Bice Chair Emeritus in healthcare law, policy, and ethics at the Gould School of Law, Professor Emeritus of law and medicine at the Keck School of Medicine, and Founding Codirector of the Pacific Center for Health Policy and Ethics at the University of Southern California. In addition to writing and editing a dozen books and more than three hundred scholarly articles and chapters, Professor Alexander has made significant contributions to public policy in fields such as the ethics of research with human beings, organ transplantation, death and dying, genetic research and therapies, and public health. He is an elected member of both the National Academy of Medicine and of the American Law Institute and a Fellow of the American Association for the Advancement of Science.

Hui Yun Chan is a law scholar with research interests in health law, technology, and bioethics. She holds a PhD from the Law Faculty at the University of Otago. She has taught in universities in the United Kingdom and has published on the legal and ethical aspects of issues related to COVID-19 and the regulation of health technologies. Her current work focuses on the legal and ethical aspects of cross-border data transfer under the Future Health Technology research program on trustworthy data governance at the Centre for Biomedical Ethics in the Yong Loo Lin School of Medicine at the National University of Singapore and Singapore–ETH Centre.

Anna Chiumento is a Lecturer and Co–Program Director for the Global Mental Health and Society MSc Program at the School of Social and Political Sciences at the University of Edinburgh. Her research, which uses qualitative social science and empirical ethics methods, sits at the interface of global mental health, research ethics, and bioethics. She has a particular interest in the normative dimensions of research and practice in the field of global mental health and is a member of the Steering Committee of the Global Forum on Bioethics in Research.

Nadav Davidovitch is an Epidemiologist and Public Health Physician and Head of Ben-Gurion University of the Negev's School of Public Health. He is the Chair of the Association of Public Health Physicians in Israel and a member of various committees of the Israeli Ministry of Health. During the COVID-19 pandemic, he served as the chair of the cabinet of the Magen Israel program (the national program for fighting the coronavirus).

Heather Draper is Professor of Bioethics in Warwick Medical School at the University of Warwick (United Kingdom), where she coordinates, designs, delivers, and assesses values, law, and ethics teaching for medical students and clinical ethics training for healthcare practitioners. She has published widely in bioethics and was a member of an Arts and Humanities Research Council (AHRC)/ UK Research and Innovation (UKRI)–funded NHS Reset Ethics project research team. She has degrees in theology and philosophy and a doctorate in bioethics awarded by the University of Manchester.

Tobias Eichinger works as Senior Teaching and Research Assistant at the Institute of Biomedical Ethics and History of Medicine at the University of Zurich, where he is coordinating the institute's teaching program and PhD program in biomedical ethics. Tobias has degrees in philosophy and film studies from the University of Freiburg and the Free University of Berlin. His research interests focus on ethical issues regarding the identity of medicine, regarding enhancement and medicalization, on principles of teaching and training medical ethics, and on issues of the relationship of film and medicine.

Sara Fovargue is a Professor of Law at the University of Sheffield in England. She is one of the Editors-in-Chief of the *Medical Law Review* and has a law degree from the University of Leicester and a PhD from the University of Manchester. She is a nonpracticing barrister. She has published widely on matters relating to health law and ethics. Her interests include the regulation of emerging biotechnologies, organ transplantation and reproduction, and decision-making for the vulnerable. Currently, she is a Coinvestigator on a Wellcome-funded project, the Future of Human Reproduction.

Lucy Frith is Reader in bioethics and social science in the Centre for Social Ethics and Policy in the Department of Law at the University of Manchester. Her research focuses on the social and ethical aspects of improving healthcare practice and policy, with a particular interest in empirical ethics and public involvement. She has carried out research on pregnancy and childbirth, research ethics (clinical trials and public involvement and cross-cultural issues in consent), the organization and funding of healthcare provision (priority setting), and the use of evidence in practice and policy and has a long-standing interest in the social and ethical aspects of reproductive technologies. She has held visiting professorships at the Centre for Medical Ethics and Law at the University of Hong Kong and Charles University (Prague). An overview of her research can be found at https://www.researchgate.net/profile/Lucy-Frith.

Yimin Ge is a Postdoctoral Fellow at the Johns Hopkins Bloomberg School of Public Health, with affiliations at the Hopkins Business of Health Initiative and the Center for Mental Health and Addiction Policy. Her research spans health economics and health policy, focusing on how policies and health care systems shape access to care, quality, and health outcomes. She earned her PhD in Public Policy and Management from the University of Southern California, an MA in Analytical Political Economy from Duke University, and a BS in Actuarial Science and Statistics from the University of Illinois Urbana-Champaign.

Viktoriya Gurash is a postdoctoral researcher at the University of Zurich. She holds an LLM in public international law from Leiden University and a PhD from Ivan Franko National University of Lviv and is a former Registry Lawyer at the European Court of Human Rights.

Jakub Hlávka is the Director of the Health Economics, Policy, and Innovation Institute at Masaryk University in the Czech Republic and a Clinical Associate Professor (Adjunct) of Population and Public Health Sciences at the University of Southern California (USC). He is also a Scholar at the Leonard D. Schaeffer Center for Health Policy and Economics at USC. His academic research focuses on the economics of aging, Alzheimer's disease, and healthcare financing, and he has advised policymakers in the United States and Europe, including the President of the Czech Republic, U.S. Centers for Disease Control and Prevention, NASA, the U.S. Department of Defense, and the U.S. Department of Health and Human Services. He has also contributed to research supported by the National Academies of Sciences, Engineering, and Medicine. Hlávka holds a PhD in public policy analysis from the Pardee RAND Graduate School, a master's degree in international affairs from Georgetown University, and a bachelor's degree from the University of Economics in Prague.

Calvin Wai-Loon Ho (JSD Cornell; PCLT, MIT; FRSPH) is Associate Professor with the Faculty of Law at Monash University in Melbourne (Australia), Research Fellow of the Centre for Medical Ethics and Law at the University of Hong Kong (China), and Fellow of PHG Foundation at the University of Cambridge (United Kingdom). His research is on global health law and ethics and the governance of health and biomedical technologies with a focus on health technologies based on artificial intelligence and data analytics. He is Co-Chair of the Expert Group on the Ethics of Social Listening and Infodemic Management and a Member of the COVID-19 Ethics and Governance Working Group of the WHO. Calvin is also an Ethics Board Member of Médecins Sans Frontières (Doctors Without Borders), and he was the Co-Chair of the Accountability Work Group of the Regulation and Ethics Work Stream of the Global Alliance for Genomics and Health.

Felicitas Holzer holds a master's degree in history and philosophy of science from the University of Cambridge and a doctorate in political philosophy with a focus on global justice from Sorbonne University. Trained as a philosopher (BA, MPhil, PhD), economist (BSc), and bioethicist (MPhil), her research interests include topics at the intersection of bioethics, socioeconomic justice, political philosophy, and philosophy of science. Felicitas holds several awards and scholarships from the German Academic Exchange Service, the National Research Council of Argentina, the Brocher Foundation (Switzerland), and the MTZ Foundation (Germany). She is affiliated with the program of bioethics at *Facultad Latinoamericana de Ciencias Sociales* (FLACSO) Argentina, a WHO Collaborating Centre, and a Member of the editorial board of the journal *Development World Bioethics.* She also gained interdisciplinary and international experience during research and work stays abroad at the Hastings Center and the Yale Interdisciplinary Center for Bioethics, as an Intern at the WHO (Switzerland), and as a member of the UK-Latin American Network of Political Philosophy (Argentina and Mexico). She recently worked as a policy assistant at the Directorate-General for International Partnerships (DG INTPA) of the European Commission in Brussels (Belgium).

Jonathan Hunger studied human medicine in Magdeburg, Paris, and Haifa and received an MSc in public health with focus on health policy and innovation management from Maastricht University. He works as a medical doctor in the field of emergency medicine and specializes in neurology and internal medicine. His current research interests include pain in neurological disorders, public health, and biomedical ethics and healthcare innovation.

Brian Hutler is an Assistant Professor of philosophy at Temple University in Philadelphia. He holds a JD and PhD from the Law and Philosophy Joint Degree Program at the

University of California, Los Angeles. Brian works on topics related to law, government, human rights, public health, and technology.

Kristen Jafflin has a PhD in sociology from the University of California, Berkeley. She has been working in Switzerland for over a decade and currently works as a Senior Scientific Collaborator at the Swiss Tropical and Public Health Institute. Her research focuses on public health, particularly regarding public health promotion, maternal and infant health, vaccination, and vaccine hesitancy. Her research uses mixed methods, combining quantitative approaches such as survey and qualitative approaches, including interviews, documentary analysis, and qualitative surveys.

Euzebiusz (Zeb) Jamrozik is an Internal Medicine Physician and Bioethicist focusing on infectious diseases, with previous training in philosophy and epidemiology. Euzebiusz is Coeditor-In-Chief of *Monash Bioethics Review* and Coeditor of the Public Health Ethics Analysis book series and has coauthored several WHO guidance documents. He is currently a Fellow at the Ethox Centre and Pandemic Sciences Institute at the University of Oxford and Honorary Clinical Associate Professor at the University of Melbourne.

Athmeya Jayaram is a Research Scholar at the Hastings Center in Garrison (New York). He holds a PhD in political theory from the University of California, Berkeley, and an MA in bioethics from New York University. Athmeya's research focuses on the intersection of political philosophy and technology ethics, particularly on the justification of decisions to design and deploy emerging technologies.

Jeff Jones is a research assistant at the Johns Hopkins Berman Institute of Bioethics and a DPhil student at the University of Oxford. He holds a master's in bioethics from Johns Hopkins University. Jeff's work focuses on public health ethics, distributive justice, moral disagreement, and public input in health policymaking.

Shelly Kamin-Friedman (LLB, MHA, PhD) is a Specialist in health law and public health law. Her research focuses on the ethical and legal aspects of public health policy and curative medicine. She is a Research Fellow at Zulat Institute for Equality and Human Rights and works to promote health rights via policy papers, media, and Knesset Committee meetings.

Helen Keller is a professor of law at the University of Zurich with a special expertise in human rights law, international climate and environmental law, and constitutional law. From 2011 until 2020, she served as a Judge at the European Court of Human Rights. From 2008 to 2011, she was a Member of the UN Human Rights Committee. Since December 2020, she has served as a Judge at the Constitutional Court of Bosnia-Herzegovina. She holds an honorary doctorate from the University of Fribourg recognizing her contributions to bridging doctrine and practice, and she holds the title of Dr. honoris causa from the University of Geneva. Her work has earned numerous accolades, such as a nomination in the 75 Women in 75 Years of Council of Europe History project and the Robert Kennedy Prize in 2024, underscoring her global impact in advancing justice and human rights.

Eva Kuhn is affiliated with the Clinic for Psychiatry and Psychotherapy at Charité – Universitätsmedizin Berlin. She serves as a Clinical Ethicist at the University Hospital Bonn, and acts as Ethics Advisor for various research projects. She holds degrees in Catholic Theology (Mag.Theol.) and Medical Law (LL.M.).

Rodrigo López Barreda is an Anesthetist from Chile, where he studied medicine at the Pontificia Universidad Católica de Chile. He holds a PhD in biomedical ethics and law from the University of Zurich (Switzerland), a master's degree in public health from the London School of Hygiene and Tropical Medicine (United Kingdom), and is currently pursuing a PhD in innovation, economics, governance and sustainable development at United Nations University–Maastricht Economic and Social Research Institute on Innovation and Technology (the Netherlands). He is an adviser to a number of NGOs working on global and public health issues.

Alice M. Miller , JD, is the Codirector of the Global Health Justice Partnership of Yale Law and Public Health Schools, Professor in the Practice at the Yale School of Public Health, Affiliated Faculty at the Yale Jackson School for Global Affairs, and Associate Professor (Adjunct) at the Yale Law School. She has taught at Yale, the University of California, Berkeley, and Columbia University on the theory and practice of gender, sexuality, and health rights in the context of criminal, human rights, and humanitarian law. Her three decades of advocacy and training experience include collaborating with local, national, and international NGOs in the United States and globally and with the WHO, the OHCHR, and other intergovernmental agencies. She coedited *Beyond Virtue and Vice: Rethinking Human Rights and Criminal Law* (University of Pennsylvania Press 2019).

Fruzsina Molnár-Gábor is Professor of international medical and health law as well as data protection law at the University of Heidelberg. She holds a doctorate in law from the University of Heidelberg and was Research Group Leader at the Heidelberg Academy of Sciences and Humanities. She is a Member of the European Group on Ethics in Science and New Technologies. She has been awarded the Heinz Maier-Leibnitz Prize (2020). She is deputy judge at the Constitutional Court of the State Baden-Württemberg.

Settimio Monteverde holds degrees in theology, applied ethics, and medical education from different Swiss universities and a doctorate in biomedical ethics with a focus on nursing ethics from the University of Zurich. Trained as a nurse, nurse anesthetist, clinical ethicist, and nurse educator, his research interests cover the teaching of ethics in undergraduate and postgraduate curricula, foundations and concepts in nursing ethics, clinical ethics consultation, and the ethics of assisted dying. He works as a Clinical Ethicist at the University Hospital of Zurich and the Institute of Biomedical Ethics and History of Medicine at the University of Zurich, and as a Lecturer (Prof. FH) in the Department of Nursing at the Bern University of Applied Sciences. He is Associate Editor of *Nursing Ethics*.

Rishita Nandagiri is a lecturer in global health and social medicine and Deputy Program Director (taught postgraduate program) in the Department of Global Health and

Social Medicine at King's College London (KCL). Prior to joining KCL, she held post-doctoral positions at the London School of Economics and Political Science (LSE). In 2020–2021, she was an Economic and Social Research Council (ESRC)-funded Postdoctoral Fellow at LSE's Department of Methodology. She currently represents KCL in the ARUA–The Guild's "Gender, Health and Sexualities" Cluster of Excellence. Rishita has previously worked with several feminist collectives and advocacy groups and has consulted for multilateral organizations, including the WHO and UNFPA. Rishita serves on the International Union for the Scientific Study of Population's Scientific Panel on Abortion Research and is a Visiting Fellow, Department of International Development, London School of Economics and Political Science.

Daniel Newton is a lawyer, currently working as a StaX Attorney with Mobilization for Justice. He was previously the Gender and Sexuality Fellow at the Global Health Justice Partnership (GHJP) of Yale Law and Public Health Schools, where he cosupervised student projects for the GHJP Health Justice Practicum and worked on projects on LGBTQ youth mental health, sex workers' rights, and synergies among queer, LGBTQ, and women's rights advocates across borders and in intergovernmental fora. Daniel has also worked on children's rights litigation, forensic investigations and war crimes accountability, human rights-based education for community-led development, and community-based mental and sexual health services for LGBTQ people. He holds a Master of Laws from Columbia Law School and a Bachelor of Laws and a Bachelor of Arts from the University of Western Australia.

Ivette María Ortiz Alcántara is a Physician from the Faculty of Medicine at the National Autonomous University of Mexico, with two medical specializations: pharmaceutical medicine and anesthesiology. She also holds a master's degree in bioethics. Currently, she is pursuing a PhD at the Institute of Biomedical Ethics and History of Medicine at the University of Zurich, supported by the Swiss Government Excellence Scholarships. Her dissertation focuses on the allocation of healthcare resources during emergencies. Before beginning her PhD, Ortiz Alcántara worked as a medical specialist at the Federal Commission for the Protection Against Health Risks. She later served as Deputy Director of Research Ethics Committees at the National Bioethics Commission of the Mexican Ministry of Health, where she coordinated the national registry of these committees. In addition to her academic and administrative roles, Ortiz Alcántara has practiced as an anesthesiologist in various hospitals across Mexico City and the state of Guerrero. She is also a member of the Mexican College of Anesthesiologists.

Jordan A. Parsons is Associate Professor in Health Law at Royal Holloway University of London (United Kingdom) and Honorary Senior Research Associate at the University of Bristol Medical School (United Kingdom). He has also held various visiting posts internationally, most recently at the Institute of Biomedical Ethics and History of Medicine at the University of Zurich (Switzerland). Jordan's training and expertise cuts across bioethics, healthcare law, and health policy, and his work has a particular focus on practical application. His research interests span reproductive healthcare, human tissue regulation, mental capacity, and more, including both normative and empirical approaches.

Maya Peled Raz (LLB, MPH, PhD) is a Member of the Israeli National Health Council. She is an associate professor of law and ethics and Head of the Division of Bioethics and Public Health in the School of Public Health at the University of Haifa. She is the Chair of the University of Haifa Research Ethics Review Board and serves as a Clinical Ethicist and the Chair of the Ethics Committee at Bnei Zion Medical Center in Haifa.

Caroline Redhead is a Research Fellow in the Centre for Social Ethics and Policy in the Department of Law at the University of Manchester and a nonpracticing Solicitor qualified in England, Wales, in Hong Kong. She has a degree in Chinese Studies from Durham University (with periods of study at Renmin University in Beijing and Taiwan Normal University in Taipei), an LLM (child law) from Northumbria University, and a PhD (palliative care and mental capacity) from Lancaster University. Her research lies broadly in the dynamic interplay among law, (bio)ethics, and social change.

Graeme Reid is the UN Independent Expert on Protection against violence and discrimination based on sexual orientation and gender identity. He is a Research Scholar and Lecturer at the Yale Jackson School of Global Affairs and an Extraordinary Lecturer at the Center for Human Rights at the University of Pretoria. An anthropologist from South Africa, Graeme has conducted research, taught, and published extensively on gender, sexuality, LGBT issues, and HIV/AIDS. His published monographs are *How to be a 'Real Gay': Gay Identities in Small-Town South Africa* (2013) and *Above the Skyline: Reverend Tsietsi Thandekiso and the Founding of an African Gay Church* (2010). Previously Reid was Director of the LGBT Rights Program at Human Rights Watch. He has taught as a Lecturer in Women's Gender and Sexuality Studies department and the Department of Anthropology at Yale University and at the School of International Public Affairs at Columbia University. Reid is the Founding Director of the Gay and Lesbian Archives of South Africa and has previously worked as a researcher at the Wits Institute for Social and Economic Research. Reid attended the University of Witwatersrand, where he received his bachelor's degree in literature and master's degree in anthropology. He also holds a PhD from the University of Amsterdam.

Travis N. Rieder is an Associate Research Professor and Director of Education Initiatives at the Johns Hopkins Berman Institute of Bioethics. He holds a PhD in philosophy from Georgetown University and is the author of two books: *Catastrophe Ethics: How to Choose Well in a World of Tough Choices* (Dutton 2024) and *In Pain: A Bioethicist's Personal Struggle with Opioids* (HarperCollins 2019).

Elizabeth Chloe Romanis is an Associate Professor in biolaw at the University of Durham (United Kingdom). She is also an Adjunct Researcher with the University Research Priority Program (URPP) Human Reproduction Reloaded group at the University of Zurich. In 2022–2023 she was a fellow in residence at Harvard University's Edmon and Lily Safra Center for Ethics and the Petrie-Flom Center for Biotechnology, Bioethics, and Health Law and Policy at Harvard Law School. She has degrees in law and healthcare ethics and a PhD in bioethics and medical jurisprudence from the University of Manchester. Chloe specializes in health law and bioethics with a special interest in reproduction and the body (abortion, gestation, pregnancy, birth, and reproductive technologies).

Bettina Schwind holds a PhD in public health from the University of Basel, Switzerland. She has spent the last ten years researching the Swiss health and social care system from the perspective of lay people, patients, and health professionals with a special focus on diversity and equity, including (feminist) care ethics. Her focus is on qualitative and participatory research methods, including citizen science approaches. She is a Lecturer on health social science methods in various academic institutions and supervises master's and postgraduate students.

Violetta Sefkow-Werner is a doctoral candidate and Research and Teaching Assistant at the University of Zurich (Switzerland). She has studied law at the University of Heidelberg (Germany) and the University of Geneva (Switzerland) with a special focus on international law. She has worked as a Student Assistant at the Max Planck Institute for Comparative Public Law and International Law in Heidelberg (Germany) and was an Editor at the *Heidelberg Law Review*. She has completed her second state exam in 2021 at the Higher Regional Court of Dresden and has clerked at the Foreign Ministry of Germany. In her doctoral thesis, she examines the legal framework of international climate and environmental law.

Jerome Amir Singh (BA, LLB, LLM, MHSc, PhD) serves as the Principal Investigator of the Scientific Advisory Group on Emergencies, which operates under the auspices of the Academy of Science of South Africa. He currently serves as a Consultant to the WHO on climate change, health, and ethics. He is Adjunct Professor in the Dalla Lana School of Public Health at the University of Toronto (Canada) and Honorary Research Fellow at the Howard College School of Law at the University of KwaZulu-Natal (Durban, South Africa). He serves on several advisory and oversight bodies related to research, policy, humanitarian, and emergency issues, including the International Ethics Review Board of Médecins Sans Frontières, the WHO's Emergencies Ethics Review Committee, the WHO Technical Advisory Group for Emergency Use Listing, and the WHO Expert Group on the Ethics and Governance of Infectious Disease Outbreaks and Other Emergencies of Public Health Importance. Jerome Amir chairs the Ethics Working Group of the US NIH-funded HIV Prevention Trial Network and serves as a member of the South African National AIDS Council Legal and Human Rights Technical Task Team and the Bioethics Advisory Panel of the South African Medical Research Council. He has previously provided support to the Bill and Melinda Gates Foundation and its partners and grantees.

Giovanni Spitale has a background in philosophy and a PhD in medical sciences, obtained at the Institute of Biomedical Ethics and History of Medicine at the University of Zurich, where he currently works as a postdoctoral researcher. He is specialized in empirical ethics and citizen science. His research focuses on public health ethics, risk and crisis communication ethics, healthcare quality improvement, and AI ethics. He uses diverse methods, including natural language processing, computational linguistics, and philosophical analysis. He also serves as a special rapporteur for the WHO on the development of ethical frameworks for social listening and infodemic management. Spitale's research has been published in journals such as *Science Advances* and *NEJM Catalyst* and featured in outlets like *The Times*, *Forbes*, and *Wired*. He is also a TEDx speaker, a MENSA member, and an avid paragliding pilot.

Luca Valera studied philosophy (BA, MA) at the Università Cattolica del Sacro Cuore di Milano (Italy). He holds a PhD in bioethics and philosophy from the Università Campus Bio-Medico di Roma (Italy). His thesis was on the topic of human ecology, in the field of environmental ethics. He has been a Professor at the Pontificia Universidad Católica de Chile since 2015, and he was the Director of the Bioethics Centre from 2018 to 2021. He is now an Associate Professor at the Universidad de Valladolid (Spain) Department of Philosophy and an Associate Researcher at the Cape Horn International Center (Chile).

Shengjia Xu is a health researcher at Mathematica. Her research uses Medicare claims and enrollment data to analyze how the aging population utilizes and spends money on healthcare. Some of her ongoing work evaluates the impact of various CMS Innovation Center's value-based care models on Medicare beneficiaries. She holds a PhD in Public Policy and Management from the University of Southern California, a master's degree in mental health from Johns Hopkins University Bloomberg School of Public Health, and a bachelor's degree in Economics and Psychology from Smith College.

Introduction

Nikola Biller-Andorno, Julian W. März, Corine Mouton-Dorey, and Stéphanie Dagron

Public health strategies must navigate the complex interplay of legal, ethical, and political factors by drawing on expertise from various disciplines at all levels—local, regional, national, and international. A fundamental challenge in this domain is reconciling the obligation to foster population health through disease prevention, detection, and intervention with the imperative to respect and protect individual rights, including autonomy and privacy. The principle of proportionality serves as the established legal and ethical standard for navigating this balance. However, during times of severe crisis and uncertainty, determining the proportionality of public health actions is extremely complex endeavor, particularly when decisions are made without conclusive evidence or uniformly applicable international standards.

This book is the result of a process spanning more than four years, a period that seems like centuries when considering the evolution of knowledge, policies, and public attitudes regarding COVID-19. Since we began work in April 2020, over 450,000 articles about COVID-19 have been published in MEDLINE-indexed journals alone—more than on any other disease in such a short time frame. Most countries have experienced fundamental policy shifts in their response to the pandemic, in some cases moving from virtually no restrictions to complete lockdowns and vice versa in other cases, often within only a matter of days. We have seen several public health measures, such as COVID-19 vaccine mandates, COVID-19 immunity passports, and vaccine priority programs for at-risk populations, initially discussed in academia and theoretical policy debates and later implemented in countries worldwide. Conversely, we have seen some pandemic response measures, such as stay-at-home orders or strict no-visit policies in nursing homes, amended or abolished after criticism from lawyers, ethicists, and civil society.

While COVID-19 no longer dominates newspaper headlines and political debates as it did in the past, reviewing COVID-19 pandemic management remains a major task for lawyers, ethicists, policymakers, and civil society, with a view to improving pandemic management strategies in the future. Many countries, including Australia, Denmark, the Netherlands, Sweden, Switzerland,

Nikola Biller-Andorno et al., *Introduction*. In: *Proportionality*. Edited by: Nikola Biller-Andorno et al., Oxford University Press. © Oxford University Press (2026). DOI:10.1093/9780197759370.003.0001 and the United Kingdom, have set up parliamentary commissions to review their respective COVID-19 pandemic response measures and issue recommendations for future improvement. Other jurisdictions, including Chile, the European Union (EU), Germany, and the United States of America, are considering doing so at the time of writing this introduction. Additionally, numerous civil society organizations, global health actors, and academic organizations have issued reviews and recommendations on COVID-19 response measures.

Many of the restrictions on civil, political, economic, social, and cultural rights imposed to prevent disease and death from COVID-19 and the collapse of healthcare systems—such as curfews, travel bans, restrictions on private gatherings and public events, and school and business closures—were unimaginable before the pandemic. Political decisions had to be made in emergencies characterized by high degrees of uncertainty, urgency, and conflicting policy interests.

In this context of large-scale restrictions of individual liberties and fundamental rights for the sake of public health, proportionality has been a crucial issue for policymakers, lawyers, ethicists, and the general public alike. Virtually all pandemic response measures were defended by some as strictly necessary and criticized by others as clearly inappropriate. Some measures, such as vaccine mandates, no-visit policies in nursing homes, and school closures, stirred high levels of political controversies. For political, legal, and ethical debates throughout the COVID-19 pandemic, proportionality issues seemed to be a common denominator.

Proportionality in International Law

The principle of proportionality, although not universally understood as a general principle of international law (Cottier et al. 2017), is central in the field of human rights protection.[1] Originally inspired by the use of a proportionality test in German administrative and constitutional law (Lang 2020), the principle of proportionality has spread to most human rights protection systems worldwide. As such, this principle applies (or should apply) in the decision-making processes of states when decisions containing restrictions on human rights are to be

[1] Other fields such as the field of humanitarian law are concerned with the application of the principle of proportionality, which is expressed in art. 51(5)(b) of the Additional Protocol I of June 8, 1977 to the Geneva Conventions of August 12, 1949, which prohibits indiscriminate attacks "expected to cause incidental loss of civilian life, injury to civilians, damage to civilian objects, or a combination thereof, which would be excessive in relation to the concrete and direct military advantage anticipated." More precisely on humanitarian law, see Cohen and Zlotogorski (2021).

taken, and its application requires that a fair balance between the rights of an individual and the interests of the community be achieved.

Under international and regional human rights law, with the exception of nonderogable rights that cannot be restricted or reduced under any circumstances (e.g., the right not to be tortured or subjected to forced labor), states may restrict human rights in the case of an emergency. This possibility is formulated in general terms in international human rights conventions, such as the International Covenant on Civil and Political Rights (ICCPR art. 4) and the International Covenant on Economic, Social, And Cultural Rights (ICESCR art. 4) and in regional conventions such as the European Convention on Human Rights (ECHR art. 15; concerning specific rights, see also arts. 8–11) and the American Convention on Human Rights (art. 27).

The principle of proportionality is not explicitly mentioned in these texts, but it is integral. The above texts, however, enumerate in very broad terms specific conditions in which limitations that indirectly imply that a balance between different objectives has been reached can be found to be valid: They can only be adopted "for the purpose of promoting the general welfare in a democratic society" during a crisis situation that implies a threat to the life of the nation (war or other public danger) (ICESCR art. 4) and "to the extent strictly required by the exigencies of the situations" (ICCPR); finally, limitations must be determined by law and must not be inconsistent with other international law obligations.

However, the principle has also been expressly recognized by judicial and quasi-judicial bodies and by the literature as an interpretative principle to be used to qualify the state's interference with individual rights (Crawford 2011). It is often presented through its three constitutive elements: (a) suitability, which requires "that the measures in question are appropriate to the objective sought," (b) necessity, which requires states to always choose the least restrictive measure to attain their objective, and (c) proportionality sensu stricto, which requires states to strike a fair balance between the interests of individuals on the one hand and the community on the other.

The general requirements formulated by international legal norms for the limitations imposed on human rights in the name of the protection of public interests have been considered on many occasions as insufficient to support states in their decision-making in times of emergency. In 1984, the Economic and Social Council of the United Nations (ECOSOC) adopted the so-called Siracusa Principles (International Commission of Jurists 1984), formulated by international experts in an effort to clarify the standards applicable for derogation requirements to be applied. Limited to civil and political rights, these standards have proven inadequate in the context of a public health emergency and have been supplemented through the formulation of additional principles, such as those found in the 2023 Principles and Guidelines on Human Rights and Public Health Emergencies (Global Health Law Consortium and the International Commission of Jurists 2024).

These recent principles provide more details concerning states' obligations to promote and protect all human rights during a public health emergency; they also tailor the requirements for acceptable limitations and derogations to human rights to the public health objective at stake and reaffirm the principle of proportionality as a central element for the review of restrictive measures (see principle 16). Additionally, the principles propose a definition of the type of public health measures that may be likely to fulfill the proportionality requirements: Indeed, in accordance with principles 15 and 16, only "rights-based and evidence-informed public health measures" that result in a limitation on human rights may be adopted. This implies a meticulous analysis of the human rights implications of each public health measure (principles 15.2b–d, e) and "a risk assessment grounded in scientific principles and scientific, epidemiological and other available evidence" conducted by an independent and interdisciplinary scientific body (principle 15.2a).

Proportionality in Public Health Ethics

Proportionality is also a fundamental principle in public health ethics that guides decisions that may limit individual freedoms to achieve broader public health goals.

In public health, there is often a delicate balance between the welfare of the community and the rights of the individual (Gostin 2003). For example, while high vaccination rates are essential for preventing disease outbreaks like measles, enforcing mandatory vaccination can conflict with the principle of autonomy. Proportionality helps manage these conflicts by ensuring that restrictions on personal rights are reasonable and justified by significant public health benefits. In addition, this principle also emphasizes fairness by requiring that any limitations on rights are justified by reasons that apply equally to everyone and do not unfairly affect vulnerable groups.

Proportionality is framed within the context of the rule of double effect (RDE) in the *Oxford Handbook of Bioethics* (Sulmasy 2007). The RDE posits that an action with both positive and negative consequences may be permissible if the positive outcomes outweigh the foreseeable negative effects. However, the application of this principle is complex and requires careful deliberation on the agent's intent and the balance between benefits and harms. Beauchamp and Childress (8th ed., 167–171) contend that invoking the RDE without thorough analysis is insufficient; it is crucial to assess whether the positive effects truly justify all potential negative outcomes.

As Childress and colleagues (2002) emphasize, proportionality necessitates that restrictions on individual rights be carefully weighed against the anticipated benefits and potential risks and that due consideration must be given to their respective likelihoods. This evaluative process must also consider the respective political, social, cultural, and economic context. In public health, proportionality serves as a bridge between legal norms and ethical imperatives that guides policymakers in the implementation of measures that are both justified and equitable. Ethicists, though often sidelined in the initial stages of public health crises, play a critical role in assessing the ethical legitimacy of public health actions, thereby influencing governance and informing the evolution of laws and jurisprudence (Cohen and Ezer 2013).

An application of the proportionality principle to a policy faces the crucial challenge of the incommensurability of the restrictions to individual rights and the anticipated risks and benefits. Take the example of a policy that mandates vaccination with a hypothetical vaccine, which is 100% safe and 100% effective. In a given hypothetical population, one thousand persons are vaccinated and one thousand persons are unvaccinated. Mandating the vaccination of the 1,000 unvaccinated persons could—statistically—avert the death of one person, who could belong either to the initially vaccinated or unvaccinated group.

Proportionality requires the balancing of the restrictions of the autonomy of the one thousand initially unvaccinated persons with the (statistical) benefit of saving one person. The stakes (preserving the autonomy of one thousand persons vs. the statistical life of one person) are incommensurate—that is, the balancing act is not logically possible as such. As a solution, the proportionality assessment could resort to the statistically measurable preferences of a certain group (e.g., the population of a certain country). Empirical approaches to proportionality in a public health crisis, however, face the issues of volatility and the polarization of public opinion, as illustrated in the chapter by Corine Mouton-Dorey, Bettina Schwind, Giovanni Spitale, Kristen Jafflin, and Nikola Biller-Andorno to this edited book (Chapter 4).

Alternatively, the proportionality of a certain measure could be analyzed through its consistency or inconsistency with other measures. Take, for example, a hypothetical scenario in which two vaccines are available. Vaccine A is less effective (95%) than vaccine B is (100%); both are sufficiently available and authorized in a given state. If that state only offers Vaccine A to its citizens and introduces a vaccine mandate for all citizens with the stated goal of fully protecting those not sufficiently protected by Vaccine A, this policy could be deemed disproportionate.

However, in most cases, neither empirical research nor consistency analyses can solve the issue of incommensurability. What becomes crucial is to perceive proportionality not only as a substantive principle but also as a core part of procedural justice. The WHO (2016) *Guidance for Managing Ethical Issues in Infectious Disease Outbreaks* defines procedural justice as follows: "Procedural justice . . . refers to a fair process for making important decisions. Elements of procedural justice include *due process* (providing notice to interested persons and an opportunity to be heard), *transparency* (providing clear and accurate information about the basis for decisions and the process by which they are made), *inclusiveness / community engagement* (ensuring all relevant stakeholders are able to participate in decisions), *accountability* (allocating and enforcing responsibility for decisions), and *oversight* (ensuring appropriate mechanisms for monitoring and review)."

Outline of the Volume

The aim of this book is to shed light on the principle/process of proportionality in order to better decide and apply proportionate measures in the face of future public health crises, whether infectious, ecological, or linked to armed conflict.

Our edited book brings together the expertise of fifty scholars and practitioners from around the world on the theme of proportionality. What started as a general discussion among academics with expertise mostly in public health ethics and international human rights law four years ago has transformed into an ambitious project to understand the role of the principle of proportionality in public health crises, using the example of the COVID-19 pandemic.

We have structured our discussions on proportionality around four main axes:

- Public health decision-making in a pandemic
- The impact of pandemic management on vulnerable populations
- Judicial review of pandemic response measures
- The digitalization of pandemic response measures

Chapters 1–6 present key challenges when it comes to integrating proportionality into public health decision-making in a pandemic. Justin Bernstein, Athmeya Jayaram, Brian Hutler, Jeff Jones, Travis Rieder, and Anne Barnhill (Chapter 1) discuss how uncertainty complicates acting proportionately in a pandemic context, using the example of physical distancing policies in US states. Rodrigo López Barreda and Luca Valera (Chapter 2) and Felicitas Holzer, Ivette María Ortiz Alcántara, Tobias Eichinger, Nikola Biller-Andorno, and Julian W. März (Chapter 6) illustrate how the proportionality principle can and should be adapted to the specific socioeconomic and cultural contexts of a country's pandemic management. Silvia Camporesi (Chapter 3) and Corine

Mouton-Dorey, Bettina Schwind, Giovanni Spitale, Kristen Jafflin, and Nikola Biller-Andorno (Chapter 4) analyze public discourses and political narratives around the proportionality of pandemic response measures, using the examples of Italy and Switzerland. This section is completed by a contribution from Euzebiusz Jamrozik (Chapter 5), who analyzes the role of evidence in proportionality assessments of pandemic response measures.

Chapters 7–12 present the impact of pandemic response measures on vulnerable populations as a key consideration in assessing their proportionality. This section is opened by contributions from Stewart Adelson, Alice Miller, Daniel Newton, and Graeme Reid (Chapter 7) and Heather Draper, Caroline Redhead, Anna Chiumento, Sara Fovargue, and Lucy Frith (Chapter 8), who discuss the disproportionate impact of COVID-19 response measures on sexual and gender-minority youth and children hospitalized in long-stay wards. Hui Yun Chan (Chapter 9) analyzes the proportionality of travel restrictions for migrant healthcare workers in Singapore. Jakub P. Hlávka, Yimin Ge, Shengjia Xu, and Alexander M. Capron (Chapter 10), Settimio Monteverde (Chapter 11), and Jonathan Hunger and Eva Kuhn (Chapter 12) analyze the proportionality of different restrictions imposed on the residents of nursing homes and long-term care facilities during the COVID-19 pandemic.

Helen Keller and Viktoriya Gurash (Chapter 13), Helen Keller and Violetta Sefkow-Werner (Chapter 14), and Shelly Kamin-Friedman, Maya Peled-Raz, and Nadav Davidovitch (Chapter 15) discuss the application of the proportionality principle to pandemic response measures by the European Court of Human Rights, the Swiss Federal Supreme Court, and the Israeli High Court of Justice, respectively.

Chapters 15–19 discuss the application of the proportionality principle in the context of the digitalization of pandemic response measures. Shelly Kamin-Friedman, Maya Peled-Raz, and Nadav Davidovitch (Chapter 15) analyze contact-tracing measures in Israel. Calvin Ho (Chapter 16) analyzes the digitalization of epidemic countermeasures in Hong Kong Special Administrative Region. Fruzsina Molnár-Gábor (Chapter 17) discusses the application of the proportionality principle to the processing of sensitive data for scientific research purposes in a pandemic context. The book concludes with two chapters, authored by Jordan Parsons and Chloe Romanis (Chapter 18) and Rishita Nandagiri and Lucía Berro Pizzarossa (Chapter 19), respectively, who discuss the proportionality of abortion regulations in a pandemic in the context of the adoption of telemedicine consultations.

We extend our sincere gratitude to all the contributing authors and the independent external reviewers whose efforts made this collection possible. The principle of proportionality frequently emerges as a focal point of discussion—whether in support of, or in opposition to, policy decisions. The chapters in this volume demonstrate the critical importance of a multidisciplinary perspective on proportionality in public health. Legal and ethical considerations are grounded in the respect for human dignity as affirmed in the Universal Declaration of Human Rights: "All human beings are born free and equal in dignity and rights." The policies examined are deeply connected to the specific processes and contexts they are meant to address, including the type of governance, the healthcare system's structure, the identification of vulnerable populations, and the levels of communication, education, and technological progress. More than five years after the onset of the COVID-19 pandemic—a time marked by high scientific and political uncertainty and significant challenges in determining the proportionality of public health measures—this book provides a wealth of experience and insight. It seeks to inform the ongoing evolution of international standards surrounding proportionality and their adaptation at local levels by contributing to the continual learning process that is essential to the resilience and effectiveness of health systems.

Competing Interests

There are no competing interests to declare.

Funding

The project was funded jointly by the Universities of Geneva and Zurich (UNIGE-UZH Joint Funding for Collaboration in Research and Teaching) under the Call 2021—"Shaping Resilient and Responsive Societies and Ecosystems in View of Global Crises."

References

Beauchamp, T. L., and J. F. Childress. 2019. *Principles of Biomedical Ethics*. 8th edition, pp. 167–171. Oxford University Press.

Childress, J. F., R. R. Faden, R. D. Gaare, L. O. Gostin, J. Kahn, R. J. Bonnie, N. E. Kass, A. C. Mastroianni, J. D. Moreno, and P. Nieburg. 2002. "Public Health Ethics: Mapping the Terrain." *Journal of Law, Medicine & Ethics* 30:170–178.

Cohen, J., and T. Ezer. 2013. "Human Rights in Patient Care: A theoretical and Practical Framework." *Health & Hum Rights* 15: 7–19.

Cohen, A., and D. Zlotogorski. 2021. *Proportionality in International Humanitarian Law: Consequences, Precautions, and Procedures*. Oxford University Press.

Cottier, T., et al. 2017. "The Principle of Proportionality in International Law: Foundations and Variations." *Journal of World Investment and Trade* 18:628–672.

Crawford, E. 2011. *Proportionality. Max-Planck Encyclopedias of International Law.* https://opil.ouplaw.com/display/10.1093/law:epil/9780199231690/law-9780199231690-e1459.

Gostin, L. 2003. "Public Health Ethics: Traditions, Profession, and Values." *Acta Bioethica* 9:177–188.

International Commission of Jurists. 1984. *Siracusa Principles on the Limitation and Derogation Provisions in the International Covenant on Civil and Political Rights.* https://www.icj.org/wp-content/uploads/1984/07/Siracusa-principles-ICCPR-legal-submission-1985-eng.pdf.

International Commission of Jurists. 2024. *Human Rights in Public Health Emergencies.* https://www.icj.org/wp-content/uploads/2024/01/Human-Rights-Public-Health-Emergencies.pdf.

Lang, A. 2020. "Proportionality Analysis by the German Federal Constitutional Court." In *Proportionality in Action: Comparative and Empirical Perspectives on the Judicial Practice*, edited by M. Kremnitzer, T. Steiner, and A. Lang. Cambridge Studies in Constitutional Law, 22–133.

Sulmasy, D. P. 2007. "'Reinventing' the Rule of Double Effect." In *Oxford Handbook of Bioethics*, edited by B. Steinbock, 114–149. Oxford University Press.

WHO. 2016. *Guidance for Managing Ethical Issues in Infectious Disease Outbreaks.* June 30, 2025. https://iris.who.int/bitstream/handle/10665/250580/9789241549837-eng.pdf?sequence=1.

1

Proportionality and Uncertainty in Physical Distancing Policies in US States

Justin Bernstein, Athmeya Jayaram, Brian Hutler, Jeff Jones, Travis Rieder, and Anne Barnhill

Introduction

In the early stages of the COVID-19 pandemic, the United States—like nearly all countries—enacted a wide variety of physical distancing policies to mitigate the harmful effects of the coronavirus. Because individual state governors in the United States have broad powers during a public health emergency, the precise response varied, but all states issued at least some guidelines or orders limiting social interaction (Villa 2020), such as closing some businesses, shifting from in-person to virtual schooling, and limiting the number of people who were permitted to gather in person together, and at least 42 states and territories enacted a stay-at-home order at some point (Moreland 2020). Typically, states implemented multiple physical distancing policies simultaneously—for example, shifting to virtual schooling and also limiting other in-person gatherings. These physical distancing policies were designed to slow coronavirus infections—in order to accomplish aims such as preventing the healthcare system from being overwhelmed, protecting vulnerable people, and saving lives. But these policies also severely curtailed the personal freedoms of movement and association, caused businesses to fold, increased unemployment and food insecurity, caused or exacerbated mental health problems—including a marked increase in drug overdose deaths—and prevented people from gathering for religious worship, funerals, and family celebrations, among other negative effects (Badr et al. 2020; Nicola et al. 2020; Smith et al. 2021; Clair et al. 2021; Tanz et al. 2022).

These effects were also often inequitable and had disproportionate impacts on already disadvantaged groups. To take one of many examples of such inequity, the people least likely to be able to telework were from the lowest income quartile, so shutting down nonessential businesses was more likely to harm lower-income than higher-income workers (Bateman and Ross 2021). And

Justin Bernstein et al., *Proportionality and Uncertainty in Physical Distancing Policies in US States*. In: *Proportionality*. Edited by: Nikola Biller-Andorno et al., Oxford University Press. © Oxford University Press (2026).
DOI: 10.1093/9780197759370.003.0002

stay-at-home orders were more burdensome for those from lower-income backgrounds to the extent that they have less living space on average, and so the costs of personal confinement were especially pronounced (Wortzel et al. 2021).

The question of the justifiability of physical distancing policies thus seems like a prime candidate for exploring the proportionality principle and the role of proportionality judgments—that is, judgments about whether the public health benefits of policies (or suites of policies) are sufficient to justify the costs. Indeed, the language of proportionality can be found in public discourse about lockdowns (Plant and Singer 2020). Some American politicians seemed to invoke it as well—for instance, then-President Donald Trump stated that when it comes to physical distancing policies, the cure must not be worse than the disease (Haberman and Sanger 2020). However, in this chapter we consider the application of the proportionality principle in one specific context: the decisions about physical distancing policies made by US governors in the early months of the COVID-19 pandemic. We will identify several forms of significant uncertainty that complicate applying the proportionality principle in this context. Despite the widespread endorsement of some form of proportionality condition by ethicists and other scholars, our analysis of this case raises serious questions about the applicability of the proportionality principle in the early stages of a pandemic, particularly in political contexts like the United States. We close by exploring where this may leave the ethics of pandemic policy.

Proportionality and Uncertainty

As presented by Childress et al. (2002) and per the sense in which we understand it, proportionality is a justificatory condition for policies, and it is one justificatory condition among others. A policy must satisfy proportionality as well as these other conditions to be an ethically justified policy. Satisfying the proportionality condition requires showing

> that the probable public health benefits outweigh the infringed general moral considerations . . . . For instance, the policy may breach autonomy or privacy and have undesirable consequences. All of the positive features and benefits must be balanced against the negative features and effects. (Childress et al. 2002, 173)

In the case of physical distancing policies, this means that the public health benefits (and any other benefits) of these policies must outweigh all the ways in which the policies have negative effects and infringe moral considerations.

The balancing and weighing inherent in judgments of proportionality, then, requires assessing the effects—positive and negative—of various policies and the effects of not enacting policies. Because assessing proportionality requires knowledge of the effects of a policy, any challenges in knowing just how much a policy benefits public health will make it harder to determine whether a policy is proportionate. In other words, if one cannot know the effects of a policy, then one cannot know whether the policy is proportionate.

Perhaps the most familiar kind of uncertainty that complicates proportionality assessments of physical distancing policies involves uncertainty about the virus, SARS-CoV-2, and the disease it causes, COVID-19—particularly in March, April, and May 2020. For instance, if modeling results are used to estimate the health benefits of lockdowns but modelers have overestimated the infectiousness of the virus, then the health benefits of shuttering nonessential businesses will be significantly lower than the models show, and so there is reason to worry that the policy measures that have been judged to satisfy proportionality in fact do not. Modelers did provide significantly different estimates of COVID-19-related deaths that depended on assumptions they were forced to make about the R0 of the coronavirus, how contagious asymptomatic carriers would be, and the deadliness of the virus, among other things (Biggs and Littlejohn 2021; Gnanvi et al. 2021).

In addition to uncertainty about the virus itself, there was also well-documented, significant uncertainty about the benefits and harms of physical distancing policies. In February–March 2020, experts struggled to determine how many lives physical distancing policies might save; indeed, there were a variety of models with markedly different predictions about the benefits of shutting down (Holmdahl and Buckee 2020). It was similarly challenging to determine the various (economic and noneconomic) costs of the policies implemented. For instance, because public schools (at least in the United States) had never attempted to make primary education entirely remote for an extended period of time, there was considerable uncertainty about the extent to which school closure would harm children—including harms from educational losses, loss of opportunities to socialize, and, in many cases, the loss of childcare and other social services that schools provide.

In addition to the difficulties of assessing the extent of the benefits and costs of physical distancing policies, there was a further question about how to weigh these benefits and burdens against each other. Some proceeded as though it was obvious that the benefits of physical distancing policies outweighed the burdens. For instance, consider this March 20, 2020, quote from then–New York Governor Andrew Cuomo (2020): "When we look back at this situation ten years from now, I want to be able to say to the people of New York I did everything we could do. I did everything we could do. This is about saving lives and if everything we do saves just one life, I'll be happy." However, others could question this assessment because they could contend that saving lives is not the only consideration that matters; they could (reasonably) counter that the relevant economic harms, hardships for children, loss of employment for lower-income workers, restrictions on liberty, and other burdens matter more than saving a single life does (see, e.g., Singer and Plant 2020).

Such disagreement is an example of what we will label *normative uncertainty*: cases in which salient values at stake are not (straightforwardly) commensurable and in which people reasonably disagree about the weights or priorities of the relevant values. This normative uncertainty is, of course, a feature of all proportionality judgments, which require weighing different positive and negative features of policies—such as improvements to public health and limitations on freedom—against each other in the absence of an agreed-upon metric. However, the challenge was particularly acute in the early stage of the pandemic because of the importance of the values on both sides, the novelty of the comparisons, and the lack of prior public discussion to guide policymakers.

Thus, policymakers were forced to make decisions quickly (owing to the urgency of the threat from the virus), but they did not know exactly how the virus or disease worked, they did not know precisely what the harms and benefits of any policy would be, and they did not know how to weight these values against each other. In these moments, if policymakers were to apply the proportionality condition, they would need to make judgments about the benefits and downsides of policies, but those judgments could not have been precise as to the extent of the gains or costs of such policies. Even though policymakers were informed by experts and others (e.g., epidemiologists on the spread of the disease, community leaders on the effects of policies on their communities), in such circumstances the information provided by experts and others included significant uncertainty. Moreover, the kind of uncertainty faced during the early months of the pandemic went far beyond lacking data on the virus or some interventions' effects; we had precious little information about many variables, which essentially left policymakers to conduct a massive, high-stakes social experiment.

This uncertainty about the benefits and downsides of a physical distancing policy arises in no small part because of the sheer scope of the policies under consideration. But it also arises from uncertainty about how pandemic policies will interact with each other. Childress et al.'s (2002) discussion of their justificatory conditions, including proportionality, focuses on individual policies. For instance, Childress et al. (2002) apply their proportionality test to assess an imaginary case in which public health agents decide whether to screen for various infectious diseases such as tuberculosis or HIV/AIDS. In the context of the COVID-19 pandemic, by contrast, governors implemented a host of policies simultaneously—not just whether to enact a stay-at-home order or shutter nonessential businesses but also whether to require virtual learning for school-aged children, to ban public gatherings, to mandate the use of masks in public places, and to make it easier to access unemployment benefits.

The fact that several policies are being introduced simultaneously matters in part because the burdens or benefits of any one policy are difficult to assess in isolation from other policies, and this, in turn, makes it that much more challenging to determine whether any particular policy satisfies proportionality. For instance, some policies might be more burdensome in light of others. Schools and houses of worship provide a variety of social services to children and parents who depend on them—especially services such as free lunch or childcare. We might worry, then, that shuttering schools and houses of worship is more harmful than shuttering just one of the two would be. Conversely, a policy might be less burdensome if other policies, including policies meant to mitigate the harmful effects of the initial policy, are also implemented. Business closures caused a sharp increase in unemployment in the United States, which was mitigated, to some extent, by increased unemployment benefits. If we are attempting to determine how burdensome a policy is, then, it matters whether other policies are currently in place or will be implemented.

Obviously, even outside of the context of a pandemic, policies can interact in ways that affect the overall benefits and burdens of the policy being introduced. The program Childress et al. (2002) used as an example of a screening program for HIV/AIDS may be more beneficial if there is also a policy subsidizing contraception or antiretroviral drugs; the potential health benefits of such a screening program might be greater in this case, and so one's judgment of proportionality will be different.

However, the COVID-19 pandemic was importantly different from these ordinary contexts for the reasons discussed. First, in the first few months of the pandemic, there was greater uncertainty about the features of the virus and the expected benefits of the relevant interventions. Second, the scale of the interventions was far greater than in ordinary contexts; the relevant physical distancing policies had profound effects on the lives of almost all members of society. Third, in many cases pandemic policies, such as shifting to virtual schooling and closing houses of worship, were introduced simultaneously. Determining whether one (relatively small-scale) policy is proportionate is difficult enough; assessing the proportionality of several large-scale policies simultaneously will strike many as bordering on unfeasible.

The United States

It is challenging enough to overcome the general uncertainty about the benefits and burdens of lockdown policies. However, the United States has two features that make proportionality judgments even more difficult: federalism and polarization. The federalist system in the United States grants significant yet limited powers to individual states to enact lockdown measures. This means that state governors cannot antecedently assess the interactions between a policy under consideration and other policies that will be enacted simultaneously, because they can neither control nor predict the policies that will be enacted by other states or by the federal government. For example, while state governors have the power to enact physical distancing policies in their own state, they cannot control which policies are adopted by governors in other states. And given that it is difficult both practically and legally to restrict the flow of people and goods across state borders, the beneficial effects of one state's physical distancing policies may depend on the policies enacted in the neighboring state.

Moreover, state governments lack the financial tools and resources of the federal government and, therefore, often had to rely on the federal government to provide financial assistance, such as aid to businesses, unemployment benefits, and food assistance. Although the US Congress ultimately allocated funds for such financial assistance in the early phase of the pandemic, governors could not be sure ahead of time whether such assistance would be forthcoming, how much it would be, or how long it would last. Because governors can neither control nor predict which policies that reduce the costs of lockdown will be enacted, they cannot know the total costs of the lockdown policies they are considering; likewise, they cannot know the total benefits of lockdown policies.

If we assume that governors' decision-making should be guided by the proportionality condition, how should governors have deliberated about lockdown policies, given these features of the federalist structure? For instance, when considering whether a lockdown policy satisfies the proportionality condition, should governors assume that the federal government will enact robust measures that mitigate the harms of these policies? That seems to stack the deck in favor of lockdown policies. Should governors instead assume that the federal government will not enact those measures? That seems to stack the deck against the lockdown policy.

Perhaps governors could use a more nuanced method that takes into account the uncertainty about what other actors will do. For example, perhaps they could estimate the expected value of a particular policy choice by multiplying the value of different possible outcomes by the probability that they will occur. So governors would still have to estimate the benefits and costs of different sets of policies (e.g., state lockdown policies + federal unemployment benefits, state lockdown policies + no federal unemployment benefits). But they would now have to multiply that expected value by the probability that the package of policies comes about (e.g., the probability that federal government provides that level of unemployment benefits, the probability that it provides no benefits). This adds another layer of uncertainty into the calculations; this is also an opportunity to stack the deck in the direction of one's favored outcome. How likely is it that the federal government will enact policies sufficient to reduce the harms of lockdown? Estimating high makes it more likely that lockdowns come out to be justified, whereas estimating low makes such justification more difficult. Thus, it is not workable for governors to try to take into account uncertainty about what other actors will do.

The second feature of the US political system that makes proportionality judgments challenging is its polarized electorate, which matters for assessing the levels of compliance that policymakers can expect from citizens. To some degree, compliance issues arise with any policy. In Childress et al.'s (2002) example, if people refuse to comply with the screening program, then clearly its health benefits are lower than they would be if people do comply, and thus it is less likely to satisfy requirements of proportionality. To give another example, imagine that government officials are considering whether to ban the sale of trans fats, the consumption of which is thought to be associated with higher risks of heart disease. The government is trying to assess just how beneficial the public health benefits of a ban will be. It stands to reason that if some vendors were to disobey this requirement, then the benefits of such a policy would be reduced. But it doesn't seem that there is a threshold for compliance such that falling below that compliance threshold would significantly or entirely undermine the benefits of the policy.

In the pandemic context, however, there are real worries that if there is insufficient compliance, some policies will not yield the intended benefits. In the case of bans on public gatherings or the shuttering of non-essential businesses, we should worry that sufficiently widespread noncompliance will significantly reduce public health gains, especially if the goal of lockdown policies was to flatten the curve—to slow infection rates, prevent hospitals from being overrun, and give the health system time to respond to the crisis. If there is sufficiently high noncompliance, then society may fail to flatten the curve anyway, as the number of people socializing provides plenty of opportunity for the virus to spread. In that case, we might end up with the worst of both worlds: the costs of imposing strict policies on those who respect them, while failing to realize the benefit they were designed to produce.

In the United States, it was hard to predict the level of noncompliance in part because pandemic policies quickly polarized along party lines. Political partisanship became a determining factor both in the way that political actors communicated policies and the extent to which members of the public complied with them (Grossman et al. 2020). This leads to some difficult questions about assessing proportionality, questions that are familiar from earlier in this section. Should policymakers assume that there will be perfect compliance with a policy? If so, that would seem to stack the deck in favor of the policy—and lead policymakers to implement policies even when doing so is not especially effective despite being quite burdensome. Of course, assuming an especially low rate of compliance will yield the converse result: It will lead policymakers to expect a policy to fail, even if it could have been successful. For policymakers to gauge the benefits of physical distancing policies, then, they would have to predict the levels of compliance region by region and policy by policy.

Conclusion

In the United States, various forms of uncertainty generated significant challenges for rigorously applying a proportionality condition to suites of physical distancing policies during the COVID-19 pandemic. We have not taken a stance on whether these uncertainties generalize to other political contexts, but we do take the challenge of uncertainty to be worth serious consideration in the future when dealing with pandemics and other novel threats.

Where does this recognition of uncertainty leave us, though? If proportionality judgments are often taken to be important for morally and politically justified policy, and if uncertainty undermines justified proportionality judgments, it's unclear what we should say about the situation in which we are left. One way to frame this question concerns who, amid uncertainty, has the burden of proof: those seeking to enact physical distancing policies such as stay-at-home orders and business closures or those arguing against these policies? Childress et al. (2002), in their discussion of proportionality, seem to suggest that the burden of proof sits on those enacting policies: The policy must be shown to satisfy the proportionality condition. However, the fact that so many governors enacted lockdown policies amid great uncertainty perhaps suggests that they—and the portion of the public that supported these policies—thought otherwise.

A natural response to these difficulties in applying the proportionality condition would be to consider another normative principle. Perhaps another justificatory condition would be more suitable for assessing policy in the early stages of a pandemic, given the high level of uncertainty. An example is some version of the precautionary principle, according to which policy is justifiable if it potentially prevents a very bad outcome even in the absence of a precise understanding of the severity of the bad outcomes, convincing evidence that the outcome will occur in the absence of action, and convincing evidence that the policy will prevent that outcome (e.g., Nordgren 2023). Once we recognize the full extent of the uncertainties that impede the application of the proportionality condition in the early stages of a pandemic, a precautionary principle of this sort becomes more attractive. However, even if a precautionary principle is more suitable early in a pandemic, it is important to consider whether, and when, the proportionality condition should once again replace the precautionary principle as a justificatory condition applied to policies. As a pandemic proceeds, the forms of uncertainty we have discussed—including uncertainty about how a pathogen is transmitted, how deadly the pathogen is, what the effects are of different public health polices, what policies will be enacted by different parts of government, and other political uncertainties—may recede. At some point, it may become feasible to apply the proportionality condition with more precision. However, we have articulated some of the challenges that arise for applications of the proportionality in the face of uncertainty, and we have suggested further avenues for thinking about such challenges.

Competing Interests

There are no competing interests to declare.

Funding

This research was funded by a grant from the US National Science Foundation.

References

Badr, H. S., H. Du, M. Marshall et al. 2020. "Association Between Mobility Patterns and COVID-19 Transmission in the USA: A Mathematical Modelling Study." *The Lancet Infectious Diseases* 20 (11): 1247–1254. https://doi.org/10.1016/S1473-3099(20)30553-3.

Bateman, Nicole, and Martha Ross. 2021. "The Pandemic Hurt Low-Wage Workers the Most—and So Far, the Recovery Has Helped Them the Least." Brookings, July 28. https://www.brookings.edu/research/the-pandemic-hurt-low-wage-workers-the-most-and-so-far-the-recovery-has-helped-them-the-least/.

Biggs, A. T., and L. F. Littlejohn. 2021. "Revisiting the Initial COVID-19 Pandemic Projections." *The Lancet Microbe* 2 (3): e91–e92. https://doi.org/10.1016/S2666-5247(21)00029-X.

Childress, J. F., R. R. Faden, Ruth D. Gaare et al. 2002. "Public Health Ethics: Mapping the Terrain." *The Journal of Law, Medicine & Ethics* 30 (2): 170–178. https://doi.org/10.1111/j.1748-720x.2002.tb00384.x.

Clair, Ruta, Maya Gordon, Matthew Kroon, and Carolyn Reilly. 2021. "The Effects of Social Isolation on Well-Being and Life Satisfaction During Pandemic." *Humanities and Social Sciences Communications* 8 (1): 1–6. https://doi.org/10.1057/s41599-021-00710-3.

Cuomo, A. 2020. "Governor Cuomo Signs the 'New York State on PAUSE' Executive Order." YouTube, March 3. https://www.youtube.com/watch?v=XxA4HL-I8sc.

Gnanvi, Janyce Euince, Kolawolé Valère Salako, Gaëtan Brezesky Kotanmi, and Romain Glèlè Kakaï. 2021. "On the Reliability of Predictions on Covid-19 dynamics: A Systematic and Critical Review of Modelling Techniques." *Infectious Disease Modelling* 6:258–272. https://doi.org/10.1016/j.idm.2020.12.008.

Grossman, Guy, Soojong Kim, Jonah M. Rexer, and Harsha Thirumurthy. 2020. "Political Partisanship Influences Behavioral Responses to Governors' Recommendations for COVID-19 Prevention in the United States." *Proceedings of the National Academy of Sciences* 117 (39): 24144–24153. https://doi.org/10.1073/pnas.2007835117.

Haberman, M., and D. E. Sanger. 2020. "Trump Says Coronavirus Cure Cannot 'Be Worse Than the Problem Itself.'" *The New York Times*, March 23. https://www.nytimes.com/2020/03/23/us/politics/trump-coronavirus-restrictions.html.

Holmdahl, I., and C. Buckee. 2020. "Wrong but Useful—What Covid-19 Epidemiologic Models Can and Cannot Tell Us." *New England Journal of Medicine* 383 (4): 303–305. https://doi.org/10.1056/NEJMp2016822.

Moreland, A. 2020. "Timing of State and Territorial COVID-19 Stay-at-Home Orders and Changes in Population Movement—United States, March 1–May 31, 2020." *Morbidity and Mortality Weekly Report (MMWR)* 69 (35): 1198–1203. https://doi.org/10.15585/mmwr.mm6935a2.

Nicola, M., Z. Alsafi, C. Sohrabi et al. 2020. "The Socio-Economic Implications of the Coronavirus Pandemic (COVID-19): A Review." *International Journal of Surgery* 78:185–193. https://doi.org/10.1016/j.ijsu.2020.04.018.

Nordgren, A. 2023. "Pandemics and the Precautionary Principle: An Analysis Taking the Swedish Corona Commission's Report as a Point of Departure." *Med Health Care Philos* 26 (2): 163–173. https://doi.org/10.1007/s11019-023-10139-x.

Plant, M., and P. Singer. 2020. "When Will the Pandemic Cure Be Worse Than the Disease?" *Project Syndicate.* https://www.project-syndicate.org/commentary/when-will-lockdowns-be-worse-than-covid19-by-peter-singer-and-michael-plant-2020-04.

Singer, Peter, and Michael Plant. 2020. "When Will the Pandemic Cure Be Worse Than the Disease?" *Project Syndicate*, April 6. https://www.project-syndicate.org/commentary/when-will-lockdowns-be-worse-than-covid19-by-peter-singer-and-michael-plant-2020-04.

Smith, S., R. Edwards, and H. Duong. 2021. "Unemployment Rises in 2020, as the Country Battles the COVID-19 Pandemic." *Monthly Labor Review*, June. https://www.bls.gov/opub/mlr/2021/article/unemployment-rises-in-2020-as-the-country-battles-the-covid-19-pandemic.htm.

Tanz, L., A. Dinwiddie, S. Snodgrass, J. O'Donnell, C. Mattson, and N. Davis. 2022. "A Qualitative Assessment of Circumstances Surrounding Drug Overdose Deaths During Early Stages of the COVID-19 Pandemic." *CDC Injury Center.* https://www.cdc.gov/overdose-prevention/media/pdfs/SUDORS-Data-Brief-2.pdf, Accessed October 3, 2022.

Villa, V. 2020. "Most States Have Religious Exemptions to COVID-19 Social Distancing Rules." *Pew Research Center*, April 27. https://www.pewresearch.org/fact-tank/2020/04/27/most-states-have-religious-exemptions-to-covid-19-social-distancing-rules/.

Wortzel, J. D., D. J. Wiebe, G. E. DiDomenico et al. 2021. "Association Between Urban Greenspace and Mental Wellbeing During the COVID-19 Pandemic in a US Cohort." *Frontiers in Sustainable Cities* 3. https://www.frontiersin.org/articles/10.3389/frsc.2021.686159.

2

Proportionality and Resource Allocation in a Pandemic

The Example of Chile

Rodrigo López Barreda and Luca Valera

Introduction. The COVID-19 Pandemic and the Ethical Criteria for Fair Resource Allocation

During a pandemic, the allocation of limited sanitary resources becomes a crucial issue. Hospitals, often facing a shortage of resources, are forced to make difficult decisions. This problem is not unique to a single country, as it has arisen worldwide (Valera et al. 2020). In some countries, the scarcity of resources has led to tragic outcomes, particularly in regions with preexisting economic and social vulnerabilities. The Latin American region, in particular, was dramatically affected by the COVID-19 pandemic because of existing healthcare and social inequalities. Moreover, it is worth noticing that Latin American countries generally have two different health systems (i.e., the public and the private), which coexist in parallel; there are public and private health insurance and public and private health providers. Like all insurance, the premiums paid depend on individuals' risks, which are more highly concentrated in lower-income and older populations. People with higher incomes who, consequently, have a lower burden of disease tend to opt for private insurance and providers with abundant resources. In contrast, the population with a greater burden of disease cannot pay for private insurance and is covered by the public system, which has fewer resources compared to the number and complexity of its beneficiaries. This is one of the many factors that explain health inequalities in Latin American. Indeed, the decisions made during the pandemic had to consider all of these factors, which made them especially complex and often extreme (Tambone et al. 2020).

Thus, the COVID-19 pandemic triggered a new reflection on the criteria—including the ethical ones—to be adopted in critical situations and circumstances of a scarcity of healthcare resources (e.g., mechanical ventilators

Rodrigo López Barreda and Luca Valera, *Proportionality and Resource Allocation in a Pandemic*. In: *Proportionality*. Edited by: Nikola Biller-Andorno et al., Oxford University Press. © Oxford University Press (2026).
DOI: 10.1093/9780197759370.003.0003

or available beds) or human resources (e.g., healthcare personnel) (Wax and Christian 2020). To draft these criteria, international reflection on the topic took into account the "classic" ethical paradigms (e.g., principlism) and adapted highly validated international guidelines (e.g., Emanuel et al. 2020; Sokol 2020) to the existing situation of each country.

Thus, once again, in bioethics and public health ethics, the Anglo-Saxon tradition was imported and applied to the problems existing in Latin America without considering that those problems largely depend on the social context in which they originated (Sánchez et al. 2020). The idea that health, for example, is an individual and, at the same time, a social good is almost inseparable from its social context. Indeed, the COVID-19 pandemic showed us that our conception of health is strongly connected to different social factors, such as "poverty, physical environment (e.g., smoke exposure, homelessness), and race or ethnicity" (Abrams and Szefler 2020, 659). In this regard, as we argued in a previous article (Valera and López Barreda 2022), "a strong focus on socioeconomic status is more urgent than ever: our health basically depends on factors that go beyond our organism. Or better: our organism could not be isolated from its context and socioeconomic environment."

Following our previous considerations, we argue that the different socioeconomic contexts of the world's diverse regions are highly relevant to the public health and clinical decision-making process. Consequently, we need to do more than apply existing guidelines to concrete situations and concerns. To support this analysis, we will analyze the case of Chile, where the debate on the fair allocation of resources and the "last bed dilemma" (Valera et al. 2021) dominated discussions about how to respond to the COVID-19 pandemic. In particular, a central theme in this debate has been the dilemma between, on the one hand, using proportional treatments for individual patients and, on the other hand, the need to save as many lives as possible.

The Case of Chile

Chile was severely affected by the COVID-19 pandemic, with a total of 3,466,425 people infected by SARS-CoV-2 and 45,093 deaths attributed to this disease (Ministry of Health of Chile 2022). The first case was detected on March 3, 2020. From March 18, the government decreed a constitutional state of exception, which allows for the implementation of a series of restrictive measures in order to reduce the spread and mitigate the effects of a disease (Aguilera et al. 2022). Among the restrictive measures used were the closure of borders for nonresident foreigners (from March 18, 2020, to July 25, 2021), mobility restrictions (including lockdowns) following a plan called "step by step," which had five different stages depending on the level of contagion, and the mandatory use of facial masks (from April 8, 2020, to September 30, 2022) (Aguilera et al. 2022). In the educational sector, face-to-face classes were replaced by distance or hybrid activities from March 2020, as allowed by the step-by-step plan. Still, it is estimated that by March 2021, only 51.5% of schools had resumed their normal activities (Aguilera et al. 2022).

From a socioeconomic point of view, Chile was in the middle of a difficult political period that was characterized by social unrest, which led to the establishment of a convention to change the current constitution, which had been written during the dictatorship of Augusto Pinochet. Because of this, several subsidies were delivered to the most vulnerable of the population (Aguilera et al. 2022), but one of the most debated measures was the voluntary withdrawal of individual pension funds (Ramírez 2021). In terms of healthcare, a set of policies aimed at strengthening diagnostic capacity, integrating the public and private systems (Aguilera et al. 2022), and universal vaccination (reaching up to 92.5% of the population) were put in place (Our World in Data 2022).

Despite all of these measures, the pandemic took a significant toll in terms of health and social consequences. Poverty increased by about 20%, and income differences also increased (Aguilera et al. 2022). The distribution of mortality echoed what was reported in other countries, affecting populations with fewer resources to a greater extent, particularly those with a lower level of educational and who live in overcrowded conditions (Bilal et al. 2021). These results made the deep structural inequities that affect the country even more evident.

Even if the integration between the public and private healthcare systems had generated a significant number of resources to care for the large number of patients, Chile might not have been able to replicate situations like those that occurred in other Latin American countries, where there were shortages of supplies like oxygen. Various organizations prepared Chile for the eventuality that its health institutions would be overwhelmed and that it would face what was called "the last bed dilemma" (Valera et al. 2021). The media played a significant role, often alarming the population without promoting a real debate (López et al. 2021). In this context, several bioethical guidelines were drafted, such as those of the Chilean Society of Internal Medicine (Echeverría et al. 2020), the Bioethics Center at Pontificia Universidad Católica de Chile (Valera et al. 2020), and the Dr. Gustavo Fricke Hospital (Toro 2020; see also Paredes et al. 2020; Sánchez et al. 2020).

The Chilean Guidelines for Fair Resource Allocation

Compared to most European and North American guidelines, in Chile most proposals called for a rational use of resources without making an explicit call to leave some social groups behind in terms of receiving medical treatment. Moreover, they advocated for the right of the elderly to receive healthcare and criticized any predefined age as a cutoff for admission into hospitals (Ramos Vergara et al. 2021). At the same time, they admitted that under special circumstances, such as those during a pandemic, when healthcare resources may be scarce, an adequate proportionality judgment is more urgent than ever. If therapeutic stubbornness is morally reprehensible in conditions of affluence, it is even more so in conditions of limited resources: Not only is the individual patient harmed, but also potential patients are deprived of medical treatment (Valera et al. 2021).

Hence, much emphasis was placed on the fact that it is morally appropriate to limit therapeutic measures to patients who may not receive the anticipated reasonable benefits from them (Vega Toro and Novoa Satta 2020).

Another interesting feature was that many guidelines (e.g., Carrasco et al. 2020; Micolich et al. 2020; Valera et al. 2020) made a call to remember that the most important duty of medicine is to care rather than to cure. How clinicians assess the proportionality and the number of resources required for a given measure may differ when the intention is rectified. A very sick patient with severely affected lungs may require a high-flow nasal cannula to have normal arterial oxygen content in the lab tests, which entails significant use of resources. However, a patient may need less oxygen to calm dyspnea. In contexts of limited resources, delivering oxygen at the high doses necessary to improve a patient's clinical condition could be disproportionate, while administering oxygen at low doses to seek symptomatic relief would be proportionate. This shows the difference between *caring* and *curing*: Even if curing is disproportionate in some cases, caring is almost always adaptable to different contexts ("What can I do for this patient here and now?") and, hence, it is proportionate.

Most of the guidelines acknowledged that making these types of decisions was difficult for clinicians, who in Chile do not typically make proportionality judgments every day. At the same time, they recognized the limitations of bioethics committees that did not have the resources to do this type of evaluation as often as needed. Thus, the guidelines proposed an accompaniment to clinicians charged with patient care so that they could share the weight of the decision with more people and not feel that the responsibility was exclusively theirs as individuals.

Redeeming Proportionality in the Era of Public Health Ethics

Obviously, what has been said so far does not reflect in detail all the directives proposed in Chile. We have tried, as far as possible, to gather some crosscutting ideas. In fact, while it is quite true that Chile generally avoided resorting to utilitarian proposals or those that discriminate based on the patient's age or the estimated years of survival, individual Chilean scholars (e.g., Aguilera 2020; Aurenque et al. 2020; Micolich et al. 2020; Burdiles and Pommier 2021) supported that kind of criteria.

Overall, distancing from these criteria meant, in fact, broadening the factors to be considered in the decision-making process—extending the view and not restricting it. In this sense, the priority of "caring over curing" (Carrasco et al. 2020) implied redeeming and deepening the concept of proportionality (Burdiles and Pommier 2021). Indeed, while the proportionality assessment is a prudential judgment (Miranda 2021) that aims to carefully consider the concrete clinical conditions in which an individual patient is actually placed, a public health crisis requires "considering the patient as a whole" and beyond—that is, taking into account the social context of a public health crisis.[1] This "beyond" is the novel element that emerges profoundly from the Chilean context. This means, following Carrasco et al. (2020), remembering that (a) the consideration of the patient's condition is ethically prior to the consideration of the resources available, (b) each patient deserves an ad hoc treatment and represents a unicum in clinical care, and (c) every patient's condition is different, so treatments will not necessarily be the same. Differences between the patients also depend on their socioeconomic conditions and culture. This is particularly relevant in contexts with a considerable gap between the poorest and the richest people—Chile is an excellent example of such a situation. In this sense, considering the social determinants of health (Valera and López Barreda 2022) is particularly appropriate, especially during a pandemic. This fact is helpful in making an adequate diagnosis of a patient's condition and looking for better treatments and cures so as not to discriminate against the patient. Thus the environmental or social context may be a critical element in offering to that particular patient the best cure in that concrete situation. This integration of environmental and socioeconomic context in the decision-making process may be a relevant contribution from Chile in the debate on proportionality during a pandemic.

[1] This means carefully taking into account both the psychological and emotional dimensions of the patient (Portales and Beca 2020) and healthcare workers (Alvarado et al. 2021).

Conclusion

The pandemic, rather than making us face the scarcity of resources, forced us to deal with the limits of medicine itself, reminding us of its purpose—to care rather than to cure—and of the value and importance of social context for judging therapeutic proportionality. Moreover, owing to the concrete socioeconomic situation (e.g., the two health systems, poverty, a lower educational level, and overcrowded conditions) and the existing social culture of solidarity (Sánchez et al. 2020), a nonutilitarian approach to proportionality was dominant in Chile during the pandemic. In this sense, the Chilean case may help us rethink the main focus of medicine: the patient, not the resources.

Acknowledgments

The authors wish to thank the reviewers and editors of this book for their valuable contributions.

Competing Interests

There are no competing interests to declare.

Funding

The authors received no specific funding for this work.

References

Abrams, E. M., and S. J. Szefler. 2020. "COVID-19 and the Impact of Social Determinants of Health." *Lancet Respir Med* 8:659–671.

Aguilera, B. 2020. "Asignación ética de recursos sanitarios escasos en el contexto de crisis por COVID-19." *Medwave* 20 (5): e7935.

Aguilera, B., T. Cabrera, J. Duarte et al. 2022. "COVID-19: Evolución, efectos y políticas adoptadas en Chile y el mundo," March. *Dirección de Presupuestos del Ministerio de Hacienda. Serie de Estudios de Finanzas Públicas.* http://www.dipres.cl/598/articles-266625_doc_pdf.pdf.

Alvarado, R., J. Ramírez, Í. Lanio et al. 2021. "El impacto de la pandemia de COVID-19 en la salud mental de los trabajadores de la salud en Chile: Datos iniciales de 'The Health Care Workers Study.'" *Rev Med Chile* 149 (8): 1205–1214.

Aurenque, D., M. Espinosa, J. A. Lecaros, D. Loewe, and R. Villarroel. 2020. "Orientaciones ético-médicas para la atención de pacientes críticos en contexto de pandemia por COVID-19." *Bioética Complutense* 39:34–40.

Bilal, U., T. Alfaro, and A. Vives. 2021. "COVID-19 and the Worsening of Health Inequities in Santiago, Chile." *International Journal of Epidemiology* 50 (3): 1038–1040.

Burdiles, P., and A. O. Pommier. 2021. "El triaje en pandemia: Fundamentos éticos para la asignación de recursos de soporte vital avanzado en escenarios de escasez." *Revista médica clínica las condes* 32 (1): 61–74.

Carrasco, M. A., R. López, L. Valera, P. Pérez, and R. Castro. 2020. "Orientaciones éticas ante el llamado 'problema de la última cama.'" https://facultadmedicina.uc.cl/wp-content/uploads/2020/04/Orientaciones-eticas-ante-el-llamado-%E2%80%9Cproblema-de-la-ultima-cama%E2%80%9D.pdf.

Echeverría, C., C. Rojas, P. Taboada et al. 2020. "Consideraciones éticas en relación con la atención de pacientes en la situación de pandemia por coronavirus SARS-CoV-2 (COVID-19)." Santiago Medical Society. https://www.smschile.cl/new/2020/03/29/consideraciones-eticas-en-relacion-con-la-atencion-de-pacientes-en-la-situacion-de-pandemia-por-coronavirus-sars-cov-2-covid-19/.

Emanuel, E. J., G. Persad, R. Upshur et al. 2020. "Fair Allocation of Scarce Medical Resources in the Time of Covid-19." *NEJM* 382:2049–2055.

López, O., G. Rivera-Aguilera, R. González Benavente, C. Nova, B. García Villamil, and V. Forján Espinoza. 2021. "Narrativa épica, profesionales de la salud y pandemia: Análisis de medios en Chile y Colombia." *Psicoperspectivas* 20 (3). https://doi.org/10.5027/psicoperspectivas-vol20-issue3-fulltext-2403.

Micolich, C., S. P. Salas., A. Arriagada et al. 2020. "Consideraciones éticas y propuesta de priorización para la asignación de recursos escasos durante la pandemia de SARS-CoV-2: Reflexiones del departamento de ética del Colegio Médico de Chile." https://www.colegiomedico.cl/wp-content/uploads/2022/05/Consideraciones-eticas-para-la-priorizacion-de-recursos-escasos.pdf.

Ministry of Health of Chile. 2022. "Plan de acción coronavirus COVID-19; casos confirmados en Chile COVID-19." https://www.minsal.cl/nuevo-coronavirus-2019-ncov/casos-confirmados-en-chile-covid-19/.

Miranda, A. 2021. "Criterios de justicia para la asignación de recursos médicos escasos en situaciones de pandemia." *Veritas* 49 (August). https://doi.org/10.4067/S0718-92732021000200055.

Our World in Data. 2022. "Coronavirus (COVID-19) Vaccinations." https://ourworldindata.org/covid-vaccinations?country=CHL.

Paredes, M. C., K. Pesse-Sorensen, and K. Barros Rubio. 2020. "Ética de la salud pública: Propuesta sobre los principios fundamentales que guían las responsabilidades éticas del estado en el contexto pandemia COVID-19." *Rev Med Chile* 148:1481–1488.

Portales, M. B., and J. P. Beca. 2020. "Buen morir en pandemia." *Rev Med Chile* 148:707–714.

Ramírez, F. 2021. "¿Qué efectos puede tener un cuarto retiro o un retiro completo de los fondos de pensiones?" Universidad de Chile, October 8. https://www.uchile.cl/noticias/180499/que-efectos-puede-tener-los-nuevos-retiros-de-fondos-de-pensiones.

Ramos Vergara, P., L. Valera, H. Gac, and C. Richards Yáñez. 2021. "El adulto mayor en el contexto del covid-19: ¿en el centro del cuidado o al margen por su edad?" *Cuad bioet* 32(106): 329–339.

Sánchez, I., R. López, and L. Valera. 2020. "COVID-19 and Ethics: A Latin-American Perspective." *Asia Pacific Journal of Public Health* 32:505–506.

Sokol, D. 2020. "The Life and Death Decisions of Covid-19" (blog). *The BMJ Opinion*, March 20. https://blogs.bmj.com/bmj/2020/03/20/daniel-sokol-the-life-and-death-decisions-of-covid-19/.

Tambone, V., D. Boudreau, M. Ciccozzi et al. 2020. "Ethical Criteria for the Admission and Management of Patients in the ICU Under Conditions of Limited Medical Resources: A Shared International Proposal in View of the COVID-19 Pandemic." *Front Public Health* 8:284. https://doi.org/10.3389/fpubh.2020.00284.

Toro, F. 2020. *Guía ética para atención de pacientes COVID-19*. Hospital Dr. Gustavo Fricke, June. http://www.hospitalfricke.cl/wp-content/uploads/2019/10/GUIA.pdf.

Valera, L., M. A. Carrasco, and R. Castro. 2021. "Fallacy of the Last Bed Dilemma." *J Med Ethics* 48 (11): 915–921. https://doi.org/10.1136/medethics-2021-107333.

Valera, L., M. A. Carrasco, R. López et al. 2020. "Orientaciones éticas para la toma de decisiones médicas en el contexto de la pandemia de COVID-19 en Chile." *Rev Med Chile* 148:393–398.

Valera, L., and R. López Barreda. 2022. "Bioethics and COVID-19: Considering the Social Determinants of Health." *Front Med* 9:824791. https://doi.org/10.3389/fmed.2022.824791.

Vega Toro, S., and F. Novoa Satta. 2020. "Aspectos éticos de la pandemia por COVID-19 en pediatría." *Rev Chil Pediatr* 91 (4): 495–499. https://www.scielo.cl/pdf/rcp/v91n4/0370-4106-rcp-rchped-vi91i4-2466.pdf.

Wax, R. S., and M. D. Christian. 2020. "Practical Recommendations for Critical Care and Anesthesiology Teams Caring for Novel Coronavirus (2019-nCoV) Patients." *Can J Anaesth* 67 (5): 568–576.

3

Proportionality in Public Health Ethics, Fear, and State of Exception

A Critical Narrative Approach

Silvia Camporesi

Italy, January 2020: The First Signs of the Outbreak

I lived lockdown in Italy during the first European outbreak of the COVID-19 pandemic. I was expecting and at term in early 2020. My family and I had decided to spend those first few weeks of our child's life in my hometown of Forlì, in the region of Emilia-Romagna in Northern Italy. One morning in late January, I went down to the café below our apartment and ordered an espresso before settling in to read one of the communal newspapers. Standing shoulder to shoulder with the other patrons at the *bancone*, I scanned the news about the outbreak of a new pathogen in Lodi, a town in Lombardy about 260 kilometers from where I was standing. The news was comparing the new pathogen to the seasonal flu, only "a bit stronger." Those were the very early days of the pandemic: The new pathogen did not even have a name yet. Only later, on February 11, 2020, would the "novel coronavirus" receive its official name: SARS-CoV-2 (severe acute respiratory syndrome coronavirus 2) (World Health Organization [WHO] 2020). The disease would be called COVID-19. In a personal essay written while confined to my home and published in AEON in April 2020, just a few weeks after that morning when I read the first news of the outbreak in the café below our apartment, I wrote,

> In the café, the consensus was that the reaction was "over the top." We're not like China, we said to one another, where people can be locked up in their homes. It was Carnival season; that Sunday, we had a neighborhood party. Our older son dressed up as King Arthur, with a red cape and foam sword, and enjoyed throwing streamers and confetti along with dozens of other kids.

When re-reading that essay in preparation to write this chapter four years later, those events seem cloaked under a surreal mantle. That Mardi Gras party would

Silvia Camporesi, *Proportionality in Public Health Ethics, Fear, and State of Exception*. In: *Proportionality*. Edited by: Nikola Biller-Andorno et al., Oxford University Press. © Oxford University Press (2026). DOI: 10.1093/9780197759370.003.0004 be the last social engagement for months to come, as the region of Emilia-Romagna would be in lockdown two days later, on February 23. It is hard to believe that the norms of societies to which we are so accustomed were, and can be, completely dismantled in only a few days or weeks. But that was the case. In the name of an unprecedented tragedy and health crisis, exceptional public health measures, which became known collectively as lockdown, were implemented. Now, more than four years later, it is important to reconnect to those feelings and reflect on the following questions: What does the fact that the norms of society were dismantled so easily in the name of an unprecedented emergency tell us about the fabric of our society and about the fragility of our reality? What can it tell us about the principles of public health ethics, which we thought were unassailable tenets of how public health measures restricting individual freedoms are implemented? Finally, were other, less toxic counter-narratives available that would make sense of what was happening and of the breaking down of the reference points in the world? It is of vital importance to reconnect to those feelings from lockdown and to critically engage with these questions. Narratives make sense of the world and *do things* in the world: They influence individual agency. They create heroes, victims, and villains. They are the repositories of our reactive attitudes of blame, resentment, and even hatred. Narratives create the cultural and biopolitical legacy of the pandemic.

This chapter proceeds as follows: I first provide background on lockdown measures in Italy in 2020 and on the institutional framework for crisis management in Italy. I then outline the public health ethics principles used in the ethical management of a novel infectious disease outbreak and assess whether they were respected in the case of the ban on outdoor exercise in Italy in 2020. I then discuss the master narratives that were used implicitly to justify it, before moving on to discuss the performativity of the master narratives of war, heroism, and sacrifice mobilized in the pandemic in Italy and elsewhere in the world. I conclude by discussing the implications of specific narratives on the public perception and lived experiences of citizens in lockdown in Italy in 2020 for the construction of cultural memory of the pandemic and for its biopolitical legacy.

Background on the Lockdown Measures in Italy in 2020

The first COVID-19 case was recorded in Italy around the same time that my second child was born, in late January 2020. Two Chinese tourists from Wuhan holidaying in Italy were hospitalized at Spallanzani hospital in Rome for a new viral form of pneumonia (Severgnini 2020). The first person in Italy to have locally acquired COVID-19, known as Patient 1, was documented on February 19, 2020, in Codogno, a town of fifteen thousand southwest of Milan, in the Lombardy region (ANSA 2020). It soon became evident how the two Chinese tourists who ended up in the Spallanzani hospital in Rome had driven from the north to the south through the regions where clusters of cases were later identified. On January 31, 2020, Italy declared a national state of emergency, and all flights to and from China were suspended (Council of Ministers 2020). The Italian government first attempted a phase of contact tracing and case isolation. Restrictions to freedom of movement that were enforced through the mobilization of military forces were initially applied (from February 23, 2020) only to eleven towns in the Northern Italian regions of Lombardy, Emilia-Romagna, and Veneto. When this first phase failed to contain the outbreak, in the night between March 8 and 9, 2020, the government declared a national lockdown effective from the following day, Monday, March 9, 2020. This announcement was delivered over the evening news by at that time Italian Prime Minister Giuseppe Conte: "We all have to renounce something for the good of Italy." The announcement led to a frenzy of people competing to catch the last night trains that would take them elsewhere in Italy where they could join their families, which obviously led to an acceleration in the spreading of the new pathogen in Italy (Sole 24 ore 2020).

What did lockdown look like in Italy in the first phase of the pandemic in 2020? The question of a pandemic preparedness plan was at the center of a harsh media controversy, as were conspiracy theories, in Italy and elsewhere in the world (Cable et al. 2021). In 2003, following the outbreak of the A/H5N1 virus in Asia, the WHO recommended that all countries prepare a pandemic preparedness plan following the established guidelines and WHO recommendations of 2005–2006 (WHO 2005). Italy had developed a pandemic preparedness plan in 2006 according to the six pandemic phases identified by the WHO. The plan set out clear organizational guidelines to be followed if the Council of Ministers were to declare a state of emergency (Italian National Plan for Preparedness and Response 2006). The preparedness plan detailed that, in the case of an emergency, coordination functions are the responsibility of the Prime Minister, who is advised by the Civil Protection Department. The latter, in turn, is in charge of setting up the Technical and Scientific Committee (Comitato Tecnico-Scientifico; CTS), which stays in place for the entire duration of the national emergency (in the case of COVID-19, this was January 31, 2020–March 31, 2022) and whose expert advice played a key role in managing the crisis in Italy in 2020, as highlighted in Camporesi et al. (2022). The CTS provided expert advice to the government on public health containment measures. The government, in turn, produced hundreds of decrees that had the force of law and that closely reflected the expert advice produced by the CTS—so closely that in the first phase of the pandemic, the minutes of the CTS meetings were copied and pasted into the decrees of the following day and outlined increasingly severe public health containment measures (Camporesi et al. 2022).

After a first phase of regional lockdowns in the Northern Italy regions of Emilia-Romagna, Veneto, and Lombardy (from February 23 to March 9), national lockdown in Italy lasted for ten weeks, from March 9 until May 5, 2020. Schools at all levels, museums, libraries, theaters, cinemas, and gyms were shut down. Severe restrictions on freedom of movement were implemented. Movements from *a* to *b* were allowed only for necessities. A self-declaration was needed and had to be produced on request to the police and other public officials involved in lockdown enforcement (Simoni 2020). In addition, Italy was the only country in Europe to adopt a ban on outdoor exercise (Camporesi 2020). From March 9 to May 4, 2020 walking (but not jogging, cycling, or other outdoor exercise) was permitted within two hundred meters of one's home (Michelini et al. 2021). All factories and production lines that were not considered absolutely essential were shut down. The limited set of essential sectors that remained operational during the pandemic were sectors deemed necessary to sustain citizens' livelihoods and to produce and deliver goods necessary to navigate the pandemic (e.g., grocery stores, factories that manufacture medical equipment, and banks) (Horowitz 2020; Di Porto et al. 2022). Firms in other sectors could remain active only if they could allow remote work. Outdoor activities and gatherings of any size, in public *or private*, were prohibited. Parks and playgrounds were closed to the public and monitored with drones. Not respecting the lockdown in Italy was a criminal offense punishable by fines of up to €3,000 and, potentially (in case of violations of lockdown following a positive COVID-19 test), a criminal charge of crimes against public health and up to five years in jail (Wanted in Rome 2020). In 2020 alone, Italy reportedly charged *more than forty thousand individuals* for violating its quarantine rules (Sun and Zilli 2020).

Lived Experiences of Lockdown in Italy in 2020

In 2020, for the first time in my life aside from during a World Cup, I started seeing Italian flags sprouting from windows. These were soon accompanied by rainbow flags, which signified the overarching, optimistic narrative in the first phase of the pandemic: "Andrà tutto bene" (Everything will be all right). The international media were quick to pick up those unprecedented sentiments. *The New York Times* talked about Italians finding "a moment of joy amidst a moment of anxiety" (Horowitz 2020). Indeed, videos started going viral of Italians proudly singing arias by Verdi and Puccini and playing live music on their balconies in solidarity with healthcare workers. However, lockdown in the spring of 2020 had other, darker shades, which were picked up to a lesser extent by the international media.

Neighborhood vigilantism emerged as a new, concerning social phenomenon in Italy in 2020. Reports of lockdown violations were conveyed in a plurality of ways, including mass public participation in community-based policing activities: Photos of alleged transgressors were reported to the police and posted for public shaming on social networks (Scalia 2021). In some municipalities, citizens were explicitly encouraged by local governors to report lockdown violations: In March 2020, an online reporting system was launched by the mayor of Rome at that time, Virginia Raggi, to enable citizens to report infringements (Favale 2020). Drones were used in towns across Italy to spot transgressors, including in my own city of Forlì, in Emilia-Romagna (Camporesi 2020; Redazione 2020), and in other municipalities. In the town of Messina, in Sicily, the mayor deployed drones with prerecorded messages that insulted the transgressors ("Where . . . are you going? Go back home!") ("Coronavirus" 2020, my translation). A woman driving a car while waiting at a traffic light with her window down was verbally attacked by a person watching her from a window: "Stay home, you murderer!" (Stai a casa assassina!) (Accolla 2020). It turned out she was one of those people who had an essential job that couldn't be performed remotely.

In the city of Padua (Veneto Region), in April 2020, a fifty-year-old man who was jogging with his dog was assaulted by two passersby, resulting in multiple fractures and hospitalization (Pietrobelli 2020). The case of the jogger assaulted in Padua was not an isolated incident in Italy in 2020; evidence of several other cases of verbal and physical assaults of joggers and runners and discretionary and discriminatory abuses of force by police against Italian citizens was reported by various sources in Italy in the first half of 2020 (Accolla 2020; De Vivo 2020; Scalia 2021; Fontefrancesco 2022). What soon became evident to citizens in lockdown is that, in practice, police forces enjoyed broad discretion on whether to authorize individuals to leave their homes, with the result being that "the meeting between law enforcement officers and citizens [ended up] in a negotiation, where the power of the officer is counterbalanced by the capacity of the citizen to appear as a 'mainstream' person, possibly one with significant cultural, social, and relational capital" (Simoni 2020, 10).

Master Narratives at Play: Heroes, Victims, and Villains in Italy in 2020

Narratives help individuals and collectives make sense of their experience and the world while, at the same time, doing things in the world (Camporesi et al. 2025; Davis and Lohm 2020; Meretoja 2022). Narratives have a performative dimension whereby they do not simply describe states of affairs or things but do things in the world by influencing the agency of individuals and their representation of the world. There are dominant or master narratives, and there are counter-narratives or oppositional narratives (Hansen 2018; Meretoja 2021), also sometimes called "narratives of resistance" (Squire and De Lemos 2022). Squire et al. (2014) have written that narratives constitute a form of explanation and build knowledge. In her works, Meretoja (2020; 2021; 2022) has highlighted how master narratives, which are often implicit, function in the world as interpretative tools and models of sense-making and how they are performative: They influence the agency of the individuals by shaping how they interpret the world and act in the world.

The war narrative was the narrative most widely mobilized worldwide to make sense of the pandemic. Meretoja (2020) has argued that the master narrative of war deployed across the world in reference to the pandemic is problematic not just for healthcare workers but also for potential patients, as it urges them "to prepare for the fight by keeping [ourselves] fit and alert" and by creating "an illusion of control." However, as we know from the literature on illness narratives—in particular in the case of cancer, from 'quest' counter narratives—it is not those patients who are prepared to fight or who fight better who survive (Hansen 2018). Within the pandemic war narrative, several elements or subnarratives can be identified: the heroism subnarrative, the "worthwhile" sacrifice subnarrative, and the fear subnarrative. The heroism subnarrative has been critically unpacked by several commentators (Cox 2020; Khan et al. 2021; Kinsella and Sumner 2022). Cox has pointed out how the continuing dominance of the hero narrative for healthcare workers is problematic in several ways, from portraying the duty of care as limitless and independent of the level of personal risk and other duties in one's own life (e.g., toward family members), to downplaying the responsibilities for structural interventions, such as better-resourced personal protective equipment. As the pandemic unfolded, an increasing number of healthcare workers started resisting a narrative that, on the one hand, depicted them as heroes and, on the other, depicted them as "expendable collaterals" (Lohmeyer et al. 2021). This representation of healthcare workers burdened them with supererogatory moral duties toward their patients, as if they had the moral obligation (which they did not) to save patient lives at all costs, even at the cost of risking their own lives, or of abandoning other duties that they might have had toward family members, relatives, or close friends. In addition to characterizing healthcare workers as heroes, the master narratives at play behind the scenes in the management of the health crisis in Italy in 2020 led to, by way of collateral, the creation of victims and villains. Verbal attacks against alleged violators such as the one narrated by Accolla (2020)—"Stay home, you murderer!"—and reported earlier in this chapter were documented daily by bloggers in 2020 (e.g., De Vivo 2020; Manzotti 2020).

The unique stigma and public shame joggers and runners experienced in Italy in 2020 can be further explained, I argue, by looking back at the specificities of Patient 1 in Italy. Mattia Maestri, from the city of Codogno, in Lombardy, is a marathoner and Ironman athlete who, at the age of thirty-eight, spent twenty days in intensive therapy between late February and early March 2020 (Visotti 2020). During the days in February when he was positive and asymptomatic, Mattia ran two half marathons and was active daily in an amateur soccer league (Donadio 2020). The links between his active social engagement with sports and the first outbreak in Italy, in the city of Codogno, were widely reported in the media. In addition, some preliminary data postulated a possible link between strenuous exercise and severe cases of COVID-19. According to a "viral auto-inhalation" hypothesis, the transient immune system depression found in athletes—combined with the increased ability of SARS-CoV-2 to move farther down the airway, which is facilitated by intense exercise—led to severe manifestations of COVID-19 (Matricardi et al. 2020). These postulations were published in 2020 and picked up by media, which concluded that "running is bad for your health" (Manzotti 2020). Furthermore, a remarkable fact—although it was not well known to the international press—happened in 2021, when the Public Prosecutor's Office in Lodi opened an investigation into Maestri. This was based on strong suspicions that the man had not disclosed the whole truth to the relevant authorities about contacts preceding the illness. At the end of the preliminary investigations, the public prosecutor requested the dismissal of the proceedings. According to the judge for preliminary investigations, Maestri "had not committed any offense," because when he arrived at the Codogno hospital, the SARS-CoV-2 virus had already been circulating in Italy for several weeks (Redazione Ambasciator 2021). Still, it seems quite significant that Italy's Patient 1 was, although eventually acquitted, criminally prosecuted. Overall, a variety of narratives were mobilized that can explain the hatred against runners unique to Italy during year one of the pandemic.

Proportionality, Fear, and State of Exception in Italy in 2020

According to the WHO (2016) guidelines, three main tenets should guide public health policies for the ethical management of a novel infectious disease outbreak. The first tenet is the principle of proportionality, according to which the interventions restricting individual freedoms need to be proportional to the severity of the risks being offset. The second tenet pertains to evidence: When it comes to specific guidance for restricting freedom of movement, which is relevant for our discussion, decisions "should be grounded on the best available evidence about the outbreak pathogen," and "no such interventions should be implemented unless there is a reasonable basis to expect they will significantly reduce disease transmission" (WHO 2016). The third tenet is the principle of least infringement: Wherever it is possible to achieve an aim with less infringement on freedoms, there is a *moral obligation* to do so. A final point related to the necessity of justifying restricting freedom of movement on the basis of the best available evidence at that time is *transparency of the rationale* for the implemented restrictions—that is, the implementation of public health policies should be justified transparently on the basis of the best available evidence at that time and revised (toward the direction of least infringement) as soon as new evidence emerges. The WHO's (2016, 25–26) *Guidance for Managing Ethical Issues in Infectious Disease Outbreaks* is quite clear in that regard insofar as

> the rationale for relying on these measures should be made explicit, and the appropriateness of any restrictions should be continuously re-evaluated in light of emerging scientific information about the outbreak. If the original rationale for imposing a restriction no longer applies, the restriction should be lifted without delay.

Let's analyze how the WHO tenets for the ethical management of a novel pathogen outbreak apply to the restriction on movement in Italy in 2020, starting from the first one.

1. Proportionality: Were the restrictions proportional to the severity of the risks that they offset?
2. Evidence: Was the prohibition based on the best available evidence at that time? And was it revised as soon as new evidence emerged?
3. Least infringement: Could the same aim have been achieved with less infringement on freedoms?

To be fair to the policymakers who had to come up with public health measures at time of emergency, the question of how to measure proportionality is easier in hindsight. During a public health emergency, it might be justified to adopt a precautionary approach (WHO 2016). In addition, in practical terms, assessing proportionality can be challenging because of (a) the uncertain estimation of the probability and magnitude of various policy outcomes and (b) the possible incommensurability of the expected benefits and harms achieved by certain policies (Jamrozik et al. 2022). In the research conducted by me and my colleagues of the public health policies in Italy and the United Kingdom, we have shown how policymakers have come to very different conclusions based on the same available evidence (Angeli et al. 2021; Camporesi et al. 2022). Different stakeholders can implicitly assign a higher weight to one of three key values—utility, liberty, and equality (see Selgelid 2009)—underlying public health ethics and thereby privilege policies that are more or less restrictive of individual freedoms. For example, Italy adopted measures that were consistently more restrictive than were those of the United Kingdom in terms of wearing facemasks, which remained mandatory until May 1, 2022, in outdoor settings and until June 15, 2022, in schools and universities, public transport, cinemas and theaters, hospitals and care homes, and sporting events and concerts (Angeli et al. 2021; Wanted in Rome 2022).

Because of the precautionary principle, the stringent restrictions on freedom of movement might have been justifiable in Italy at the beginning of the outbreak, and during the early peak of the emergency in March 2020, when the level of uncertainty regarding the ways in which the new pathogen was spreading was highest. It was not yet known how long the virus could survive on surfaces nor what the safe distance between individuals should be. Hence, although we can say that at that time, adopting measures that prohibited running could achieve the aim of not spreading the virus, we can also say that by April 2020, there were epidemiological data emerging from China and soon confirmed elsewhere showing that viral transmission was concentrated in indoor settings, with reports of outdoor transmission being extremely rare (Salje et al. 2020). Hence, to the question, Was the same aim achievable with a lesser infringement on individual freedoms?, the answer seems to be a straightforward yes, as the same aim could have been achieved in different ways. For example, public health guidelines could be enforced by staggering exercise times by age group instead of prohibiting exercise for all or by requiring outdoor exercise to be done while wearing a facemask. Instead, the tout court ban on outdoor exercise implemented in Italy in 2020 exacerbated existing inequalities, as it disproportionately affected those without access to a private outdoor space in the absence of other measures aimed at mitigating those differences. We knew, even before the COVID-19 pandemic, that outdoor exercise is key to maintaining mental health and physical well-being. Access to outdoor and green spaces is consistently associated with better general and mental health across strata of urbanization, socioeconomic status, and genders (Triguero-Mas et al. 2015). These data are particularly strong in children (Abraham et al. 2010). In Italy, children and adolescents did not have access to in-person schooling for over twenty-six weeks in 2020 (Fubini 2021). The ban on running that was exercised in Italy for a prolonged period of time (ten weeks) exacerbated existing inequalities in access to the outdoors, with long-term effects, especially for children and adolescents (Barbieri et al. 2022).

The final point I would like to discuss here is the need for a transparent rationale for any public health policy restricting individual freedoms. From a legal point of view, the burden of proof for demonstrating that restricting the right of freedom of movement is proportional rests on the state that enacts the restrictions (Rivers 2014). In other words, the state must demonstrate that the individual right to freedom of movement has been breached in a way that is justifiable because of a recognized exception. Instead, in Italy in 2020, the rationale for the ban on outdoor exercise in 2020 was never made explicit. On the contrary, it was considered self-evident, and the direness of the situation was taken to be a sufficient, nonverbal explanation for the lack of explicit evidence for the restriction, as analyzed in Camporesi (2020).

An Ethical Crisis in Public Health

Historian of medicine and anthropologist Ilana Lowy (2020) has shown how the "draconian" containment measures enacted to manage the COVID-19 crisis were similar to those put in place in 2003 in mainland China to contain the SARS epidemic. In both cases, such measures were presented to the citizens, and mostly accepted by them, as a "worthwhile sacrifice" in the name of an extraordinary health situation (Lowy 2020). At the peak of the outbreak in Italy in 2020, Italian philosopher Giorgio Agamben (2020) was one of the few voices critical of the containment measures that were being implemented. Referring to the arguments of his 2005 book, *The State of Exception*, Agamben described the concerning indefinite temporal expansion of the sovereign power of states in 2020 and pointed to the increasing tendency of governments, including Italy, to use the "state of exception as a normal governing paradigm." The language of *exception* or *exceptionalism* assumes that an emergency creates special conditions in which the usual standards and practices no longer apply: The ethical perspective itself is affected, and it is argued that special circumstances justify actions and policies that normally would not be ethically acceptable. Diedericks (2022, 8) has analyzed how securitization operates within the exceptional state and how a security threat is "responded to with extraordinary measures that fall outside the bounds of 'normal' (democratic) politics." Kirk and McDonald (2021) have similarly shown how the language of *security* and *threat* serves to enable extraordinary measures that would not be justifiable in normal times. Kirk and McDonald (2021) have analyzed the links between the *securityness* of the COVID-19 disease by political figures and the justification of exceptional measures put in place in several countries throughout the world in 2020. Securityness is established when an actor in a position of political authority "speaks security" and a relevant "audience" accepts this connection, leading to the acceptance of extraordinary measures that would otherwise not have been accepted (Kirk and McDonald 2021, 3). Ndiritu and coauthors (2021) have analyzed the linguistic means and strategies that political leaders have used to appeal to their citizens to observe control measures. Among the linguistic strategies adopted, Aristotle's appeals to logos, ethos, and pathos were widely used in speeches by heads of state from four countries (the United States, the United Kingdom, Russia, and Kenya) analyzed by the authors as a means to exercise soft power. In Italy, the appeal to pathos and to exceptionalism was used as means to accompany the use of power in the form of hundreds of decrees produced during the state of emergency (over two years), all with the binding force of law (Camporesi 2020). It seems evident that the narrative of exceptionality was widely resorted to in Italy in 2020 to justify restrictions on freedom of movement, although implicitly so and without the need for a transparent evidence base.

In 2020, citizens all over the world were asked by their governments to make extraordinary sacrifices to match what were portrayed as extraordinary circumstances. Such extraordinary measures, according to the public health literature, can be justified only in a situation of emergency, for a limited time, with a clear expectation that the severity of the restriction will be balanced by the severity of the risk being offset and will need to be continually re-evaluated to avoid the normalization of an exception. Jamrozik (2022) comparatively analyzed key pandemic public health policies in light of widely accepted ethical principles for public health ethics, among which were the principles already mentioned of proportionality, least infringment, and the need for evidence, and showed how public health policies worldwide have failed to conform to these ethical principles that were widely accepted before the pandemic. Jamrozik (2022, 1) speaks of "an ethical crisis in public health." Given all of the above, I think it is fair to conclude that the ban on outdoor exercise in Italy in 2020 was an example of a prolonged use of stringent measures in the absence of a clear and transparent rationale, which was not revised as soon as new evidence emerged and whose public health aim could have been met with less-infringing measures as those spelled out earlier in this chapter, and as such it was not ethically justified.

Conclusions

What does the fact that the norms of society were dismantled so easily in 2020 in the name of an unprecedented emergency tell us about the fabric of our society? What can it tell us about the tenets of public health ethics, which we thought were unassailable and necessary for the implementation of public health measures restricting individual freedoms? Finally, in what ways did master narratives do things in the world and lead to the creation of heroes, victims, and villains in the pandemic and to long-standing societal fissures still visible today?

Narratives are performative: They function as the cultural mediation of sense-making and lead to the creation of selective memories. Master narratives of war, fear, and sacrifice fueled public health responses that went against consolidated principles for the ethical management of public health crises. The implications and consequences of the deployed narratives are clear: In a dominant war narrative, there can be only heroes, victims, and villains. There were, of course, the victims. The only victims who counted within this framing, though, were those who died of COVID-19 or those who contracted severe COVID-19 or perhaps, though to a lesser extent, those who are suffering from long COVID. Those who were ill in other ways and saw their planned surgeries or care being refused or postponed because of the COVID-19 health emergency were not portrayed as victims but as expendable sacrifices or unavoidable collaterals. A clear hierarchy of illnesses and of sick bodies ensued, something that was analyzed by Diedericks (2022) in her work on negotiating ordinary and extraordinary TB in South Africa. In Italy in 2020, there were those who felt entitled by the narratives of fear and exceptionality to establish a self-led surveillance and invigilation system and happily complied and cooperated to the point of feeling entitled to attack (verbally or, in some instances, physically) those who did not conform to the widespread *social mores* of the moment. Those who refused to comply with the restrictions on freedom of movement, were portrayed as 'irresponsible villains'.

A different framing of the COVID-19 emergency, a different cultural memory of the pandemic, beyond a health emergency only, would have been possible and is possible. This different framing would not resort to a war narrative but to different counter-narratives: of solidarity between different generations, of shared responsibility for the planet and future generations, of an intergenerational pact between the younger and older demographics.[1] A different framing during the first year of the pandemic would have highlighted other aspects of the crisis, including the long-term impact on mental health of prolonged lockdown, the economic impact of the near-total shutdown of factories and production lines, the societal fissures resulting from the widespread resort to narratives that created only heroes, victims, and villains. A different framing of the pandemic would have, possibly, asked citizens to sacrifice less, out of mindfulness for the longer-term consequences of restrictive public health policies in terms of social instability, economic losses, recessions, and mental health concerns. The pandemic happened and unfolded in a certain way. The way it unfolded was not the only possible way. The curtailment of individual freedoms for prolonged periods of time through extraordinary measures was excessive, was unjustifiable,

[1] In a separate OUP volume, edited with Sanny Mulubale and Mark D. M. Davis, we have collected pandemic narratives from scholars working in Africa, Asia, Australia, the Americas, the United Kingdom, and Europe, to further dialogue on the pandemic across geographical, cultural, and social diversity and considers how COVID-19 intersects with privilege and inequity in diverse social circumstances (Camporesi et al. 2025).

is unjustifiable, will be unjustifiable. Future readers, it is to you whom I talk. The virus happened. Other viruses will spill over. Other pandemics will happen. However, it is we, as humans, who choose the narratives we use to make sense of the world. Some narratives are better than others. It did not have to go this way. It does not have to go this way when it happens again.

Acknowledgments

I am grateful to the attendees of a symposium held in person at King's College London on June 18, 2022, in honor of the retirement of Professor Brian Hurwitz and to the attendees of a seminar held online on September 7, 2022, as part of the Institute of Medical Ethics seminar series for their questions and feedback. I am also deeply grateful to Professor Mark Davis for his long-standing mentorship and friendship and for sparking my interest around questions of public trust, narratives, and expert knowledge. Finally, I am personally indebted to the readers of my AEON 2020 piece narrating lockdown in Italy from a personal perspective, whom I have never met and will likely never meet in person but who reached out to me to express their sympathy for some of the views included in that piece and to share their own personal experiences of lockdown in 2020 elsewhere in the world. Your messages and stories helped give meaning to my lockdown and inspired me to work more on this topic. Thank you!

Competing Interests

There are no competing interests to declare.

Funding

There is no funding to declare.

References

Abraham, A., K. Sommerhalder, and T. Abel. 2010. "Landscape and Well-Being: A Scoping Study on the Health-Promoting Impact of Outdoor Environments." *International Journal of Public Health* 55:59–69.

Accolla, D. 2020. "Runner, untori e il bisogno di odiare chi esce da casa." *Linksiesta Blog*, March 19. https://www.linkiesta.it/2020/03/blog-post-2020-03-19-runner-untori-e-il-bisogno-di-odiare-chi-esce-da-casa-28891/.

Agamben, G. 2020. "Lo stato d'eccezione provocato da un'emergenza immotivata." *Il Manifesto*, February 26. https://positionspolitics.org/giorgio-agamben-the-state-of-exception-provoked-by-an-unmotivated-emergency/.
Angeli, F., S. Camporesi, and G. Dal Fabbro. 2021. "The COVID-19 Wicked Problem in Public Health Ethics: Conflicting Evidence, or Incommensurable Values?" *Humanities and Social Sciences Communications* 8 (1). https://www.nature.com/articles/s41599-021-00839-1.
ANSA. 2020. "Coronavirus: Un contagiato in Lombardia," February 21. https://www.ansa.it/sito/notizie/cronaca/2020/02/21/coronavirus-un-contagiato-in-lombardia_dda62491-4ae1-40af-9cd4-e7dc8402b493.html.
Barbieri, V., C. J. Wiedermann, A. Kaman et al. 2022. "Quality of Life and Mental Health in Children and Adolescents After the First Year of the COVID-19 Pandemic: A Large Population-Based Survey in South Tyrol, Italy." *International Journal of Environmental Research and Public Health* 19 (9): 5220.
Cable, J., D. L. Heymann, A. Uzicanin et al. 2021. "Pandemic Diseases Preparedness and Response in the Age of COVID-19—a Symposium Report." *Annals of the New York Academy of Sciences* 1489 (1): 17–29.
Camporesi, S. 2020. "It Didn't Have to Be This Way: Reflections on the Ethical Justification of the Running Ban in Northern Italy in Response to the 2020 COVID-19 Outbreak." *Journal of Bioethical Inquiry* 17 (4): 643–648.
Camporesi, S., F. Angeli, and G. D. Fabbro. 2022. "Mobilization of Expert Knowledge and Advice for the Management of the Covid-19 Emergency in Italy in 2020." *Nature Humanities and Social Sciences Communications* 9 (1): 1–14.
Camporesi, S., S. Mulubale, and M. D. M. Davis. 2025. *Crisis, Inequity, and Legacy Narrative Analyses of the COVID-19 Pandemic.* Oxford University Press.
Carinci, F. 2020. "Covid-19: Preparedness, Decentralisation, and the Hunt for Patient Zero." *BMJ* 368. https://doi.org/10.1136/bmj.m799.
"Coronavirus, a Messina i droni con la voce del sindaco De Luca: 'Dove c . . . vai? Torna a casa.'" 2020. *La Repubblica*, March 25. https://video.repubblica.it/dossier/coronavirus-wuhan-2020/coronavirus-a-messina-i-droni-con-la-voce-del-sindaco-de-luca-dove-c-vai-torna-a-casa/356733/357298.
Council of Ministers. 2020. "Delibera del consiglio dei ministry." *Gazzetta Ufficiale*, January 31. https://www.gazzettaufficiale.it/eli/id/2020/02/01/20A00737/sg.
Cox, C. L. 2020. "'Healthcare Heroes': Problems with Media Focus on Heroism from Healthcare Workers During the COVID-19 Pandemic." *Journal of Medical Ethics* 46 (8): 510–513. https://www.gazzettaufficiale.it/eli/id/2020/02/01/20A00737/sg.
Davis, M., and D. Lohm. 2020. *Pandemics, Publics and Narrative.* Oxford University Press.
De Vivo, P. 2020. "È colpa di quelli come te se c'è il contagio! Abusi in divisa e strategia del capro espiatorio nei giorni del coronavirus." WuMing Foundation, March 22. https://www.wumingfoundation.com/giap/2020/03/vendicatori-in-divisa-coronavirus/.
Di Porto, E., P. Naticchioni, and V. Scrutinio. 2022. "Lockdown, Essential Sectors, and COVID-19: Lessons from Italy." *Journal of Health Economics* 81:102572.
Diedericks, L. 2022. "'We've Come to Live with This Thing, Like It's Our Birthright': Negotiating Ordinary and Exceptional TB in the South African Colonial Present." PhD diss., King's College London.
Donadio, R. 2020. "I Can't Stop Thinking About Patient One." *The Atlantic*, April 16. https://www.theatlantic.com/international/archive/2020/04/italy-patient-one-family-coronavirus-covid19/610039/.
Favale, M. 2020. "Coronavirus, raggi ai cittadini: 'Segnalateci chi non rispetta l'isolamento.'" *La Repubblica* (Rome), March 27. https://roma.repubblica.it/cronaca/2020/03/27/news/coronavirus_raggi_invita_alla_delazione_non_e_spiare_ma_un_aiuto_a_tutti_-252445873/.

Fontefrancesco, M. F. 2022. "A Running Enemy: Jogging at the Time of COVID-19 Pandemic." In *Sport and Quality of Life: Practices, Habits and Lifestyles*, edited by Paolo Corvo and Fabio Massimo Lo Verde. Springer International.

Fubini, F. 2021. "Davvero l'Italia ha chiuso le scuole più degli altri, per il Covid?" *Corriere della sera*, February 21. https://www.corriere.it/scuola/secondaria/21_febbraio_01/davvero-l-italia-ha-chiuso-scuole-piu-altri-il-covid-2c2f8432-64a1-11eb-aad7-ece6884524fa.shtml.

Hansen, P. K. 2018. "Illness and Heroics: On Counter-Narrative and Countermetaphor in the Discourse on Cancer." *Frontiers of Narrative Studies* 4 (s1): s213–s228.

Horowitz, J. 2020. "Italy Announces Restrictions Over Entire Country in Attempt to Halt Coronavirus. *The New York Times*, March 9. https://www.nytimes.com/2020/03/09/world/europe/italy-lockdown-coronavirus.html.

Italian National Plan for Preparedness and Response. 2006. Piano Nazionale di Preparazione e Risposta a una Epidemia Influenzale. https://www.salute.gov.it/imgs/C_17_pubblicazioni_501_allegato.pdf.

Jamrozik, E. 2022. "Public Health Ethics: Critiques of the 'New Normal.'" *Monash Bioethics Review* 40 (1): 1–16.

Khan, Z., Y. Iwai, and S. DasGupta. 2021. "Military Metaphors and Pandemic Propaganda: Unmasking the Betrayal of 'Healthcare Heroes.'" *Journal of Medical Ethics* 47 (9): 643–644.

Kinsella, E. L., and R. C. Sumner. 2022. "High Ideals: The Misappropriation and Reappropriation of the Heroic Label in the Midst of a Global Pandemic." *Journal of Medical Ethics* 48 (3): 198–199.

Kirk, J., and M. McDonald. 2021. "The Politics of Exceptionalism: Securitization and COVID-19. *Global Studies Quarterly* 1 (3): ksab024.

Lohmeyer, B. A., and N. Taylor. 2021. "War, Heroes and Sacrifice: Masking Neoliberal Violence During the COVID-19 Pandemic." *Critical Sociology* 47 (4–5): 625–639.

Lowy, Ilana. 2020. "The Unknown Known: The SARS Past of COVID-19." *Medical Anthropology Quarterly*, June 5. Rapid Response Blog Series. https://medanthroquarterly.org/rapid-response/2020/06/the-unknown-known-the-sars-past-of-COVID-19/.

Manzotti, R. 2020. "#iostoacasa: Come la paura e la mancanza di ragione uccidono la libertà e la democrazia." *Leoniblog*, April 8. https://www.leoniblog.it/2020/04/08/iostoacasa-come-la-paura-e-la-mancanza-di-ragione-uccidono-la-liberta-e-la-democrazia/.

Matricardi, P. M., R. W. Dal Negro, and R. Nisini. 2020. "The First, Holistic Immunological Model of COVID-19: Implications for Prevention, Diagnosis, and Public Health Measures." *Pediatric Allergy and Immunology* 31 (5): 454–470.

Meretoja, H. 2020. "Stop Narrating the Pandemic as a Story of War." *Open Democracy*, May 19. https://www.opendemocracy.net/en/transformation/stop-narrating-pandemic-story-war/.

Meretoja, H. 2021. "A Dialogics of Counter-Narratives." In *Routledge Handbook of Counter-Narratives*, edited by K. Lueg and M. W. Lundholt. Routledge.

Meretoja, H. 2022. "Implicit Narratives and Narrative Agency: Evaluating Pandemic Storytelling." *Narrative Inquiry* 33 (2): 288–316. https://doi.org/10.1075/ni.21076.mer.

Michelini, E., N. Bortoletto, and A. Porrovecchio. 2021. "Outdoor Physical Activity During the First Wave of the COVID-19 Pandemic: A Comparative Analysis of Government Restrictions in Italy, France, and Germany." *Frontiers in Public Health* 9:615745.

Ndiritu, N., and J. Maina2021. "Delivering COVID-19 Containment Measures: A Case of Persuasion and Power." *Asian Journal of Social Science and Management Technology* 3 (1): 67–76.

Pietrobelli, G. 2020. "Coronavirus, pestato perché senza mascherina a Padova." *Il fatto quotidiano*, April 19. https://www.ilfattoquotidiano.it/2020/04/19/coronavirus-pestato-perche-senza-mascherina-a-padova-ero-uscito-a-fare-una-corsa-con-il-mio-cagnolino-mi-trovavo-a-100-metri-da-casa/5775064/.

Redazione. 2020. "Coronavirus, a Forlì droni in volo contro chi infrange le regole." *Corriere romagna*, March 16. https://www.corriereromagna.it/coronavirus-forli-droni-volo-infrange-regole/.

Redazione Ambasciator. 2021. "Mattia maestri: Accusa archiviata per il paziente 1 di Codogno," October 29. https://www.ambasciator.it/paziente-1-mattia-maestri-accusa-COVID/.

Rivers, J. 2014. "The Presumption of Proportionality." *The Modern Law Review* 77 (3): 409–433.

Salje, H., C. Tran Kiem, N. Lefrancq et al. 2020. "Estimating the Burden of SARS-CoV-2 in France." *Science* 369 (6500): 208–211.

Scalia, V. 2021. "'Stay Home You Murderer!': Populist Policing of COVID-19 in Italy." *International Journal of Police Science & Management* 23 (3): 242–252.

Selgelid, M. J. 2009. "A Moderate Pluralist Approach to Public Health Policy and Ethics." *Public Health Ethics* 2(2): 195–205.

Severgnini, C. 2020. "Coronavirus, First Two Cases in Italy: It's Two Chinese Tourists." *Corriere della sera*. https://www.corriere.it/cronache/20_gennaio_30/coronavirus-italia-corona-9d6dc436-4343-11ea-bdc8-faf1f56f19b7.shtml.

Simoni, A. 2020. "Limiting Freedom During the COVID-19 Emergency in Italy: Short Notes on the New 'Populist Rule of Law.'" *Global Jurist* 20 (3): 20200023.

Squire, C., M. Andrews, M. Davis et al. 2014. *What Is Narrative Research?* Bloomsbury Academic.

Squire, C., and J. B. De Lemos. 2022. "Narrating Resistant Citizenships Through Two Pandemics." *Social Sciences* 11 (8): 358.

Sun, N., and L. Zilli. 2020. "COVID-19 Symposium: The Use of Criminal Sanctions in COVID-19 Responses—Enforcement of Public Health Measures, Part II." *OpinioJuris*, April 3. https://opiniojuris.org/2020/04/03/COVID-19-symposium-the-use-of-criminal-sanctions-in-COVID-19-responses-enforcement-of-public-health-measures-part-ii/.

Triguero-Mas, M., P. Dadvand, M. Cirach, et al. 2015. "Natural Outdoor Environments and Mental and Physical Health: Relationships and Mechanisms." *Environment International* 77: 35–41.

Visotti, G. 2020. "Un mese dopo: Mattia, il paziente 1 di Codogno, può tornare a casa." *La Repubblica*, March 10. https://www.repubblica.it/cronaca/2020/03/19/news/coronavirus_mattia_paziente_1-301067614/.

Wanted in Rome. 2020. "Coronavirus in Italy: Fines of up to €3,000 for Violating Quarantine Rules," March 25. https://www.wantedinrome.com/news/coronavirus-in-italy-fines-of-up-to-3000-for-violating-quarantine-rules.html.

Wanted in Rome. 2022. "Where You Need to Wear a Mask in Italy from 1 May," May 10. https://www.wantedinrome.com/news/where-you-need-to-wear-a-mask-in-italy-from-1-may.html.

WHO (World Health Organization). 2005. *International Health Regulations 2005*. https://www.who.int/publications/i/item/9789241580410.

WHO (World Health Organization). 2016. *Guidance for Managing Ethical Issues in Infectious Disease Outbreaks*. https://www.who.int/publications/i/item/9789241549837.

WHO (World Health Organization). 2020. *Naming the Coronavirus Disease (COVID-19) and the Virus That Causes It*. https://www.who.int/emergencies/diseases/novel-coronavirus-2019/technical-guidance/naming-the-coronavirus-disease-(COVID-2019)-and-the-virus-that-causes-it.

4

Perceptions of Proportionality

An Empirical Study of Swiss Residents' Moral Considerations about COVID-19 Containment Measures

Corine Mouton-Dorey, Bettina Schwind, Giovanni Spitale, Kristen Jafflin, and Nikola Biller-Andorno

Introduction

The World Health Organization (WHO) declared the coronavirus outbreak a pandemic on March 11, 2020. In response to the rapid spread of the coronavirus, the Swiss government declared a national lockdown on March 17, 2020, which partially ended in early May 2020 (Weck 2020). Thereafter, Switzerland relaxed containment measures faster than other European countries did (Balthasar et al. 2022, 140).

In Switzerland, containment measures in the first half of 2020 were based on the Federal Act on Controlling Communicable Human Diseases of September 28, 2012 (Epidemics Act; Epid A)which provided a legal basis for public health measures . The government also relied on the constitutional right of necessity to support socioeconomic measures taken in response to the epidemic (Swiss Federal Constitution of April 18, 1999, art. 185)). As the constitutional right of necessity is limited to six months, the Federal Council (FC) was obliged to submit a bill to Parliament to provide further support for the economy, the COVID-19 Act, which was passed by Parliament in September 2020 and came into force immediately. In order to maintain the measures for as long as necessary, the FC and the Parliament called on Swiss citizens to vote for the COVID-19 Act on the grounds of necessity and solidarity. Opponents of the COVD-19 Act contested these reasons, pointing to the primacy of the Swiss people in a direct democracy. They argued that the law violated a number of constitutional rights and did not fulfil the legal obligation to evaluate the effectiveness of containment measures. They also claimed that the risk of adverse effects on certain groups of the population was being neglected. (Swiss Confederation 2021a, 42–43). The government won the popular vote (60.2%) on June 13, 2021, but a significant proportion of

Corine Mouton-Dorey et al., *Perceptions of Proportionality*. In: *Proportionality*. Edited by: Nikola Biller-Andorno et al., Oxford University Press. © Oxford University Press (2026). DOI: 10.1093/9780197759370.003.0005 the population (39.8%) expressed their disagreement with the law, which they felt was neither useful nor respectful of their rights (Swiss Confederation 2021b). Such a result demonstrated the majority's acceptance of the measures taken and, implicitly, of their proportionality.

The concept of proportionality is central to Swiss law: It is a constitutional principle (Swiss Constitution art. 5, al. 2), according to which all state activities must be proportionate to the objectives pursued. The Swiss Constitution (art. 2 al. 1; art.5 al. 2) protects the liberty and rights of the people and requires the state to act in the public interest. Rights and duties must be balanced: Everyone has rights and also duties to the community to secure the rights and freedom of others (UN General Assembly Resolution 217A [III], Universal Declaration of Human Rights, A/RES/217[III] [December 10, 1948] art. 29). Therefore, measures that may restrict the fundamental rights of individuals are permissible if they meet constitutional conditions (Swiss Constitution art. 36). That is, the restrictions must

1. have a legal basis (e.g., the COVID-19 Act),
2. be justified in the public interest or for the protection of the fundamental rights of others,
3. be proportionate.

In July 2021, the opponents of the COVID-19 Act obtained the possibility of a new referendum, this time arguing that the COVID Certificate discriminated against unvaccinated people. COVID Certificates were electronic or paper certificates with QR codes that showed whether people were vaccinated against COVID-19, recovered from a COVID-19 infection, or had a recent negative COVID-19 test (FOPH 2021b). These opponents again lost the vote on November 28, 2021 (38% against and 62% in favor of the government) (Swiss Confederation 2021c). In the run-up to this second referendum, public tensions rose, and opponents of the law called for demonstrations, some of which led to violent clashes. The heated debates in the run-up caused a deep rift in Swiss society, to which the Swiss Nonprofit Society responded with a campaign titled "Through the Crisis Without Division," which promoted values such as respect, tolerance, and working together instead of against each other (Bütler 2021).

These dynamics raise the question of how Swiss citizens[1] understand proportionality as they experience its application during a global health crisis. The Swiss government, for example, regularly communicated containment measures in press conferences from the beginning of the pandemic. At the same time,

[1] In this chapter we use *citizens* to refer to all residents of Switzerland, regardless of nationality, residency status or other.

Swiss citizens began to express different opinions about whether containment measures were proportionate.

The Swiss Constitution emphasizes the obligation to deploy *proportionate restrictions* without explaining precisely what is meant by *proportionate*. For a measure restricting human rights to be proportionate, Swiss jurisprudence requires the authorities to take restrictive measures to meet the following criteria:

1. Adequacy: The measure must be suitable for achieving the intended purpose.
2. Necessity: The state must limit itself to the least possible restriction of fundamental personal rights.
3. Proportionality in a narrower sense: If the measure is appropriate and necessary, authorities must examine whether the restriction is proportionate to the objective pursued (Mahon 2015, 46–47).

Empirically, however, the investigation of these dimensions, although central to public health ethics, remains challenging. Not every important public health interest is necessarily a major public interest, and if it is, its evolution over time and space must be taken into account (Mahon 2015, 44–45). This makes the principle of proportionality a complex issue in practice.

Surveys were carried out to assess the adequacy and effectiveness of the Swiss government's measures during the pandemic—one such survey resulted in a detailed report from the Federal Office of Public Health (FOPH) (Balthasar et al. 2022)—but no study has examined the population's perspective on the principle of proportionality. A cross-sectional survey run in April 2020 reported high adherence to the government containment measures while acknowledging differences depending on age and health literacy and the need for further research on the public's concerns and needs regarding the measures (Selby et al. 2020). It is important to note that public perceptions of what is proportionate may change over time and differ between segments of the public. This variation may also affect how citizens understand the meaning of proportionality and its justification by policymakers. A survey across eleven European countries showed significant differences between countries in the citizens' perception of COVID-19 protection measures when it came to the limitation of their freedom and the balance of benefits and risks. The authors stressed the importance of better understanding citizens' points of view for the governments to build on trust or persuasion when facing a major public health problem such as the COVID-19 pandemic (Georgieva et al. 2021). To our current knowledge, there was no empirical research on how Swiss citizens perceive, understand, or criticize the proportionality of government actions in their daily lives.

This knowledge gap led us to pose the following research questions: How do people understand proportionality? How do they describe it, and what are their thoughts on how it should be achieved, who should make decisions about it, and how it should be evaluated? The answers to these questions could help assess the relevance and application of the principle of proportionality in times of crisis and uncertainty in public health.

Aim

The aim of this study was to better understand which containment measures Swiss citizens perceived as (dis)proportionate and which actors and conditions they would consider most appropriate to ensure that decisions on containment measures are proportionate in a public health context such as the COVID-19 pandemic. As such, we wanted to learn more about proportionality from the Swiss citizen's point of view.

Pandemic Context

Data collection took place from December 10, 2021, to January 10, 2022, which encompassed a particularly dynamic moment in the pandemic. As seen in Figure 4.1, case counts were surging to the highest registered levels of the pandemic, and the number of deaths and hospitalizations were also rising quickly, although not reaching peaks seen in earlier waves.

At this point in the pandemic, COVID-19 vaccination for adults had been underway for almost a year, and all adults were eligible for vaccination. Vaccination of youth aged twelve and older had been underway for approximately three months, and the first recommendations for booster doses had been issued just six weeks prior (FOPH 2023). However, vaccination coverage remained relatively low at 65%, a rate considered insufficient by public health authorities at a time when unvaccinated individuals were far more likely to be hospitalized than their vaccinated peers were.

In addition to vaccination, a limited number of authorized COVID-19 treatments were available at this time, including two antiviral medications that improved outcomes in patients with severe COVID-19 requiring supplemental oxygen (Remdesivir and Baricitinib) and a treatment using monoclonal antibodies (Ronapreve) that improved outcomes in patients at high risk of developing severe COVID-19. All three treatments had to be administered at healthcare facilities by injection or intravenously under close supervision from healthcare providers (National Institutes of Health [NIH] 2020; European Medicines Agency (EMA) 2021; Swissmedic 2021; Selvaraj et al. 2022).

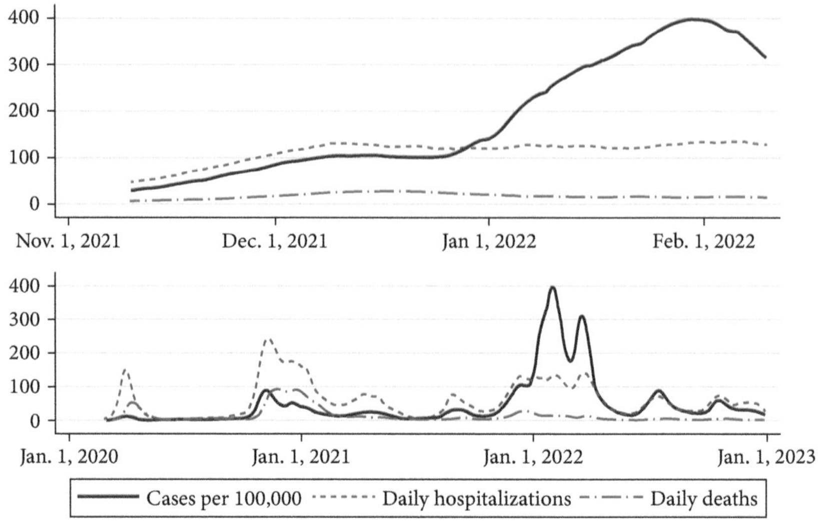

Fig. 4.1 Daily cases per one hundred thousand population, daily hospitalization, and daily deaths from November 10, 2021, to February 10, 2022, and for the whole pandemic on a fourteen-day moving average.
Source: FOPH (2023).

On November 28, 2021, Swiss citizens voted in support of the second COVID-19 Act. This vote validated the use of COVID Certificates in Switzerland. They were widely used in Europe at this period in the pandemic. Being fully vaccinated gave people access to a certificate valid for one year, as did recent recovery with an infection confirmed by a polymerase chain reaction (PCR) test. Recent recovery with an infection confirmed by an antigen test gave access to a valid certificate for a period of ninety days, and negative tests qualified people for a valid certificate for two to three days, depending on the test used (FOPH 2021c). People without a valid certificate could not engage in many social activities in public, including dining in restaurants, attending shows, or going to museums.

The debate surrounding the implementation of COVID Certificates included intense discussion about which vaccination, recovery, or testing requirements would apply in which places. Options were widely discussed using a German-derived short-hand of 1G, 2G, and 3G ("G" standing for "Geimpfte" [vaccinated], "Genesene" [recovered] or "Getestete" [tested].).[2]

[2] A 3G requirement meant that an individual needed to be vaccinated, had recently recovered, or had a recent negative test, whereas 2G required someone to be vaccinated or to have recently recovered, and 1G required someone to be vaccinated only.. In addition, there were debates about adding testing requirements to vaccination or recent recovery—so-called 3G+, 2G+, and 1G+ requirements (FOPH 2021d).

This period also saw growing concerns about new, more transmissible virus variants (Shiehzadegan et al. 2021). The Delta variant, which was approximately twice as transmissible as the original variant with no notable decrease in severity, had first emerged that summer and made up the vast majority of cases in Switzerland (over 90%) at the beginning of data collection. However, a new, even more transmissible variant, the Omicron variant, was just beginning to spread in Switzerland and made up over 90% of cases by the end of data collection (FOPH 2021a).

The WHO first classified Omicron as a variant of concern on November 26, 2021, just two weeks before data collection began. In early December 2021 and January 2022, it was clear that this variant was more transmissible than earlier variants were, but it was still unclear how great the risk of infection was for vaccinated or previously infected individuals and whether disease severity differed notably from the original variants (WHO 2021).

Table 4.1. provides a brief overview of the pandemic context during the study period.

Table 4.1 Pandemic landscape in Switzerland during data collection. Data on cases, hospitalizations, ICU beds, deaths, main variants, share of positive tests, and vaccination status were obtained from the FOPH (2021a). On reproduction rates: Our World in Data (2020); Arroyo-Marioli et al. (2021); Hale et al. (2021). On stringency indexes: Hale et al. (2021).

	Beginning of data collection (Dec. 10, 2021)	**End of data collection (Jan. 1, 2021)**
Weekly laboratory-confirmed cases per 100,000 population	729.9	1673.6
Weekly laboratory-confirmed hospitalizations per 100,000 population	10.3	9.9
Weekly laboratory-confirmed deaths per 100,000 population	2.1	1.3
Share of ICU beds occupied by COVID-19 patients	32.5%	31.2%
Reproduction rate	1.21	1.39
Main variant	Delta (90.7%)	Omicron (92.1%)
Share of positive tests		
PCR tests	19.6%	37.7%
Antigen tests	8.3%	28.1%
Vaccinated with at least one dose of vaccine	67.5%	68.6%
Stringency index (unvaccinated)	50	56.48
Stringency index (vaccinated)	38.89	38.89

Methods

Data Collection

We collected the data presented in this paper using PubliCo, a novel risk and crisis communication platform specifically developed using a citizen-science approach in the context of COVID-19 (Spitale et al. 2021). The system comprises three main components: a survey interface, a diary interface, and an analytics interface.

We developed a qualitative survey (Braun et al. 2021) using the survey component of PubliCo. This allowed us to collect demographic information and in-depth written reflections in an anonymous manner. The survey included informed consent information, demographics (nationality, age, gender, highest degree of school completed, marital status, and whether the respondent has children), and four free-text fields for respondents to provide their reflections in response to the following structured prompts, which investigated their understanding of proportionality:

- In your opinion, which pandemic control measures are most proportionate, and why?
- In your opinion, which pandemic control measures are least proportionate, and why?
- How should decisions about which measures are proportionate be made? By whom and based on what criteria?
- What needs to be weighed when considering whether a measure is proportionate?

These questions were introduced with a brief prompt:

> The ongoing COVID-19 pandemic has prompted governments around the world, including the Swiss government, to institute unprecedented restrictions on residents in an effort to slow or prevent the spread of COVID-19 and protect hospital capacity to cope, over the last two years. It is important to be able to evaluate the proportionality of these different measures in Switzerland: How are the restrictions imposed proportionate with the harms caused by the pandemic? Please share your thoughts on the proportionality of current pandemic control measures with us.

The qualitative survey was developed in English and subsequently translated in German, French, and Italian by native speakers.

Recruitment

Once we programmed the survey, we started distributing the link to recruit our participants. We did so from December 10, 2021, to January 10, 2022, using a Facebook ads campaign (Carter-Harris et al. 2016; Wozney et al. 2019). Further details on the recruitment are available as supplementary material, structured as follows: The campaign collected a total of 38,586 visualizations, 1,874 clicks, and 546 responses. Out of 546 responses, 512 respondents gave their informed consent. The total cost was of €774.98, with a cost per click of €0.41 and a cost per response of €1.51—cheaper than the mean reported in a recent systematic review (Thornton et al. 2016). The enrollment rate, calculated as the ratio of answers to clicks, is 27.32%.

Analysis

CMD and BS used MAXQDA 2020 to analyze the qualitative data following Braun and Clarke's (2006) thematic analysis, including five analytic steps:

1. Familiarization with the data
2. Designation of preliminary codes
3. Search for preliminary themes
4. Revision and definition of themes
5. Provision of a written record

CMD and BS discussed the results of the analysis in order to validate the findings.

Results

Participants

Table 4.2 shows the characteristics of people who gave consent to participate in the reflections and of those who then submitted reflections. A total of 512 consented to participate in the project, with 495 submitting reflections. Participants had a wide variety of perspectives on the pandemic, with most (73.3%) accepting that it was a major public health concern. However, a substantial minority (26.7%) rejected this idea. Among those who submitted reflections and those who accepted the pandemic as a major public health concern, the vast majority were Swiss nationals (90.5% and 91.7%, respectively); slightly over half were

Table 4.2 Descriptive statistics of respondents

	Total (N = 512)		Reflection submitted (N = 495)		Accepts pandemic as public health concern (N = 363)	
	N	(%)	*N*	(%)	*N*	(%)
Nationality						
Swiss	460	(89.8%)	448	(90.5%)	333	(91.7%)
Other / no answer	52	(10.2%)	47	(9.5%)	30	(8.3%)
Gender						
Male	275	(53.7%)	265	(53.5%)	190	(52.3%)
Female	213	(41.6%)	210	(42.4%)	163	(44.9%)
Other / no answer	24	(4.7%)	20	(4.0%)	10	(2.8%)
Age						
35 and younger	79	(15.4%)	74	(14.9%)	62	(17.1%)
36–45	107	(20.9%)	107	(21.6%)	82	(22.6%)
46–55	122	(23.8%)	118	(23.8%)	82	(22.6%)
56-65	127	(24.8%)	123	(24.8%)	87	(24.0%)
66 and older	68	(13.3%)	67	(13.5%)	49	(13.5%)
No answer	6	(1.2%)	3	(0.6%)	1	(0.3%)
Civil status						
Single, never married	88	(17.2%)	85	(17.2%)	67	(18.5%)
Married or domestic partnership	288	(56.3%)	281	(56.8%)	209	(57.6%)
Divorced, separated, or widowed	93	(18.2%)	91	(18.4%)	64	(17.6%)
No answer	38	(7.4%)	33	(6.7%)	23	(6.3%)
Has children						
Yes	296	(57.8%)	291	(58.8%)	218	(60.1%)
No	183	(35.7%)	176	(35.6%)	131	(36.1%)
No answer	33	(6.4%)	28	(5.7%)	14	(3.9%)

Table 4.3 Characteristics of reflections, number of responses, average number of characters, maximum and minimum number of characters, and interquartile range

	N	(%)	Mean	Min	Max	Interquartile range
Question 1	490	(99.0%)	154.1	2	1624	47 –185
Question 2	483	(97.6%)	183.6	3	1874	49 –228
Question 3	476	(96.2%)	215.2	1	3053	72 –272
Question 4	458	(92.5%)	145.3	1	1565	45 –181

male (53.5% and 52.3%, respectively); and most were married (56.8% and 57.6%, respectively), had children (58.8% and 60.1%, respectively), and were between 36 and 65 years of age (70.2% and 69.2%, respectively).

As seen in Table 4.3, most participants who submitted reflections gave answers to all of the prompts.

Question 1 received the most responses and question 4 the fewest. Responses were the length of a short paragraph on average, with the longest responses being approximately one page long, and the shortest consisting of only one word or character (e.g., "0," "2g," "2G+," "alle" or "kein").

Research Findings

Two overarching themes emerged: Respondents who rejected and those who accepted the pandemic as a major public health concern. Since the consideration of any proportionality of containment measures presupposes the existence of a public health emergency such as the COVID-19 pandemic (as required by Art. 36 of the Swiss Constitution), we focus in this study primarily on the reflections of those who recognized the pandemic as a justified major public health problem. Excerpts cited below are English translations of the original texts, which are available in the supplementary materials.

Rejection of the Pandemic as a Major Public Health Concern

The theme *rejection of pandemic as a major public health concern* describes the reflections of individuals who either questioned the pandemic itself or considered any containment measures to be disproportionate and therefore did not consider the pandemic situation to be a public health concern.

> This was and is not a pandemic at all. (Response 378)
> None [is proportionate], as all measures are of no use. (Response 441)

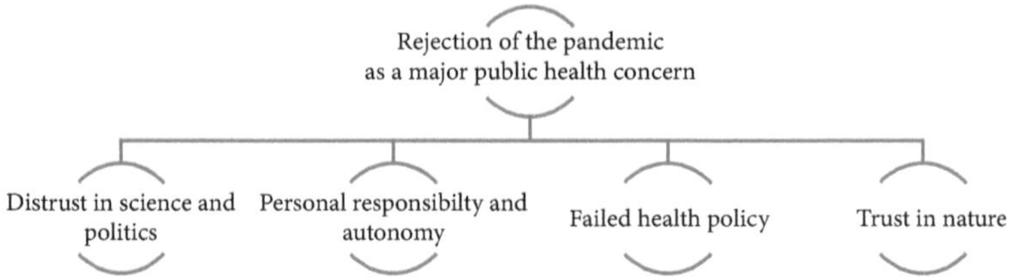

Fig. 4.2 Overview of the theme *rejection of the pandemic as a major public health concern.*

The data collected revealed the following further subthemes as summarizes in the Figure 4.2.

1. Distrust in science and politics
2. Personal responsibility and autonomy
3. Failed health policy
4. Trust in nature

The following excerpts give examples of each in turn:

> Activist propaganda by an overtaxed government that has no ideas and allows itself to be shown up by some experts. (Response 327)
>
> Common sense and personal responsibility. (Response 356)
>
> If hospitals reach their capacity limits, it will not be due to a "pandemic" but to a completely misguided health policy. (Response 358)
>
> There are no proportionate measures. People die—some sooner; others later. (Response 439)

Overall, quotes from this theme showed a rejection of the pandemic as a public health issue, with the pandemic being seen as primarily caused by failed public health policies. Mistrust of government and science was central. Each was portrayed as malevolent, in contrast with the individual, who was portrayed as responsible for making autonomous decisions and having a healthy mind and trust in the natural course of life.

Acceptance of the Pandemic as a Major Public Health Concern

The theme *acceptance of the pandemic as a major public health concern* describes quotes from individuals who recognized the existence of the pandemic and/or that some kind of containment measure could be proportionate while also reflecting on how and who should best decide on the proportionality of containment measures. Figure 4.3 summarizes the thematic overview and its subthemes.

Fig. 4.3 Overview of the theme *acceptance of the pandemic as a major public health concern.*

What Measures Are Considered Proportionate?

Perceptions of what constituted a proportionate response to the pandemic varied widely, forming the subtheme *What measures are considered proportionate.*It consists of the codes (1) *acceptance of basic hygiene measures* and (2) an *array of measures*, which were combined with the first in different ways (protect people at risk, improve clinical measures, test everyone, ban large events, strengthen the immune system).

What distinguishes the responses of these participants from those who rejected the notion that the pandemic or any measures were proportionate is that there was a broad *acceptance of basic hygiene measures*, such as hand washing, wearing a mask, or staying at home when sick, as being appropriate, especially when undertaken freely by the individual.

> Distance, hygiene, like a normal flu. (Response 187)

This broad consensus on hygiene measures was combined with an *array of measures* that were considered proportionate. Some favored protecting people at risk or strengthening the immune system.

> Only distance and compulsory masking [are proportionate]. 2G and mandatory vaccination [are disproportionate]. When it comes to protection, [at-]risk groups should be protected in isolation. And not healthy people who tend to have only mild cases. (Response 49)
>
> Strengthening the immune system to be as resistant as possible [is proportionate]. Reduce risk factors where possible (obesity, [being] overweight). Protect people at risk (hand hygiene, appropriate masks, distancing, vaccination). Let children get infected (they have a lower health risk with covid than with influenza). (Response 15)

Some respondents were in favor of testing everyone—both vaccinated and unvaccinated—which was not required at the time. Only unvaccinated people and people who had not recently recovered from a COVID-19 infection had to be tested to take part in certain events.

> Testing vaccinated AND unvaccinated people. Distance, masks[,] and common sense. (Response 141)
>
> Test all, whether vaccinated or not. Certificate only for those who have a test. No more special treatment of vaccinated people. Every vaccinated person lives in false security. Every vaccinated person can pass on the virus. (Response 23)

It is clear from the above quotes that even some of those who considered certain containment measures as proportionate felt that they had been implemented in an unfair manner. Conversely, others supported the existing measures.

> Mandatory masks, distance, hygiene, 3G, 2G [are proportionate, as are] all small restrictions. (Response 52)

This quote shows that some felt that the containment measures in place at that time were appropriate and fair, which overall underscores the diverse perspectives among respondents who recognized the pandemic as a public health concern.

Decision-Making Process for Proportionate Containment Measures

The subtheme *decision-making process for proportionate containment measures* is grounded in respondents' reflections on *who should decide on proportionate measures* and on *how the proportionality of containment measures should be decided.* For more details on (sub)codes described hereafter, see Figure 4.3.

Who Should Decide on Proportionate Measures? Perceptions of who should decide on containment measures varied widely across the reflections of those who accepted the pandemic as a public health concern. Some thought *political stakeholders,* particularly the FC, should make decisions on containment measures, either alone or in consultation with the COVID-19 task force.

> The Federal Council alone. (Response 442)
>
> Decisions should be made by the federal government with a sense of proportion, as this is the only way to avoid a patchwork quilt[,] as is currently the case. (Response 364)
>
> The Federal government[,] as it is an emergency situation, after consultation with the task force. (Response 260)

The quotes underlined a preference for and trust in the FC as the primary decision-making body. Respondents highlighted the desirability of avoiding a patchwork of decisions and measures, which could occur if the twenty-six cantons were the primary decision-makers on containment measures.[3] Others, however, thought that the FC should decide together with other Swiss political stakeholders.

> Consensus between the Confederation and cantons. (Response 353)
>
> Federal Council together with Parliament. (Response 434)

These quotes, and the following quotes, reflect the—albeit very different—perceptions and desires for more direct public involvement in the decision-making process (subtheme: *public*), beyond the direct votes on the COVID-19 law in Switzerland:

[3] In Switzerland, health laws exist at cantonal level, and the cantons express their views at federal level via the Conference of Health Directors. Federal health laws, such as the Epidemics Act and the COVID-19 Act, are applied in accordance with the constitutional principle of subsidiarity. The cantons are attached to a high degree of decision-making independence in healthcare matters.

> I think every measure should be discussed and voted on. (Response 79)
>
> In a democratic process, by a group of randomly selected citizens, informed by experts who have various specialties and orientations. (Response 386)

Others, however, did not consider decisions on the proportionality of measures to be a political decision and preferred expert assessments (subtheme: *experts*). Some favored the expertise of the Swiss National COVID-19 Science Task Force (2020), which was composed of experts in epidemiology, virology, pediatrics, intensive care medicine, mental health, laboratory work and testing, communication, data sciences, and ethics.

> By the Task Force because it is in contact with hospitals and infectiologists. (Response 408)
>
> The measures should be decided by taskforce/specialists. (Response 402)

Still other participants preferred the involvement of expertise beyond public health and medicine.

> Pool of experts (NOT only doctor or epidemic experts, solving a problem may create other problem, we don't want that!). (Response 209)
>
> From people from different fields. Instead of only virologists and physicians, psychologists, sociologists, and many more should also be involved. Otherwise, the negative effects of the measures will be totally forgotten. (Response 339)

These quotes indicate a wish for the decision-making body to include expertise beyond the health sciences in order to consider and weigh other aspects, such as social and economic consequences of the pandemic, against the health aspects.

In addition, a certain distrust of the neutrality of decision-makers was apparent even among those who supported containment measures in principle.

> By people with no ties to Pharma, obviously. (Response 428)
>
> Neutral posts and not purchased. (Response 466)
>
> Independent subject matter experts who represent neither government, nor pharmaceutical interests. (Response 432)

The quotes suggested skepticism about the influence of industries, especially pharmaceutical companies, on the decision-making processes in both science and politics.

Furthermore, even among those who supported basic hygiene measures to contain the pandemic, some wanted *the individual* to be free to decide whether to comply.

> I think it's not upon any government to tell me what I should do to stay healthy. If the governments had let the virus run its course people would have built their own antibodies and the virus would have been gone already. (Response 131)
>
> The free choice of each individual must not be impaired. Everyone has the choice of where to go or not to go. Which place to visit or avoid. Everyone is aware that one can become infected and that it can be fatal. But it is free will. (Response 371)

The quotes imply a primacy of individuals, their autonomy, and free will.

More rarely, the individualized decision is based on a worldview.

> What is the value of a human life? How old do we want to become. Measures should be voluntary. The Federal Council should [make recommendations]. (Response 352)

Some respondents argue that the decision should be made first and foremost by the individual's *personal doctor*.

> By physicians who are trained and not bound by conflicts of interest and who are able to know the problem from the beginning of the patient's contamination and its subsequent staged evolution. (Response 420)
>
> By practicing physicians and common sense! (Response 226)

The quotes indicate that medical doctors should decide on the appropriateness of personal containment and treatment measures.

Overall, the data show that there was no clear consensus on who should decide on measures to achieve proportionality.

How Should the Proportionality of Containment Measures Be Decided? From the data analyzed, we were able to identify the aspects that participants felt needed to be considered in order to decide on appropriate mitigation measures from the viewpoint of the participants. However, the ways to achieve this varied considerably between respondents. In the view of some, the decision on proportionality should be *in accordance with the law* with a clear articulation of the public health interest and the measures deemed necessary and suitable for achieving it.

> The assessment of whether a federal law is proportionate or not is a purely theoretical one, regardless of who makes it. Ultimately, the sovereign decides on the law—and the sovereign approved the Covid law in November[,] completely disregarding the fact that, according to the usual legal criteria for assessing

> proportionality, the law completely overshoots the mark and is clearly disproportionate . . . . [There are] three criteria: Is there a legal basis? Is the measure *probably* suitable to achieve the intended goal. Is the measure absolutely necessary, i.e., is there no milder measure with an equivalent result? If the answer to any of the questions is no, the measure is disproportionate. (Response 419)

> There is a clear and proven legal basis for this, as well as extensive literature and case law. In principle, the measure must be the mildest possible, which is nevertheless suitable for achieving a clearly set purpose. In addition, the weighing of private interests against public interests must be in favor of the public interests. (Response 357)

For others, *hospital capacity* appeared as a major criterion for making decisions on containment measures.

> As long as we're dealing with an infectious disease that seriously affects only a few people, apart from the very vulnerable, the only criterion should be the saturation of the care system. Provided, of course, that we don't reduce the capacities of this system in the midst of a pandemic. (Response 423)
>
> Hospital utilization rates, number of new cases. (Response 354)
>
> Medical capacity (ICU) and whether access to other medical areas could still be provided. (Response 402)

The responses noted that decisions should involve *balancing benefits and risks.* This involved balancing the benefits of the measures against their possible negative consequences for mental health, economic impacts, and societal tensions while also balancing short-term benefits against long-term consequences.

> Risk[:]benefit ratio on all aspects of health (physical, physiological, psychological, social . . . . so many aspects forgotten in the last 2 years). (Response 368)
>
> That the cost (in every sense) does not outweigh the benefits. (Response 45)
>
> Overall consideration of benefits/harm in the economic and psychological, ethical realms. (Response 427)
>
> Social cohesion must be preserved. Federalism must not harm the country. The FC must show itself to be a federating body that defends national unity. (Response 328)
>
> Risks and benefits, short & long term. (Response 200)
>
> Social damage not only in direct economic terms but also in future and indirect terms. (Response 5)

Moreover, from the standpoint of respondents, balancing risks and benefits also required prioritizing the objectives to be achieved and deciding on trade-offs.

> Basis [case fatality rate] = Measures to protect vulnerable groups (approximately 70 and over and younger with pre-existing conditions). (Response 432)
>
> How much of the population is constrained and annoyed versus how much of the population faces real risks to their lives. (Response 38)
>
> Knowing that destroying an economy and the future of young people to save old people with one foot already in the grave is a disgrace to the human species. (Response 46)

The quotes illustrate the perspective that it was necessary to identify vulnerable and less vulnerable groups in order to decide on group-specific appropriate interventions. Participants argued that risk varied across social groups, which in their view justified different measures. It is clear from the quotes that greater restrictions on the physical integrity or autonomy and isolation of certain high-risk groups were considered appropriate. This approach is related to *a sense of justice*, as it evokes a desire to protect the vulnerable without discriminating against other groups. More broadly, quotes show the search for the common good of the whole society, a public interest that goes beyond public health alone.

> What kind of society do we want to be? (Response 65)
>
> Criteria for political decision-making must take into account the interests of society as a whole. (Response 392)

It is also clear from the quotes that even among those who consideredthe pandemic to be a public health problem, some wanted *the quality of the data* to be better than was then the case in order to make appropriate decisions.

> There definitely needs to be more and more accurate data collected to make decisions. This has been criminally neglected . . . . Moreover, the decisions seem to be subject to a political, international narrative and not evidence-based. (Response 475)
>
> The principle is in order. but inclusion of contrary and independent opinions imperative. Also, clear facts continuously collected and evaluated, which is not happening! (Response 338)

The above quotes show dissatisfaction with the data used and with knowledge generation for decision-making, but they also reveal a mistrust of policy and research and question their independence and transparency in informing decisions.

Moreover, respondents stressed that the quality of information was also linked to how data were used and shared to assess the efficacy and impact of measures taken. To achieve this, some also advocated for taking into account data from other countries.

> Decisions should be made with an international task force; we are all in the same [situation]. (Response 65)
>
> The efficiency/usefulness according to figures from abroad. (Response 399)

Additionally, respondents stated a clear desire for broader support for decisions and measures linking science, policy, and practice, seeing this as the only way to decide on the appropriateness of measures and their implementation and impact in practice and daily life.

> If there is dissemination of information, the creation of knowledge[,] and the practical applicability of the material taught, there is no doubt that all the right behaviors will be adopted. (Response 381)
>
> Its real impact, the results expected/obtained. (Response 416)

It is also clear from the quotes that respondents wanted policies to be applicable to everyday life, but the decision-making process seemed, from their point of view, to be far removed from their reality of life.

Discussion

Given the study goal, we have not analyzed in detail responses from respondents who did not consider the pandemic of major public interest and who consequently judged all governmental measures as disproportionate. Rather, their stance prompts the question of how to convey to different segments of the public that managing a public health crisis is a major public interest that at times leads to the necessary limitation of fundamental rights.

Our core findings are based on insights provided by those respondents who saw the pandemic as a major threat to public health and on their reflections on the proportionality of the measures deployed. While distancing and hygiene measures promoted by the FOPH are considered proportionate, other measures give rise to a broad diversity of opinions on their proportionality, particularly regarding COVID Certificates, generalized testing, protection of specific at-risk groups, and the stimulation of the immune system with or without vaccination.

Respondents also had diverse perspectives on the best decision-making process for proportionate measures. While several respondents recognized the role of the FC because of the legitimacy of its role and the urgency of the situation, others thought that the FC should not be the only entity to judge and decide on the proportionality of the measures. According to participants, other political stakeholders, especially the cantons and experts must be involved. Some called for multidisciplinary expertise, including representatives from outside the health field, such as ethicists, economists, and sociologists; conversely, others thought expert input should be limited to virologists and epidemiologists. Of note, the taskforce advising the FC was sometimes judged to be too close to pharmaceutical interests. The respondents proposed several collegial solutions, including the direct participation of citizens in decisions on the proportionality of measures, and an international perspective. Respondents also recommended giving a voice to patients, people at risk, or personal doctors in the field. In addition, respondents valued individual responsibility, autonomy, and free will in matters of health. Some even took a distanced approach to the epidemic based on their personal worldview, suggesting that we ought to let the pandemic take its course without intervening in any major way. The subject of what needs to be considered to determine whether a measure is proportionate tells us how respondents conceptualize proportionality—that is proportionality for them is a principle that:

- needs to be grounded in law;
- is triggered by a major public health concern, such as hospital capacity;
- requires balancing risks to and benefits for not only health (personal or public) but also other aspects of well-being and social life that are affected by containment measures, such as psychology, economics, (the avoidance of) stigmatization and societal polarization, and intergenerational (in)justice;
- should protect the most vulnerable and avoid discrimination;
- relies on the quality of data and of communication (i.e., it should be transparent, truthful, based on evidence, and free from conflicts of interest, and it should take into account data from other countries);
- must consider data on the impact of measures in several domains within and outside health and over time.

In this study, our aim was to learn more about proportionality from the Swiss residents' point of view. The diversity of opinions on the decision-making process regarding the proportionality of measures argues in favor of a principle of proportionality that cannot be univocally defined. While the feeling of disproportionality is easily expressed by the population, the principle of proportionality is more difficult to define and involves some moral judgment. A multiwave panel survey conducted in France and Austria considered the appropriateness of the government measures as a good proxy for trust in government. It showed that the dynamic of trust in government varied with the political system and over time, and that the government needed to rely on a partisan consensus to maintain the public's trust (Kritzinger et al. 2021). Our study observed a similar divide in society regarding trust and proportionality. In particular, respondents who did not recognize the seriousness or even the existence of the pandemic exemplified that, in the absence of trust, no measures are considered proportionate. Trust in policymakers was linked to citizens' information and participation, with the type and quality of information playing a key role in this matter, as we found under the subtheme *quality of data*. A survey conducted in February 2022 in the United States showed that American adults value scientific expertise to maintain trust in government and health agencies; fear of scientific information being biased by political or commercial interests, conversely, undermined trust (SteelFisher et al. 2023). Empirical studies in different countries have explored the citizen perceptions in terms of behavior related to (Silubonde et al. 2023) or perception of the pandemic course (Baggio et al. 2022), reporting that trust in official bodies eroded overtime, which subsequently compromised the implementation and effectiveness of protective/containment measures. These studies also showed that the impact of secondary effects (economic and psychologic) of the containment measures varied with the socioeconomic level of the people, as in our study with the subthemes *balancing benefits and risks* and *with a sense of justice*.

These insights show a broader understanding of proportionality than is found in Swiss jurisprudence—namely, by necessity, appropriateness, and proportionality in the strict sense. The findings thereby emphasize the limits of a purely legal approach to the principle of proportionality. Indeed, the three Swiss jurisprudence conditions appeal to and rely on a consensus among legislators and decision-makers that explicitly and implicitly resorts to a moral reasoning (i.e., an ethical approach to proportionality). Beauchamp and Childress (2019, chap. 5) introduced the notion of proportionality as part of the principle of nonmaleficence, "a prima facie principle that requires the justification of harmful actions." Harm is defined broadly to include infringement of fundamental human rights and privacy. In some circumstances, however, the desired benefit is accompanied by harmful side effects. Then it is important that "the intended purpose be the good one and that the secondary consequences be as limited as possible, in no case the means to achieve the desired beneficial effect, and proportional." The authors retain the need for proportionality, as "the good effect must outweigh the bad effect. That is, the bad effect is permissible only if a proportionate reason compensates for permitting the foreseen bad effect" (Beauchamp and Childress 2019, chap. 5). This balance of interests depends on many factors, and ethical assessment in practice may lead to different decision-making processes and outcomes. We saw this during the COVID-19 pandemic between different European countries, despite their close social and democratic political contexts. The same cause provoked different responses in different countries—for example, school closures or vaccine mandates. In the context of the pandemic, the meaning of what is proportionate and what is not is factually open to interpretation and requires resolving moral conflicts, which by their very nature are context sensitive and context specific (Eidgenössische Departement des Innern 2022).

This is also what emerged from our empirical study: The legal principle of proportionality must be respected in Swiss democracy, but it also calls for moral reflection based on personal experiences of the measures implemented. We identify three main areas of respondents' moral reflections:

- The question of who should decide reveals the role of individual choice in relation to top-down containment measures. This relates to the concept of relational autonomy.
- The question of how proportionality should be determined identifies the importance of balancing different interests in different segments of the population, such as between vulnerable people and other groups (i.e., it is an issue of social justice).
- Truth and trust in decision-makers and the trustworthiness of decision-makers, which we summarize under the notion of trust, should be recognized as a core, foundational pillar.

Our research methodology does not allow us to dictate normative recommendations, but we can suggest further exploring these three intertwined ethical considerations when deciding on proportionate measures to restrict fundamental rights during a public health emergency.

Relational Autonomy

In clinical ethics the concept of autonomy focuses on autonomous choice. As illness could impair the ability to appropriately self-manage (Beauchamp and Childress 2019, chap. 4). The concept of autonomy has been enriched by the notion of a bond with loved ones who are "indispensable in the process of coming to terms with illness, and deciding about treatment" (Van Nistelrooij 2017). This relational approach is relevant to care at the population level. Indeed, in public health, autonomy is a broad concept based on human rights and external influences; it is described as relational autonomy (i.e., autonomy in relation to others who are able to inform and guide) as opposed to narrowly defined individual autonomy in isolation (Zimmerman 2017). Public health measures should not only avoid restricting autonomy in an unnecessary and disproportionate way, but they should also include positive measures to offer people a range of possible choices. Autonomy in this broader multidisciplinary approach is about agency and the ability for governance as developed in the capabilities approach to life by Sen (1993). Our respondents advocated this need for self-governance as an issue of personal responsibility, free will, and worldview. Relational autonomy is a right that can be experienced differently by Swiss citizens, depending on their specificities and environment. To reduce the risk of disproportionate measures or perception of disproportionality, decision-makers need to listen to experts, inform and educate citizens, and listen to them through transversal interactions with different groups, so that an idea of the common good can emerge from empowered people. The relational autonomy thus developed enables citizens to make a valuable contribution to public health decisions. This approach including relational considerations has already been recommended in health promotion policies (Wardrope 2015). It is possible that at the start of a crisis such as a pandemic, the need to take action in a state of emergency and uncertainty may lead to these relational factors being overlooked, particularly if the public health framework has not previously highlighted them. Evaluating the impact of measures, informing people, and listening to them in their different environments and diversity, with true dialogical engagement and collaborative social work, should make it possible to (re-)establish a framework that fosters relational autonomy—as also stipulated by the Sendai Framework (UN Office for Disaster Risk Reduction 2015). However, a common social project cannot be reduced to the mere exercise of autonomy in different relational contexts. The relational autonomy of some is limited by the relational autonomy of others (Childress 2022). The respondents rejecting the pandemics as a public health concern can be seen as privileging their own autonomy and that of their relational group at the expense of others by denying the impact on public health. To establish the proportionality of public health measures, it is important to balance different relational interests; this is what social justice contributes.

Social Justice

A sense of justice emerges from respondents' desire to avoid discrimination, exclusion, and the division of society. Balancing different group interests while avoiding excessive paternalism is a difficult task. Some measures were considered disproportionate because the well-being of some groups represented public interests—for instance, the future of the young generation, the isolation of the elderly, the social and health consequences of an economic collapse, the neglect of other health problems, the weakening of the local healthcare system—that were greater than the sole pandemic public health issue. These concerns for those who are the most affected by the federal measures are broader than a utilitarian aim to yield as much health as possible (e.g., the lowest number of deaths) while balancing measures with individual respect or freedom. Faden and Powers have introduced a public health ethics approach that fits these concerns (Powers and Faden 2006): They argue that the foundational moral justification for the social institution of public health is social justice. Therefore, the aim of public health is to secure for everyone a sufficiency of health according to six separate and interconnected dimensions of well-being: *health*, *personal security*, *reasoning*, *respect*, *attachment*, and *self-determination*. This approach encompasses not only the WHO definition of health as a state of complete physical, mental, and social well-being but also the particular circumstances of vulnerable and marginalized groups (Walker and Fox 2018).

The Swiss Epidemics Act provides for measures to be taken in terms of control and protection of personal data (*personal security*), isolation and quarantine (*attachment*), and constraints on *reasoning* and *self-determination*. Containment measures must respect public well-being over and above health, and it is in this balance of interests that social justice is exercised. The principle of proportionality applied to public health is reflected in these different dimensions. At the beginning of the pandemic, key ethical concepts were identified and defined: *solidarity*, *equity*, *trust*, *autonomy*, *equal moral respect*, and *vulnerability* (Dawson et al. 2020). These ethical concepts are also reflected in the previously described dimensions of social justice and solidarity and equity, with consideration given to disadvantaged groups. Therefore, the public is not uniform nor monolithic, and the principle of proportionality must weigh well-being as a common good for different segments of different publics. This is also what our study shows in times of public health crisis: Respondents criticized several inequalities and divisions in society. However, they also called for prioritization and positive discrimination, which would use measures targeting people at risk. It follows that solidarity will ask for nondiscrimination and support to the most vulnerable people and that equity may consider that different situations deserve different measures. These observations demonstrate that it is challenging for the government to apply measures uniformly across the entire population when trying to ensure they are proportionate. The Epidemics Act includes a division of tasks between the cantons and the federal government, which respects the principle of subsidiarity enshrined in the constitution (Swiss Constitution arts. 3, 5). This balance may have been undermined by the need for urgency and the COVID-19 Act, which gave greater authority to the federal level. However, because the cantons sometimes took slightly different decisions, doubts about the proportionality of the measures may have arisen and fed a feeling of mistrust, which we saw in all groups of respondents. This is why, in addition to relational autonomy and social justice, trust is a key principle in establishing the proportionality of public health containment measures.

Trust

In managing the pandemic, containment measures may have been taken or applied differently from one country to another and, in Switzerland, from one canton to another. This lack of consistency led to questioning and even to mistrust among respondents. Our empirical data contain concerns about the lack of information; the need for evidence-based data, truth, and data independent from commercial interests; and the need for information from different sources and from foreign countries. These considerations were also reflected in the way respondents judged who should be responsible for the decision-making process. Respondents called for experts to guide politicians in their decision-making or even to have the experts make decisions themselves. But there was no consensus on who experts are: experts in epidemics, or experts in any other discipline, and sometimes experts who merely provide contradiction. This plurality of conceptions poses the problem of whom to believe in a context of epistemic underdetermination (Upshur 2002) or at least of who is considered sufficiently trustworthy by the population so that they will have confidence in the accuracy and proportionality of the measures taken. Doubts about institutions and their decisions and infodemics (WHO 2020) undermine confidence and social cohesion and lead people to refuse protective measures such as vaccination because of fears that they are dangerous or ineffective. We saw this in some reflections that highlighted mistrust in the public health system and political institutions related to issues of vaccination and the use of COVID Certificates.

The role of communication during a pandemic was acknowledged as crucial even before COVID-19 (Lee et al. 2008). Providing reliable information by for example "disclosing information as well as speaking honestly and truthfully [often grouped under transparency] . . . and building and maintaining trust" (Childress et al. 2002) is an important condition for trust in public health ethics. From the onset of the COVID-19 pandemic, trust has been a key ethical issue: Decision-makers in public health had to provide truthful answers and respect confidentiality to build and maintain trustworthiness—that is, by offering other people reasons to trust them. Particularly during a pandemic, trust plays a role in several contexts related to, for example, the reliability of testing, the protection of privacy when surveillance is required, the communication of understandable information, building trustworthiness in experts, and the provision of transparent and understandable explanations about what is known and unknown in addition to taking the proposed rights-restricting actions. Poor communication management can erode public trust in politics and scientists, especially as any shortcomings in this area leave room for infodemics that are difficult to counter (Spitale et al. 2023). The concept of trust is a complex one and cannot be isolated from the other two ethical concepts of relational autonomy and social justice. Altogether, relational autonomy, social justice, and trust, although not forming an exhaustive ethical framework for public health, are key ethical values informing Swiss residents' understanding of the principle of proportionality in their practical life during the COVID-19 pandemic. When federal law leads to containment measures, respecting these three ethical values could help ensure that the decision-making process and implementation of measures are more clearly perceived as proportionate by citizens.

Limitations and Strengths

The limitations of the study include the slight underrepresentation of women in the qualitative survey, which may indicate a gender bias in the response rate. Additionally, recruitment was based on Facebook ads only, as opposed to a broad random sample, which may present a limitation, especially as social media has been identified as a major source of misinformation during the pandemic (Burki 2020). The quality of the data collected were partly limited, as some responses were short and lacked breadth and depth, while others provided extended answers that allowed for in-depth thematic analysis. Such limitations may hamper the generalizability of the findings, although the overall themes resonate with the public discourses present during this time of the pandemic in Switzerland. Further, analysis and validation of themes was conducted by a multilingual team to discuss and validate analysis results. We used a qualitative survey to gain insight into people's situated knowledge, thus depicting their unique perspectives on COVID-19 policy in Switzerland while reaching a large number of individuals. Therefore, we believe the results are of key importance, as they provide in-depth insights into the variety of perceptions on issues around proportionality and containment measures (Braun et al. 2021).

Conclusion

Our research sheds light on Swiss residents' perception of how to develop and deploy proportionate containment measures in a public health crisis. This study provides insights into what should be considered when policymakers apply the principle of proportionality to decisions that restrict fundamental rights in the interest of major public policy. The analysis of the responses leads us to conclude that an ethical perspective must be considered in the legal decision-making process and in the implementation of measures that are intended to be proportionate. What we have learned about proportionality from our results goes beyond simply deciding on proportionate measures: Proportionality, as perceived by our study, involves a multidimensional approach that touches the entire social fabric in ways that guarantee the founding principles of human rights: justice, autonomy (relational and for all), and trust. To ensure that the measures decided upon are perceived as proportionate when they are applied, good effects should not only outweigh bad effects (per the ethical principle of nonmaleficence) but also be balanced with the use of the ethical concepts of relational autonomy, social justice, and trust. Respect for these three ethical values when national law leads to containment measures will help develop a shared common good in a bottom-up public health perspective and, consequently, lead to a better assessment of proportionality in the choice of containment measures.

Acknowledgments

The authors thank Professor Dr. Sonja Merten (Swiss Tropical and Public Health Institute [TPH]) and Dr. Andrea Grolimund (Swiss TPH) for their valuable collaboration in realizing this project. Our thanks also go the peer reviewers of the manuscript for their remarks on advancing the insights presented here.

Competing Interests

There are no competing interests to declare.

Funding

The work presented here was supported by the Swiss National Science Foundation under project numbers 31CA30_195905—PubliCo—an Experimental Online Platform for COVID-19-Related Public Perception (BS, KJ, GS

Supplementary Materials

Recruitment

- Daily budget: €25
- Start: December 10, 2021
- End: January, 1, 2022
- Country: Switzerland
- Age groups: 18–65+
- Languages: Italian, English, French, German
- Visual element: A neutral video animation representing the concept of proportionality and asking potential respondents to share their opinion, developed in English and translated in German, French, and Italian by native speakers.
- Facebook ad text: "We've been faced with a lot of pandemic control measures over the last 2 years of the COVID-19 pandemic. How proportionate do you find the pandemic response? Share your thoughts with us."

Original Text

The quotes were originally in different languages: German, French, Italian, and English. We have translated them all into English in the chapter. Here we reproduce each quote in its original language, indicating the respondent's number.

Rejection of the Pandemic as a Public Health Concern

Das war und ist keine Pandemie. (Response 378)
Keine [ist verhältnismässig]. Da alle Massnahmen nichts nützen. (Response 441)
Aktionistische Propaganda einer überforderten Regierung, die keine Ahnung hat und sich von irgendwelchen Experten vorführen lässt. (Response 327)
Gesunder Menschenverstand und Eigenverantwortung. (Response 356)
Falls die Spitäler an ihre Auslastungsgrenzen geraten sollten, liegt das nicht an einer "Pandemie" sondern an einer völlig verfehlten Gesundheitspolitik. (Response 358)
Es sind keine Massnahmen verhältnismässig. Leute sterben nun mal, die einen früher die anderen später. (Response 439)

Acceptance of the Pandemic as a Public Health Concern

What Measures Are Considered Proportionate?

Abstand, Hygiene, wie bei einer normalen Grippe. (Response 187)

Nur noch Abstand und Maskenpflicht [sind proportional]. 2G und Impfzwang/pflicht [sind unproportional]. Wenn es um Schutz geht, sollte man Risikogruppen isoliert schützen. Und nicht gesunde Menschen die eher nur leichte Verläufe haben. (Response 49)

Das Immunsystem stärken, um möglichst widerstandsfähig zu sein [ist proportional].—Risikofaktoren nach Möglichkeit verringern (Fettleibigkeit, Übergewicht). Risikopersonen schützen (Handhygiene, angemessen getragene Masken, Distanzierung, Impfung)—Kinder immun werden lassen (sie haben bei Covid ein geringeres Gesundheitsrisiko als bei der Grippe). (Response 15)

Das Testen von geimpften UND ungeimpften Personen. Abstand, Maske und ein gesunder Menschenverstand. (Response 141)

Alle testen, egal ob geimpft oder nicht. Zertifikat nur noch wer einen Test hat. Keine Sonderbehandlung mehr von Geimpften. Jeder Geimpfter lebt in falscher Sicherheit. Jeder Geimpfter kann das Virus weiter geben. (Response 23)

Maskenpflicht, Abstand, Hygiene, 3G, 2G, [sind proportional und] alles kleine Einschränkungen. (Response 52)

Decision-Making Processes for Proportionate Containment Measures

Der Bundesrat alleine. (Response 442)

Die Entscheidungen sollten vom Bund mit Augenmass getroffen werden, nur so kann ein Flickenteppich, wie derzeit vermieden warden. (Response 364)

Le gouvernement fédéral car il s'agit d'une situation d'urgence, après consultation de la task force. (Response 260)

Consensus confédération et canton—sur la base de la mortalité seulement. (Response 353)

Bundesrat zusammen mit Parlament. (Response 434)

Penso che ogni misura vada discussa e votata. (Response 79)

Dans un processus démocratique, par un groupe réunissant des citoyens tirés au sort, éclairés par des experts qui sont de plusieurs spécialités et d'orientation diverses. (Response 386)

Par la Task force car elle est en relation avec les hopitaux et les infectiologues. (Response 408)

Die Massnahmen soll von Taskforce/Fachspecialisten entschieden. (Response 402)

Pool of expert (NOT only doctor or epidemic experts, solving a problem may create other problem, we don't want that!). (Response 209)

Von Menschen aus verschiedenen Bereichen. Anstatt nur Virologen und Mediziner sollten auch Psychologen, Soziologen, und viele mehr miteinbezogen werden. Sonst werden die negativen Effekte der Massnahmen total vergessen. (Response 339)
Par des personnes n'ayant aucun lien avec les pharmas, évidemment. (Response 428)
Neutrale Stellen und nicht gekaufte. (Response 466)
Unabhängige Fachexperten, welche weder staatliche, noch pharmazeutische Interessen vertreten. (Response 432)
I think it's not upon any government to tell me what I should do to stay healthy. If the governments had let the virus run its course people would have [built] their own antibodies and the virus would have been gone already. (Response 131)
Die Freie Entscheidung eines jeden einzelnen darf nicht beeinträchtigt werden. Jeder hat die Wahl wo man hingeht oder nicht. Welchen Ort man besucht oder meidet. Jedem ist bewusst das man sich anstecken kann und es tödlich enden kann. Doch es ist der freie Wille. (Response 371)
Was ist ein Menschenleben Wert. Wie alt wollen wir werden. Massnahmen sollen freiwillig sein. Bundesrat soll empfehlen. / What is the value of a human life? (Response 352)
da medici preparati e non vincolati da conflitti di interesse e che siano in grado di conoscere il problema da subito, dall'inizio della contaminazione del paziente e la susseguente evoluzione a stadi. (Response 420)
Par les médecins pratiquants et le bon sens! (Response 226)

How Should the Proportionality of Containment Measures Be Decided?

Die Beurteilung ob ein Bundesgesetz verhältnismässig ist oder nicht ist eine rein theoretische, egal wer sie anstellt. Letztendlich bestimmt der Souverän über das Gesetz—und dieser hiess das Covid Gesetz im November gut. Völlig ungeachtet dessen, dass nach den gängigen juristischen Kriterien zur Beurteilung der Verhältnismässigkeit das Gesetz völlig über das Ziel hinausschiesst und klar unverhältnismässig ist. . . . 3 Kriterien: Besteht eine gesetzliche Grundlage? Ist die Massnahme NACHWEISLICH geeignet, das angestrebte Ziel zu erreichen. Ist die Massnahme zwingend erforderlich, also gibt es keine mildere Massnahme mit gleichwertigem Ergebnis? Ist eine der Fragen mit Nein zu beantworten, ist die Massnahme unverhältnismässig. (Response 419)
Dazu gibt es klare und bewährte rechtliche Grundlagen bzw. ausführliche Literatur und Rechtsprechung. Grundsätzlich muss die Massnahme die mildest mögliche sein, welche dennoch geeignet ist zur Erreichung eines klaren gesetzten Zwecks. Zudem hat die Abwägung der privaten gegeüber der öffentlichen Interessen zugunsten der öffentlichen Interessen auszufallen. (Response 357)

Tant qu'on a affaire à une maladie infectieuse qui ne touche gravement que peu de personnes, en dehors des personnes très vulnérables, le seul critère devrait être la saturation du système de soins. Pour autant bien sûr qu'on ne réduise pas les capacités de ce système en pleine pandémie. (Response 423)
Auslastung der Krankenhäuser, Anzahl neuer Fälle. (Response 354)
Medizin-Kapazität (ICU) und ob der Zugang zu andere Medizinbereich nocht gewährleistet werden könnte. (Response 402)
Rapport bénéfice risque sur tout les aspects de la santé (physique, physiologique, psychologique, sociale . . . tant d'aspect oublié depuis 2 ans). (Response 368)
Che il costo (in tutti i sensi) non sia maggiore dei benefici. (Response 45)
Gesamtabwägung Nutzen / Schaden im wirtschaftlichen und psychologischen, ethischen Bereich. (Response 427)
La cohésion sociale doit être préservée Le fédéralisme ne doit pas nuire au pays. Le CF doit se montrer comme un organe fédérateur qui défend l'unité nationale. (Response 328)
Risques et avantages, à court et à long terme. (Response 200)
Il danno sociale non solo in termini economici diretti ma anche futuri e indiretti. (Response 5)
Grundlage CFR [case fatality rate] = Massnahmen zum Schutz der vulnerablen Gruppen (ca. ab 70 und jüngere mit Vorerkrankungen). (Response 432)
Quelle part de population est contrainte et embêtée par rapport à la part de population qui risque réellement sa vie. (Response 38)
Sachant que détruire une économie et l'avenir des jeunes pour sauver des vieillards avec déjà un pied dans la tombe est une honte pour l'espèce humaine. (Response 46)
Che tipo di società vogliamo essere? (Response 65)
Kriterien zum politischen Entscheid müssen die Interessen der Gesellschaft als Ganzes berücksichtigen. (Response 392)
Es müssen definitiv mehr und genauere Daten gesammelt werden um Entscheidungen zu treffen. Das wurde sträflich vernachlässigt . . . Zudem scheinen die Entscheide einem politischen, internationalen Narrativ zu unterliegen und nicht Evidenz basierend. (Response 475)
Grundsatz ist in ordnung. aber einbezug gegenteiliger und unabhängiger meinungen zwingend nötig. ebenso klare fakten laufend sammeln und auswerten. was nicht geschieht! (Response 338)
Le decisioni vanno prese con una task force internazionale, siamo tutti nella stessa. (Response 65)
Die Effizienz / der Nutzen gemäss Zahlen aus dem Ausland. (Response 399)

Ist eine Informationsverbreitung, die Wissensschaffung und der praktischen Anwendbarkeit der vermittelten Materie gegeben, so besteht kein Zweifel dass alle richtigen Verhaltensweisen auch gelebt werden. (Response 381)
Son impact réel, les résultats escomptés/obtenus. (Response 416)

References

Arroyo-Marioli, F., F. Bullano, S. Kucinsk, and C. Rondón-Moreno. 2021. "Tracking *R* of COVID-19: A New Real-Time Estimation Using the Kalman Filter." PLOS One 16 (1): e0244474. https://doi.org/10.1371/journal.pone.0244474.

Baggio, M., H. Nohlen, and A. Proestaki. 2022. "Perceptions of the COVID-19 Pandemic Phases and Future Waves." *JRC Publications Repository*, June 27. https://publications.jrc.ec.europa.eu/repository/handle/JRC129853.

Balthasar, A., S. Essig, T. von Stolkar et al. 2022. "Evaluation der Krisenbewältigung Covid-19 bis Sommer 2021." https://www.bag.admin.ch/dam/bag/de/dokumente/e-f/evalber-mt/2022-evaluation-krisenbewaeltigung-covid-19-schlussbericht.pdf.download.pdf/2022-schlussbericht-evaluation-krisenbewaeltigung-covid-19-d.pdf.

Beauchamp, T. L., and J. F. Childress. 2019. *Principles of Biomedical Ethics*. 8th edition. Oxford University Press.

Braun, V., and V. Clarke. 2006. "Using Thematic Analysis in Psychology." *Qualitative Research in Psychology* 3 (2): 77–101. https://doi.org/10.1191/1478088706qp063oa.

Braun, V., V. Clarke, E. Boulton, L. Davey, and C. McEvoy. 2021. "The Online Survey as a Qualitative Research Tool." *International Journal of Social Research Methodology* 24 (6): 641–654. https://doi.org/10.1080/13645579.2020.1805550.

Burki, T. 2020. "The Online Anti-Vaccine Movement in the Age of COVID-19." *The Lancet Digital Health* 2 (10): e504–e505. https://doi.org/10.1016/S2589-7500(20)30227-2.

Bütler, R. 2021. "Was das Virus mit uns macht—SGG startet Kampagne gegen Spaltung der Gesellschaft." *Schweizer Radio und Fernsehen*, November 21. https://www.srf.ch/news/schweiz/was-das-virus-mit-uns-macht-sgg-startet-kampagne-gegen-spaltung-der-gesellschaft.

Carter-Harris, L., R. Bartlett Ellis, A. Warrick, and S. Rawl. 2016. "Beyond Traditional Newspaper Advertisement: Leveraging Facebook-Targeted Advertisement to Recruit Long-Term Smokers for Research." *Journal of Medical Internet Research* 18 (6): e117. https://doi.org/10.2196/jmir.5502.

Childress, J. F. 2022. "Respecting Personal Autonomy in Bioethics: Relational Autonomy as a Corrective?" In *Thick (Concepts of) Autonomy*, edited by James F. Childress and Michael Quante. Philosophical Studies Series. Springer International. https://doi.org/10.1007/978-3-030-80991-1_9.

Childress, J. F., R. R. Faden, R. D. Gaare et al. 2002. "Public Health Ethics: Mapping the Terrain." *Journal of Law, Medicine & Ethics* 30 (2): 170–178. https://doi.org/10.1111/j.1748-720X.2002.tb00384.x.

Dawson, A., E. J. Emanuel, M. Parker, M. J. Smith, and Teck Chuan Voo. 2020. "Key Ethical Concepts and Their Application to COVID-19 Research." *Public Health Ethics* 13 (2): 127–132. https://doi.org/10.1093/phe/phaa017.

Eidgenössische Departement des Innern. 2022. "Aperçu des mesures prises contre le coronavirus dans plusieurs capitales européennes." https://www.newsd.admin.ch/newsd/message/attachments/70296.pdf.

EMA (European Medicines Agency). 2021. "Ronapreve," November 10. https://www.ema.europa.eu/en/medicines/human/EPAR/ronapreve.

FOPH (Federal Office of Public Health). 2021a. "COVID-19 Switzerland, Information on the Current Situation." https://www.covid19.admin.ch/en/epidemiologic/virus-variants?variantZoomHospSeg=2022-04-10_2023-06-18&variantZoomMonitoringSeg=2021-11-18_2022-02-03.

FOPH. 2021b. "COVID Certificate," October 25. https://web.archive.org/web/20211025042226/https://www.bag.admin.ch/covid-certificate.

FOPH. 2021c. "Where and How to Get a COVID Certificate and How Long It Is Valid," November 30. https://web.archive.org/web/20211130195235/https://www.bag.admin.ch/bag/en/home/krankheiten/ausbrueche-epidemien-pandemien/aktuelle-ausbrueche-epidemien/novel-cov/covid-zertifikat/covid-zertifikat-erhalt-gueltigkeit.html.

FOPH. 2021d. "Coronavirus: Information for Checkers and Issuers and Technical Details on the COVID Certificate," December 22. https://web.archive.org/web/20211222154455/https://www.bag.admin.ch/bag/en/home/krankheiten/ausbrueche-epidemien-pandemien/aktuelle-ausbrueche-epidemien/novel-cov/covid-zertifikat/covid-zertifikat-pruefer-aussteller-technische-informationen.html/.

FOPH. 2023. "COVID-19 Switzerland." https://opendata.swiss/en/dataset/covid-19-schweiz.

Georgieva, I., T. Lantta, J. Lickiewicz et al. 2021. "Perceived Effectiveness, Restrictiveness, and Compliance with Containment Measures Against the Covid-19 Pandemic: An International Comparative Study in 11 Countries." *International Journal of Environmental Research and Public Health* 18 (7): 3806. https://doi.org/10.3390/ijerph18073806.

Hale, T., N. Angrist, R. Goldszmidt et al. 2021. "A Global Panel Database of Pandemic Policies (Oxford COVID-19 Government Response Tracker)." *Nature Human Behaviour* 5 (4): 529–538. https://doi.org/10.1038/s41562-021-01079-8.

Kritzinger, S., M. Foucault, R. Lachat, J. Partheymüller, C. Plescia, and S. Brouard. 2021. "'Rally Round the Flag': The COVID-19 Crisis and Trust in the National Government." *West European Politics* 44 (5–6): 1205–1231. https://doi.org/10.1080/01402382.2021.1925017.

Lee, C., W. A. Rogers, and A. Braunack-Mayer. 2008. "Social Justice and Pandemic Influenza Planning: The Role of Communication Strategies." *Public Health Ethics* 1 (3): 223–234.

Mahon, P., and N. Zimmermann. 2015. *Droit constitutionnel: Droits fondamentaux*. 3rd edition. Vol. 2. Helbing Lichtenhahn Verlag. https://www.helbing.ch/fr/detail/ISBN-9783719034085/Droit-constitutionnel-Volume-II.

NIH (National Institutes of Health). 2020. "Final Report Confirms Remdesivir Benefits for COVID-19," October 19. https://www.nih.gov/news-events/nih-research-matters/final-report-confirms-remdesivir-benefits-covid-19.

Our World in Data. 2020. "COVID-19 Data Explorer." https://ourworldindata.org/explorers/coronavirus-data-explorer.

Powers, M., and R. R. Faden. 2006. *Social Justice: The Moral Foundations of Public Health and Health Policy. Issues in Biomedical Ethics*. Oxford University Press.

Selby, K., M.-A. Durand, A. Gouveia et al. 2020. "Citizen Responses to Government Restrictions in Switzerland During the COVID-19 Pandemic: Cross-Sectional Survey." *JMIR Formative Research* 4 (12): e20871. https://doi.org/10.2196/20871.

Selvaraj, V., A. Finn, A. Lal, M. S. Khan, K. Dapaah-Afriyie, and G. P. Carino. 2022. "Baricitinib in Hospitalised Patients with COVID-19: A Meta-Analysis of Randomised Controlled Trials." *EClinicalMedicine* 49 (July): 101489. https://doi.org/10.1016/j.eclinm.2022.101489.

Sen, A. 1993. "Capability and Well-Being." In *The Quality of Life*, edited by Martha Nussbaum and Amartya Sen. Oxford University Press. https://doi.org/10.1093/0198287976.003.0003.

Shiehzadegan, S., N. Alaghemand, M. Fox, and V. Venketaraman. 2021. "Analysis of the Delta Variant B.1.617.2 COVID-19." *Clinics and Practice* 11 (4): 778–784. https://doi.org/10.3390/clinpract11040093.

Silubonde, T. M., L. Knight, S. A. Norris, A. Van Heerden, S. Goldstein, and C. E. Draper. 2023. "Perceptions of the COVID-19 Pandemic: A Qualitative Study with South African Adults." *BMC Public Health* 23 (1): 684. https://doi.org/10.1186/s12889-023-15450-z.

Spitale, G., F. Germani, and N. Biller-Andorno. 2023. "The PHERCC Matrix. An Ethical Framework for Planning, Governing, and Evaluating Risk and Crisis Communication in the Context of Public Health Emergencies." *The American Journal of Bioethics* 24 (4): 67–82. https://doi.org/10.1080/15265161.2023.2201191.

Spitale, G., S. Merten, K. Jafflin, B. Schwind, A. Kaiser-Grolimund, and N. Biller-Andorno. 2021. "A Novel Risk and Crisis Communication Platform to Bridge the Gap Between Policy Makers and the Public in the Context of the COVID-19 Crisis (PubliCo): Protocol for a Mixed Methods Study." *JMIR Research Protocols* 10 (11): e33653. https://doi.org/10.2196/33653.

SteelFisher, Gillian K., Mary G. Findling, H. L. Caporello et al. 2023. "Trust in US Federal, State, and Local Public Health Agencies During COVID-19: Responses and Policy Implications: Study Reports the Results of a Survey of Public Trust in US Federal, State, and Local Public Health Agencies' Performance During the COVID-19 Pandemic." *HealthAffairs* 42 (3): 328–337. https://doi.org/10.1377/hlthaff.2022.01204.

Swiss Confederation. 2021a. "Arguments of the Referendum Committee, Popular Vote June 13, 2021." https://www.admin.ch/dam/gov/de/Dokumentation/Abstimmungen/juni2021/Abstimmungsbroschuere_13-06-2021_WEB_de.pdf.download.pdf/Abstimmungserl%C3%A4uterungen%20Juni%2021.pdf.

Swiss Confederation. 2021b. "Volksabstimmung vom 13.06.2021." https://www.bk.admin.ch/ch/d/pore/va/20210613/index.html.

Swiss Confederation. 2021c. "Volksabstimmung vom 28.11.2021." https://www.bk.admin.ch/ch/d/pore/va/20210613/index.html.

Swiss National COVID-19 Science Task Force. 2020. "Organisation—Swiss National COVID-19 Science Task Force." https://sciencetaskforce.ch/en/organisation-expert-groups/.

Swissmedic. 2021. "Current Status of Authorisations for Combating COVID-19," December 30. https://web.archive.org/web/20211230031257/https://www.swissmedic.ch/swissmedic/en/home/news/coronavirus-covid-19/stand-zl-bekaempfung-covid-19.html.

Thornton, L., P. J. Batterham, D. B. Fassnacht, F. Kay-Lambkin, A. L. Calear, and S. Hunt. 2016. "Recruiting for Health, Medical or Psychosocial Research Using Facebook: Systematic Review." *Internet Interventions* 4 (May): 72–81. https://doi.org/10.1016/j.invent.2016.02.001.

UN Office for Disaster Risk Reduction. 2015. *Sendai Framework for Disaster Risk Reduction 2015–2030.* https://www.undrr.org/publication/sendai-framework-disaster-risk-reduction-2015-2030.

Upshur, R. E. G. 2002. "Principles for the Justification of Public Health Intervention." *Canadian Journal of Public Health* 93 (2): 101–103. https://doi.org/10.1007/BF03404547.

Van Nistelrooij, I., M. Visse, A. Spekkink, and J. de Lange. 2017. "How Shared Is Shared Decision-Making? A Care-Ethical View on the Role of Partner and Family." *Journal of Medical Ethics* 43 (9): 637–644. https://doi.org/10.1136/medethics-2016-103791.

Walker, A. K., and E. L. Fox. 2018. "Why Marginalization, Not Vulnerability, Can Best Identify People in Need of Special Medical and Nutrition Care." *AMA Journal of Ethics* 20 (10): e941–e947. https://doi.org/10.1001/amajethics.2018.941.

Wardrope, A. 2015. "Relational Autonomy and the Ethics of Health Promotion." *Public Health Ethics* 8 (1): 50–62. https://doi.org/10.1093/phe/phu025.

Weck, J. de. 2020. "Switzerland Is Choosing Austerity Over Life." *Foreign Policy* (blog), November 10. https://foreignpolicy.com/2020/11/10/coronavirus-switzerland-is-choosing-austerity-over-life/.

WHO (World Health Organization). 2020. "Infodemic." https://www.who.int/health-topics/infodemic#tab=tab_1.

WHO. 2021. "Coronavirus Disease (COVID-19): Variants of SARS-COV-2," December 4. https://www.who.int/news-room/questions-and-answers/item/coronavirus-disease-(covid-19)-variants-of-sars-cov-2.

Wozney, L., K. Turner, B. Rose-Davis, and P. J. McGrath. 2019. "Facebook Ads to the Rescue? Recruiting a Hard to Reach Population into an Internet-Based Behavioral Health Intervention Trial." *Internet Interventions* 17 (September): 100246. https://doi.org/10.1016/j.invent.2019.100246.

Zimmerman, F. J. 2017. "Public Health Autonomy: A Critical Reappraisal." *Hastings Center Report* 47 (6): 38–45. https://doi.org/10.1002/hast.784.

5

Proportionality and the Need for Evidence

A Case Study of Outdoor Public Health Interventions for Respiratory Viruses in Australia

Euzebiusz Jamrozik

Background

The proportionality principle requires that the expected benefits of a public health intervention outweigh its expected harms. By *harms*, I mean anything that makes a person's life worse (Rid 2014), including, for example, harms related to the liberty restrictions of mandated interventions (Table 5.1). While this appears straightforward, assessments of proportionality can be complex in practice.

One difficulty in assessing proportionality is the epistemic challenge of determining the probability and magnitude of (expected) benefits and harms, including accounting for relevant uncertainties (Figure 5.1). In order to claim that a policy measure will be proportionate, policymakers arguably should provide data regarding (a) the existence of a significant public health risk, (b) the effectiveness of an intervention in reducing the risk (i.e., evidence of expected benefits), and (c) evidence of expected harms that would be outweighed by expected benefits. This provides a clear link between the principle of proportionality and the principle of the need for evidence (Table 5.1): Ethical justification of public health policy requires evidentiary justification.

As they are in most risk-benefit assessments, data regarding expected benefits and harms will have some degree of uncertainty. Uncertainty will typically be reduced insofar as (a) more data are collected, (b) data are of high quality, and (c) data regarding the efficacy or effectiveness of an intervention are collected in well-designed and well-controlled studies.

Restrictions of individual liberty often cause harm. Harms of restrictive public health interventions might therefore include mental health harms, economic harms, physical harms, missing out on certain pleasures of daily life, and so on (Godfrey-Smith 2022; Lawford-Smith 2022). While it is conceivable that some restrictions of liberty would not cause harm (but might nevertheless be ethically problematic), I will not focus on such cases here. The principle of the least

Euzebiusz Jamrozik, *Proportionality and the Need for Evidence*. In: *Proportionality*. Edited by: Nikola Biller-Andorno et al., Oxford University Press. DOI: 10.1093/9780197759370.003.0006 restrictive alternative requires policymakers to select a policy that involves the least liberty restriction, other things being equal (i.e., assuming the benefits of the policy options are similar; see Table 5.1). There might therefore be cases in which more than one policy option is proportionate (because the expected benefits of each policy outweigh relevant risks), but among such options, policymakers should choose the policy with the least restriction of liberty (and, in corollary, the least amount of harm related to liberty restrictions). This is why mandatory policies (i.e., those associated with legal, financial, and other penalties for noncompliance), as opposed to recommendations, arguably should be a last resort.

Table 5.1 Selected principles of public health ethics

Principle	Interpretation
Proportionality	The expected harms involved in an intervention should be outweighed by expected benefits.
Need for evidence	Evidence of likely benefits is needed to justify imposition of potentially burdensome public health interventions.
Least restrictive alternative	Where two interventions are expected to be equally effective, the intervention that involves the fewest restrictions of liberty should be selected.

Source: Adapted from Jamrozik and Selgelid (2019).

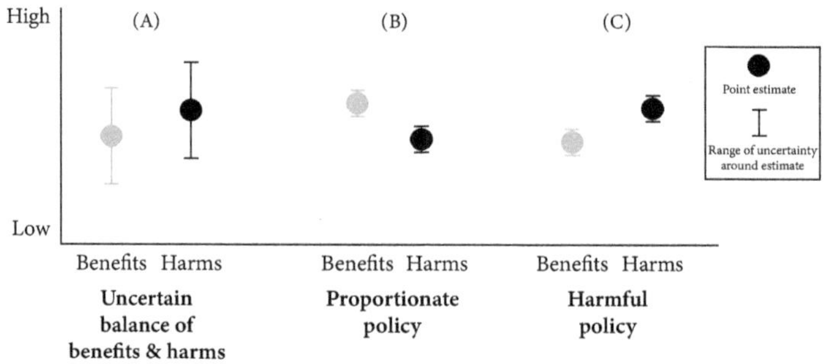

Fig. 5.1 Balance of benefits and harms in situations of uncertainty, proportionality, and net harm. (A) In situations of uncertainty about the balance of (expected) benefits and (expected) harms, estimates of benefits and/or harms are imprecise, and a wide range of uncertainty means that it is possible that benefits outweigh harms or the reverse. (B) In situations of proportionality, (expected) benefits outweigh (expected) harms. (C) In situations of net harm, (expected) harms outweigh (expected) benefits. Note that (A) is consistent with (B) or (C) or both being true because the point estimates in (B) and (C) are within the range of estimates in (A).

In this case study of outdoor nonpharmaceutical interventions (NPIs) used during the COVID-19 pandemic, I will argue that policymakers implementing *mandatory* interventions have an especially strong *ethical obligation to provide data* showing that benefits outweigh harms (with an adequate degree of certainty). One source of moral obligation here is the proportionality principle; the other is the principle of the least restrictive alternative. I will argue that mandated outdoor NPIs for SARS-CoV-2 (and other respiratory viruses) fail the proportionality principle since (a) there is no significant risk of acquiring respiratory viral infection outdoors, (b) there is no evidence that outdoor NPIs produce benefits, (c) many outdoor NPIs involve significant harm, and (d) mandates increase the harms of outdoor NPIs.

Case Study: Outdoor NPIs for COVID-19 in Australia

The population of Melbourne in Victoria, Australia, was subject to the longest (by some estimates) combined period of lockdown in any democratic country, which involved the use of multiple mandatory NPIs. Many of these NPIs lacked robust evidence of effectiveness yet were punitively enforced—often with police support, even in outdoor areas. Examples of mandated but evidence-poor outdoor interventions include (a) outdoor mask use, (b) limitations on outdoor activities (e.g., bans on leaving home except for essential purposes and one hour of exercise per day), and (c) the closure of children's playgrounds. During the pandemic, restrictions on *indoor* activities were implemented in many countries; in some countries with few or no restrictions on *outdoor* activities, this resulted in increased use of outdoor space. Yet movement data suggest that Australian residents' use of outdoor space did not increase to the same degree as in comparable countries that adopted indoor NPIs without punitive outdoor policies (Ritchie 2020).

Proportionality is a key ethical (and in many cases legal) requirement for public health policy. It is widely recognized that proportionality requires that the benefits of an intervention outweigh the associated harms (including those arising owing to the liberty restrictions involved in mandatory policies) (Childress et al. 2002; Selgelid 2009; Jamrozik and Selgelid 2019; Jamrozik 2022). However, it is rarely noted that proportionality has implications for the duty of public health agencies to provide evidence that, for example, interventions are effective in reducing a significant risk to public health. Australian public health agencies failed to fulfill this duty regarding outdoor restrictions and in some cases persisted with restrictive outdoor NPIs for many months (e.g., Tomazin and Cunningham 2021).

I argue that given the principles of proportionality and the least restrictive alternative, the more coercion or harm involved in a policy, the stronger the duty of public health agencies to collect and share evidence demonstrating (with reasonable certainty) that expected benefits outweigh expected harms. Highly coercive or harmful interventions should therefore be accompanied by high-quality evidence of (net) benefit or by a plan to collect such evidence.

By April 2020, it was known that outdoor transmission of SARS-CoV-2 was extremely rare. Only one episode of outdoor transmission had been reported worldwide, involving two people in China who had a prolonged conversation on an outdoor bench (Qian et al. 2021). In this context of low-to-minimal risk, even an intervention that might be highly effective would not produce large public health benefits. How then could outdoor public health interventions be justified?

One standard response to such questions has been to appeal to uncertainty (including various forms of the precautionary principle) (Greenhalgh et al. 2020). Public health agencies might claim that in early 2020 there was uncertainty about the probability of outdoor transmission. Following from this, it might be claimed that within these uncertainties, it was possible that the risk of outdoor transmission was higher than it initially appeared to be, and thus outdoor public health interventions—perhaps even mandated interventions—aimed at mitigating this risk would be justifiable.

However, even if the benefits of public health interventions were high (i.e., because the risks of outdoor transmission turned out to be high and interventions were effective), the possibility of large benefits alone does not necessarily mean that policies that implement these interventions would be proportionate and that stringent interventions would be justified, especially if implemented for long periods of time. First, uncertainty concerns not only the degree to which a policy will produce benefits but also uncertainty about policy-related harms. All policies involve harms, even if the only harms are economic costs or well-being costs caused by restrictive policies, and these harms may be uncertain at the time the policy is implemented. The fact that there is uncertainty about a public health risk (and therefore about the benefits of mitigating this risk) does not entail that the benefits of a policy aimed at reducing this risk will (or will be likely to) outweigh its harms. One way of thinking about uncertainty is that it represents a range of potential values of an estimated outcome (e.g., a benefit or a harm). This approach is similar to the confidence intervals used by epidemiologists: The narrower the interval (or range) around an estimate, the higher the certainty that the estimate is true (other things being equal).

What matters for proportionality is that expected benefits outweigh expected harms. Uncertainty arguably requires that the *lower* bound of the range of potential estimates of benefits is higher than the *higher* bound of the range of potential estimates of harms (Figure 5.1). When this is not the case, it remains possible that harms outweigh benefits (although the smaller the overlap between the range of potential benefits and the range of potential harms, the more likely it is that one outweighs the other). In other words, in situations of uncertainty (in which there are overlaps between estimated benefits and harms) the policy may not be proportionate (Figure 5.1). In the case of outdoor NPIs adopted by Australia, expected harms were significant (Table 5.2), even accounting for uncertainties regarding how harmful they might be. It is implausible to claim that health agencies could have been confident (i.e., sufficiently certain) that these harms would be outweighed by public health benefits.

Perhaps this standard may be too stringent, especially at the start of an epidemic due to a novel pathogen. Many people might endorse the initial use of an intervention even if it is not clear whether likely benefits outweigh likely harms (or there might be disagreement about the uncertainty bounds around estimates of such outcomes or the relative weight of different benefits and harms). Yet, at a minimum, as discussed in the next paragraph, such situations arguably entail an obligation to collect data to reduce uncertainty and reassess the proportionality of interventions over time.

Second, public health agencies are typically empowered to collect data on health risks (and policy outcomes). While uncertainty might justify the *initial* introduction of a policy without evidence that it is proportionate, the proportionality principle arguably requires that there should be a plan to collect data in order to reduce relevant uncertainties and demonstrate proportionality. Regarding the risk of outdoor transmission, Australia conducted detailed contact tracing of every case in the country (until international borders reopened in November 2021) with viral genetic sequencing of almost all samples positive for SARS-CoV-2. Only one case of possible outdoor transmission was reported in Australia with epidemiological and viral genetic data to confirm linkage. This case was reported by a local public health agency in June 2021 ("Woman" 2021) and has not yet been published in academic literature. No confirmed cases of outdoor transmission were reported in any other jurisdiction worldwide; although outdoor transmission was sometimes reported, this has not been accompanied by evidence that the cases were genetically linked and/or that no indoor contact between the cases occurred. Given these findings, it is implausible to claim that there were data demonstrating a significant risk of outdoor transmission that would have justified the imposition of mandatory outdoor NPIs, yet such interventions continued for many months of the pandemic. Although defenders of outdoor NPIs might claim that the effectiveness of such policies prevented the detection of outdoor transmission events, this is also implausible given that no such events were detected in other countries with less stringent policies.

In addition to using the proportionality principle to select policies, public health agencies arguably should select less restrictive policies unless there are data to show that this would significantly increase public health risks (Table 5.1).

Table 5.2 Examples of coercive outdoor policies during the COVID-19 pandemic in Australia

Policy	Example of penalty for noncompliance	Harms
Outdoor mask use	Fine of $200	Cost of masks Environmental harms of mask disposal Financial harms
Meeting outdoors for purposes other than exercise	Fine of $5,000 per person	Mental health harms Financial harms
Leaving the house for more than one hour per day	Fine of $5,000	Mental health harms Physical health harms Financial harms
Traveling more than 5 km from home address	Fine of $5,000	Mental health harms Financial harms

This is because liberty is an important value—in addition to utility and well-being (i.e., benefits and harms), among others—for such agencies to consider in pluralistic societies (Selgelid 2009). Mandatory policies involve significant liberty infringements and related harms. In the case of mandatory outdoor interventions implemented during the coronavirus pandemic, it was clear that there were significant harms (Table 5.2), and many of these harms could have been mitigated by adopting policies involving recommendations about outdoor activities rather than mandates. Given that initial data demonstrated that the benefits of outdoor interventions would be low (despite uncertainties), it was highly likely that the harms of mandatory outdoor NPIs would outweigh their benefits—in other words, that such policies would not be proportionate.

Proportionality and the Obligation to Collect Data

Proportionality remains a key ethical requirement for public health policy. The requirement that expected benefits outweigh expected risks entails the need for data that demonstrate net benefit with certainty: Ethical justification requires evidentiary justification. Of course, there may be practical and philosophical challenges at the start of a public health emergency that is due to a novel pathogen. Practical challenges include a lack of data about the pathogen as well as the benefits and harms of proposed interventions. The philosophical challenges include potential incommensurability between different (types of) benefits and harms, and this means that policymakers and societies need to make ethical judgments about the balance of benefits and harms that go beyond the quantification of likely outcomes, including evaluations of the bounds of uncertainty around such estimates.

However, even if many people might accept highly stringent policies in the face of uncertainty, proportionality requires, at a minimum, a plan to collect data to demonstrate proportionality. In other words, novel policies implemented without a plan to collect data are prima facie unjustifiable. Improved quantification of benefits and harms may at least better inform judgments about proportionality (i.e., the balance between benefits and harms). Given the rate of data collection in recent emergencies, including COVID-19, it is likely that within a few months there will be much less uncertainty than at the start of an emergency (Barosa et al. 2023). Therefore, even if certain policies might initially be widely accepted in the face of uncertainty, the ethical and evidentiary justification for such policies must be revised over time as certainty increases.

Further, more restrictive policies, such as mandates, arguably entail an even stronger moral responsibility for public health agencies to collect and provide data demonstrating that benefits outweigh harms. This is because restrictive policies often cause harm and because liberty restriction, in any case, requires ethical justification. This means that public health agencies must be especially certain (or aim to collect robust data that would increase certainty) about benefits and harms in the case of mandatory policies. Where such certainty is lacking, a more ethical approach may be to issue recommendations for behavior change while more data are collected rather than to implement stringent policies with significant penalties for noncompliance.

Conclusion

Outdoor interventions for COVID-19 failed the proportionality principle. There was no evidence of benefit, and significant harms were exacerbated by restrictive policies, including draconian penalties for noncompliance and by the prolonged duration of such restrictive interventions in some settings, including in Australia. Uncertainty (or precaution) was not an adequate justification for these policies, especially for their use over prolonged periods, and future attempts to claim that outdoor interventions for respiratory viruses are proportionate should be met with skepticism. More generally, for mandatory policies in particular, there should be a requirement that public health agencies produce data regarding benefits and harms in order to satisfy the proportionality principle.

Competing Interests

There are no competing interests to declare.

Funding

This research was supported by funding from the Wellcome Trust [203132] and [221719].

The Trust and Confidence research program at the Pandemic Sciences Institute at the University of Oxford is supported by an award from the Moh Foundation.

References

Barosa M., E. Jamrozik, and V. Prasad. 2023. "The Ethical Obligation for Research During Public Health Emergencies: Insights From the COVID-19 Pandemic." *Medicine, Health Care and Philosophy* 27:1–22.

Childress, J. F., R. R. Faden, R. D. Gaare et al. 2002. "Public Health Ethics: Mapping the Terrain." *Journal of Law, Medicine & Ethics* 30 (2): 170–178.

Godfrey-Smith, P. 2022. "Covid Heterodoxy in Three Layers." *Monash Bioethics Review* 40 (1): 17–39.

Greenhalgh, T., M. B. Schmid, T. Czypionka, D. Bassler, and L. Gruer. 2020. "Face Masks for the Public During the Covid-19 Crisis." *BMJ* 369:m1435.

Jamrozik, E. 2022. "Public Health Ethics: Critiques of the 'New Normal.'" *Monash Bioethics Review* 40:1–16.

Jamrozik, E., and M. J. Selgelid. 2019. "Surveillance and Control of Asymptomatic Carriers of Drug-Resistant Bacteria." In *Ethics and Drug Resistance: Collective Responsibility for Global Public Health*, edited by Euzebiusz Jamrozik and Michael Selgelid. Springer.

Lawford-Smith, H. 2022. "Was Lockdown Life Worth Living?" *Monash Bioethics Review* 40:1–22.

Qian, H., T. Miao, L. Liu, X. Zheng, D. Luo, and Y. Li. 2021. "Indoor Transmission of SARS-CoV-2." *Indoor Air* 31 (3): 639–645.

Rid, A. 2014. "Setting Risk Thresholds in Biomedical Research: Lessons from the Debate About Minimal Risk." *Monash Bioethics Review* 32 (1): 63–85.

Ritchie, H. 2020. "Google Mobility Trends: How Has the Pandemic Changed the Movement of People Around the World?" Our World in Data, June 2. https://ourworldindata.org/covid-google-mobility-trends.

Selgelid, M. J. 2009. "A Moderate Pluralist Approach to Public Health Policy and Ethics." *Public Health Ethics* 2 (2): 195–205.

Tomazin, F., and M. Cunningham. 2021. "Push for Playgrounds to Reopen Amid Fears for Children's Mental Health." The Age, August 18. https://www.theage.com.au/politics/victoria/push-for-playgrounds-to-reopen-amid-fears-for-children-s-mental-health-20210818-p58jwz.html.

"Woman in 70s Contracted COVID from 'Fleeting Exposure' to Bondi Limo Driver." 2021. The Australian, June 18. https://www.theaustralian.com.au/news/woman-in-70s-contracted-covid-from-fleeting-exposure-to-bondi-limo-driver/video/1ddf9ea0cc074f4fc192492f4e2e3324.

6

Inaction and the Proportionality Principle

A Review of the Management of the COVID-19 Pandemic in Mexico

Felicitas Holzer, Ivette María Ortiz Alcántara, Tobias Eichinger, Nikola Biller-Andorno, and Julian W. März

Introduction: Proportionality and Pandemic Management in Mexico

Mexico's administration has been criticized for its hesitance to control the COVID-19 pandemic. This called into question not only the leadership of President Andrés Manuel López Obrador but also that of Mexico's chief epidemiologist, López-Gatell Ramírez, against whom complaints were filed for failing to comply with administrative and ethical obligations as a public servant. According to the charges, he had misdiagnosed the situation, underestimated its severity, and used statistical models that resulted in inaccurate information about the development of the disease, which affected COVID-19 mortality projections (Álvarez and Ramírez 2020). While in other countries the primary apprehension regarding emergency powers revolves around their potential for abuse, Mexico faced a different initial concern at the onset of the pandemic: the hesitancy of executive powers to respond to the emergency (Velasco-Ibarra 2020). The criticism not only has been brought forward in the public debate but also has been echoed by the parliamentary group Movimiento Ciudadano, which accused the government of taking disproportionately small actions to manage the pandemic, despite the government's legitimate aim of protecting socioeconomic welfare (De La Cruz-Hernández and Álvarez-Contreras 2022).[1] Thus, a pivotal question emerges: Have the efforts of the Mexican executive branch to control the pandemic been insufficient, as critics of the government's pandemic management strategies suggested? While we acknowledge the significance of legal discussions

[1] The exhortation directed to the federal government by several Members of Parliament contains the precise allegations against Subsecretary López-Gatell Ramírez for neglecting his duty to adequately manage the COVID-19 pandemic (http://sil.gobernacion.gob.mx/Archivos/Documentos/2022/01/asun_4294625_20220112_1641582288.pdf).

Felicitas Holzer et al., *Inaction and the Proportionality Principle*. In: *Proportionality*.
Edited by: Nikola Biller-Andorno et al., Oxford University Press. © Oxford University Press (2026).
DOI: 10.1093/9780197759370.003.0007

on proportionality as an important phenomenon for study,[2] our exclusive focus in this chapter will be on public policy.

The first aim of this chapter will be to illuminate the concept of *inaction* by initially defining it as executive underreach by the government. Following this, we will conduct a proportionality assessment of the public policies implemented during the COVID-19 pandemic to evaluate whether executive underreach indeed occurred. To do this, we will first and foremost provide an overview of the pandemic situation in Mexico in 2020; then we will outline the pandemic governance strategies pursued by the health administration in light of important socioeconomic parameters by focusing on (a) the health system, mortality rates, and dissemination of accurate health information and (b) the socioeconomic challenges the government faced regarding poverty and work. We then offer an account of inaction using the concept of proportionality and examine whether the apparent inaction from the Mexican executive branches could be labeled as *disproportionate*. We discuss potential challenges to the viewpoint suggesting that the government's response was disproportionate. Instead of offering a succinct framework and categorically determining Mexico's response to the pandemic threat as disproportionately small, we aim to delve into specific aspects relevant to the context of a Latin American middle-income country. Consequently, we conclude that a multitude of factors and conflicting interests may complicate the perception of inaction in this case, making it more complex than initially perceived.

Mexico's Pandemic Management

Mexico's federal health secretary ordered the nationwide suspension of all nonessential activities on March 30, 2020. However, the first COVID-19 cases were confirmed in late February, and the World Health Organization (WHO) declared a global pandemic on March 11 (Hollingsworth et al. 2020), and many countries had already taken action by that time. Furthermore, while it is true

[2] Over the last fifteen years, proportionality analysis has gradually become a common feature of Mexican jurisprudence (Velasco Ibarra 2020). Note that several court cases use the test of proportionality to evaluate Mexico's COVID-19 pandemic public policies. Most notably, Judge Ana Luisa Hortensia Priego Henríquez, head of the thirteenth district court in administrative matters, ordered the Mexican government on March 19, 2020, to take "more aggressive" action against the spread of COVID-19 virus disease within twenty-four hours of her ruling (Rangel Laguna 2020). The court decided that the administration had not taken enough precautions to protect the population from the spread of the disease. The District Court's decision particularly put forward that "the authorities [were] not adopting the general sanitary measures effective and proportional to the risk faced by the country for the prevention, avoidance of contagion, detection, and reaction to the SARS-CoV-2 virus and the COVID-19 disease" (Perseo Programa Universitario de Derechos Humanos, Universidad Nacional Autónoma de México, No. 86, April 2020, http://www.pudh.unam.mx/perseo/juez-ordena-al-ejecutivo-federal-tomar-acciones-para-atender-la-emergencia-por-el-coronavirus/#more-29442).

that the Federal Ministry of Health had issued responses to the COVID-19 challenges in several decrees containing measures such as the temporary suspension of all educational activities and the ban on large public gatherings, no lockdowns[3] or curfews had been set—the government only recommended people stay at home. Actions by the government have been criticized for, among other things, being "uncoordinated" on the state and local levels (Velasco-Ibarra 2020).

Defenders of the performance of Mexico's public health administration argued that the government had to deal with relatively bad conditions. A chronically underfunded public health system complicated efforts to track the disease and coordinate the response. Previous administrations had a history of a lacking medical infrastructure and a fragile economy with a high degree of economic and social inequality—all factors that fueled the negative effects of the pandemic (García Ramírez and Martínez Martínez 2020). Moreover, Mexico had previously shut down the country for two weeks during the H1N1 (swine flu) pandemic in 2009, and the country had scrambled to curb the virus spread at that time. This experience led Hugo López-Gatell Ramírez, the head of the Undersecretariat of Prevention and Health Promotion at the Mexican Secretariat of Health, to the assumption that any measure during the COVID-19 pandemic should be well considered and free from political meddling. President Obrador gave López-Gatell Ramírez full decision-making power and protected him from political criticism (Perez Ortega 2020).

To further explore whether Mexico's weak measures to contain the COVID-19 pandemic can be seen as a disproportionate pandemic response, it is worth looking at the estimated positive and negative effects of Mexico's pandemic plan and related policies. Important factors to consider are Mexico's high excess mortality and the overburdening of the hospitals (Figure 6.1). Here, the hypothesis is that proportionate public health measures, if taken earlier, would have prevented premature deaths and would have relieved hospitals from treating an overwhelming number of COVID-19 cases. In addition, this analysis must be considered alongside a broader view on other socioeconomic parameters in Mexico. Most notably, we will discuss the government's response in the context of existing poverty rates, work-related migration, and the large informal sector (Figure 6.2).

[3] We follow the *Merriam-Webster* definition of a *lockdown* as "a temporary condition imposed by government authorities (such as during the outbreak of an epidemic disease) in which most people are required to refrain from or limit activities outside the home that involve public contact (such as dining out or attending large gatherings)" (https://www.merriam-webster.com/dictionary/lockdown).

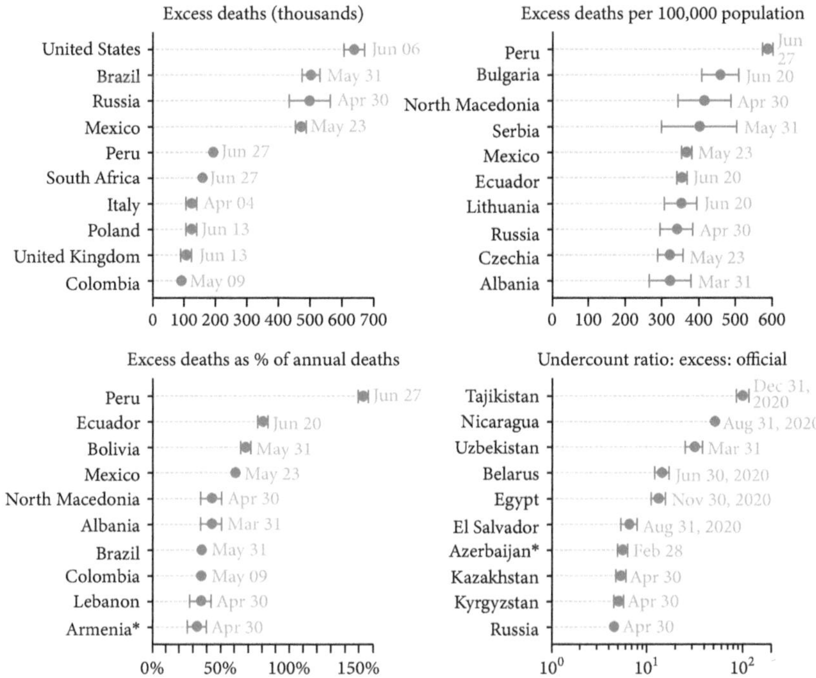

Fig. 6.1 Top ten countries in the World Mortality Dataset by various excess mortality measures. Each subplot shows the top ten countries for each of our four excess mortality measures: total number of excess deaths, excess deaths per one hundred thousand, excess deaths as a percentage of baseline annual mortality, and the undercount ratio (excess deaths to reported COVID-19 deaths by the same date).
Source: Karlinsy and Kobak (2021).

Challenges to the Health System: Mexico's COVID-19 Mortality, Crowded Hospitals, and Dissemination of Accurate Health Information

Mexico was among the most affected countries during the COVID-19 pandemic, with excess mortality greater than 50% of the expected annual mortality, per the World Mortality Dataset (Karlinsky and Kobak 2021; see Figure 6.3).[4] Dahal and colleagues (2021) estimated a Mexican excess mortality rate at around sixteen per ten thousand individuals during the COVID-19 pandemic. According

[4] Yet Karlinsky and Kobak (2021) state that obtaining statistics on the precise mortality rates was difficult, as not all countries reported accurate data.

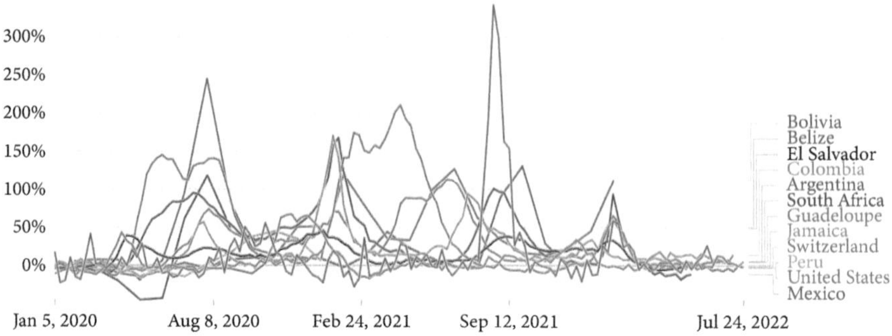

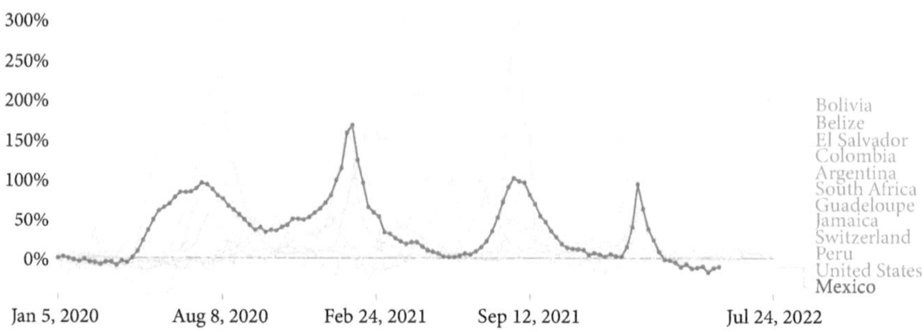

Figs. 6.2 and 6.3 Excess mortality over time: deaths from all causes compared to projections based on previous years. The percentage difference between the reported number of weekly or monthly deaths in 2020–2022 and the projected number of deaths for the same period based on previous years. The reported number might not count all deaths that occurred because of incomplete coverage and delays in reporting. Comparisons across countries are affected by differences in the completeness of death reporting.

Sources: Human Mortality Database (2022), https://www.mortality.org/; World Mortality Dataset (2022), https://www.who.int/data/data-collection-tools/who-mortality-database.

to Dahal and colleagues (2021), this constitutes a reliable estimate of a hard-hit Latin American country with a low testing rate. Mexico City reported the highest excess death rate (63.5 per 100,000) compared to the rest of the country. However, COVID-19 deaths only accounted for 39% of total excess deaths, which were in total 333,538 in 2020 (Dahal et al. 2021, 1). Excess mortality not clearly linked to COVID-19 might, nevertheless, reflect the effect of low testing rates or hint at the fact that other causes during the pandemic could have led to an increased death rate (Dahal et al. 2021, 1).

Estimates show that from the onset of the pandemic until the end of April 2020, excess mortality rates in Mexico were lower than those in some other countries—for instance, the United States. However, Mexico then overtook the

United States and showed a higher mortality rate, at least until October 2020. Compared to the other countries in the region, Mexico seemed to have relatively high excess mortality yet without exceptional peaks or outliers (see Figure 6.3). Figures 6.2 and 6.3 suggest that it is generally challenging to come to any concise conclusion about disproportionately bad health outcomes in Mexico, at least in comparison to other countries. We acknowledge that intercountry comparisons are difficult to make, as contexts, variables, and parameters change considerably from country to country. Additionally, evidence-based intercountry comparisons regarding decision-making and governmental responses become especially challenging during a pandemic crisis. This challenge stems partly from the inability to apply historical data to the unprecedented COVID-19 context and partly from the dynamic nature of emerging evidence. The pre-COVID-19 public health preparedness and response landscape in Mexico had been characterized as weak in the literature; measures were largely not evidence based (Rubin et al. 2021).

The pandemic crisis revealed underlying deficiencies in the healthcare system and reinforced existing inequalities between different social groups. Essentially, Mexico's public health administration failed to effectively govern the healthcare system at both the state and federal levels. According to the authors Bautista-González et al. (2021), these issues are partly due to the lack of preparedness for the outbreak and the uncoordinated and hugely heterogeneous measures taken. The authors argue that the translation and adaptation of scientific evidence were deficient and resulted in an important delay in the healthcare system's response during the first months of the pandemic (Snilstveit et al. 2020; Bautista-González et al. 2021).

Moreover, Mexico underwent a transformation, including the reprioritization of public health responses. During the pandemic, COVID-19 patients were prioritized, and the number of beds to treat those patients was expanded. The overwhelming number of COVID-19 cases shifted the focus away from other important public health problems, such as obesity, diabetes, measles, and violence. Immunization campaigns became disrupted, and other health policies, such as programs to address gender violence, were temporarily suspended (Bautista-González et al. 2021, 5). Thus, beyond COVID-19 deaths, the high levels of excess mortality were also rooted in the neglect of other illnesses owing to overburdened health services (Frenk and Gomez Dantés 2020).

Another important point of concern was the ability of populations and subgroups, such as children and health personnel, to access health services, especially COVID-19-related immunization (Kane Jiménez and Gandy 2021). The Mexican government was, indeed, able to vaccinate a significant part of its population: 70% of all adults were immunized by the end of September 2021.

However, there was no systematic immunization and prioritization plan for healthcare workers, which had severe consequences for those working in the sector (Bautista-González et al. 2021, 5). Neither was there an elaborate strategy to vaccinate other subgroups, such as children. According to Amnesty International, Mexico was the country that registered the highest number of deaths of health personnel in 2020 (Velázquez Leyer 2021). The president announced in April 2021 that health personnel working in private institutions, which were not officially recognized as COVID-19 care centers, would not be vaccinated until vaccines were distributed according to their age range, which caused confusion and even resulted in lawsuits against the government (Latinus 2021).

While the Mexican government made efforts to distribute the available vaccine doses, geographic and socioeconomic disparities remained salient. Northern states had significantly better access to vaccines than did the respective populations in southern states, where public service capacity, economic development, and civilian security usually tend to be weaker (Kane Jiménez and Gandy 2021).

Regarding the dissemination of information, Bautista-González et al. (2021, 5) criticize the Mexican government for issuing confusing recommendations. For instance, the simultaneous recommendations for social distancing and staying at home led to public uncertainty. Moreover, the country should have collected more reliable and timely epidemiological data to appropriately adapt the COVID-19 response and provide more efficient access to updated scientific information. The lack of unification regarding policies and guidelines across institutions and regions considerably undermined a coherent and efficient distribution of information (Bautista-González et al. 2021, 6).

Socioeconomic Challenges: Poverty, Informal and Precarious Working Conditions, and the Enforceability of Measures

A key measure taken by many countries to mitigate the pandemic's devastating consequences was the enforcement of lockdowns. The strict imposition of quarantine lockdown rules significantly reduced mobility. However, the success of such measures largely depended on effective enforcement and the ability of the policies to restrict the movement of individuals and groups. In Mexico, persons who were socioeconomically deprived or part of marginalized groups and who depended on daily work opportunities often refused to follow the recommendation to stay at home during the COVID-19 pandemic. These individuals typically depended on the informal sector for their income.

According to Hernández Trujillo (2020, 187), 59.1% of workers in 2020 occupied jobs in the informal sector in Mexico City, Baja California, Nueva León, or Querétaro. Informal workers are not legally protected in the case of unemployment, and a break in activity usually implies the absence of income. At the same time, it should also be mentioned that Mexican federal law protects formal workers for only up to one month, during which time the formally unemployed can claim the amount of the legal minimum salary. Many poor workers search for jobs in metropolitan areas and bigger cities that frequently offer better economic possibilities, healthcare services, and education facilities. They commute from rural areas where the living expenses are comparatively low (Sobrino 2014, 446). Thus, it is not surprising that 76.6% of informal work is concentrated in metropolitan areas and larger cities (Robles et al. 2019). This phenomenon substantially exacerbated the spread of the virus—which was prevalent in metropolitan areas and in bigger and middle-size cities—to peripheral regions and, more specifically, to economically disadvantaged areas (Hernández Trujillo 2020, 186).

Despite Mexico's relatively lenient COVID-19 restrictions on mobility and work opportunities (especially in comparison with other countries), unemployment still became a problem. Millions of people lost their jobs, including those in the informal sector. The official unemployment rate rose from 3.7% at the end of the third quarter of 2019 to 5.1% in the corresponding period of 2020. Likewise, the rate of underemployment, which reflects workers who are available to work more hours than the ones they are currently employed to work, jumped from 7.8% to 17% over the same time frame (Velázquez Leyer 2021). The inadequate unemployment protection offered by the state, a long-standing issue, plunged many former workers into severe hardship.

Implications for Proportionality in Mexico's Response to the COVID-19 Pandemic: A Preliminary Assessment

When evaluating the functioning of the health system, it appears justifiable to state that the Mexican government failed to adequately respond to the challenges of an overburdened health system. While failures in the government's information strategy were due to mismanagement by the administration at that time, other shortcomings may have stemmed from a previous absence of reforms in the healthcare sector. Additionally, given the socioeconomic circumstances of Mexico's working class and poorer population, any consideration of proportionate measures against the COVID-19 pandemic would need to address the potentially negative socioeconomic impacts on informal and low-income formal workers.

The government never required strict compliance with its recommendations. One result of this weak enforcement was that informal workers who depended on daily work for subsistence wages rarely complied with recommendations to stay at home. The ongoing migration of workers from the peripheries to economic centers aggravated the spread of the COVID-19 virus within a population that was already vulnerable and often cut off from the healthcare system. Consequently, this situation worsened existing social inequalities, particularly placing poorer workers at risk of contracting COVID-19 disease (Velázquez Leyer 2021). According to Velasco-Ibarra (2020), the government's reluctance to impose strict measures might be interpreted as concern regarding the effects of its decrees on employment relations. In practice, a temporary suspension of all labor relations would have sharply cut vulnerable workers' income despite any compensation they would have been entitled to under the Federal Labor Law of 2015.

This issue can also be viewed through the lens of a lack of political determination to take decisive actions to effectively mitigate severe impacts of the COVID-19 crisis, including the lack of implementation of economic and fiscal measures such as the ones taken by other countries. Robust fiscal policies to bolster the economy were never implemented (Velasco-Ibarra 2020). This strategy of austerity was pursued despite the fact that the global economic recession affected the country during the pandemic. Consequently, individuals reliant on daily income for survival remained exposed to both economic hardship and public health risks.

Has Mexico's Inaction Been Disproportionate?

To determine whether Mexico's health administration effectively did too little, we must define *inaction*. Inaction can be considered as not only the absence of measures but also weak actions amounting to underperformance. Inaction could be considered an underreach by the country's executive branches as compared to the baseline of *actions* necessary to adequately address the effects of the pandemic.

For instance, Pozzen and Scheppele (2020, 609) define *executive underreach* as "a national executive branch's willful failure to address a significant public problem that the executive is legally and functionally equipped (though not necessarily legally required) to address." This definition, according to Pozzen and Scheppele (2020), would need to be complemented by a substantive analysis of how *failure* is precisely understood. They propose that failure can be weighed using relative expectations for executive action enshrined in a state's own laws and in applicable international legal norms. Underreach occurs when domestic and international legal sources are widely seen to authorize, if not also encourage or oblige, an executive to address a particular problem—be it climate change, a pandemic, or other issues of normative concern—and the executive fails to do so. Differently put, there must be good (moral) reasons why executive branches ought to do more, given the severity of the threat or the moral force of the rationale backing such actions (Pozzen and Scheppele 2020). Furthermore, it is crucial to recognize that executive underreach may pave the way for later executive overreach by creating conditions of precarity or unrest that might then be addressed through more legally questionable means. This also has a transnational dimension, as harms caused by underreach may spill over to other regions, which is notably pertinent in the context of pandemics.

What Is *(Dis)proportionate* Action?

Proportionality, as a principle, requires that a constitutionally legitimate justification underlie implemented measures for guaranteeing and/or limiting certain (sometimes divergent) interests (Martínez Zorrilla 2014). Following South African scholar Etienne Mureainik's approach, the principle has also given moral and political weight to shifting constitutional law from a culture of authority to a culture of justification. Court rulings, in which the proportionality test also comes into play, are part of a deliberative culture and justification of political power and, thus, play a central role in how plural societies arbitrate and deliberate conflicting interests (see Cohen-Eliya and Porat 2011). A culture of justification requires that executive powers provide substantive justification for all their actions. This is reflected in the requirement of *rationality* and *reasonableness*, such as in constitutional interpretation. Here, public law is thought to delimit the borders of public action and to ensure that decisions are taken by those who have the legal competences to do so. Proportionality in a culture of public justification and deliberation permits disputes based on reason and rational argument about these limits of legitimate law making (Cohen-Eliya and Porat 2011). In this sense, public policy, legislation, and jurisdiction are all aspects of the same fundamental paradigm.

The interests of different societal groups are usually enshrined in constitutional rights, or *basic rights*, which are themselves based on international conventions (Grimm 2007; Cianciardo 2010). According to Cianciardo 2010, whether a certain action is proportionate can be analyzed based on three subprinciples: adequacy, necessity, and proportionality sensu stricto. The first subprinciple, adequacy,[5] establishes the condition that a chosen means must be the right one for achieving a particular goal; the second principle, necessity, stipulates that the means chosen is the least restrictive to a basic right under

[5] Sometimes adequacy is introduced as *rationality* together with *legitimate aim* (Cohen-Eliya and Portat 2011).

question; the third principle requires that any measure must be proportionate sensu stricto—that is, there must be a positive balance between costs and benefits.[6] When applying the proportionality principle, one must evaluate the limits of the rights in play, the relationship between the specific basic rights involved, and their relationship to the public interest. A measure—or means—taken to attain a certain aim is considered *disproportionate* if one of the subprinciples is violated. There are mainly two types of violations of the principle of proportionality: the alteration of the content of a basic right and, more salient for our purposes, the lack of a proper *justification* of the restriction in light of the subprinciples (Cianciardo 2010; Khosla 2010).

Most discussions examine the proportionality principle in light of measures that *constrain* certain basic rights. The three subprinciples of proportionality—adequacy, necessity, and proportionality sensu stricto—can then be reframed as principles used to minimize harm to basic rights under the measures taken to achieve a given purpose and under the constraint that the benefits of the means outweigh the caused costs. However, it does not seem self-evident that this would apply to the *omission* of adequate measures (e.g., *inaction*).

However, in the past decades, it has been increasingly accepted that basic rights can be violated not only by actively violating (negative) liberty rights, such as the right to freedom of expression or free movement, but also by underfulfilling certain (positive) rights, usually framed as socioeconomic rights to certain goods or basic services that the state has a duty to provide or guarantee access to (Karp 2015; Nampewo et al. 2022). The currently internationally recognized "respect, protect, and fulfill" framework of human rights seems to include both the state's duty to refrain from action and its duty to provide specific goods and services. While *respect* has traditionally been associated with the no-harm principle, *protection* and *fulfillment* can be seen as a reaction to past human rights abuses by third parties. Moreover, *fulfilling rights* clearly addresses the positive duty to provide resources and make the objectives of human rights (i.e. healthcare, security, freedom) directly accessible (Karp 2015). This framework is also backed by the 1948 UN Universal Declaration of Human Rights, in which some rights contain not only freedoms but also entitlements to the provision of certain goods and service systems. This backing furthermore implies that such entitlements can be legally binding and require action by state actors.

Proceeding from these considerations, *inaction* by an executive branch may render it morally and legally accountable if the inaction leads to the insufficient

[6] Sometimes, these subprinciples are complemented by a fourth requirement—namely, that the interest must be legitimate (Cianciardo 2010; Cohen-Eliya and Porat 2011).

respect, protection, and fulfillment of basic constitutional rights. Hence, it is reasonable to maintain that *inaction* can be considered a disproportionate response in certain circumstances—namely, if there is sufficient evidence of the infringement of a basic right resulting from not only the violation of a negative duty but also the neglect of positive duties. In such instances, it must also be demonstrated that the executive branch's inaction violates the subprinciples of adequacy, necessity, and proportionality sensu stricto.

In the specific context of inaction, (a) adequacy requires proof that the government has violated a basic right through the nonfulfillment or insufficient fulfillment of a constitutional duty[7] and that there were other feasible means to completely or partially fulfill the neglected duty. Furthermore, (b) regarding the subprinciple of necessity, it must be demonstrated that there would have been, hypothetically, a feasible manner of fulfilling the respective duty without excessively impinging on other basic rights and (c) that proportionality stricto sensu would have been fulfilled if a hypothetical alternative action had been taken, which means that there is sufficient evidence that a hypothetical alternative would be associated with a better cost-benefit ratio.

Considerations Relevant to Mexico's Pandemic Management in Light of the Proportionality Principle

There are numerous considerations when applying the proportionality principle to Mexico's pandemic management and its attempts to mitigate the negative effects of the spread of COVID-19. Rather than focusing on epidemiological details of the presented case, we would like to shed light on some general lines of reasoning by referring to the proportionality principle and its corresponding subprinciples and by raising relevant questions linked to parameters that might have (so far) been insufficiently applied to the context of public policy.[8] The general strategy of our analysis will be to widen the lens to include more potential obstacles than when applying the proportionality principle in a unidimensional way—for example, when the sole focus remains the underfulfillment of the right to health, as usually put forward by critics of the Mexican government (Velasco-Ibarra 2020). Through this approach, we seek to introduce more complexity into the assessment.

[7] The potential violation of basic rights through executive underreach has been sustained in the literature, most notably by Pozzen and Scheppele (2020).

[8] The proportionality principle has been widely discussed as guidance for public policy in the COVID-19 pandemic in several contexts (see, e.g., Rubin and de Vries 2020; Cronert 2022).

The Right to Health and the Insufficient Fulfillment of Duties Through Inaction

The Mexican health administration's response to the COVID-19 crisis has been criticized for neglecting duties concerning the rights to physical integrity and health. The basic interests and rights of individuals, particularly those exposed to the virus, were jeopardized (see the introduction to this chapter), and key duties of the government were, at best, insufficiently fulfilled if not completely neglected. Although the federal government did, indeed, adopt measures, they were criticized for being delayed and incomplete. Some, but not all, of the available public health tools were utilized, and implementation was deemed deficient by many commentators (Velasco-Ibarra 2020).

In light of the epidemiological situation, it might be reasonable to say that the Mexican government and its health administration violated the duty to ensure sufficient access to public health facilities, especially for the poor and the vulnerable who have lacked the financial means to fall back on private hospitals. Furthermore, the authorities failed to fund measures to adequately test contagious persons, to trace contacts, and to order quarantines. Neither did they immunize all relevant groups in a socially justifiable and fair order. It is furthermore reasonable to assume that because of the lack of containment measures, specific vulnerable groups—notably, the diseased and the elderly—were excluded from essential medical services simply because the situation was out of control. Since information concerning the sanitary measures in place was unclear and caused confusion in the general population, the duty to publish reliable data and provide access to adequate information and education on COVID-19 virus disease was insufficiently fulfilled.

Considering several interpretations of the right to health in the current literature, the government's executive underreach could be interpreted as constituting a violation of human rights. According to International Covenant on Economic, Social, and Cultural rights (ICESCR) Article 12, the right to health contains "the prevention, treatment and control of epidemic, endemic, occupational and other diseases" (ICESCR Art. 12). Moreover, the Mexican Constitution (Art. 4) acknowledges the right to health by guaranteeing every citizen the progressive realization of high-quality health services that are accessible and free of charge.

Montel and colleagues (2020) put forward several core duties of governments during the COVID-19 pandemic derived from the right to health, in line with General Comment No. 14, on the right to the highest attainable standard of health, of the UN Committee on Economic, Social and Cultural Rights. One important duty of the state consists of ensuring the right of access to health facilities, goods, and services on a nondiscriminatory basis, especially for vulnerable or marginalized groups. For these purposes, the WHO recommended that states contain the spread of disease by testing individuals, tracing contacts, quarantining suspected cases, and treating confirmed cases (Montel et al. 2020).

Additionally, nondiscriminatory access to healthcare demands paying attention to specific vulnerable groups, including elderly persons with chronic conditions, minority ethnic populations, persons from the lowest wealth quintile, and non-COVID-19 patients with other preexisting conditions. Another duty related to the COVID-19 pandemic has been to provide education and access to information concerning issues related to the pandemic. First, states should report on their progress and publish reliable data on indicators such as incidence and mortality. Second, states have a duty to ensure that health information of sufficient quality is circulated to the public. Third, according to Montel and colleagues (2020), the right to health would also imply that health professionals and other vulnerable groups be adequately protected and trained during a pandemic.

Adequacy (in the COVID-19 Context): Feasible Means to Fulfill the Duties at Stake

Commentators have suggested that feasible and more aggressive measures—for example, curfews, contact tracing, and immunization strategies, including more (vulnerable) population groups—could have improved Mexican pandemic management in terms of reduced excess mortality, lower infection rates, consistent and effective communication, and an increased availability of treatment centers at hospitals (Guthrie 2020).

However, as Rubin and colleagues (2021) show, there have been—especially at the onset of the pandemic—major obstacles to assessing the effectiveness of measures. In noncrisis situations, governments and health administrations can often refer to past data to understand local health impacts of their actions. But in emergencies, many factors change, making it harder to make decisions based on previous evidence. The shortage of reliable evidence regarding how effective a health measure is at containing the harmful effects of the pandemic, moreover, is exacerbated by the high potential for public health risks from inaction. Furthermore, the fact that health measures are crosscutting issues that affect not only health but also other sectors such as transport, finance, the police, agriculture, or education is another obstacle. Hence, incoherent scientific data and recommendations seem to be almost unavoidable (Rubin et al. 2021, 3).

The fact that millions of Mexican workers carry out their activities in the informal sector calls into question whether people would have widely respected stricter rules (see Velasco-Ibarra 2020). More aggressive measures only qualify as feasible means to control a pandemic if they show enough *enforceability*. In this regard, we can question whether curfews and very strict mobility constraints would have been realistic. Were resource constraints in other social sectors an obstacle to helping individuals, and especially the vulnerable, cope with the COVID-19 spread? Additionally, one might consider curfews and very strict mobility constraints unsuitable in comparison to other, more fruitful measures, such as contact tracing, testing, and a better information policy.

Necessity (in the Context of COVID-19): Feasible Means to Fulfill the Respective Duties Without Overrestricting Other Basic Rights

Apart from enforceability and resource concerns, other significant moral, social, and economic costs might result from more aggressive measures. A general economic recession induced by overly restrictive measures on economic activity has the ability to produce a significant negative impact, especially on the ability of informal workers to maintain their jobs and to afford shelter and food (based on the assumption that the national budgetary restrictions do not allow for governmental assistance to the very poor). Economic costs would then directly translate into social and moral costs regarding the poorest populations, often illegal immigrants and ethnic minorities. When considering the proportionality principle, the state must also consider how the state actions outside the healthcare context relate to the duty to provide equal access to public services, basic goods, and a basic income. It remains to be seen whether measures would have evoked a clash between the right to health and the right to subsistence when imposing lockdowns, enforcing curfews, closing nonessential economic activities, and quarantining for longer periods. However, this might not necessarily be true for contact tracing and testing or the appropriate dissemination of information and data management (as far as budgetary constraints allow for these measures). Furthermore, there is also the issue of negative spillovers beyond national borders caused by executive underreach (Pozzen and Scheppele 2020).

Hence, it remains unclear how the proportionality principle arbitrates between different types of rights and the correlative state duties regarding those basic socioeconomic rights. At least for policymakers, it seems more complex to solve these conflicts than to opt precipitously for the right to health and physical integrity while potentially neglecting other state duties at stake (see Cronert 2022).[9]

Proportionality Sensu Stricto: Benefits and Costs of Action Versus Inaction

Based on Rubin's et al. (2021) analysis, it appears that conducting a strict proportionality analysis during the initial stages of the COVID-19 pandemic was challenging because of epistemic uncertainty—that is, a lack of reliable evidence (Holzer et al. 2023). An estimate of the impact of policy measures on a complex system of different sectors, such as healthcare and the economy, was difficult to

[9] We previously argued that rights conflicts are not necessarily categorical but can often be addressed and even resolved. Inevitable rights conflicts need to be addressed by *second-order* reasons that reweigh reasons that are usually thought to regulate rights conflicts and trade-offs of rights, which are conceived as pro tanto rights. We should not think of rights as correlative of single duties but as generating a multiplicity of duties, which implies that there is no single-minded (moral) account of the way in which the resolution of rights conflicts should be approached. For instance, one possible (hypothetical) line of argument could be that the emergency at the beginning of the pandemic and the indeterminable magnitude of the infectious risk possibly justify the application of the precautionary principle and giving priority to the right to health over other socioeconomic rights (Holzer et al. 2023).

ascertain. Consequently, many decision-makers opted to pursue strategies under the rationale of applying the *precautionary principle* rather than a proportionality analysis in the absence of concrete evidence (Taleb et al. 2014; Rubin et al. 2021).

Despite this, in terms of proportionality, some argue that decision-makers should have conducted a more comprehensive cost-benefit analysis that considered the potential of containing the pandemic in the short and medium terms as well as wider socioeconomic factors that could affect different subgroups of the population in the short, medium, and long terms. This would have also necessitated timely, evidence-based evaluations of measures to verify or adjust the expected costs and benefits (see Rubin et al. 2021).

The potential benefits of more aggressive measures and expanded immunization strategies could include reducing excess mortality and improving the delivery of health services, which could avoid overburdening hospitals. However, these benefits must be weighed against the costs of the envisaged measures. As previously discussed, under the subprinciple of necessity, costs might rise in the economic sector in both the short term and long term, depending on Mexico's ability to recover from an economic recession and the capacity of individuals who work in the informal sector to survive temporary income losses. While it is certain that the economic recession was multifactorial and caused by a global dynamic, strict lockdowns have a high probability of worsening the socioeconomic situation for both formal and informal workers, a dynamic compounded by the absence of social protection mechanisms or regimes, in the case of unemployment. Nevertheless, stricter, coordinated, and unanimous actions by state actors might have come along considerable advantages, particularly by alleviating pressure on the healthcare system (especially when COVID-19 infections peaked) and facilitating overdue, long-term reforms in the health system. This, in turn, would have protected the poorest and most vulnerable individuals and offered them better possibilities for accessing healthcare.

Conclusion

We have argued that *inaction*, conceptualized as executive underreach, can qualify as a violation of the proportionality principle if the state fails to honor its correlative duties to respect, protect, and fulfill basic rights. To evaluate whether a rights violation is taking place, the principle of proportionality and its corresponding subprinciples serve as tools for assessing public policies. However, assessing the actual and hypothetical moral, social, and economic benefits and costs of inaction remains a challenge. Furthermore, adopting measures with regard to the principle of proportionality may also necessitate making institutional changes and correcting known deficiencies in the healthcare system while remaining within the constraints of the available resources.

Following the public critique and a parliamentary movement against the public policy pursued by the Mexican government in response to the COVID-19 pandemic, we intended to unfold our analysis by proposing a possible interpretation of state duties during the COVID-19 pandemic corresponding to the right to health and other important socioeconomic rights. When highlighting possible benefits and costs that might have been associated with more aggressive measures to curb the negative effects of the pandemic on individuals and the health system, we also understand that a full analysis would require a more in-depth inquiry and an extensive cost-benefit analysis. Thus, our intention has merely been to *raise pertinent questions* about the conceptual and real-life obstacles related to applying the proportionality principle to inaction. One clear conclusion is that Mexico's socioeconomic context, characterized by large income disparities, a large informal sector, and considerable resource constraints on public assistance and income support, caused challenges that differ greatly from those in high-income environments and even other, structurally distinct middle-income countries. Our analysis aimed to use the proportionality principle as a lens to evaluate Mexico's pandemic response, inviting future discourse on harmonizing public health priorities with socioeconomic rights amid Mexico's socioeconomic landscape.

Competing Interests

There are no competing interests to declare.

Funding

There is no funding to declare.

References

Álvarez Máynez, J., and J. Ramírez Velasco. 2020. *La denuncia contra López-Gatell: Un caso jurídico contra la negligencia.* https://eljuegodelacorte.nexos.com.mx/la-denuncia-contra-lopez-gatell-un-caso-juridico-contra-la-negligencia/.

Bautista-González, E., J. Werner-Sunderland, P. P. D. Mendiola et al. 2021. "Health-Care Guidelines and Policies During the COVID-19 Pandemic in Mexico: A Case of Health-Inequalities." *Health Policy OPEN* 2:100025.

Cianciardo, J. 2010. "The Principle of Proportionality: The Challenges of Human Rights." *Journal of Civil Law Studies* 3 (1): 177–182.

Cohen-Eliya, M., and I. Porat. 2011. "Proportionality and the Culture of Justification." *The American Journal of Comparative Law* 59 (2): 463–490.

Cronert, A. 2022. "Precaution and Proportionality in Pandemic Politics: Democracy, State Capacity, and COVID-19-Related School Closures Around the World." *Journal of Public Policy* 42 (4): 705–729.

Dahal, S., J. M. Banda, A. I. Bento, K. Mizumoto, and G. Chowell. 2021. "Characterizing All-Cause Excess Mortality Patterns During COVID-19 Pandemic in Mexico." *BMC Infectious Diseases* 21 (1): 1–10.

De La Cruz-Hernández, S. I., and A. K. Álvarez-Contreras. 2022. "COVID-19 Pandemic in Mexico: The Response and Reopening." *Disaster Medicine and Public Health Preparedness* 16 (6): 2264–2266.

Frenk, J., and O. Gómez Dantés. 2020. "Covid-19: Balance catastrófico." *Nexos* 42 (514): 32. https://www.nexos.com.mx/?p=50282.

García Ramírez, M., and P. Martínez Martínez. 2020. "Cuál es el camino después de la pandemia por COVID-19?" In *Mexico ante el COVID-19: Acciones y retos*, edited by Carmen Medel Palma, Abigail Rodríguez Nava, Giovanni R. Jiménez Bustos, and Ricardo Martínez Rojas Rustriá. Casa de libros abiertos - UAM. https://www.casadelibrosabiertos.uam.mx/contenido/contenido/Libroelectronico/Mexico-ante-covid-19-acciones-retos.pdf.

Grimm, D. 2007. "Proportionality in Canadian and German Constitutional Jurisprudence." *University of Toronto Law Journal* 57 (2): 383–397.

Guthrie, A. 2020. "Mexican Court Orders Federal Government to Act More Aggressively Against COVID-19." *Law.com*, March 19. https://www.law.com/international-edition/2020/03/19/mexican-court-orders-federal-government-to-act-more-aggressively-against-covid-19/?region=/international-edition/region/north-america/.

Hernández Trujillo, J. M. 2020. "Pobreza, migración y movilidad en la propagación del COVID-19 en Mexico ante el COVID-19: Acciones y retos." In *Mexico ante el COVID-19: Acciones y retos*, edited by Carmen Medel Palma, Abigail Rodríguez Nava, Giovanni R. Jiménez Bustos, and Ricardo Martínez Rojas Rustriá. Casa de libros abiertos - UAM. https://www.casadelibrosabiertos.uam.mx/contenido/contenido/Libroelectronico/Mexico-ante-covid-19-acciones-retos.pdf.

Hollingsworth, Julia, Adam Renton, and Joshua Berlinger. 2020. "March 31 Coronavirus News." CNN. https://edition.cnn.com/world/live-news/coronavirus-pandemic-03-31-20/h_9a640db0d74d14113ca4dc7a748fbb54.

Holzer, F., I. M. O. Alcántara, T. Eichinger, and J. W. März. 2023. "Proportionality and Mexico's Pandemic Management During the COVID-19 Crisis." *Developing World Bioethics*, October 17. https://doi.org/10.1111/dewb.12429.

Kane Jiménez, S., and A. Gandy. 2021. "Mexico's Vaccine Supply and Distribution Efforts." Wilson Center, October 4. https://www.wilsoncenter.org/article/infographic-mexicos-vaccine-supply-and-distribution-efforts.

Karlinsky, A., and D. Kobak. 2021. "The World Mortality Dataset: Tracking Excess Mortality Across Countries During the COVID-19 pandemic." MedRxiv, January 29. https://www.ncbi.nlm.nih.gov/pmc/articles/PMC7852240/.

Karp, D. J. 2015. "The Responsibility to Protect Human Rights and the RtoP: Prospective and Retrospective Responsibility." *Global Responsibility to Protect* 7 (2): 142–166.

Khosla, M. 2010. "Proportionality: An Assault on Human Rights? A Reply." *International journal of Constitutional Law* 8 (2): 298–306.

Latinus. 2021. "Juez ampara a médicos privados para que sean vacunados contra la Covid-19," May 4. https://latinus.us/mexico/2021/5/4/juez-ampara-medicos-privados-para-que-sean-vacunados-contra-la-covid-19-37444.html.

Martínez Zorrilla, D. 2014. "El Principio de proporcionalidad como criterio de resolución de conflictos constitucionales." in *Argumentación jurídica: Fisonomía desde una óptica forense*, edited by R. Aguilera and R. López. Universidad Nacional Autónoma de México. https://archivos.juridicas.unam.mx/www/bjv/libros/8/3706/5.pdf.

Montel, L., A. Kapilashrami, M. P. Coleman, and C. Allemani. 2020. "The Right to Health in Times of Pandemic: What Can We Learn from the UK's Response to the COVID-19 Outbreak?" *Health and Human Rights* 22 (2): 227–241.

Nampewo, Z., J. H. Mike, and J. Wolff. 2022. "Respecting, Protecting and Fulfilling the Human Right to Health." *International Journal for Equity in Health* 21 (1): 1–13.

Ooms, T. 2022. "Mexico, First Collegiate Court of the 24th Circuit, 25 October 2021, No. 582/2021 [reg no Tesis XXIV.1o.1 K (11a.)]." Covid-19 Litigation: Open-Access Case Law Database, April 13. https://www.covid19litigation.org/case-index/mexico-first-collegiate-court-24th-circuit-no-5822021-reg-no-tesis-xxiv1o1-k-11a-2021-10.

Our World in Data. 2022. "COVID Vaccinations." https://ourworldindata.org/covid-vaccinations.

Perez Ortega, R. 2020. "Mexico's Coronavirus Czar Faces Criticism as COVID-19 Surges." *Science*, December 9. https://www.science.org/content/article/mexico-s-coronavirus-czar-faces-criticism-covid-19-surges.

Pozen, D. E., and Kim L. Scheppele. 2020. "Executive Underreach, in Pandemics and Otherwise." *Am. J. Int'l L.* 114(4): 608. https://scholarship.law.columbia.edu/faculty_scholarship/2735.

Rangel Laguna, R. 2020. "Juez ordena adoptar medidas eficaces contra COVID-19." *MVS noticias*, March 19. https://mvsnoticias.com/nacional/2020/3/19/juez-ordena-adoptar-medidas-eficaces-contra-covid-19-434862.html.

Rubin, O., and D. H. de Vries. 2020. "Diverging Sensemaking Frames During the Initial Phases of the COVID-19 Outbreak in Denmark." *Policy Design and Practice* 3 (3): 277–296.

Rubin, O., N. A. Errett, R. Upshur, and E. Baekkeskov. 2021. "The Challenges Facing Evidence-Based Decision Making in the Initial Response to COVID-19." *Scandinavian Journal of Public Health* 49 (7): 790–796.

Snilstveit, B., L. Langer, and T. Lotfi. 2020. "Addressing the Need for Timely and Reliable Evidence in the Time of COVID-19: International Initiative for Impact Evaluation." *Reliefweb*, May 18. https://reliefweb.int/report/world/addressing-need-timely-and-reliable-evidence-time-covid-19.

Sobrino, J. 2014. "Migración interna y tamaño de localidad en México." *Estudios demográficos y urbanos* 29 (3): 443–480.

Taleb, N. N., R. Read, R. Douady, J. Norman, and Y. Bar-Yam. 2014. "The Precautionary Principle (with Application to the Genetic Modification of Organisms)." arXiv, October 17. https://arxiv.org/abs/1410.5787.

Velasco-Ibarra, E. 2020. "Mexico: Emergency Powers and COVID-19." Verfassungsblog. https://verfassungsblog.de/mexico-emergency-powers-and-covid-19/.

Velázquez Leyer, R. 2021. "Mexico's Social Policy Response to Covid-19: A Path of Minimal Action." CRC 1342 Global Dynamics of Social Policy. Covid-19 Social Policy Response Series 5. https://www.ssoar.info/ssoar/bitstream/handle/document/71809/ssoar-2021-velazquez_leyer-Mexicos_Social_Policy_Response_to.pdf?sequence=1&isAllowed=y&lnkname=ssoar-2021-velazquez_leyer-Mexicos_Social_Policy_Response_to.pdf.

7

Public Health Proportionality for Sexual and Gender Minority Youth

Stewart Adelson, Alice Miller, Daniel Newton, and Graeme Reid

Introduction

The treatment and prevention of disease among the populace are basic public health goals and core obligations of states under human rights. Achieving these goals and fulfilling these obligations requires public health strategies suited to the specific needs of diverse populations. Sexual and gender minority (SGM) youth have public health needs that are in some ways identical to those of the non-SGM youth population and in other ways unique. SGM youth have distinct developmental needs and health predictors related to their sexual orientation, gender identity, or gender expression that may affect health. They may also be exposed to anti-SGM discrimination and stigma, which are associated with important health disparities. Therefore, it is important that public health programs for SGM youth consider the adverse health effects of stigma and not augment them. Doing so partly entails states' responsibility to protect the SGM populations' health and human rights, and it calls for tailored protections by states. For these reasons, public health programs for SGM youth sometimes require unique public health strategies that should be developed in line with ethics and fundamental rights protections found under both national and international laws. Proportionality in public health can therefore encompass obligations to assess the potential benefits of public health policies, programs, and practices in light of their bioethical and human rights risks. This chapter discusses the rationale and principles for considering proportionality in public health programs serving SGM youth and strategies for serving these individuals.

Public Health Proportionality and SGM Youth

When determining optimal public health strategies, the bioethical imperatives of *beneficence* and *nonmaleficence* require public health officials to weigh the

Stewart Adelson et al., *Public Health Proportionality for Sexual and Gender Minority Youth*. In: *Proportionality*. Edited by: Nikola Biller-Andorno et al., Oxford University Press.
DOI: 10.1093/9780197759370.003.0008

relative risks and benefits of policy, program, and practice options to determine the best course of action. For example, a vaccination program for preventing a given disease might carry risks of widespread disease if not implemented, but the vaccine might also carry some risk of adverse side effects if the program were implemented. If undertaken, benefits must outweigh risks to minimize ethical hazards among alternatives to justify the program. In addition, the bioethical *justice imperative* requires that health resources be distributed equitably among diverse populations. For example, in comparison with those who can work remotely, manual laborers might be disproportionately adversely affected by quarantine lockdown. Similarly, children might have unique cognitive and social-emotional developmental needs that differ from those of adult populations, and their experiences of the advantages of social distancing might also differ from those of adults. Beyond these bioethical imperatives, human rights imperatives require that public health programs and policies ensure respect for a range of key rights while promoting health. Good public health requires optimally assessing health benefits of program, policy, and practice options and their health and human rights risks.

Proportionality is a tool for elucidating, analyzing, and synthesizing bioethical and human rights imperatives when they are in contention in practices adopted by states ostensibly in the service of public health. Childress and colleagues (2002) define proportionality as showing "that the probable public health benefits outweigh the infringed general moral considerations," including in the spheres of both health and rights. Proportionality can be considered a public health practice of minimizing apparently competing bioethical and human rights hazards within public health policies and programs in the overall pursuit of distributive justice. This chapter discusses the concept of proportionality that must be brought into any proportionality-based review of benefits over harms in the case of SGM youth.

Public health proportionality can be developed regarding both ethics and rights law frameworks, albeit while taking care to recognize the distinct obligations of each frame. Tests of the justifiability of state action include whether the action is not arbitrary, is rationally related to the goal (effectiveness), is not discriminatory, and uses the least restrictive actions, which courts can sum up as *proportionality*.[1] At the same time, both US antidiscrimination law and nondiscrimination in international human rights law recognize the need for specific attention to the removal of historical barriers to equality in health research and healthcare. However, common public health strategies in infectious disease crises such as quarantine and contact tracing have been found to be in

[1] UN Human Rights Committee, "General Comment No. 31 (80): The Nature of the General Legal Obligation Imposed on States Parties to the Covenant; International Covenant of Civil and Political Rights." UN Doc. CCPR/C/21/Rev.1/Add. 13 (March 24, 2004).

tension with other rights such as those to nondiscrimination, privacy, freedom of movement, and assembly. Governments have a duty to strike the right balance between generalized and effective protection of their citizens' well-being and the protection of rights and liberties, especially of minoritized or stigmatized classes of people (Yamin 2005). As a recent text on health law notes, "Principles such as equity, solidarity and proportionality may emerge as foundational principles of global health law" (Toebes 2018).

This chapter will use examples of proportionality in public health responses to infectious disease such as HIV/AIDS and COVID-19, although these are not the only health crises that command attention to ethics and rights, to examine the use of proportionality as a lens for intervention. In times of infectious disease outbreaks, typical public health tools might include prevention through not only education and the communication of information but also quarantine and contact tracing. Ideally, such programs would be based on broad public consensus. Achieving such consensus requires public health officials not to use public health tools in discriminatory ways but to ensure that information be created and shared in ways that effectively support the target communities. However, historically, "many of the controls that governments use to identify, prevent, and respond to infectious diseases limit individuals' liberty of movement, privacy, freedom to travel and immigrate, and freedom to control their own body .... Frequently, these social controls are imposed disproportionately on vulnerable populations. Sometimes these controls provide little or no public health benefit" (Parmet 2010). Public health responses are most effective when they are responsive to successful community-generated measures (Hastings et al. 2021).

Definitions and Demographic Estimates

One cross-culturally salient definition of SGMs used by the UN Development Program (UNDP) refers to

> people whose biological sex, sexuality, gender identity and/or gender expression depart from majority norms. The concept of sexual and gender minorities includes considerable diversity as well as a multiplicity of identities and behaviors, including lesbians, gay men, bisexuals and transgender people (LGBT); intersex people . . . ; gender non-conforming people who may not see themselves as transgender; and people involved in same-sex relations who may not see themselves as lesbian, gay or bisexual, possibly preferring another word to self-identify . . . or possibly preferring no label at all. (O'Malley and Holzinger 2018)

As noted by Victor Madrigal-Borloz (2019), the UN independent expert on sexual orientation and gender identity (SOGI), "There is currently no globally-accepted definition, or international classification scheme, to facilitate internationally comparable data between subpopulations according to sexual orientation and gender identity." There have been efforts to measure the global SGM population. Research definitions are important because of their effect on estimates of demographic denominators and any associated disease prevalence. In addition, population classification thresholds will affect the statistical significance of any associations found between risk exposures and mental health outcomes. This is important to bear in mind when discussing the evidence base.

The UN Office of Economic Co-Operation and Development (OECD), in seeking to estimate the global lesbian, gay, bisexual, transgender, and intersex (LGBTI) population, has found that "few population-based surveys include direct questions on sexual orientation, and even fewer ask respondents about their gender identity . . . . Tentative but conservative measures suggest that LGBTI [constitute] a sizeable minority. They represent approximately 4.5% of the total population in the US" (Valfort 2017). Based upon available population data sets in thirty-eight countries and indices of discriminatory laws and policies affecting SGMs in 197 countries, it is estimated that up to 83% of the sexual minority individuals conceal their sexual orientation (Pachankis and Bränström 2019). For SGMs, concealment of identity is associated with exposure to stigma. Exposure to stigma is associated with poor physical and mental health outcomes in LGBT populations (Lick et al. 2013; Meyer and Frost 2013; White Hughto et al. 2015). Youth who are LGBT constitute a unique group comprising various subpopulations. Stigma such as family nonacceptance and school bullying can begin in youth and is associated with poor long-term outcomes in physical and mental health (van der Star et al. 2021).

Estimates from the US 2019 Youth Risk Behavior Surveillance Survey, a representative national sample of high school students, showed a median of 2.7% who said they were gay/lesbian, 6.4% who said they were bisexual, and 4.0% who reported that they were unsure of their sexual orientation. Despite changing social attitudes, youth still struggle with nonheterosexual identities. For example, one finds important differences between identity, attraction, and behavior. In New York City in 2005–2007, 38.9% of adolescents who reported only same- or both-sex partners nevertheless identified as "straight." More recently in 2015, a US median 25% of adolescents with only same- or both-sex partners identified as "heterosexual or straight" (Kann et al. 2016). In some cultural contexts, incongruence between identity and attraction and behavior may be associated with identity concealment (in some places, this is called being in the closet). Identity concealment owing to developmental struggles that youth experience in reconciling identity, behavior, and attraction domains is an important mediator of mental and physical health risk.

Gender identity refers to one's experience of gender, which for some youth does not match their birth sex and assigned gender. One definition of *transgender youth* is those whose gender experience matches the *Diagnostic Statistical Manual* (*DSM-5-TR*) diagnosis of gender dysphoria or the International Classification of Diseases' (ICD-11) diagnosis of gender incongruence or both diagnoses. Both diagnoses refer to distress associated with a person's marked discomfort with their own birth sex. This can involve secondary sex characteristics and/or gender role and expression, the latter of which is salient for prepubertal children.

Demographic estimates of US and European adult patients seeking specialty treatment for gender dysphoria, as defined by the *DSM*, are as follows: 0.005% to 0.014% for birth-assigned males and from 0.002% to 0.003% for birth-assigned females. However, the diagnosis of gender dysphoria is controversial. Many youths whose gender identity doesn't match their birth sex in some way but who don't meet *DSM's* strict criteria identify as transgender and gender nonconforming (TGNC). For example, Eisenberg and colleagues (2017) analyzed population surveillance on approximately eighty-two thousand ninth- and eleventh-grade students in Minnesota. Students who self-reported being "transgender, genderqueer, genderfluid or unsure about their gender identity" made up 2.7% ($n =$ 2,168).

Stigma and Health Disparities Among SGM Youth

The inclusion of SGM youth in healthcare is a basic pediatric goal (Hadland et al. 2016). Assessing the proportionality of public health measures regarding SGM youth requires a consideration of their unique developmental needs and health determinants such as stigma. *Stigma* refers to the negative stereotyping of marginalized groups. Examples of anti-LGBT youth stigma include the experience of family nonacceptance, school bullying, rejection anticipation, and identity concealment and the existence of stigmatizing laws, policies, and norms. Minority stress theory relates exposure to stigma to health disparities (Meyer and Frost 2013; Hatzenbuehler 2016). A proportional analysis of public health programs for SGM youth must consider the effects of stigma on health outcomes.

An important consideration in designing and implementing public health policies and programs for SGM youth is to recognize that their identity development and decisions about whether to reveal it to others (i.e., to come out) are typically uniquely salient life issues for them, including with regard to their cultural, social, political, and familial contexts (Khuzwayo 2021). SGM youth at different developmental stages and from diverse cultural and socioeconomic backgrounds may experience possibilities and limitations related to sexual and gender development and public expression that differ from those of the non-SGM population. This may influence whether a given youth recognizes their own same-sex attraction or gender-diverse feelings, acts upon them in social or sexual ways, experiences themselves as having an SGM identity, and reveals to others any such attraction or feelings and, if so, to whom.

SGM youth who are exposed to stigma experience health disparities, including elevated rates of depression, suicidality, anxiety, substance abuse, HIV, and disordered eating in comparison with the general population (Hatzenbuehler and Pachankis 2016; Santarossa et al. 2019; van der Star et al. 2021). These health disparities among SGM youth are major causes of mortality. Stigma and associated mental health disparities—including risks to mental health—are important mediators of secondary health behaviors and risk taking that affect areas like HIV prevention (Pachankis et al. 2017). Minimizing stigma and its adverse effects may improve LGBT youths' rates of engagement in and the results of public health initiatives.

Public health programs for marginalized populations can work better when these efforts fight stigma and promote equity and inclusion. Successful programs are those that decrease stigma. For example, programs to prevent, detect, and treat HIV among populations that are diverse in terms of race and gender (including across SOGI, sex/gender, and ethnicity) are most successful when they use strategies to decrease stigma (El-Sadr 2021). Conversely, stigma and discrimination decrease the likelihood that those affected by HIV will avail themselves of public health services including testing, treatment, and prevention (Wouters et al. 2020).

To be successful, public health programs for SGM youth must minimize stigma. These principles apply equally to all youth. For example, a study (Miller et al. 2018) of a diverse sample of 1,793 youth that controlled for the age, HIV status, and race of youth in sexual partnerships in which HIV was more likely to be transmitted found that

> structural HIV stigma had deleterious indirect effects on youth's participation in HIV-risky sexual partnerships. Concentrated disadvantage and structural sexual and gender minority stigma had direct negative effects on youth's perceptions of their communities as supportive and on their participation in prosocial activity. Support perceptions had direct, protective effects on avoidance of HIV-risky sexual partnerships.

Congregate spaces may be uniquely safe spaces for some SGM youth. In considering a public health intervention such as quarantine that might limit access to congregate spaces, the use of proportionality assessments for actions around SGM youth requires weighing the purported benefit of the quarantine against the risks of limiting access to spaces that promote health and well-being. Having safe spaces and trusted sources of information may take on a special significance for such youth. Public health tools such as quarantine and contact tracing often operate at cross-purposes with public health opportunities for SGM populations—for example, the closure of congregate spaces for SGM communities to prevent the spread of communicable diseases like HIV can inadvertently restrict the dissemination of useful public health information about infection control. Continuing these practices can lead needlessly to other health risks affecting mental health and health behavior and can increase the risk of abuse and exploitation. These factors may further adversely affect an SGM youth's amenability to public health messaging and to receiving information and motivation for healthy behaviors. Rather than eliminating safe spaces, using them for outreach could be a way to promote and optimize public health. Good public health programs must consider these unique factors for SGM youth in order to ensure they meet the tests of proportionality, especially the features of nondiscrimination and the focus on direct and indirect benefits and harms in designing and implementing programs.

Decreasing stigma does not mean avoiding truth in public health campaigns. For example, it would not require downplaying HIV prevalence among SGM youth in an effort to avoid a potentially stigmatizing association between epidemics such as HIV and SGM people. Rather, it means promoting health behaviors that are effective and useful to those populations simultaneously while providing protections against discrimination, thus preserving human rights, equity, and dignity around shared public health goals. Public health officials responsible for SGM youth must understand which options can be effective while avoiding unnecessary stigmatization in public health messaging and practice. They must also not aid or abet sociopolitical repression such as the criminalization of same-sex conduct, which can discourage adaptive health behaviors such as testing, treatment, and prophylaxis and thereby increase vulnerability to HIV and other illnesses (Purcell 2021). SGM youth are also disproportionately affected by restrictions on comprehensive sexuality education, which renders their experiences invisible. Globally, state actions that seek to limit movement or access to services or to comprehensive information vis-à-vis SOGI have been found to be in violation of rights and to fail key aspects of proportionality (i.e., they are discriminatory and not the least-restrictive means) (Madrigal-Borloz 2020a; 2020b).

Using proportionality in public health to assess key aspects, such as the avoidance of stigma among SGM youth, need not be a zero-sum game pitting their interests against those of other groups. Moreover, attention to stigma and discrimination makes clear when purported public health measures are in fact illusory in their claimed success for public health. By making public health interventions proportionate, the actions are more effective: Not stigmatizing marginalized groups can simultaneously protect them and the general population by decreasing disease reservoirs and vectors. In this way, improving the health of SGM youth can benefit them and others at the same time. Therefore, in addition to being justified ethically, proportionality can be strategically advantageous in achieving public health outcomes. Weighing factors such as actions that generate stigma in a lens of proportionally, public health practitioners can see how their actions can do more harm than good through revealing the hidden messages that harm some groups, and they can re-tailor their actions to optimize equity and concrete public health outcomes across the full population simultaneously.

Proportionality in Population Measurement and Program Design

If sufficient data is available from research, weighing risks and benefits to meet proportionality tests can be possible using quantitative tools. To obtain the data necessary to design and implement a public health program, it is first necessary to accurately define the target population and its health-related exposures and outcomes. Achieving public health compliance with both rights- and ethics-based tests of proportionality for SGM youth requires clarity and equity in conceptualizing what is being measured and counted. It also requires a careful enumeration of multiplicities of expressions, conduct, and identity in terms of both intersectional identities and life experience over time among SGM youth. Doing so begins by identifying them in and across the range of health-related surveys and needs assessments.

Developing empirical instruments to count SGM youth populations requires valid conceptualization. This includes a consideration of face, construct, and discriminant validity of a measure and its constructs. Constructs of sexuality and gender must be conceptually appropriate and clinically relevant. Research instruments must be statistically sensitive and specific and must have satisfactory positive and negative predictive value (Cimpian 2017). Using them requires an appropriate operationalization of measures. Fear of being publicly exposed as having a stigmatized sexual or gender identity (i.e., as being outed) must be a special public health consideration for SGM youth. It is important to consider confounders of significance for such youth, such as nondisclosure—for example, from fear of consequences or inadequate inclusivity of measures (Pachankis and Bränström 2018; 2019). These may require special strategies to ensure privacy, anonymity, and/or control of information in ways that are consistent with standard pediatric sexual health best practices. Public health programs should also consider the appropriateness of health screening strategies for use with SGM youth. For example, SGM youth facing stigma might be more willing to provide information in anonymous and confidential formats.

Measures used in empirical health research must also define and operationalize sex- and gender-related variables in sociocultural and historical contexts. These influence individuals' experience of sexual orientation and gender experience, including gender expression and identity. The effective design and implementation of public health programs requires acknowledging sociocultural contexts. Research constructs regarding sex and gender may also need to be revised from time to time to deal with shifting political, economic, and historical contexts. For example, measures of minority stress have been adapted to TGNC youth (Hidalgo et al. 2019) and Black, Latino, and Asian sexual minority men (McConnell 2018; DiGuiseppi et al. 2022).

Existing tools for evaluating public health programs such as measures of burden of disease, medical decision analysis, and cost-benefit analysis (Detsky et al. 1997; Adunlin et al. 2015) could be adapted to SGM youth populations proportionally by including salient variables. One strategy for generating empirical methods for meeting proportionality tests in medical decision analysis could be to include variables related to health exposures (e.g., stigma) and to outcomes (e.g., health-promoting behavior) in standard tools, such as decision trees (Detsky et al. 1997), estimates of probabilities and utilities (Naglie et al. 1997), decision model analysis and interpretation (Krahn et al. 1997), and Markov modeling of epidemics (Naimark et al. 1997). Programs could also evaluate the cost effectiveness of options factoring in the potential adverse effects of exposure to stigma. Outcomes for LGBT populations can be measured using qualitative outcomes—for example, quality-adjusted life years (QALYs), which measures both the quality and duration of life—and quantitative measures of disease burden—for example, disability-adjusted life years (DALYs), which measure disability and premature mortality.

When insufficient data exist are available for making robust judgments about whether actions meet the test of proportionality on an empirical quantitative basis, it is necessary to weigh the risks and benefits of such actions for SGM youth using clinical and programmatic judgment. In some circumstances, a mixture of existing data, clinical judgment, and ethical and rights analysis can provide a framework for program design, measurement, and analysis. Existing research data can be supplemented by the empirical study of program needs, benefits, and risks; by including methods such as surveys and program outcome

Table 7.1 Accurately measuring and analyzing SGM youth health information

- Enumerate SGM youth
- Use valid screening instruments
- Measure the burden of the disease
- Understand the relationship between stigma and health outcomes (minority stress)
- Factor these into medical decision analysis
- Perform a cost-benefit analysis
- Determine cost effectiveness, taking minority stress into consideration and including qualitative (morbidity, QALYs) and life-year health outcomes (DALYs)

measures; and by using qualitative methods of program assessment. These can be weighed simultaneously with issues of human rights and freedoms.

One strategy for designing public health programs that consider youths' needs appropriately is to include youth advisory boards in program planning and implementation. When included as leaders, co-collaborators, or participants in research, stakeholder populations can help frame hypotheses and design studies that capture salient factors influencing health outcomes. It is important that public health researchers use accurate classification and intersectional strategies in conducting studies and analyzing data—an approach that, when applied appropriately to LGBT populations, has been dubbed the queering of research (Reid and Ritholtz 2020). The concept of recognizing and incorporating populations' own understanding of the area being researched has been called a component of epistemic justice (Fricker 2007). One model for stakeholder leadership in research includes participatory action research methodologies (Cornish et al. 2023; Iacono et al. 2023).

Feasibility, Acceptability, and Utility

At a minimum, healthcare programs and practices require *clinical competence*—that is, adequate knowledge and skill to treat and prevent illness and promote health in populations at risk. SGM youth may have special clinical needs in areas such as mental and physical health. These specific needs are described in systematic reviews, guidelines, and other healthcare knowledge resources (Adelson and Schuster 2020; Bockting 2020). Knowledge of these may help in planning and implementing public health programs for SGM youth by weighing their unique clinical needs appropriately. Information is also available through community resources such as the National Center for Youth with Diverse Sexual

Orientation, Gender Identity, and Expression (the National SOGIE Center)[2] and the National LGBTQIA+ Health Education Center.[3] To meet any review of ethics- or rights-based proportionality in program planning and implementation, public health officials can obtain technical assistance from these and similar reputable sources of information.

While clinical competence is a necessary component of public health, it is not in itself sufficient. For any public health program or policy to work, it must be feasible, pragmatically accessible, and useful to the population served, and its facilities, goods, information, and services must be evidence based and appropriate.[4] Examples of strategies that might be considered include advance crisis plans, targeted screening programs, dedicated crisis hotlines, SGM-competent child welfare services, safe and affirmative medical spaces, and support groups.

Achieving feasibility, acceptability, and utility considering both ethical and rights-based proportionality tests for SGM populations requires public health officials to have competencies in addition to clinical competence. These include cultural competence, cultural humility, and structural competence. *Culture* refers to systems of knowledge and social rules (Jenks 2011; Boroughs et al. 2015), including domains of language, thoughts, communications, actions, customs, beliefs, and values (CDC 2023). *Cultural competence* in working with SGM youth across age, race, place, class, disability, religion, and indigeneity includes establishing welcoming and affirmative healthcare spaces (Hadland et al. 2016). *Cultural humility* refers to the health program and caregiver attributes required for providing healthcare to diverse populations experiencing power imbalances; it has been further defined as

> a process of openness, self-awareness, being egoless, and incorporating self-reflection and critique after willingly interacting with diverse individuals. The results of achieving cultural humility are mutual empowerment, respect, partnerships, optimal care, and lifelong learning. (Foronda et al. 2016)

Structural competence refers to understanding the structural social factors influencing health—for example, access to healthcare resources (Hansen and Metzel 2019). Without adequate economic and societal resources, other healthcare competencies and attitudes are in and of themselves bootless.

A combined understanding of cultural and structural social factors influencing health is referred to as *sociocultural competence* (Weiss et al. 2021).

[2] https://sogiecenter.org.
[3] https://www.lgbtqiahealtheducation.org.
[4] Committee on Economic, Social and Cultural Rights (CESCR), "General Comment No. 22 on the Right to Sexual and Reproductive Health," UN Doc. E/C.12/GC/22 (May 1, 2016); CESCR, "CESCR General Comment No. 14: The Right to the Highest Attainable Standard of Health (Art. 12)," UN Doc. E/C.12/2000/4 (May 11, 2000); Wiley et al. 2022.

Table 7.2 Areas of public health competence with SGM populations

- Attain the required cultural, structural, and clinical competence
- Use systematic reviews and guidelines
- Consider targeted strategies and dedicated programs in collaboration with SGM technical assistance if required. Examples include the following:
    - o Advance crisis plans
    - o Targeted screening
    - o Crisis hotlines
    - o Child welfare needs
    - o Safe and affirmative medical spaces
    - o Support groups
- Choose messaging carefully in collaboration with community partners and key opinion leaders
- Obtain human rights consultations
- Use SGM-relevant outcome research

Public health messaging for SGM youth should be carefully chosen with structural and cultural competence and humility in mind. In addition to technical assistance as described earlier in this chapter, program planning can be undertaken in consultation and collaboration with key opinion leaders from the target community. Public health planners can consider obtaining or seeking referrals for human rights guidance and/or consultations from relevant UN agencies that have incorporated rights and ethics principles in their work—ranging from the WHO, the Joint UN Program on HIV/AIDS, branches of UNDP, and the Office of the UN High Commissioner for Human Rights to national and international human rights-based NGOs such as Human Rights Watch,[5] Amnesty International,[6] and Physicians for Human Rights[7]—to understand how to address SGM youth needs related to human rights and freedoms while meeting their legitimate public health needs.

General Recommendations and Conclusions

Proportionality in public health involves appropriately considering potential benefits of policies, programs, and practices in light of their bioethical and human rights risks. Bioethical imperatives and human rights law require public health policymakers, officials, and practitioners to assess proportionality. Doing

[5] http://www.hrw.org.
[6] http://www.amnesty.org.
[7] http://www.phr.org.

so includes assessing potential human rights impingements of state or nonstate actors, preserving rights and liberties, and minimizing stigma while protecting or improving population health. Doing so can be achieved through quantitative and qualitative methods or through a combination of methods.

SGM youth have unique developmental needs and are disproportionately exposed to stigma and discrimination, including threats to their human rights. Among SGM youth, exposure to stigma is associated with disparities in physical and mental health. Avoiding stigma and protecting rights and liberties is a special consideration in public health programs for SGM youth. Considering stigma can help make visible the ways that traditional tools for managing public health crises require unique operationalization, feasibility, and risk/benefit trade-offs for SGM youth populations compared with general population. Successful public health programs for SGM youth optimize avoiding bioethical hazards and adhering to human rights principles while taking their unique health needs and predictors into full consideration.

Proportional public health management on behalf of SGM youth is not a zero-sum game that pits their health interests against those of non-SGM populations. Achieving proportionality can simultaneously help protect SGM youths' human rights, minimize their mental and physical health risk, and enhance the effectiveness of public health programs. Doing so benefits both SGM youth and the general population concurrently.

Acknowledgments

The authors gratefully acknowledge the support of the Tides Foundation and Broadway Cares/Equity Fights AIDS, which supported this project through the Youth Equity Science Project of the Yale Law and Public Health Schools' Global Health Justice Partnership (GHJP). The GHJP receives Fellowship support from the Gruber Program for Global Justice and Women's Rights.

Competing Interests

There are no competing interests to declare.

Funding

There is no funding to declare.

References

Adelson, S., and M. Schuster. 2020. "Gay, Lesbian & Bisexual Adolescents." In *Nelson Textbook of Pediatrics*, edited by Robert M. Kliegman and Joseph W. St. Geme III. Elsevier.

Bockting, W. O. 2020. "Gender and Sexual Identity." In *Nelson Textbook of Pediatrics*. Robert M. Kliegman and Joseph W. St. Geme III. Elsevier.

CDC. 2023. National Prevention Information Network. https://npin.cdc.gov/.

Cimpian, J. R. 2017. "Classification Errors and Bias Regarding Research on Sexual Minority Youths." *Educational Researcher* 46 (9): 517–529.

Cornish, F., et al. 2023. "Participatory Action Research." *Nature Reviews Methods Primers* 3:34. https://www.nature.com/articles/s43586-023-00214-1.

Detsky, A. S., et al. 1997a. "Primer on Medical Decision Analysis: Part 1—Getting Started." *Med Decis Making* 17 (2): 123–125.

Detsky, A. S., et al. 1997b. "Primer on medical decision analysis: Part 2—Building a Tree." *Med Decis Making* 17 (2): 126–135.

DiGuiseppi, G. T., et al. 2022. "Multiple Minority Stress and Behavioral Health Among Young Black and Latino Sexual Minority Men." *LGBT Health* 9 (2): 114–121.

Eisenberg, M. E., A. L. Gower, B. J. McMorris, G. N. Rider, G. Shea, and E. Coleman. 2017. "Risk and Protective Factors in the Lives of Transgender/Gender Nonconforming Adolescents. "*J Adolesc Health* 61(4): 521–526.

Fricker, M. 2007. *Epistemic Injustice: Power and the Ethics of Knowing*. Oxford University Press.

Hadland, S. E., B. R. Yehia, and H. J. Makadon. 2016. "Caring for Lesbian, Gay, Bisexual, Transgender, and Questioning Youth in Inclusive and Affirmative Environments." *Pediatr Clin North Am* 63 (6): 955–969.

Hansen, H., and J. Metzel 2019. *Structural Competency in Mental Health and Medicine: A Case-Based Approach to Treating the Social Determinants of Health*. Springer International.

Hatzenbuehler, M. L. 2016. "Structural Stigma: Research Evidence and Implications for Psychological Science." *Am Psychol* 71 (8): 742–751.

Hatzenbuehler, M. L., and J. E. Pachankis. 2016. "Stigma and Minority Stress as Social Determinants of Health Among Lesbian, Gay, Bisexual, and Transgender Youth: Research Evidence and Clinical Implications." *Pediatr Clin North Am* 63 (6): 985–997.

Iacono, G., L. Holle, E. Loveland et al. 2023. "Community-Based Participatory Action Research with LGBTQIA+ Youth During the COVID-19 Pandemic: Reflections from a Collaborative Autoethnography." *Qual. Social Work* 23 (6): 970–989. https://doi.org/10.1177/14733250231194783.

Jenks, A. C. 2011. "From 'Lists of Traits' to 'Open-Mindedness': Emerging Issues in Cultural Competence Education." *Cult Med Psychiatry* 35 (2): 209–235.

Kann, L., T. McManus, W. A. Harris, et al. 2016. "Youth Risk Behavior Surveillance–United States, 2015." *MMWR Surveill Summ* 65(6):1–174.

Khuzwayo, Z. 2021. "'Why Do I Need to Come Out If Straight People Don't Have To?' Divergent Perspectives on the Necessity of Self-Disclosure Among Bisexual Women." *Front Sociol* 6:665627.

Krahn, M. D., et al. 1997. "Primer on Medical Decision Analysis: Part 4—Analyzing the Model and Interpreting the Results." *Med Decis Making* 17 (2): 142–151.

Madrigal-Borloz, V. 2019. "Data Collection and Management: An Essential Component in Creating Awareness and Providing Effective Measures to Address Violence and Discrimination Based on SOGI." UN Doc. A/HRC/41/45 (May 14).

Madrigal-Borloz, V. 2020a. "ASPIRE Guidelines on COVID-19 Response and Recovery Free from Violence and Discrimination Based on Sexual Orientation and Gender Identity." UN Human Rights Special Procedures (June 18).

Madrigal-Borloz, V. 2020b. "Violence and discrimination based on sexual orientation and gender identity during the coronavirus disease (COVID-19) pandemic." UN Human Rights Council. UN Doc. A/75/258 (July 28).

Meyer, I. H., and D. M. Frost. 2013. "Minority Stress and the Health of Sexual Minorities." In *Handbook of Psychology and Sexual Orientation*, edited by C. J. Patterson and A. R. D'Augelli. Oxford University Press.

McConnell, E. A., et al. 2018. "Multiple Minority Stress and LGBT Community Resilience Among Sexual Minority Men." *Psychol Sex Orientat Gend Divers* 5 (1): 1–12.

Miller, R. L., et al. 2018. "Structural Effects on HIV Risk Among Youth: A Multi-Level Analysis." *AIDS Behav* 22 (11): 3451–3467.

Naglie, G., et al. 1997. "Primer on Medical Decision Analysis: Part 3—Estimating Probabilities and Utilities." *Med Decis Making* 17 (2): 136–141.

Naimark, D., et al. 1997. "Primer on Medical Decision Analysis: Part 5—Working with Markov Processes." *Med Decis Making* 17 (2): 152–159.

O'Malley, J., and A. Holzinger. 2018. *The Sustainable Development Goals: Sexual and Gender Minorities*. UN Development Program.

Pachankis, J. E., and R. Bränström. 2018. "Hidden from Happiness: Structural Stigma, Sexual Orientation Concealment, and Life Satisfaction Across 28 Countries." *J Consult Clin Psychol* 86 (5): 403–415.

Pachankis, J. E., and R. Bränström. 2019. "How Many Sexual Minorities Are Hidden? Projecting the Size of the Global Closet with Implications for Policy and Public Health." *PLOS One* 14 (6): e0218084.

Parmet, W. E. 2010. "Public Health and Social Controls: Implications for Human Rights." Northeastern University School of Law Research Paper No. 44-2010. SSRN, February 2.

Purcell, D. W. 2021. "Forty Years of HIV: The Intersection of Laws, Stigma, and Sexual Behavior and Identity." *Am J Public Health* 111 (7): 1231–1233.

Reid, G., and S. Ritholtz. 2020. "A Queer Approach to Understanding LGBT Vulnerability During the COVID-19 Pandemic." *Politics & Gender* 16 (4): 1101–1109.

Toebes, B. 2018. "Global Health Law: Defining the Field." In *Research Handbook on Global Health Law*, edited by G. L. Burci and B. Toebes. Edward Elgar Publishing.

Valfort, M.-A. 2017. "LGBTI in OECD Countries." https://www.oecd.org/en/publications/lgbti-in-oecd-countries_d5d49711-en.html.

White Hughto, J. M., et al. 2015. "Transgender stigma and health: A critical review of stigma determinants, mechanisms, and interventions." *Soc Sci Med* 147: 222–231.

Wiley, L. F., et al. 2022. "Introduction: What Is Health Justice?" *J Law, Med & Ethics* 50 (4): 636–640.

Yamin, A. E. 2005. "The Right to Health Under International Law and Its Relevance to the United States." *Am J Public Health* 95 (7): 1156–1161.

8

Responding Proportionately to the COVID-19 Pandemic in UK Long-Stay Inpatient Pediatric Wards

Heather Draper, Caroline Redhead, Anna Chiumento, Sara Fovargue, and Lucy Frith

Context: The COVID-19 Pandemic in the United Kingdom in Autumn 2020

Across Europe, countries responded differently to the COVID-19 pandemic, according to sometimes regional but usually national political judgments and the infection rates at any given time. The United Kingdom was among the most seriously affected countries in Europe. The United Kingdom comprises four countries: England, Wales, Scotland, and Northern Ireland. The last three have devolved responsibilities for public health, and the measures taken across the four countries did, therefore, differ at times. Having some understanding of how the pandemic affected England is relevant to this chapter. Rather than focusing on the proportionality of measures that affect the whole population, we will explore how the broader policies affected staff, patients, and their families at the micro level by looking at the typical restrictions placed on non-COVID-19 pediatric inpatient services in England in late autumn 2020. To give some context to this case study, we will briefly outline the progress of the virus and the measures taken in response to the pandemic from January 2020 to July 2021.

In the United Kingdom, the first COVID-19 wave struck rapidly, with reported cases rising from forty new cases on March 2, 2020, to 2,339 by March 23, 2020,[1] when a UK-wide lockdown was announced (Institute for Government 2022). New daily cases peaked at around 5,151 a month later.[2] Mass testing was not available at this time, so the case incident rate was probably much higher. Although it was clear in January that a pandemic was imminent, the World

[1] https://github.com/CSSEGISandData/COVID-19.
[2] https://github.com/CSSEGISandData/COVID-19.

Heather Draper et al., *Responding Proportionately to the COVID-19 Pandemic in UK Long-Stay Inpatient Pediatric Wards*. In: *Proportionality*. Edited by: Nikola Biller-Andorno et al., Oxford University Press. © Oxford University Press (2026). DOI: 10.1093/9780197759370.003.0009

Health Organization did not declare it as underway until March 11, 2020.[3] At this time, little was known about the SARS-CoV-2 virus. The National Health Service (NHS), along with the UK public, had little time to respond and little information upon which to base its response. In the 2009 H1N1 (swine flu) pandemic, pregnant women, children, and young adults, especially those with underlying health conditions, were found to be particularly vulnerable.[4] Understandably, therefore, these groups initially attracted greater concern, including, in some cases (e.g., those in the third trimester of pregnancy), additionally stringent measures designed to protect them from COVID-19 until more information about the virus was available. Included in these measures were others who were considered most vulnerable. This included, for example, those known to be severely immunocompromised (NHS n.d.). These measures included complete shielding: confining people to their home, except to receive urgent medical treatment. Those sharing a home with shielded patients were advised to remain as isolated as possible. These restrictions, or variations of them, remained in place in England until April 2022.[5]

In England, hospitals and other care settings moved rapidly to introduce infection control measures based on radically reducing person-to-person contact. This included minimizing footfall by limiting access to sites to patients only and asking staff whose roles could be performed from home not to come into work. Social distancing measures were initially introduced in hospitals, and more broadly within the community, against a background of limited and erratic supplies of personal protective equipment (PPE). Visiting was initially strictly prohibited, with some very limited exceptions eventually made for those who were dying. Visiting restrictions remained in place for over a year but were variously softened and hardened again in response to infection waves and were only finally lifted in June 2022. In addition, in March 2020 as many inpatients as possible were discharged to be cared for in the community. This was both to increase capacity for treating COVID-19 patients and to limit the spread of infection within hospitals. For those who could not be discharged, life on the ward was radically changed by the infection control measures. These measures were put in place not just to protect patients and the staff caring for them but also to curb the spread of COVID-19 *within* hospitals and *from* hospitals back

[3] WHO. 2020. "WHO Director-General's Opening Remarks at the Media Briefing on COVID-19." Media briefing, March 11. https://www.who.int/director-general/speeches/detail/who-director-general-s-opening-remarks-at-the-media-briefing-on-covid-19—11-march-2020.

[4] NHS Health A–Z (2020), January 1. https://webarchive.nationalarchives.gov.uk/ukgwa/20230127142206/https://www.nhs.uk/conditions/swine-flu/ (available via webarchive.org, accessed February 19, 2024).

[5] UK Government Department of Health and Social Care and UK Health Security Agency, Guidance for people previously considered extremely vulnerable from COVID-19, https://www.gov.uk/government/publications/guidance-on-shielding-and-protecting-extremely-vulnerable-persons-from-covid-19/guidance-on-shielding-and-protecting-extremely-vulnerable-persons-from-covid-19 (accessed February 19, 2024).

out into the community. The response mirrored the wider public health measures being enacted in other nonhealthcare settings. In April 2020, all nonurgent, nonessential, non-COVID-19 related services were suspended for three months. A COVID-19 NHS Test and Trace service became operational in England in May 2020, with polymerase chain reaction tests available to individuals with a raised temperature, a continual cough, or altered taste/smell.

Most parts of the United Kingdom[6] had enjoyed a brief summer with relatively few restrictions. Conforming to mask wearing in public became something of a political statement. Measures to enforce mask wearing came into force in July 2020.[7] The NHS recovery plan commenced in July 2020 with the reintroduction of normal services.

New variant strains of the virus began to cause concern in the United Kingdom in September and October 2020, however, and cases once again began to soar, reaching a peak of around 33,487 per day in mid-November. This second wave, which incorporated the emergence of the highly infectious Alpha variant in December 2020 and another peak in January 2021, continued until April 2021 (Office for National Statistics 2021). Regional, tiered restrictions were instigated in England in mid-October 2020, and a further month-long, England-wide lockdown was announced on October 31 to start on November 5, 2020. Many areas were in the highest tier, which had four measures, by December 26, 2020; some restrictions were lifted for twenty-four hours over Christmas. By January 6, 2021, England was once again in lockdown. The vaccine rollout started on December 8, 2020, with priority being given to those over eighty years old and healthcare workers; lower-risk groups were called for vaccination from April 2021 (Mounier-Jack et al. 2023). A three-step plan to remove restrictions started in March 2021 with the reopening of schools, and universally available lateral flow testing made available in April 2021. It was mid-July 2021, however, before the majority of the legal restrictions were lifted in England (Institute for Government 2022).

Background

In this chapter, we explore the ethical and legal dimensions of the effect of hospital infection control measures on patients, families, and staff in long-stay pediatric wards. Our insights were gained from a research project titled

[6] In addition to the devolved governments making decisions for Scotland, Wales, and Northern Ireland, more local regional measures meant that some areas, such as Leicester and parts of Leicestershire, remained heavily restricted from July 2020 to spring 2021. The first lockdown was for the entire United Kingdom.

[7] Health Protection (Coronavirus, Wearing of Face Coverings in a Relevant Place) (England) Regulations 2020 (SI 2020/791).

When Pandemic and Everyday Ethics Collide: Supporting Ethical Decision-Making in Maternity Care and Pediatrics During the COVID-19 Pandemic.[8] Our research took place in England between July 2020 and September 2021 over five geographically diverse NHS sites and concentrated on pediatric and maternity services that did not treat COVID-19 patients. We explored how ethical considerations underpinned healthcare decision-making during the period immediately following the first wave in the United Kingdom as nonurgent, non-COVID-19 services were being reinstated in an environment that was still being ravaged by the pandemic as the second wave hit. We received Health Research Authority approval and approval for study participation from each NHS Trust. Our methods and results have been published elsewhere (Chiumento et al. 2020). To protect site/participant confidentiality, the following case description is based on composite data drawn from all sites.

Case Description

The setting we devised as our case study for this chapter draws on composite data from all our sites to describe a fairly typical surgical ward in a specialist pediatric inner-city hospital in England in late autumn 2020. It was the designated regional center for complex orthopedic surgery, including trauma (e.g., from road traffic accidents). It was a "green" (non-COVID-19) ward with tight infection control measures. Pre-COVID-19, the ward had ten beds, but capacity was reduced to six to ensure the required two-meter distance between the beds. Children undergoing complex surgery could be expected to be in the ward for several weeks at least, sometimes many months.

Staff wore light PPE (e.g., masks, gloves, disposable aprons, and sometimes visors for specific procedures). Most children were bedbound, but when they were not, they were encouraged to remain within their bed space. This area was marked out on the floor with thick adhesive tape. The children were not required to wear masks but were tested regularly for COVID-19. Only one designated visitor per child was permitted on hospital premises at a time. This person was required to be from the child's usual household. Ideally, there was a single designated person; in most cases, this was a parent. If that person tested positive for COVID-19, became ill, or was self-isolating, another person could be designated. If the child normally lived across two households, a designated person

[8] **Frith, L. (PI)** (2020–2021). *When Pandemic and Everyday Ethics Collide: Supporting Ethical Decision-Making in Maternity Care and Paediatrics* (UKRI project AH/V00820X/1). University of Liverpool (lead), with collaborators at University of Central Lancashire, Royal College of Physicians of London, University of Exeter, Liverpool Health Partners, Liverpool Women's Hospital, UK Clinical Ethics Network, Birmingham Women's & Children's NHS FT, Alder Hey Children's NHS Foundation Trust.

from each household was permitted to visit but not at the same time. Both parents were allowed to visit together in exceptional circumstances—for example, immediately before (one hour) and after (thirty minutes) surgery or if a child was dying. Visitors were required to remain within their child's bed space and to wear a mask at all times. The parents/family common room was closed, and parents were no longer permitted to use the ward kitchen. Staff policed compliance with these requirements, and parents were encouraged to move on if they stopped to chat with other parents.

Discussion

Providing a case study is a useful way of considering how proportionate the response to the pandemic was in a specific clinical context and point in time. The focus of our discussion is the impact of the infection prevention and control measures. Clearly, these were proposed with good reason; it is worth reflecting now, however, on whether these measures were proportionate because, as our data illustrate, they were not without cost.

The infection prevention and control policies served at least four purposes. First, they were intended to prevent pediatric patients from being infected with COVID-19. By this time, children were generally known to only experience relatively mild illness if infected unless they had other medical conditions. Nonetheless, the patients in our case study would have experienced illness on top of the effects of their surgery or the conditions for which surgery was needed. Even if COVID-19 was not ultimately life-threatening, a persistent cough, for instance, could exacerbate wound pain, and respiratory viruses may predispose patients who have had recent surgery with a general anesthetic to developing a chest infection, which would be unpleasant even if treatable with antibiotics. Moreover, any patient who developed COVID-19 in a green ward would be moved to a "red" (COVID-19) ward to minimize the risk of infection for other patients and staff in the ward. Such relocations might represent unwelcome upheaval for the child and mean that specialist staff were less able to respond to a patient's underlying surgical condition, potentially resulting in setbacks to their recovery.

Second, infection control minimized the risk that staff would be infected and be off sick or need to self-isolate because of close contact with an infected person and, therefore, be absent from work until testing could demonstrate that they were not infectious. Staff absences, whether as a direct result of COVID-19 infection or because of self-isolation owing to close contact with an infected person, meant it was often challenging for the NHS to staff services safely.

Staffing problems clearly affected patients in terms of service delivery and staff well-being by putting working staff under even greater pressure.

Third, preventing transmission to parents was important in maintaining the limited visits that were allowed for patients in the ward. Isolation arrangements meant that if a parent or other family member living with the parents became infected, the patient would have no visitors (unless their parents were living in separate households).

Finally, in addition to seeking to prevent spread within the ward, the infection measures also sought to limit spread *between* wards and *from* the hospital to the community and from the community to the hospital. In this respect, the ward restrictions were often not that different to the restrictions pertaining outside the hospital (Institute for Government 2022). In England, a circuit-breaker lockdown was imposed in November 2020, though local lockdowns had started as early as July. Most areas of England emerged from the November lockdown into tiered restrictions that amounted to much of the same in terms of limiting social interactions between different households. By early January 2021, England was once again in lockdown, with all parts of the country being placed into tier 4, "stay at home" restrictions. These restrictions were, however, particularly significant in their effects on patients whose rehabilitation would ordinarily have included incremental challenges, such as moving from the ward to another space within the hospital, visiting a playground or a shopping center, or having weekend home leave.

Whether these measures were *proportionate* requires a consideration of the effects on those concerned. The effects of the measures, which included inconvenience, frustration, loneliness, fear, were arguably more significant for these patients (and their families) *because* they were children than they were for non-COVID-19 adult inpatients. At the least, the effects were highly significant, given children's general dependence on their parents. We draw on the insights from our participants to highlight some of the impacts of infection control measures in this context that are potentially less often discussed.

Effects of Broken Communities on the Wards

Infection prevention and control measures resulted in the loss of a benefit that is fairly specific to long-stay pediatric wards—the community of parents providing peer support to each other during their children's inpatient stay. In common with the staff, some parents and patients had direct experience of big changes that the arrival of COVID-19 to the United Kingdom brought to the ward environment. They had a shared experience of "before" and "now" as the infection prevention and control measures were rolled out. These parents lost peer support—a benefit that was abruptly removed/changed. For others, the measures put in place to control infection were all they had known.

> But obviously once you restarted the services, you went in your bed space, you stayed in your bed space, they couldn't you know, they can't go and sit next to [a patient's] mum in bed eight because she's upset because he's going to theater. It's a very different feel. And we policed that quite strongly . . . . And that's not, you know, we've grew up on a ward that's very sociable: The kids will often play, the physios will get the two children throwing balls to each other across the bed spaces, and you know, it's quite a friendly ward . . . . [It] is quite a community feel, especially amongst the parents, and the staff will often look after the same patients for weeks so that there's quite a relationship built up there . . . . Well obviously, . . . the more community side of the ward had to stop. (Nurse, ward manager)

Peer support is known to be a valuable resource for parents of children being treated for long-term conditions or being treated over an extended period (see, e.g., Pilona et al. 2021). Complex, specialist surgery often requires considerable inpatient recovery time and may be accompanied by setbacks that require further surgery and readmission for further reconstruction. There are different routes into a ward such as the one we described: Some children will need surgery for conditions they were born with, others as a result of accidents or recently diagnosed conditions. There will, however, often be significant elements of shared experience, such as periods of acute anxiety and uncertainty, dashed and rebuilt hopes, and long periods of time away from the home environment, which necessitate juggling work commitments and/or care for other children and trying to maintain other relationships, such as with a partner or spouse, under strained and constrained circumstances.

During the pandemic, parents were also dealing with a multitude of other problems, including COVID-19 infection and self-isolation, the illness of family members (some of whom were also dependents, others of whom were providing much-needed support at home), the loss of paid employment or reduction of income, and homeschooling during lockdown periods.

> And what it turns out to be was her fridge had broken the day before, something else had broken and then she . . . had had a parking ticket. And it just was what finished it off and then I walked onto the ward and I was just the person to talk to! . . . And I certainly have noticed in more recent months that everything seems to be sharpened and heightened, you know, so people are less resilient[,] . . . less flexible, more kind of set, more kind of irritable, almost. And I think it's to do with the fact that, you know, we haven't been able to go

> anywhere; we, some of us, haven't seen our families in a year, you know, children, . . . elderly family members. Can't even go down the pub! You know, you can't go and watch a movie in the cinema . . . . And I suppose having people at home that would normally go out to work, that can, that could be stressful. So I could see how it flares quite easily at times. (NHS senior manager)

Hence, parents whose children were admitted to hospital had a lot to cope with and were isolated from familiar means of support and isolated from each other during this phase of the COVID-19 pandemic. On top of this, they faced the strain of presenting a calm and comforting exterior to their child.

Staff told us about how, prior to the pandemic, they strove to generate a community feeling on wards like those outlined in our case study. We were told, for instance, about how staff organized film and takeout nights and about how the parents themselves formed mutual support groups and shared their experiences with others who had a good understanding of what they were going through.

> So quite often the parents become each other's support . . . . You know, [Name] in bed six and [Name] in bed eight is going to meet me for coffee at nine o'clock after ward round. And you know, we'll go for a bit of breakfast, and we'll have a chat and . . . they'll form those support groups. Well, we see that that's good for the families. But obviously at the moment, it's not . . . . It can't be the priority because none of our children would do well from being COVID positive. (Nurse, ward manager)

The forging of informal supportive networks or communities on wards may provide a benefit to some parents—though not all will benefit equally. This benefit could be regarded from the perspective of proportionality as a superlative or bonus to good care. While clearly beneficial to those participating in these networks and communities, it is not obvious that any of those helping create this benefit are *obliged* to do so. Given this, because the benefits are in addition to what could be reasonably expected and the harms prevented by the restrictions are serious, such restrictions may seem proportional and justified. We will now look at each of the parties involved in these communities to determine what their obligations to each other are and whether this affects the calculation of whether loss of peer support weighs more lightly than do the harms prevented.

Parents, as people forced together by circumstance, have some obligations to each other of the kind that could be described as common decency, such as contributing to preserving the general orderliness of communal areas, not making undue noise or being a nuisance to others, and being respectful of privacy and others' possessions. What is less clear is what is required of them in terms of offering friendship or expressing empathy. There may be some obligation to offer a fellow in distress some immediate comfort, other things being equal, or to be willing to reciprocate such comfort willingly received. In this respect, a supportive community of parents in a ward can arise organically as a result of some individual kindness that results in that kindness being reciprocated or in behaviors to others that emulate the kindnesses an individual has received. But the creation of such a mutually beneficial community seems to be supererogatory rather than obligatory, though it is easy to see how duties of reciprocity might enable it to be(come) self-sustaining. In fact, parents were still able to form limited communities by using electronic devices to engage in chat via groups hosted on social media. While this was a much-scaled-down means of support, it enabled something of a community to emerge that did not contravene social distancing measures.

Ward staff have a clear and obvious professional duty to protect and promote the best interests of their patients, not least because of the patients' legal status as minors. As most hospitalized children benefit from having the company of their parents during their stay, bolstering the parents' capabilities to support their children will, in turn, benefit the child. Pediatric healthcare professionals have long recognized that because children invariably exist—and thrive—in families, pediatric services should be family centered where possible. Moreover, parents (or those with parental responsibility) are legal proxies for their children and must, therefore, be closely involved in decision-making and understand the ramifications of treatment decisions.

At the same time, there is a limit to the support that staff are obliged to offer to family members. Harsh as it may seem, responding to a parent's distress is an expression of *personal* compassion by the staff but is, perhaps, not *professionally* required. This assumes that a parent's emotional or psychological strain is not affecting their child and that the obligation to family may be part of promoting the best interests of the patients. Time and effort are resources that are, like all other resources in the NHS, thinly spread. Across the NHS and social care, family members who are perceived to be coping may be regarded as less in need than those who are floundering and so are unable to contribute meaningfully to the ongoing care of the patient. Against this background, investing time in enabling a supportive ward community—in which parents thrive as opposed to survive—could be regarded as supererogatory in a pandemic context, and its loss could be seen as a sacrifice less costly than it may first appear, compared to infection control.

Having said that, the NHS Trust responsible for the ward has no reason to prevent initiatives that improve the experiences of everyone, provided that the costs (which in this case appeared to be minimal) do not disproportionately affect services elsewhere. It is also arguable that, from the staff perspective, there is a cost in *not* helping parents do more than survive.

> But we're very much the type of people that if . . . they come back sobbing, we'd give them a cuddle . . . . It's very difficult to see somebody crying and not give them a little bit of comfort. (Nurse, ward manager)

At the same time, under the circumstances it seems clear that restoring the community—or even implementing measures to grow it in other ways, such as through electronic means of communication—might be a low priority.

Inhibited Right to Family Life and Loss of Right to Parent

In late autumn 2020, all areas of the hospital would have been similarly affected by restrictions, and pediatric visiting arrangements were actually less restrictive than were those for adult patients, whereby, at times, no routine visiting was permitted.[9] That an exception was made for pediatric wards is a compromise between infection control imperatives, on the one hand, and the best interests of children and the rights of parents on the other. Given the speed at which infection control policies were implemented in March 2020, and given that they had changed very little by November 2020, these policies were unlikely to have been driven solely by scientific evidence. They were also possibly influenced by the expediency (at the level of hospitals) of keeping the rules for the public simple, clear, and consistent across the entire organization. Moreover, it is probably not possible for any given hospital to be able to quantify precisely what the infection risks might be of changing visiting arrangements in different ways on different wards for different categories of patient and at different points in the pandemic. Even when more was known about the COVID-19 virus, there were just too many variables. This meant that members of the public had to trust that advertised visiting arrangements were the best that could be provided under the circumstances. However, policies should always adhere to ethical standards and be fair and evenly applied. Fairness does not necessarily mean identical treatment, but it does imply that like cases should be treated alike when they are similar in morally relevant ways or differently if their differences are morally relevant.

[9] This extended to maternity care, where the nonbirthing partner was not permitted to re-enter the hospital once they had left following the birth. This led to prolonged loss of opportunities for early bonding with a new baby when either the birthing partner or baby had to remain in hospital.

The first morally relevant difference to note is that between child and adult patients. Tight visiting restrictions in the case of adults who had capacity at the time of admission remained in place. An exception was sometimes made for dying patients. Some wards permitted one person who was free of symptoms or had tested negative for COVID-19 or both to be with a noninfectious adult patient as they died, but many adult patients—especially those with COVID-19 and/or in nursing homes—died without loved ones physically present.[10] The visiting policy regarding children was, therefore, already an exception to this general rule. Equity needs to be maintained between arrangements for children and for other patients and between children. Making an exception for children is likely to be acceptable to the general population, although there was, in fact, no public consultation about any of the measures imposed in March 2020. While our public focus group participants understood that meaningful dialogue with parents of hospitalized children would have been difficult (if not impossible) under the circumstances, there was a clear sense that better preparation should be made for any future public health emergencies.

> My child's hospitals battened down the hatches effectively and started to prepare, because we didn't know how children were going to be affected by COVID-19 at all. And it could have been—it could have been awful. It could have been, especially for the very, very sick children. And they had to tackle it in a way that was immediate. And talking to us about that would have been really, really hard for them to do, but before, they could have actually done it and could have caused more problems than it was worth. So although I do think that we should have strategies for public engagement and all the time, there are circumstances like this last year that it would have probably been dangerous for them to do it. Now, as it happens, of course, we're being told that children are barely affected by this. They're not even—they don't even seem to be spreading it very much. . . . So we planned for something awful, and then it didn't turn out to be awful, from a child's point of view. I wonder whether we just need to put these strategies in in order to prepare for future events like this, now that we've been through one, and they probably should have been in beforehand to have very quick decisions being made, but it [was] unprecedented. (Participant, public focus group)

This included both imposing infection control measures and lifting them.

[10] Families were sometimes able to say their goodbyes using videoconferencing or telephones. It should also be noted that family members often caught COVID-19 from each other and were, therefore, ill or infected themselves as patients died. Very overstretched staff also needed to recognize when patients were near to death and to have enough time to alert a family member to come to the hospital. Restrictions in care homes were even more stringent.

> I agree that unprecedented time at the beginning where there was a lot, a lot of unknowns. And hospitals did have to go into sort of a, I suppose, like an emergency mode—like, it was completely understandable. But then what then seemed to subsequently happen long after having a good, empirical understanding that the actual virus itself was not a significant risk to children was there was inadequate consultation with regards to the sort of the management of coming out of that emergency phase. And it felt like a lot of decisions. Well, it felt, in our experience, it was that we had zero involvement in any of the decision . . . . The onus was on me to find out what the process was . . . . I just think that there should have—as soon as, sort of, it was clear that there was not a significant risk to children—I think that children's hospital services should have tried to well involve us with at least communication as to how they're trying to recover from it. A lot more. (Participant, public focus group)

In the United Kingdom, pediatric patients are those from birth to fifteen, with young people (those aged sixteen and seventeen) often—but not always—treated on adult wards. It would have been distressing for younger children to be physically separated from their parents for long periods, and unlike adults, they may not be capable of understanding why this was necessary. Extended separation may also have damaged the parent-child relationship. Allowing one parent to remain with the child is a compromise, since it is in the interests of all patients and staff for the risk of infection on the ward to remain as low as possible. Allowing this in the case of all minors—even those with greater capacity—could be justified on pragmatic grounds (it is difficult for hospitals to accurately assess and enforce age- and capacity-specific criteria) or because of the relative emotional immaturity of children compared to adults.

One morally relevant disparity between children is family circumstances. As reflected in our case description, children whose parents had separated could be visited by both parents, whereas parents living in the same household had to designate a single parent to visit their child. Arrangements for children whose parents live in different homes were in line with the government's approach to social distancing in the wider population. Even during the UK-wide first and tightest lockdown, no restrictions were placed on the movement of children between the homes of separated parents, even though this considerably increased the social contacts of both households. The view that the welfare interests of children are furthered by maintaining a relationship with both parents, unless proved otherwise, is stated in legislation.[11] By November 2020, the COVID-19 risks of this arrangement were generally thought not to be borne

[11] Children Act 1989 section 1 (2A)–(2B). See also the Explanatory Notes to the Children and Families Act 2014, Pt. 2, Sec. 11.

by the children, as evidence had emerged that younger children who were fit and well when infected were generally asymptomatic or only experienced mild symptoms. Instead, the risks were to the adults in both households, particularly those with specific COVID-19-related vulnerabilities.

The arrangements for separated parents were observed by our pediatric staff participants to have created some tensions on the ward. They were perceived as unfair by some parents who were not separated and who were forced to choose whom to designate as the visitor. The arrangement seemed to them to privilege parents who were separated, as both were able to visit, whereas in their case one parent (the nondesignated visitor parent) was effectively prevented from maintaining an ongoing relationship with their child.[12] Recognizing the importance of interactions with their family, the guidance around phone and tablet use in hospital settings was considerably relaxed, and many wards, such as the one in our case study, encouraged their patients to speak to and see other family members on video calls.

> So we were doing baby's cares on FaceTime for parents to be involved and to help them choose an outfit and things like that, you know, . . . which was lovely . . . . So it was just trying to do what we would normally do for our families . . . [to] find different ways . . . to try and reduce that, that the impact of things, really. (Pediatric high-dependency ward nurse)
>
> So we can set up Zoom calls, and we can set up WhatsApp calls, and we can help like that. But I would imagine [there'd] still be a portion of the parents that have been in that would very much say their views, and [their] wishes to have family with them haven't been adhered to. But I don't know how you get around that. (Pediatric nurse)

To the best of our knowledge, visiting policies on pediatric wards were not subject to court challenge. The Children Act 1989 stipulates that the welfare interests of the child should be the paramount consideration of all public bodies, which includes hospitals. It is possible that if parents could have demonstrated that their child's welfare was being damaged by the visiting arrangements, a court might have made an order on the basis of their child's best interests, particularly if they could also demonstrate how they could manage visiting without increasing the risk that the infection control measures were designed to mitigate (including the risks to their own child). Most parents, given the reduction of visitor facilities (canteen, family areas, the staff kitchen, showers, etc.) needed to return home periodically and were then mixing with the other parents and family members in their household. This made it even harder for staff to explain and for parents

[12] Later, visiting policies did change to permit both parents to visit separately.

to understand, how, nevertheless, the overall infection risk increased if those household members came into the hospital, particularly when both parents from separated families were allowed to visit.

> But during [July and August 2020], we could go to the pub with five different friends. And we were being encouraged to eat out to help out—there was all these schemes, and . . . the transmission rates were very low. But there was no movement. And there was no visiting at our trust . . . . And in September, guidance was issued . . . to say . . . trusts should review their risk assessments. And my local trust didn't do that until Christmastime, just before Christmas, and only began implementing changes then in February, and that I cannot understand. (Participant, public focus group)

Going forward, evidence and ethical rationales for these kinds of restrictions should be more clearly articulated to staff and the public alike.

Parents could also have considered a challenge under the Human Rights Act 1998. This act incorporated the European Convention on Human Rights (ECHR) into domestic law and protects UK citizens and residents against breaches of their rights by public authorities, including NHS hospitals. Article 8 of the ECHR protects the right to respect for private and family life and often underpins challenges to healthcare decision-making. But the protected rights in this article are not absolute. Accordingly, if, for example, interfering with someone's right to respect for their private and family life can be shown to be in accordance with the law, meet a legitimate aim (e.g., protecting public health in the context of a pandemic), and address a pressing social need proportionately, then it is likely to be considered justifiable.[13]

The law in England recognizes the difficult nature of some of the decisions that must be made; the key is that, in making them, human rights must be respected and promoted.[14] In the case of COVID-19 restrictions on the ward in our case study, visiting restrictions were relaxed in the most challenging of circumstances. So, for example, both parents were permitted to be present together with their child for the hour before surgery and for thirty minutes in the recovery unit[15] or

[13] See, for example, respective discussions in *Evans v. United Kingdom*, App. 6339/05, 46 EHRR 34 (2007) (Eur. Ct. H.R.); *Pretty v. United Kingdom*, App. 2346/02, 2 FCR 97 (2002) (Eur. Ct. H.R.); and *Enhorn v. Sweden*, App. 56529/00, 41 EHRR 30 (2005) (Eur. Ct. H.R.).

[14] See, for example, *R v. Secretary of State for Education* (2020), EWCA (Civ.) 1577 (Eng.), in which the secretary of state for education was found to have acted unlawfully in failing to consult the Children's Commissioner for England and other children's rights organizations before making "substantial and wide-ranging" changes to legal protections for England's seventy-eight thousand children in care.

[15] Recovery units in the UK NHS are where patients go immediately from theaters to be stabilized prior to transfer. Time spent in recovery can vary according to, for example, the depth and duration

if a child was approaching the end of life.[16] These exceptions recognized that a preoccupation with infection risks may be disproportionate in circumstances in which the harms of keeping loved ones apart were very great, such as in the last moments of life, when there would be no possibility of postponing significant family contact to some future point, thereby creating a lasting and irreversible harm.

Our participants reported not only that parents appreciated this small relaxation for surgery but also that, on occasions, the nondesignated visitor parent would become hostile when their thirty minutes were up, or when the child was moved from recovery back to the ward, or when a child thought to be dying rallied.

> We've let two people [in] because their child's been extremely sick or might die, and then actually you come to the point where they actually they don't look like they're going to die anymore. And you have to sort of go back to normal rules. And they find that quite challenging. (Advanced Nurse Practitioner [ANP], pediatric intensive care)

The above considerations are pertinent to our third theme, the effect on the ward staff who were responsible for enforcing the visiting restrictions.

The Negative Effects of Using Healthcare Staff to Police Infection Measures

Many of the staff who were required to police compliance with infection prevention and control measures had, pre-COVID-19, been actively involved in *cultivating* family friendly and supportive communities in children's wards. After the pandemic was declared, they found themselves *actively disrupting* conversations between parents on the ward, thus actively impeding the development of mutually beneficial or reciprocally supportive relationships, and they struggled with this. They also had to manage conflict situations—for example, a nondesignated parent refusing to leave or designated parents trying to smuggle

of anesthetic and patient factors such as blood pressure, pain levels, respiration rates, pulse, and temperature.

[16] This was not initially the case early in the pandemic. The first child to die as a result of COVID-19 in the United Kingdom was thirteen-year-old Ismail Mohamed Abdulwahab, whose family was not permitted to be with him when he died on March 30, 2020. On April 15, 2020, the government announced, citing the death of Ismail Mohamed Abdulwahab, that whenever possible, arrangements would be made for family to be with patients as they died, though commentary at the time said that the change had already been made as early as April 2, 2020 (BBC 2020).

nondesignated parents into the ward to visit their child by opening fire escape doors or by opening the main ward door when no one was watching.

> They're just not coping very well, and they're cross . . . so you just get that more passive-aggressiveness from them in the bed space really, or they're . . . constantly testing the rules. So they will just bring another person in—they'll sort of sneak somebody in . . . and they're like, "Oh, such and such let us [in]." And so that [is] constant, almost testing the rules. (Nurse)

Because of social distancing, it was not always possible to conduct these difficult enforcement conversations and dispute resolutions in private—and all were conducted with the additional barrier of PPE. Equally, on the rare occasion when an exception was made because of extreme circumstances, other parents would challenge staff for an explanation.

> I felt, we all felt, it was the right decision to let both parents be with this child pre-op. And then they had half an hour when he came back and then Dad checked into a hotel. And it caused an awful lot of bad feeling with the other parents. . . . It literally got to the stage where people wouldn't say good morning to this family. And it had only happened for a couple of hours. But all the surrounding parents were saying to the staff, "That's not fair, that's a choice, that's not fair." And we felt awful for allowing that to happen. (Nurse, ward manager)

Rightly evoking patient confidentiality could be perceived as evasion, leading to further tensions with staff and between parents.

> But . . . it's very difficult to explain a situation when you can't breach confidentiality, because obviously, we didn't want to say, "D'you know they just found yesterday he's got cancer, you need to lay off the family." Obviously, can't say anything. . . . And . . . it was quite difficult at the time, because [it] seems like a silly issue out of the context, [but] when you've had a mum [who's] had no other adult company [for four weeks], it's huge. . . . It's just massive. . . . And it was quite upsetting for the [other staff] . . . because that's an awful thing to have happened. (Nurse, ward manager)

Yet staff are accustomed to monitoring visitors' behavior (we include parents here) in hospital wards. Indeed, the use of infection control measures, such as washing hands or wearing gloves before performing any kind of procedure or examination with patients, was widely enforced prior to the coronavirus pandemic, with some NHS Trusts displaying posters encouraging everyone—including patients and visitors—to ensure that this was adhered to by all.

The perception of enforcing COVID-19 infection mitigation measures as policing per se may, therefore, be something of a misperception. Staff are expected to enforce a variety of organizational policies, including respectful behavior while visiting. It may be hard, but it is not unreasonable to ask them to do this.

However, staff members have the right to respectful interactions with patients and visitors, even in a pandemic, and hospitals have the responsibility and the right to protect patients from harm. Accordingly, when parents push back against policies, it may be reasonable to have additional but proportionate policies in place that support staff efforts. In the United Kingdom, NHS hospitals now promote zero tolerance for the verbal or physical abuse of staff. In the case of *adult* patients, repeated transgressions can result in the withdrawal of care. When children pose a threat to staff, additional staffing or other measures are deployed as part of the duty to act in the best interests of the child. Responses such as red carding (whereby visiting rights are completely withdrawn and visitors banned from hospital premises) are more controversial in the case of parents of child patients than visitors to adult patients, because of the potentially negative effect on children. But presumably, such measures and those that fall short of these should be imposed when necessary to protect staff. It seems important, therefore, to enact additional measures alongside visiting restrictions for de-escalating the inevitable tensions that will result. This may go some way to limiting the harms to all. It is important that policies be evenly enforced in order for them to be perceived as fair and proportionate by those most affected.

The policing of social distancing measures was, however, perceived a little differently from other interpersonal disagreements. Staff were sympathetic to the needs of parents to see their children, and they were responsive to the problems that the strict visiting restrictions created, both for parents and for their children. Such restrictions not only ran completely counter to the considerable efforts those same staff had, over many years, invested in creating family-centric, supportive ward communities, the restrictions but also added yet another barrier to the demonstration of care that was already perceived by staff as having been disrupted by wearing PPE and maintaining two meters distance.

> And I think something that I've noticed very much . . . was the number of parents that feel it's very wrong. It's wrong. They blame us . . . . We have no right to prevent them being with their child and visiting their child. . . . I had one mum who said to me, "This is not negotiable. I will be present here with my husband and the father of my child. And it is totally unethical, inappropriate, and against all of my rights as a parent, for you to say that both parents cannot be at the bedside." . . . [But] she actually was very receptive when I [told] her about my experience in adult services . . . to keep COVID out of the hospital.

Staff exhibited tremendous resilience in the face of the ethical challenges of delivering care during the pandemic. This includes those maintaining non-COVID-19 treatment services. We have discussed elsewhere (Chiumento et al. 2024) the damaging effect on staff of having their ability to demonstrate compassionate care limited by infection prevention and control measures and the need to consider the longer-term damage of fracturing compassionate care in any future pandemic. Accordingly, in the context of this chapter, we are inclined to interpret the responses of staff to policing infection control measures as further reflection on how their ability to demonstrate compassionate delivery of care was compromised. It is true that healthcare staff are accustomed to enforcing hospital policies (e.g., about infection control and visiting). During the pandemic, however, they were also enforcing policies that many regarded as undermining or compromising their professional identity as compassionate carers. Although these may have been policies that they broadly agreed were necessary for public health reasons, defending them to individuals—particularly when the costs of doing so were evident—may have felt like a betrayal of deep-seated values of clinical ethics such as "make your patient your first concern" (General Medical Council 2024).[17] Such values reflect the quality of individual patient-carer relationships to which healthcare professionals should aspire but which may be difficult to achieve in pandemic circumstances when public health considerations comes to the fore (Baines et al. 2020).

Conclusion

In this chapter, we have used a case study to describe and discuss some of the day-to-day effects of the COVID-19 infection prevention restrictions for patients, their family, and staff in non-COVID-19 long-stay pediatric hospital wards. Our wider study has clearly influenced our sense of the costs to all concerned, and, in particular, our findings related to the fracturing of compassionate care. During the worst parts of the pandemic in England, those living as patients in care environments experienced greater isolation. The dual imperatives for health organizations of protecting vulnerable patients and staff (as both employees and a precious social resource) meant that even during times when restrictions in the wider community were somewhat lifted, tighter restrictions were maintained within those organizations. As we now begin to reflect on whether the restrictions on the wider community were proportionate, it is important to remember that these dual imperatives for health organizations could have been used to justify more significant restrictions than those imposed outside these settings.

[17] The Nursing and Midwifery Council's *Code* similarly states, "Put the interests of people using or needing nursing and midwifery services first. Make their care and safety your main concern."

Infection control measures did impose considerable burdens on patients, their families, and staff—some of which may not have been obvious at the time, like the fracturing of care relationships. As we have discussed, they were probably on balance proportionate, given the dangers infection posed to patients and the broader consequences of infection spreading within the hospital and from the hospital to other parts of the community. These measures did reflect those in place elsewhere in the community and in adult NHS services, and that comparison adds weight to the argument that they were proportionate—at least in the context in which they were imposed. It is, however, important to remember that permitting limited parental visiting represented a departure from restrictions elsewhere, and further compassionate exceptions were made in addition to this. The exception made for some limited parental visiting is one that can be justified with reference to the status, rights, and needs of children. Although there were still costs, making this exception went some way to lessening the burdens experienced by everyone concerned.

Finally, as we start to reflect on what measures might be justified and proportionate in hospital settings (and beyond) in a future pandemic, we should also consider how best to utilize stakeholder engagement in this process. The COVID-19 pandemic left little time in the United Kingdom for consultation beyond core groups of experts. It is easy to forget how little was known about the virus at the start of the pandemic, when it seems patterns for how states ought to respond were set early on by the responses of those who were hit hardest first. When planning for the next pandemic of a novel pathogen, it may be difficult to re-create the sense of dealing with something completely unknown when stakeholders of all kinds will be influenced by their own memories of COVID-19 and the benefit of hindsight. Nonetheless, planning measures should include mechanisms for rapid, inclusive, and effective stakeholder involvement to help inform judgments about the acceptability of the potential range of measures being considered in response.

Acknowledgments

The authors would like to acknowledge the valuable contribution made by Dr. Paul Baines to the NHS Reset Ethics project.

Competing Interests

There are no competing interests to declare.

Funding

Our research was supported by a grant from the UKRI AHRC COVID-19 rapid response call (AH/V00820X/1). Ethical oversight and sponsorship were provided by the University of Liverpool (Central University Research Ethics Committees, REC ID: 794–8290).

References

BBC. 2020. "Coronavirus: Close Family to Be Allowed to Say Goodbye to the Dying," April 15. https://www.bbc.co.uk/news/uk-52299590.

Chiumento, A., P. Baines, C. Redhead, S. Fovargue, H. Draper, and L. Frith. 2020. "Which Ethical Values Underpin England's National Health Service Reset of Paediatric and Maternity Services Following COVID-19: A Rapid Review." *BMJ Open* 11 (6). http://dx.doi.org/10.1136/bmjopen-2021-049214.

Chiumento, A., S. Fovargue, C. Redhead, H. Draper, and L. Frith. 2024. "Delivering Compassionate NHS Healthcare: A Qualitative Study Exploring the Ethical Implications of Resetting NHS Maternity and Paediatric Services Following the Acute Phase of the COVID-19 Pandemic." *Soc Sci & Med* 344 (March): 116503. https://doi.org/10.1016/j.socscimed.2023.116503.

General Medical Council. 2024. "Good Medical Practice and More Detailed Guidance 2024." https://www.gmc-uk.org/professional-standards/good-medical-practice-2024.

Institute for Government. 2022. "Timeline of UK Government Coronavirus Lockdowns and Measures, March 2020 to December 2021." https://www.instituteforgovernment.org.uk/sites/default/files/chart-images/timeline-coronavirus-lockdown-december-2021_0.png.

Mounier-Jack, S., P. Paterson, S. Bell, L. Letley, B. Kasstan, and T. Chantler. 2023. "Covid-19 Vaccine Roll-Out in England: A Qualitative Evaluation." *PLOS One* 18 (6): e0286529.

NHS (National Health Service). n.d. "Shielded Patient List." *NHS Digital.* Last updated February 20, 2024. https://digital.nhs.uk/services/high-risk-shielded-patients.

Nursing and Midwifery Council (NMC). 2018. "The Code: Professional Standards of Practice and Behaviour for Nurses, Midwives and Nursing Associates." https://www.nmc.org.uk/standards/code/.

Office for National Statistics. 2021. "Coronavirus (COVID-19) Infection and Survey Technical Article: Waves and Lags of COVID-19 in England, June 2021." https://www.ons.gov.uk/peoplepopulationandcommunity/healthandsocialcare/conditionsanddiseases/articles/coronaviruscovid19infectionsurveytechnicalarticle/wavesandlagsofcovid19inenglandjune2021.

Pilona, B., A. Craig, M. Lemmon, A. Goeller, and the Newborn Brain Society Guidelines and Publications Committee. 2021. "Supporting Families in Their Child's Journey with Neonatal Encephalopathy and Therapeutic Hypothermia." *Seminars in Fetal and Neonatal Medicine* 26 (5): 101278. https://doi.org/10.1016/j.siny.2021.101278.

9

Proportionality in Public Health Law

A Case Study of Singapore's Travel Restrictions for Migrant Healthcare Workers

Hui Yun Chan

Introduction

This case study explores the proportionality of restricting healthcare workers in Singapore from traveling overseas during the pandemic period between 2020 and 2021. The case study proceeds as follows: This section provides an overview of Singapore in terms of the context in which the restrictive measures operate. The second section describes how the pandemic is managed in Singapore. The third section explores the travel restrictions imposed on healthcare workers and the workers' reactions to the restrictions. The fourth section examines the measure's proportionality, followed by a conclusion in the fifth section.

Singapore is a multiracial country with a population of 5.9 million (World Population Review 2022). It is an urbanized, densely populated island nation located at the south of Peninsula Malaysia (Tan et al. 2021, 2). Singapore gained independence in 1965, with the ruling People's Action Party in governance till today. Its healthcare system includes public and private health delivery, although the public health sector provides for the majority of inpatient and specialist outpatient healthcare (Chua 2020, 260). The Ministry of Health oversees the country's healthcare delivery, including the recruitment of healthcare workers. There were approximately fourteen thousand registered doctors as of 2018, corresponding to 2.4 doctors per one thousand people, which is comparable to the United States, the United Kingdom, and Japan (Ministry of Health 2019). Singapore's population has a high life expectancy and a ratio of hospital beds to the population below the OECD average, signaling a healthy healthcare system (Tan et al. 2021, 4).

Despite the robust quality of the healthcare system, a shortage of healthcare workers is a constant concern for Singapore's healthcare sector. Singapore's growing elderly population adds to the pressure of finding sufficient healthcare workers. State-level initiatives to increase the local healthcare workforce,

Hui Yun Chan, *Proportionality in Public Health Law*. In: *Proportionality*. Edited by: Nikola Biller-Andorno et al., Oxford University Press. © Oxford University Press (2026). DOI: 10.1093/9780197759370.003.0010 especially nurses, have met with limited success (Chua 2020, 261). Foreign nurses and doctors have been recruited from neighboring countries in Southeast Asia such as the Philippines, Malaysia, Myanmar, and India beginning in the 1980s to address the shortage (Yeates and Pillinger 2018, 94; Chua 2020, 261, 262). Although the migration of healthcare workers from developing to developed countries is a common occurrence, this flow of migration has resulted in detrimental consequences for the workers' countries of origin, which have faced critical shortages (OECD 2020). Thus far, only Singapore and the Philippines implemented travel restrictions for healthcare workers to prioritize the countries' healthcare provision during the pandemic. In response to the in-country shortage in the Philippines during the COVID-19 pandemic period, the Philippines—the largest contributor to other countries' healthcare workforce—banned their nurses from leaving the Philippines to live and work as nurses abroad (Alibudbud 2022). This situation highlighted the difficulty in balancing individual freedom of movement and prioritizing public health needs. The following section considers more closely how Singapore managed the COVID-19 pandemic.

Pandemic Management in Singapore

Singapore was highly praised for successfully implementing an organized, stepwise pandemic approach, especially in the first six months of 2020 (Chua et al. 2020; Tan et al. 2021; Wang et al. 2021; Kim et al. 2022). Its success could partly be attributed to the sociopolitical dynamics between the population and the ruling People's Action Party (Abdullah and Kim 2020). There is high population compliance with pandemic measures, which is based on an implicit acceptance of the trade-offs necessarily involved in relinquishing some rights in favor of long-term public goods (Abdullah and Kim 2020, 772, 774). There is a general sense of trust that the ruling party is acting in the best interest of the population. An example could be drawn from Singapore's prior experience in managing the SARS and H1N1 pandemics, which have resulted in the establishment of a multiministry taskforce, a national command and control structure, a home-front crisis management system, the Disease Outbreak Response System Condition (a system of identifying the severity of the pandemic), and most recently the National Centre for Infectious Diseases (Tan et al. 2021, 2, 5; Kim et al. 2022). Each played a role in the planning, monitoring, and implementing of pandemic measures.

A highly centralized political and administrative system has enabled the swift deployment of pandemic response policies to address the changing infection landscapes (Abdullah and Kim 2020, 771). Singapore's geographical nature as an island nation and its technology-connected population have greatly enhanced the permeability of the latest pandemic governmental measures. Pandemic policies were rapidly communicated to the population via multiple social media channels and conventional media platforms (Abdullah and Kim 2020, 772). For example, the COVID-19 (Temporary Measures) Act 2020 and COVID-19 ([Temporary Measures] [Control Orders] Regulations) 2020 were enacted to prevent the spread of COVID-19 (Chua et al. 2020, 4). The measures included border control, travel curbs, nationwide contact tracing, mandatory mask wearing, quarantine, and enhanced physical and social distancing. In tandem with these multipronged approaches, a network of Public Health Preparedness Clinics was established in preparation for an influx of COVID-19 patients. The blend of these approaches has proved effective in limiting infections in the early stages of the pandemic. However, local community transmissions arising from travelers returning to the country during the border control period prompted the government to entirely close its borders to all travelers. The strict travel restriction constitutes one of the government's successful containment policies for preventing the importation of COVID-19 infections into the country (Kim et al. 2022). However, the restriction inadvertently affected healthcare workers, resulting in a more significant exodus than in prepandemic times.

Travel Bans, the Suspension of Healthcare Workers' Leave, and the Ramifications of These Measures

Chia Shi-Lu, the chair of the Government Parliamentary Committee for Health, announced travel bans affecting healthcare workers in the public health sector, which were reported in Singapore's main news outlet. The report indicated that all travel and leave, both professional and personal, was suspended indefinitely to ensure Singapore's preparedness for healthcare delivery in the event of COVID-19 hospitalizations (Cheow 2020).[1] The report seemingly implied that the restriction arose not from a shortage of healthcare workforce but rather from the need for prevention and precaution, which underpinned the decision. Despite this emphasis, the chairman reiterated that

[1] Because of a lack of archival materials from official sources, reference is made here to news reports about internal memos rather than to published guidance in the public domain. A search in the Ministry of Health portal conducted in 2023 revealed that circulars are no longer available. I have written to the director of medical services requesting a copy of the original circular; however, I was received no response.

> this is why we need to ensure that doctors and nurses are available, and not on leave or abroad. This system requires careful rostering—the plan works only if there are enough people . . . . Should there be reason for it, personnel can still appeal for leave to be granted. (Cheow 2020)

There was an expectation that healthcare workers would abide by the decision in view of their obligations as doctors and nurses. The report further indicated that, while the restriction could unduly affect healthcare workers, national confidence in the healthcare system and the need to avoid overwhelming hospitals were prioritized.

The reactions came quickly. It was reported that within the first half of 2021, around 1,500 healthcare workers resigned from their jobs, compared to two thousand resignations annually in the prepandemic period (Abu Bakar 2021; Awang 2021; See 2021; Tan 2021; Teng 2022). Among the resignations, around five hundred foreign healthcare workers resigned in 2020, and an additional five hundred left in the first six months of 2021 (Ministry of Health 2022). It is reasonable to infer that while resignations are common occurrence in any profession, the number of resignations in 2020 and 2021 compared with those before the pandemic showed that the healthcare workers' inability to take leave and travel for any reasons under prolonged pandemic working conditions for more than twenty months pushed them to leave the profession. They might have held out as long as they could, believing from previous experience that the pandemic could be over soon. However, when there were no signs of COVID-19 abating by 2021, the psychological and physical tolls that had accumulated since 2020 became intolerable, prompting them to resign.

It was reported that only a small number of healthcare workers was granted leave to travel overseas on "exceptional and compassionate grounds" such as to visit family (Yong 2022). The travel bans, among other factors, played a significant role in prompting foreign healthcare workers to resign (Khalik 2021; Tan 2021). These bans influenced the decision to leave, as they meant that the only option available to travel to see family overseas was to resign, since the workers' leave applications would be declined and they would be unable to take any leave. The resignations led to gaps in the healthcare workforce, as the shortages were not filled quickly enough, which led to overworking existing healthcare workers.

The largely compliant population and top-down, centralized decision-making meant that any potential protests, lawsuits, or complaints were unlikely to happen publicly. Social media platforms became the outlet for healthcare workers to air their grievances, which ranged from exhaustion to discrepancies between what was happening in hospitals and what was reported in mainstream media in terms of hospital preparedness. Some healthcare workers challenged the reasoning of some pandemic measures affecting hospitals, saying that "instructions were often too mechanical and that there was no communication of the thought processes behind the containment decisions" (Abdullah and Kim 2020, 772). Local healthcare workers empathized with their foreign-born colleagues who were unable to travel to see their families for almost two years because of the restriction (Lim and Goh 2021). Requests to travel to see families who contracted COVID-19 were declined, citing staff shortage (Yip and Chia 2022). In some cases, it was reported that requests that were previously declined were subsequently approved on a no-pay leave basis when healthcare workers threatened to resign (Yip and Chia 2022). The healthcare workforce continued to be staffed by former healthcare workers (Chua et al. 2020, 3). However, nurses were reportedly reluctant to answer the government's call to return from retirement to serve the country (Teng 2022). For example, in response to the government's plea for retired healthcare workers to assist with the pandemic, Singapore Nursing—a group of advocates for nurses and nursing welfare—used their platform to allow nurses to share their struggles; the group posted on Instagram (@sgnightingales):

> Raise our pay? [Do] we deserve hazard pay? Nobody will come back seriously, people left for a reason. Use your brain.

Feelings of burnout, depression, and anxiety are some of the main concerns that plagued nurses who left as the pandemic continued (Tan 2021). A study conducted in Saudi Arabia, a country with a high number of foreign healthcare workers indicated a correlation between distress among healthcare workers and being far from families because of travel bans (Altwaijri et al. 2022).

The travel and leave restrictions were lifted in October 2021 via internal circulars to healthcare workers by the Ministry of Health (Lim and Goh 2021; Tjendro 2021). However, it was reported that the restrictions could be reinstituted should there be an increase in COVID-19 cases (Yong 2022). The restrictions were lifted, consistent with the introduction of vaccinated travel lanes (VTL), which were announced in October 2021. The lifting of restrictions was not solely due to falling infections; the progress made in COVID-19 vaccinations despite rising numbers of cases resulting from the Delta and Omicron variants also made it possible to open the borders. Despite lifting the restrictions, healthcare workers' travel permissions were subject to further internal institutional arrangements and guidance (Tjendro 2021). This implies that, should an institution declined healthcare workers' leave on any grounds, the workers would have been unable to travel, despite the VTL option. Further, the VTL was limited to specific countries such as Canada, the United Kingdom, the United States, and several EU countries. Given that most foreign healthcare workers came from less-developed countries (e.g., Philippines, Myanmar, Malaysia) that were excluded from the VTL, this measure becomes meaningless for the affected healthcare workers, as they were still unable to travel. A responsive approach in the changing circumstances would have been to allow leave for affected healthcare workers to travel to home countries not designated under the VTL.

Were the Measures Proportional?

Is the infringement of the personal rights of healthcare workers (e.g., the inability to travel to see or care for family, the risk of harm to mental well-being) proportional to the probable benefits (e.g., not overwhelming hospitals, continued healthcare delivery, protecting public health)? The following analyses will explore this issue by balancing the positive aspects of the restriction against the negative elements through an assessment of its content and implementation process. This analysis examines the purpose of the restriction, its connection to the expected benefits, its necessity, its effectiveness, and whether it ensured that there was no disproportionate burden on individuals. Proportionally restrictive measures that are necessary and effective can justify the curtailment of individual rights and liberties to protect public health in pandemics (März et al. 2022).

The travel restrictions imposed on healthcare workers aimed to protect public health through the continued delivery of healthcare services by preventing public hospitals from being overburdened. Motivated by these aims, healthcare workers were not allowed to take travel leave, which enabled hospitals to be prepared for an influx of COVID-19 patients. The restriction was necessary from the perspective of healthcare management to keep hospitals functioning with a sufficient healthcare workforce and to avoid overworking healthcare workers who would have had to replace colleagues who were on leave. Healthcare workers recognized their duty to treat patients and their moral duty to fellow healthcare professionals who might need to shoulder more work if their colleagues were allowed to leave overseas, given the possibility of having their return delayed or prevented because of border control or illness.

Additionally, Singapore has a history of recruiting a foreign workforce to build local capacity, especially in the healthcare sector, which relies substantially on foreign nurses from neighboring countries. Foreign nurses encompassed one-third of the nursing workforce, but this number has gradually increased to more than half because of new recruits from Malaysia, India, China, and Myanmar (Teo 2021b). The shortage of healthcare workers, particularly nurses, arising from a higher number of resignations than usual resignations fueled recruiters to ramp up recruitment overseas (Khalik 2021). Nonetheless, this remains complicated, given the difficulties of bringing in healthcare workers from abroad during a pandemic and the prevailing internal limitations on hiring foreigners, as with the Philippines' policy prohibiting their healthcare workers from leaving to work elsewhere during the pandemic (Teo 2021a). A recent announcement by Singapore's Ministry of Health about increasing nurses' pay to retain them (Teo 2021b) lends further weight in favor of the Singapore's restriction, as it demonstrates the critical nature of staff shortages in public healthcare and underscores the necessity of imposing travel bans for healthcare workers. Based on these considerations, the restriction is underpinned by a legitimate cause, as it was necessary for the overall functioning of the healthcare system.

The restriction appeared to be effective in the first stage of the pandemic. The low death rates and small number of cases requiring ICU care demonstrated that hospitals were not overwhelmed (Abdullah and Kim 2020; Abu Bakar 2021; Teo et al. 2021). While Singapore emerged from partial lockdown in mid-2020, the restriction on healthcare workers remained in force and was only lifted in October 2021, more than twelve months after the country lifted some restrictions. Other pandemic measures remained to contain the spread of COVID-19; these ranged from partial lockdowns to restrictions on social gatherings, physical distancing, and mandatory mask wearing, which resulted in lower death rates compared with other countries (Ng 2021, 135). This development raised misgivings about claims that hospitals were overwhelmed. When work-from-home practices began to shift to a gradual return to workplaces in June 2020, further safe management measures were in place to ensure the safety of workers, which represented a contributory effort to pandemic containment (Ng 2021, 135). Given the combination of these supporting measures, it is doubtful that leave restrictions ought to continue for healthcare workers. Further, although the suspension meant that there would be a workforce available, it had a counter-effect when higher resignation numbers than usual emerged in the later stage of the pandemic, which resulted in a labor-power restriction. Finally, while evolving variants emerged in the second half of the pandemic, evidence at that time suggested fewer hospitalizations despite rising numbers of infection in the population. The restriction does not seem to have had the desired effect on a prolonged basis and it should have been reassessed at that time.

Does the restriction create a disproportionate burden on healthcare workers? It is important to consider the nature of the COVID-19 pandemic compared to previous pandemics in determining the suitability of the restriction. Comparisons were often made to prior experiences in dealing with epidemics that were shorter in duration. For example, the SARS outbreak lasted for approximately two months in Singapore, between March and May 2003 (Ministry of Health

2003), while the H1N1 pandemic occurred between May and September 2019 in Singapore (Cutter et al. 2010) compared with the more than five years that COVID-19 has been with us. While there is an expectation that healthcare workers endure the severity of workload during comparatively shorter period of pandemics, it is doubtful that what they endured during COVID-19 was similar in scale to their experience during SARS or H1N1. As the variants continued creating wave after wave of infection, healthcare workers continued to work under heightened pressures for a substantially prolonged period. The restrictions lasted for more than twelve months (approximately twenty months), beginning in February 2020 until they were lifted in October 2021. As Tan (2021) reported,

> It feels like what started as a 2.4 km run became a marathon, and just as we are reaching the finishing line, we have to run a second marathon. Our people are exhausted physically, mentally, emotionally—whether they will admit it or not.

It is clear that weariness has taken a toll on healthcare workers. Psychological distress among healthcare workers has been widely reported and well documented (Aughtersen et al. 2021; Ali et al., 2020; Chew et al. 2020; Di Tella et al. 2020; Tan et al. 2020; Grailey et al. 2021; Jang et al. 2021; Hines et al. 2021; Altwaijri et al. 2022). Consequently, it is essential to provide educational interventions and psychological support for healthcare workers (Tan et al. 2020, 319). The workers' inability to travel to see their family may have compounded their psychosocial stress at work and led and led some to decide to leave. Despite their primary obligations as doctors and nurses, they maintain their personal rights to act in their own best interests. A siloed approach to healthcare workers risks neglecting the consideration that each of them is a person first, before their professional obligations. Members of the foreign healthcare workforce who are away from home experienced a decline in the usual psychological protective layers, such as nearness to family members and the ability to care for family members who are ill. These foreign healthcare workers risk experiencing an increased psychological toll over time. Research on healthcare workers in Singapore suggests that long-term stress and burnout persist despite exiting lockdown, indicating prolonged stress arising from constant vigilance and preparedness, which increased their adverse psychological effects (Teo et al. 2021). This lends weight to the argument that the prolonged travel ban on healthcare workers compounded their stress at work. Protecting healthcare workers during pandemics is essential for their sustainability (Kreh et al. 2021; Smallwood et al. 2021).

Research has shown that a supportive work environment lowers moral injury and that lowering stress at the workplace protects healthcare workers from additional emotional distress (Firew et al. 2020; Hines et al. 2021; Willis et al. 2021;

Miner et al. 2022; Moyo et al. 2022). The healthcare workers' feeling of being devalued by hospitals, which resulted from having unmet mental health needs and from the travel bans restricting them from seeing family, are all contributing stressors in the workplace. Measures were put in place to protect workers from infections to ensure the continuity of essential services (Ng 2021). Remedial measures such as counseling and well-being for existing healthcare workers were implemented to assist the healthcare workforce in their jobs (Ministry of Health 2022). However, it remains to be seen whether these were sufficient to ameliorate the long-term effects of the pandemic.

While it is accepted that travel restrictions could apply, the extent to which such restrictions are applied needs further evaluation. While adopting a cautious approach to avoid overwhelming hospitals is sensible, the length of time in which the restriction was in place disproportionately harmed the affected healthcare workers. They were forced to make a choice between continuing with their livelihoods or facing the inability to care for their family abroad, even temporarily. The length of the restriction could have been shortened, consistent with the implementation of VTL, and the content of the restriction could have been recalibrated to enable healthcare workers to travel on compassionate grounds rather than continuing to enforce a complete ban. While an argument can be made that their local counterparts were similarly affected by the restriction, foreign healthcare workers were separated from their families rather than simply being unable to see them at home. Given the substantial number of foreign healthcare workers in Singapore, this aspect was not given due consideration in the decision-making process. The curtailment of foreign healthcare workers' right to mobility affected their interest to psychological health, especially in the heightened stress of pandemic times. The high number of resignations is one of the signs suggesting the disproportionality of the restriction.

Conclusion

This case study illustrates the continued difficulty in striking an appropriate balance between the needs of the public (e.g., COVID-19 patients, non-COVID-19 patients) and the moral and legal obligations of healthcare providers (e.g., hospital administrators, healthcare decision-makers or managers, fellow clinicians) during pandemics. National policies in pandemics reflect considerations that are made to protect public health while seeking to minimize potential burdens that may occur to others—in this case, healthcare workers. In assessing the risks to healthcare delivery and the adverse effects on healthcare workers, the long-term negative impacts (e.g., declining mental well-being from prolonged stress, emotional and moral harm arising from being denied leave to travel) of the restrictions on healthcare workers could outweigh the positive effects (e.g., solidarity among peers during crisis). Given the reliance on foreign healthcare workers, it becomes difficult to strike this balance, and public health often takes priority. Because travel was allowed for returning residents and permitted travelers, healthcare workers were restricted from doing so, the effect was amplified among foreign healthcare workers. This has left them without many choices but to resign in order to travel to see their family or take care of their loved ones. The pandemic has amplified foreign healthcare workers' vulnerability and their needs. While healthcare workers are often relied upon to provide continued care in crisis, it is necessary to recognize their needs and vulnerabilities to provide long-term viability and sustainability. An infringement of personal rights is permitted if it is proportional to the anticipated benefits arising from such restrictions. The case study illustrates an important and continuing concern for future pandemics in balancing competing priorities.

Competing Interests

There are no competing interests to declare.

Funding

There is no funding to declare.

References

Abdullah, W. J., and S. Kim. 2020. "Singapore's Responses to the COVID-19 Outbreak: A Critical Assessment." *American Review of Public Administration* 50 (6–7): 770–776.

Abu Bakar, J. 2021. "Resignation Rates Among Healthcare Workers in Singapore up This Year: MOH to Increase ICU Capacity." *CAN*, November 1. https://www.channelnewsasia.com/singapore/resignation-rates-among-healthcare-workers-singapore-year-moh-increase-icu-capacity-2282766.

Ali, S., S. Maguire, E. Marks et al. 2020. "Psychological Impact of the COVID-19 Pandemic on Healthcare Workers at Acute Hospital Settings in the South-East of Ireland: An Observational Cohort Multicentre Study." *BMJ Open* 10:e042930. https://doi.org/10.1136/bmjopen-2020-042930.

Alibudbud, R. 2022. "When the 'Heroes' 'Don't Feel Cared For': The Migration and Resignation of Philippine Nurses Amidst the COVID-19 Pandemic." *Journal of Global Health Viewpoints*, May 23. https://jogh.org/2022/jogh-12-03011.

Altwaijri Y., L. Bilal, A. Almeharish et al. 2022. "Psychological Distress Reported by Healthcare Workers in Saudi Arabia During the COVID-19 Pandemic: A Cross-Sectional Study." *PLOS One* 17 (6): e0268976. https://doi.org/10.1371/journal.pone.0268976.

Aughterson, H., A. R. McKinlay, D. Fancourt et al. 2021. "Psychosocial Impact on Frontline Health and Social Care Professionals in the UK During the COVID-19 Pandemic: A Qualitative Interview Study." *BMJ Open* 11:e047353. https://doi.org/10.1136/bmjopen-2020-047353.

Awang, N. 2021. "1500 Healthcare Workers Resigned in First 6 Months of 2021: MOH." *Today*, November 1. https://www.todayonline.com/singapore/1500-healthcare-workers-resigned-first-6-months-2021-moh.

Cheow, S.-A. 2020. "Public Health Personnel to Defer All Travel and Leave." *The Strait Times*, February 4. https://tnp.straitstimes.com/news/singapore/public-health-personnel-defer-all-travel-and-leave.

Chew, N. W. S., G. K. H. Lee, B. Y. Q. Tan, et al. 2020. "A Multinational, Multicentre Study on the Psychological Outcomes and Associated Physical Symptoms Amongst Healthcare Workers During COVID-19 Outbreak." *Brain, Behavior and Immunity* 88:559–565.

Chua, A. Q., M. M. J. Tan, M. Verma et al. 2020. "Health System Resilience in Managing the COVID-19 Pandemic: Lessons from Singapore." *BMJ Global Health* 5:e003317. https://doi.org/10.1136/bmjgh-2020-003317.

Chua, G. P. 2020. "Challenges Confronting the Practice of Nursing in Singapore." *Asia Pacific Journal of Oncology Nursing* 7:259–265. https://doi.org/10.4103/apjon.apjon_13_20.

Cutter, J. L., L. W. Ang, F. Y. Lai, H. Subramony, S. Ma, and L. James. 2010. "Outbreak of Pandemic Influenza A (H1N1-2009) in Singapore: May to September 2009." *Annals Academy of Medicine Singapore* 39 (4): 273–310.

Di Tella, M., A. Romeo, A. Benfante, and L. Castelli. 2020. "Mental Health of Healthcare Workers During the COVID-19 Pandemic in Italy." *Journal of Evaluation in Clinical Practice* 26:1583–1587. https://doi.org/10.1111/jep.13444.

Firew, T., E. D. Sano, J. W. Lee et al. 2020. "Protecting the Front Line: A Cross-Sectional Survey Analysis of the Occupational Factors Contributing to Healthcare Workers' Infection and Psychological Distress During the COVID-19 Pandemic in the USA." *BMJ Open* 10:e042752. https://doi.org/10.1136/bmjopen-2020-042752.

Grailey, K., A. Lound, and S. Brett. 2021. "Lived Experiences of Healthcare Workers on the Front Line During the COVID-19 Pandemic: A Qualitative Interview Study." *BMJ Open* 11:e053680. https://doi.org/10.1136/bmjopen-2021-053680.

Hines, S. E., K. H. Chin, D. R. Glick, and E. M. Wickwire. 2021. "Trends in Moral Injury, Distress, and Resilience Factors Among Healthcare Workers at the Beginning of the COVID-19 Pandemic." *International Journal of Environmental Research and Public Health* 18:488. https://doi.org/10.3390/ijerph18020488.

Jang, Y., M. You, H. Lee et al. 2021. "Burnout and Peritraumatic Distress of Healthcare Workers in the COVID-19 Pandemic." *BMC Public Health* 21:2075. https://doi.org/10.1186/s12889-021-11978-0.

Khalik, S. 2021. "Hospitals and Clinics in S'pore Desperate for Nurses, Offering 'Finder's Fee' to Staff." *The Straits Times*, November 25. https://www.straitstimes.com/singapore/health/hospitals-and-clinics-in-spore-desperate-for-nurses-offering-finders-fee-to-staff.

Kim, J., J. Moon, T. Y. Jung, W. Kim, and H. C. Yoo. 2022. "Why Have the Republic of Korea, Taiwan, and Singapore Coped Well with COVID-19 and What Are the Lessons Learned from Their Experiences?" *Yonsei Medical Journal* 63 (3): 296–303. https://doi.org/10.3349/ymj.2022.63.3.296.

Kreh, A., R. Brancaleoni, S. C. Magalini et al. 2021. "Ethical and Psychosocial Considerations for Hospital Personnel in the Covid-19 Crisis: Moral Injury and Resilience." *PLoS ONE* 16 (4): e0249609. https://doi.org/10.1371/journal.pone.0249609.

Lim, J., and G. Soh. 2021. "All Healthcare Workers in S'pore Allowed to Apply for Overseas Leave: MOH Holdings." *The Straits Times*, October 20. https://www.straitstimes.com/singapore/health/all-healthcare-workers-in-spore-allowed-to-apply-for-overseas-leave-moh-holdings.

März, J. W., C. Mouton-Dorey, T. Manríquez Roa, N. Biller-Andorno. 2022. "Proportionality and Evidence-Based Pandemic Management." *Swiss Medical Weekly* 152:w30208.

Miner, S.A., B. E. Berkman, V. Altiery de Jesus, L. Jamal, and C. Grady. 2022. "Navigating Pandemic Moral Distress at Home and at Work: Frontline Workers' Experiences." *AJOB Empirical Bioethics* 13 (4): 215–225. https://doi.org/10.1080/23294515.2022.2064000.

Ministry of Health. 2003. "Special Features: SARS." https://www.moh.gov.sg/docs/librariesprovider5/resources-statistics/reports/special_feature_sars.pdf.

Ministry of Health. 2019. "Supply of Doctors in Singapore and Percentage of Local Versus Foreign Doctors." Press release, July 8. https://www.moh.gov.sg/news-highlights/details/supply-of-doctors-in-singapore-and-percentage-of-local-versus-foreign-doctors.

Ministry of Health. 2022. "Impact of Covid-19 on Resignation and Recruitment of Healthcare Professionals." Notice Paper No. 877, January 10. https://www.moh.gov.sg/news-highlights/details/impact-of-covid-19-on-resignation-and-recruitment-of-healthcare-professionals/.

Moyo, N., A. D. Bhappu, M. Bhebhe, and F. Ncube. 2022. "Perceived Risk of COVID-19 and Employee Decision-Making: How Psychological Distress During the Pandemic Increases Negative Performance Outcomes Among Healthcare Workers." *International Journal of Environmental Research and Public Health* 19:6762. https://doi.org/10.3390/ijerph19116762.

Ng, W. T. 2021. "COVID -19: Protection of Workers at the Workplace in Singapore." *Safety and Health at Work* 12:133–135.

OECD. 2020. *Policy Responses to Coronavirus (COVID-19): Contribution of Migrant Doctors and Nurses to Tackling COVID-19 Crisis in OECD Countries*, May 13. https://www.oecd.org/coronavirus/policy-responses/contribution-of-migrant-doctors-and-nurses-to-tackling-covid-19-crisis-in-oecd-countries-2f7bace2/.

See. S, 2021. "Some 1500 Medical Workers Quit in H1 2021 Amid Severe Strain on Healthcare System: MOH." *The Business Times*, November 1. https://www.businesstimes.com.sg/government-economy/some-1500-medical-workers-quit-in-h1-2021-amid-severe-strain-on-healthcare-system.

Smallwood, N., A. Pascoe, L. Karimi, and K. Willis. 2021. "Moral Distress and Perceived Community Views Are Associated with Mental Health Symptoms in Frontline Health Workers During the COVID-19 Pandemic." *International Journal of Environmental Research and Public Health* 18:8723. https://doi.org/10.3390/ijerph18168723.

Tan, B. Y. Q., N. W. S. Chew, G. K. H. Lee et al. 2020. "Psychological Impact of the COVID-19 Pandemic on Health Care Workers in Singapore." *Annals of Internal Medicine* 173 (4): 317–320.

Tan, C. 2021. "More Healthcare Workers in S'pore Quit Amid Growing Fatigue as Covid-19 Drags On." *The Straits Times*, November 1. https://www.straitstimes.com/singapore/politics/more-healthcare-workers-in-spore-resigning-amid-growing-fatigue-as-covid-19-drags.

Tan, J. B., M. J. Cook, P. Logan, L. Rozanova, and A. Wilder-Smith. 2021. "Singapore's Pandemic Preparedness: An Overview of the First Wave of COVID-19." *International Journal of Environmental Research and Public Health* 18:252–263. https://doi.org/10.3390/ijerph18010252.

Teng, R. 2022. "Nurses Still Calling It Quits Despite Health Ministry's Attempt to Retain Them." *The Home Ground*, April 15. https://thehomeground.asia/destinations/singapore/nurses-still-calling-it-quits-despite-health-ministrys-attempt-to-retain-them/.

Teo, I., J. Chay, Y. B. Cheung et al. 2021. "Healthcare Worker Stress, Anxiety and Burnout During the COVID-19 Pandemic in Singapore: A 6-Month Multi-Centre Prospective Study." *PLOS One* 16 (10): e0258866. https://doi.org/10.1371/journal.pone.0258866.

Teo, J. 2021a. "Nurse Crunch: Suspension of Filipino Nurse Permits May Affect S'pore's Nursing Workforce." *The Straits Times*, June 24. https://www.straitstimes.com/singapore/health/philippines-bars-nurses-from-working-aboard-move-could-impact-spores-nursing.

Teo, J. 2021b. "Singapore Explores All Options with Nurses in Short Supply." *The Straits Times*, July 11. https://www.straitstimes.com/singapore/health/nurses-busier-amid-shortage-govt-to-grow-spore-workforce-and-boost-productivity.

Tjendro, J. 2021. "MOH Eases Overseas Travel Rules for All Healthcare Workers." *CNA*, October 20. https://www.channelnewsasia.com/singapore/healthcare-workers-overseas-travel-leave-restrictions-moh-2255331.

Wang, X., L. Shi, Y. Zhang, H. Chen, and G. Sun. 2021. "Policy Disparities in Response to COVID-19 Between Singapore and China." *International Journal for Equity in Health* 20:185. https://doi.org/10.1186/s12939-021-01525-z.

Willis, K., P. Ezer, S. Lewis, M. Bismark, and N. Smallwood. 2021. "Covid Just Amplified the Cracks of the System: Working as a Frontline Health Worker During the COVID-19 Pandemic." *International Journal of Environmental Research and Public Health* 18:10178. https://doi.org/10.3390/ijerph181910178.

World Population Review. 2022. "Singapore Population 2022." https://worldpopulationreview.com/countries/singapore-population.

Yeates, N., and J. Pillinger. 2018. "International Healthcare Worker Migration in Asia Pacific: International Policy Responses." *Asia Pacific Viewpoint* 59 (1): 92–106.

Yip, C., and L. Chia. 2022. "Why Some Healthcare Workers in Singapore's Hospitals Have Quit—and Others Soldier On." *CNA Insider*, April 28. https://www.channelnewsasia.com/cna-insider/why-healthcare-workers-singapore-hospitals-resignations-2647746.

Yong, N. 2022. "Leave Policy for Hospital Workers May Change If COVID Cases Keep Rising: MOH Official." *Yahoo News*, January 21. https://sg.news.yahoo.com/leave-policy-hospital-workers-change-covid-cases-moh-official-103707412.html.

10

COVID-19 Restrictions in Long-Term Care Facilities in the United States

Unintended Consequences and Possible Lessons

Jakub P. Hlávka, Yimin Ge, Shengjia Xu, and Alexander M. Capron

Nursing Homes as a Case Study of the Proportionality Dilemma

Governmental policies and actions are proportional when the benefits to the public equal or exceed any resulting burdens or loss of rights. The premise of this volume is that the principle of proportionality should guide the official response to public health crises such as the COVID-19 pandemic. At the same time, the COVID-19 pandemic serves as a reminder that the policies adopted and actions taken when circumstances are at once very dire and very uncertain may later turn out not to have comported with this principle.

Nowhere was this predicament more apparent during the COVID-19 pandemic than in the restrictions imposed on nursing homes in the United States. Public health officials quickly realized that older people and those with preexisting medical conditions were at much higher risk of serious illness and death from COVID-19 than the general public was, particularly since the facilities where many such persons reside were ill-prepared to prevent or even limit the spread of the novel coronavirus among their residents and staff. The policies adopted by the government, which required nursing homes to restrict their residents' contact with each other and with outside visitors such as family members, did reduce COVID-19 morbidity and mortality among residents and staff. But the resulting isolation of residents created other forms of physical and mental harm to them and stress for their families and staff members. Was the principle of proportionality respected?

Jakub P. Hlávka et al., *COVID-19 Restrictions in Long-Term Care Facilities in the United States*. In: *Proportionality*. Edited by: Nikola Biller-Andorno et al., Oxford University Press. © Oxford University Press (2026).
DOI: 10.1093/9780197759370.003.0011

Background

The COVID-19 pandemic has had a significant negative effect on the health and well-being of billions of people around the world. In the United States, much of this harm, including many deaths, occurred among residents of nursing homes (AARP 2023). Compared with the general population, nursing homes residents have long experienced health disparities, including more adverse health outcomes, ranging from injuries from negligent care to infections that occur because the environment is contaminated (Mor et al. 2004; Levinson 2014; Li et al. 2015). Beginning in the first weeks of the public health emergency in the United States, it became obvious that SARS-CoV-2 would further worsen outcomes for nursing home residents, and as of 2022, they accounted for approximately one in six recorded deaths (AARP 2023).[1]

US Nursing Home Residents' COVID-19 Vulnerability

The unprecedented challenges that the COVID-19 pandemic generated for public health agencies were particularly evident in nursing homes. Members of the populations found there—older persons, persons recovering from severe illnesses and injuries, and persons with chronic conditions such as dementia, heart disease, diabetes, kidney disease, and respiratory illness—turned out to be especially vulnerable to the severe effects of COVID-19 (Nania 2020). In the United States, it is estimated that 83.5% of nursing home residents are sixty-five or older, among whom 32% have diabetes, 38.1% have heart disease, 46.3% have depression, 47.8% have Alzheimer's disease (AD) or other dementia, and 71.5% have hypertension (Harris-Kojetin et al. 2019). In addition to this increased disease burden, older adults are often frail, which is predictive of adverse health outcomes and mortality (Hewitt et al. 2020). A high percentage of nursing home residents need assistance with daily activities: 96.7% need bathing assistance, 92.7% need dressing assistance, 92% need walking or locomotion assistance, 89.3% need toileting assistance, 86.8% need help in getting in and out of bed, and 59.9% need assistance in eating (Harris-Kojetin et al. 2019).

Since elderly persons experience higher death rates from infections, their mortality from COVID-19 has been a special focus of epidemiological attention. Moreover, the rate of adverse outcomes increased during the pandemic, even

[1] Given the large regional and provider-level differences in the demographics of nursing home residents and in the quality of care they receive, studies to date have not provided a complete picture of the all the effects of COVID-19 on this population during the pandemic. In this chapter, we discuss key insights from publicly available data, the main sources of variability in outcomes, and some of the main trade-offs involved in the policy responses during this global public health crisis.

among those who were not infected by SARS-CoV-2; these adverse outcomes ranged from a higher frequency of depression to delayed diagnosis and treatment of other conditions, such as cancer and dementia (Sepúlveda-Loyola et al. 2020; Vose 2020; Wan 2020; Glasbey et al. 2021; Paananen et al. 2021; Barnett et al. 2022; Webber et al. 2022). For example, among Medicare enrollees aged sixty-five and older, mortality increased among individuals with dementia during 2020, even in areas where community infection of COVID-19 was low (Gilstrap et al. 2022). That year, there were 15,925 more deaths from AD and 44,729 more deaths from all dementias compared with the average of the five years before 2020 (Alzheimer's Association 2022).

At the start of the pandemic, both US nursing home residents and similarly aged counterparts in their localities faced risks of severe illness and death from COVID-19 that were much higher than the risks experienced by younger people. However, even compared to older community-dwelling adults, nursing home residents have worse health profiles. For example, dementia—which diminishes people's ability to address their own essential needs and be self-protective—is present in a third of persons over the age of sixty-four in the community but in nearly half (47.8%) of such persons living in nursing homes (Su et al. 2021).

Nursing home residents' greater vulnerability to COVID-19 arose not only from their physical and mental health status but also from their living circumstances. Besides the concentration of many at-risk individuals in an institutional setting, other nursing home-specific characteristics compound the likelihood that viruses will be transmitted to, and spread rapidly among, residents. For example, residents are usually transferred from hospitals and other high-risk settings, share rooms, and often rely on visits from family and friends for care and support. Furthermore, care delivery at nursing homes typically involves repeated, close physical contact between residents and staff, many of whom work in multiple facilities for low wages and with few benefits (Markowitz and Paulin 2022), which inclines them not to stay home and miss a day of work even when they are symptomatic. Indeed, the elevated risk of disease transmission in nursing homes was well-known even before the COVID-19 pandemic. For example, a 2014 CDC study found that 80% of US non-food-borne norovirus outbreaks occur in long-term care (LTC) facilities (Hall et al. 2014).

The Health Effects of COVID-19 in Nursing Homes

Currently, over 15,500 Medicare- and Medicaid-certified nursing homes serve more than 1.4 million residents across the United States (White House 2022). As the institutions that house the most vulnerable population, US nursing homes have reported numerous outbreaks of COVID-19 cases since the beginning

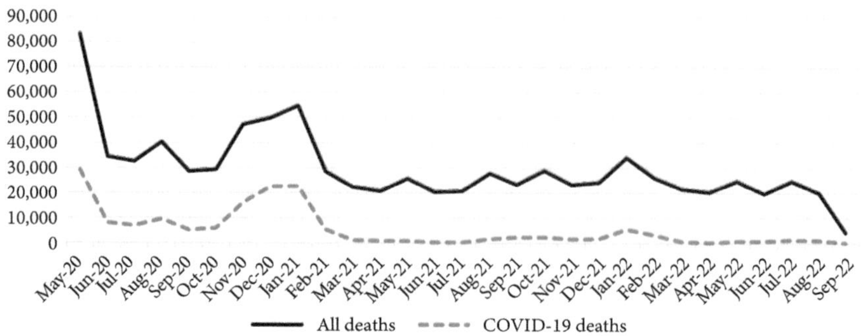

Fig. 10.1 Total deaths and COVID-19 deaths among nursing home residents, May 2020–September 2022.
Source: CMS (2022a).

of the pandemic. Nursing home residents and staff account for approximately 15.2% of all COVID-19 deaths in the United States, even though they constitute just 0.4% of the country's population (AARP 2023). As of August 2022, US nursing homes reported 1,204,959 confirmed cases of COVID-19 among residents, from which there were 155,840 deaths (Centers for Medicare and Medicaid Services [CMS] 2022a). At least as noteworthy, nursing home staff, who face a high risk of occupational exposure but who have low rates of personal vulnerability, had experienced 1,294,259 COVID-19 infections by August 2022, which resulted in just 2,629 deaths from COVID-19 (CMS 2022a).

The mortality data for nursing homes reported by the federal agency that provides public healthcare insurance, the CMS, allow the number of deaths from all causes to be compared with the number of deaths linked to COVID-19 during the first two and a half years of the pandemic—that is, through September 2022 (Figure 10.1). The two trend lines in Figure 10.1 suggest that the COVID-19 deaths are probably responsible for the two peaks in all deaths, given that the lines for all-cause deaths and deaths linked to COVID-19 run almost parallel. The reliability of the CMS trend lines in Figure 10.1 is confirmed by the death counts of US residents in 2019 and 2020, shown in Appendix Figure 1, in which the trends are similar, though the absolute numbers differ slightly because they are based on a different data source, the Underlying Cause of Death database in the Wide-Ranging Online Data for Epidemiologic Research (WONDER), maintained by the CDC.

Figure 10.2 shows that the monthly number of COVID-19 deaths in nursing homes reached its highest level at the beginning of the pandemic, followed by winter 2020–2021 (winter is the season when respiratory viral infections are most prevalent). The first SARS-CoV-2 vaccines were approved by the Food and Drug Administration (FDA) near the end of 2020 under an Emergency Use

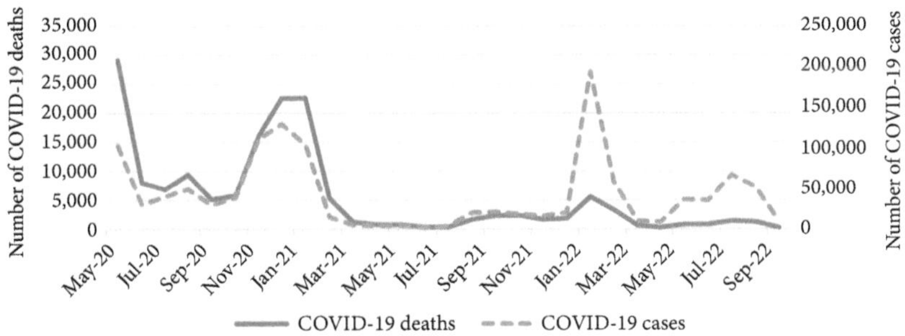

Fig. 10.2 COVID-19 cases and deaths among nursing home residents, May 2020–September 2022
Source: CMS (2022a).

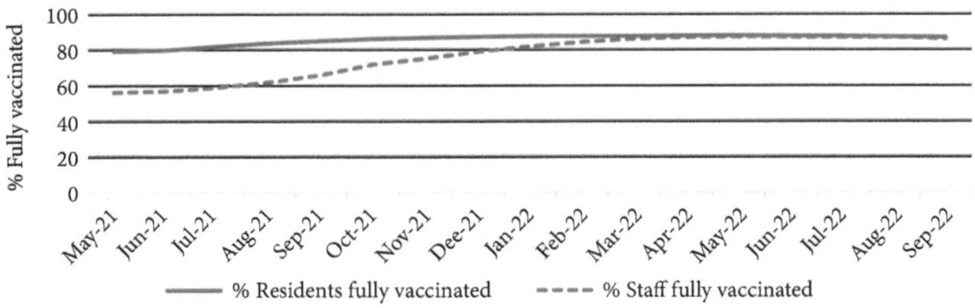

Fig. 10.3 Share of fully vaccinated nursing home residents and staff, May 2021–September 2022. Vaccination data are only available beginning in May 2021.
Source: CMS (2022a).

Authorization. Once they became available, the rapid and high rate of vaccination among nursing home residents and staff (see Figure 10.3) and the reduced lethality of the circulating virus led to a low rate of COVID-19 deaths in nursing homes between March and August 2021.

The FDA had authorized the release of the vaccines based on their ability to protect against severe infections and death rather than because they provided immunity to infection, so it was not surprising that the number of nursing home COVID-19 cases in winter 2021–2022 exceeded the peak a year earlier, because of the greater infectivity of the Omicron variant. Nonetheless, the number of deaths was much lower than in the previous waves. The death rate among nursing home residents who were infected by SARS-CoV-2 in January and February 2022 averaged less than a sixth of the rate a year earlier. Indeed, as can be seen in Figure 10.4, the case fatality rate, which was alarming at the beginning of the pandemic, rose to its highest point in February 2021 and by April had fallen to a very low level, where it has remained.

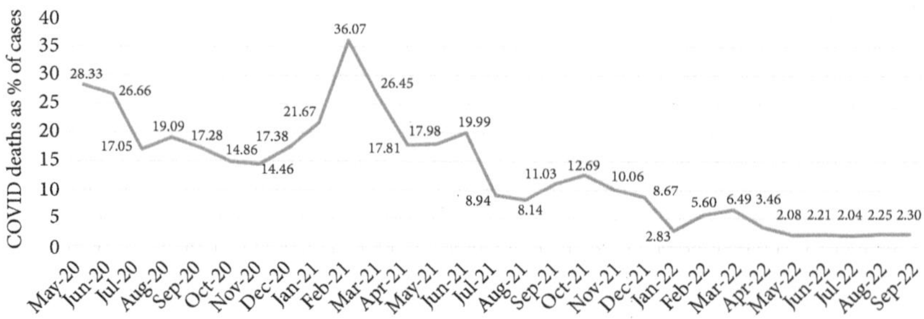

Fig. 10.4 COVID-19 case fatality rate among nursing home residents, May 2020–September 2022. The rate is calculated as the percentage of confirmed COVID-19 cases in nursing homes who died.
Source: CMS (2022a).

The rate at which nursing home residents became infected and died of COVID-19 varied substantially not only over time but also among the states. The exact ratio of the number of nursing home residents in a state to the number of deaths in this population cannot be calculated precisely because the number of actual residents in nursing homes is not systematically recorded. Nevertheless, the total number of nursing home beds by state, which is known, yields a reasonable approximation of the state-level nursing home population. Using this proxy to calculate the percentage of nursing home residents who died of COVID-19 during 2020–2022 produces striking results (Figure 10.5). Deaths in the five states (we include the District of Columbia in our calculation of states) with the lowest rates—Hawaii, Alaska, Vermont, the District of Columbia, and Idaho—occurred barely one-quarter as frequently as they did in the five states—Rhode Island, Pennsylvania, Connecticut, North Dakota, and South Dakota—where the percentage of nursing home residents who died of COVID-19 was highest.

Unlike the temporal variation in rates of COVID-19 infections and death, this state-level variation is difficult to explain. One possibility is that using the number of beds as a proxy fails to take account of differences in the percentage of beds that were occupied. The disjuncture between beds and the actual number of residents may have been particularly pronounced during COVID-19, as the combination of residents' deaths and families withdrawing their relatives from nursing homes left many beds empty. The variation in occupancy rates could, in turn, result from differences in the prevalence of COVID-19 infections in the community, in the demographic, cultural, and economic characteristics of the population (not just residents and their families but also nursing home staff), or in Medicaid reimbursement rates or from other reasons. Many of these

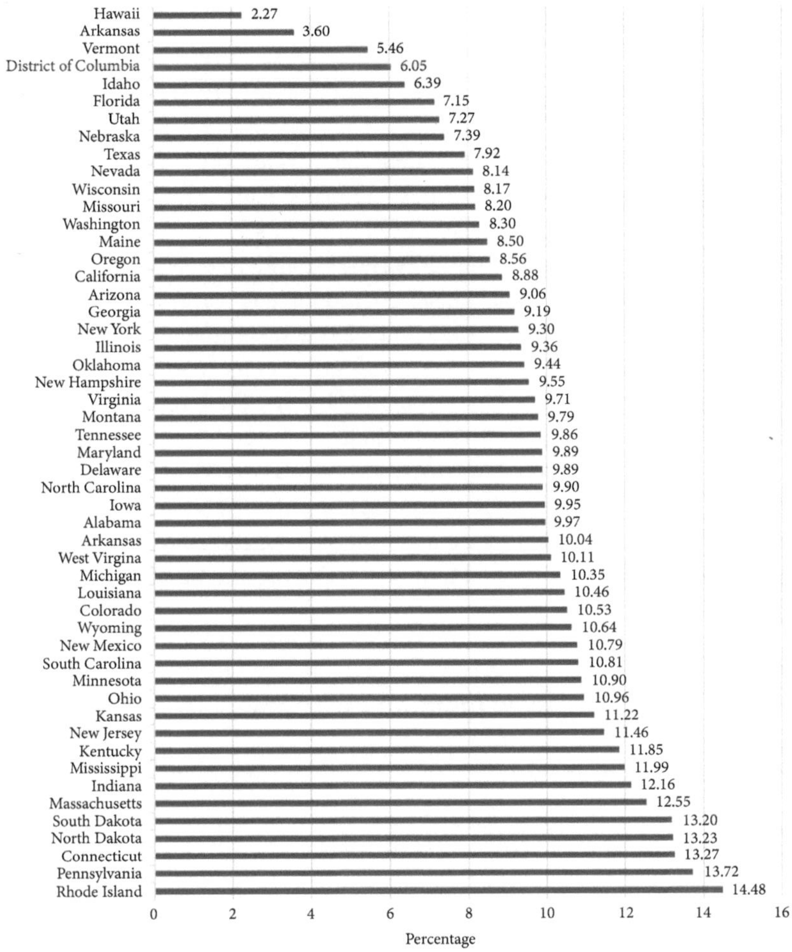

Fig. 10.5 COVID-19 nursing home resident deaths as a percentage of number of beds by state, 2020–2022. Percentages are calculated based on cumulative death numbers in each state from 2020 to 2022.
Source: CMS (2022a).

factors vary by region, and yet the differences in COVID-19 fatality rates, for the most part, do not follow a regional pattern. While the rates on the West Coast (Washington, Oregon, and California) are close together, those in New England are not (with Vermont among the lowest, Maine and New Hampshire more in the middle, and Massachusetts, Connecticut, and Rhode Island among the states with the highest rates), nor are those in the Upper West (North Dakota and South Dakota have among the very highest rates, Montana and

Wyoming are just a little lower, and Idaho is among the lowest). (An even wider variation can be seen in the percentage of a state's COVID-19 cases and deaths among nursing home residents, as shown in Figures 10.A2A and 10.A2B in the Appendix.[2])

Just as in nonpandemic times when the demanding work and low pay make it difficult to hire and retain nursing home staff (Maxouris 2021), high turnover rates and staffing shortages posed problems for maintaining residents' safety and well-being during the COVID-19 pandemic. During 2017–2018, average turnover rates among registered nurses and certified nursing assistants in nursing homes were 140% and 129%, respectively. The COVID-19 pandemic shined a spotlight on the devastating consequences of this problem (Musumeci et al. 2022). Some nursing homes even reported an annual rate of turnover of more than 300% in their total nursing staff (Gandhi et al. 2021). According to a 2021 survey by the American Health Care Association and National Center for Assisted Living (AHCA/NCAL 2021), 94% of US nursing homes reported being short of staff in the previous month, and over 50% reported losing crucial employees during the pandemic because of resignations.

Governmental Responses

In response to the COVID-19 crisis, national and international guidance for LTC facilities has concentrated on containment and mitigation strategies to reduce spread of the virus (Rocard et al. 2021). The recommended measures include improving access to personal protective equipment (PPE), prioritizing testing of LTC residents and staff, restricting access to and within facilities (e.g., prohibiting visits, adopting isolation measures), increasing the number of staff, expanding telehealth services, coordinating care among primary-care providers and providers in LTC and hospitals, and prioritizing the vaccination of residents and staff (Rocard et al. 2021). In 2020, LTC facilities in almost all OECD countries implemented visiting restrictions and limitations on group activities, such as group meals and recreational activities, though most modified the restrictions over time as COVID-19 cases began decreasing (Rocard et al. 2021).

[2] The residents' share of COVID-19 cases varied by more than tenfold between the states with the lowest (Alaska) and highest (Iowa) rates, whereas the share of deaths varied by more than fourteenfold between the states with the lowest (Alaska) and highest (Rhode Island) rates. Further, as expected—given nursing home residents' greater risk of experiencing severe illness—the percentage of a state's COVID-19 deaths that occurred among nursing home residents was at least ten times greater than residents' percentage of COVID-19 cases, which confirms the severity of the situation facing nursing homes during the COVID-19 pandemic in many states.

Federal-Level Responses

In the United States, major responsibility for protecting the health and safety of nursing home residents rests with the states and, at the federal level, with the CMS. Since 1989, regulations issued by the CMS have enumerated the requirements that facilities must meet in order to participate in the Medicare program as a skilled nursing facility (SNF) or to participate in the Medicaid program as a nursing facility. In subsequent years, these "Conditions of Participation" were amended several times before being comprehensively revised in 2016 in light of experience with the existing regulations, advances in LTC practices, and the provisions of the Affordable Care Act, which was adopted in 2010. The current regulations acknowledge residents' right to have visitors as being essential to their well-being and self-determination.[3]

Shortly after the secretary of Health and Human Services declared a public health emergency in the United States on January 31, 2020, a nursing home in King County, Washington, experienced an outbreak of respiratory illness among its 130 residents and 170 staff. At that time, in mid-February, the facility performed rapid influenza tests on some of the residents, which were negative. The medical condition of one patient with a cough, fever, and shortness of breath worsened, and she was placed on oxygen support for five days before being transferred on February 24 to a hospital for treatment, including intubation and mechanical ventilation. Four days later, her infection was identified as a new disease caused by a novel coronavirus, now known as SARS-CoV2. The patient died on March 2. Public health officials then performed polymerase chain reaction (PCR) tests at the facility and found that 81 residents (more than 60%), 34 staff, and 14 visitors tested positive for the new disease, which was later named COVID-19, for <u>Co</u>rona <u>Vi</u>rus <u>D</u>isease-20<u>19</u> (McMichael et al. 2020).

By this point, the Centers for Disease Control and Prevention (CDC) had released guidance on the use of PPE and other measures, including hand hygiene and physical distancing, to reduce the risk of infection. On March 4, 2020, the director of CMS's Quality, Safety and Oversight Group informed state survey agencies that routine surveys of all healthcare facilities were being suspended and that surveyors should immediately focus on facilities with a history of infection control problems and on "complaints alleging infection control concerns, including facilities with potential COVID-19 or other respiratory illnesses" (CMS 2020a).

Five days later, as part of the CMS's commitment to ensuring that healthcare facilities be prepared to respond to the threat of COVID-19, the Center for

[3] Medicare and Medicaid Programs; Reform of Requirements for Long Term Care Facilities 81 Fed. Reg. 68688–68872 (October 4, 2016).

Table 10.1 Timeline of CMS COVID-19 nursing home restrictions

Date	Restrictive policies
March 13, 2020	Facilities must restrict the entry of all visitors and nonessential healthcare personnel, except in certain compassionate care situations such as end-of-life situations, during which visitors must be limited to a specific room, practice appropriate hand hygiene, use PPE (such as face masks), practice physical distancing, and refrain from physical contact with residents and others while in the facility. Facilities must cancel communal dining and all internal and external group activities. Facilities must also implement active symptomatic screening (e.g., by checking for fever and for respiratory symptoms) of residents and staff and follow guidance from state and local officials that is more restrictive than CMS's.
May 8, 2020	Decisions on relaxing restrictions should be made with careful review. Factors that affect this decision include whether the nursing home has 1) a decline in the number of new cases, hospitalizations, or deaths; 2) any new COVID-19 cases; 3) staffing shortages; 4) access to adequate testing and PPE for staff; 5) the ability to transfer residents to a local hospital; 6) policies requiring visitors and residents to wear face masks and maintain social distance.
September 2020	All visits should be held outdoors whenever practicable. Facilities should create accessible and safe outdoor spaces for visits. Facilities should have a process to limit the number and size of visits occurring simultaneously.
March 2021	Residents who are fully vaccinated can choose to have close contact (including by touch) with their visitors while wearing a well-fitting facemask.
November 2021	COVID-19 vaccination is required for eligible staff at healthcare facilities participating in the Medicare and Medicaid programs. While visitors, residents, and their representatives should be made aware of the risks associated with visiting loved ones, visits should be allowed for all residents at all times. Facilities, residents, and visitors should refrain from having large gatherings where physical distancing cannot be maintained in the facility.
March 2022	Residents must be allowed to receive visitors as they choose, provided that the visitor, resident, or their representative is aware of the risks associated with visits and that the visit occurs in a manner (e.g., in the resident's room) that does not place other residents at risk. Visits can be conducted through different means based on a facility's structure and residents' needs. Facilities must allow indoor visits at all times and for all residents as permitted under regulations.

Clinical Standards and Quality issued guidance for nursing homes on infection control and the prevention of COVID-19. Facilities were instructed to monitor the information and resources released by CDC as well as advice and directives from their local health departments (CMS 2020b). Facilities were required to instruct visitors about hand hygiene and the use of PPE according to current facility policy while in a resident's room and to tell visitors to maintain physical distance and not to interact physically with residents, such as by shaking hands or hugging. Further, persons who had a fever or other COVID-19 symptoms or who could not comply with infection control techniques were to be restricted from entering the nursing home. Facilities were also encouraged to consider providing alternative means of communication, such as videoconferencing and increasing regular communication to families, to provide information about residents and changes in rules.

As deadly outbreaks occurred in nursing homes in locales across the country, CMS again revised its guidance four days later, ordering nursing homes nationwide to restrict all visitors except in compassionate care circumstances, such as an end-of-life situation (CMS 2020c). Following the CMS guidelines, nursing homes in the United States largely banned visits from family members and friends.

On May 8, 2020, the CMS issued its *Nursing Home Reopening Recommendations*, which provided nursing homes with guidance as they slowly entered the phase of reopening (CMS 2020d). However, a large number of nursing homes were not eligible to resume visits from family and friends at that time because, according to the CMS guidance, only nursing homes that were sufficiently staffed, stocked with adequate PPE and testing, and free from new COVID-19 cases for more than twenty-eight days were eligible to restart visits; otherwise, previously issued restrictions on visits had to be upheld (Karlawish et al. 2020). In September 2020, CMS revised the previous guidance to encourage outdoor visits, expand on acceptable compassionate care beyond end-of-life situations, and allow certain indoor visits on the condition that there had been no new COVID-19 cases for at least fourteen days in the facility, among other requirements per the revised guidance (CMS 2020e).

In March 2021, in light of the steady decline of COVID-19 cases nationwide and the availability of vaccines, the CMS further revised its guidance to allow physical contact with visitors if residents were fully vaccinated (CMS 2021). In November 2021, the CMS issued a regulation mandating COVID-19 vaccination among all nursing home staff as a prerequisite for participation in the Medicare and Medicaid Programs.[4]

[4] Medicare and Medicaid Programs; Omnibus COVID–19 Health Care Staff Vaccination 86 Fed. Reg. 61555 (November 5, 2021).

The CMS again revised its guidance regarding nursing home visits in March 2022. The modified guidance stated that prolonged restrictions on residents' right to visitors were no longer necessary at that time because, as of February 2022, 87% of residents and 83% staff were fully vaccinated. Per the revised guidance, visits held through various means at various locations were permitted based on residents' needs and on nursing homes' structure, subject to compliance with the core principles for COVID-19 infection prevention detailed in the guidance. In particular, the new guidance ordered that nursing homes from then on must always allow indoor visits for all residents who are defined by the guidance as eligible, with no limitations on the length or frequency of visits or the number of visitors and no requirement to schedule the visits in advance. However, outdoor visits were still considered preferable for residents and visitors whose vaccinations were not up to date with all recommended doses (CMS 2022b).

State-Level Responses

State governments have taken various actions to cooperate with the federal government and to extend federal-level efforts. Most of the states took immediate actions following the CMS's updates on nursing home restrictions.

California has the highest number of nursing home residents in the United States (Kaiser Family Foundation [KFF] 2022). Since the start of the COVID-19 pandemic, the Center for Health Care Quality (CHCQ) of the California Department of Public Health (CDPH) has worked on providing education and technical assistance to nursing homes in support of their infection control. CHCQ issued more than fifty-five COVID-19-specific policy documents during 2020–2022, which included requirements for COVID-19 mitigation plans, visits, and testing and an SNF toolkit (CDPH 2022). Specifically, in March 2020, following federal guidelines, California issued guidance for SNFs, including limiting visits, suspending collective dining and group activities inside the facilities, and restricting residents with fever or acute respiratory symptoms to their rooms (CDPH 2020a). In June 2020, the state began reopening all adult and senior care facilities. Nonessential visits were allowed if facilities met certain conditions: a decline in the number of new cases in the community, no new transmissions of COVID-19 at the facility for fourteen days, no staff shortage, adequate supplies of PPE and cleaning supplies, and sufficient access to testing (Dickfoss 2020). The state went through a gradual process of reopening. In October 2020, indoor visits were allowed in large communal spaces where six-foot distancing was possible (CDPH 2020b). Beginning in March 2021, indoor visits were allowed for fully vaccinated residents and unvaccinated residents for facilities in low-risk counties

(CDPH 2021a). Physical distancing was still required for residents who were not in quarantine and who, therefore, were allowed to eat in the same room and to engage in group activities (with face coverings) (CDPH 2021a). California lifted these requirements in June 2021 (CDPH 2021a; 2021b).

Texas, another of the three states with the highest number of nursing home residents since 2015 (KFF 2022), was the state with the ninth-lowest ratio of deaths to number of nursing homes beds during 2020–2022 (Figure 10.5). Like those in California, the restrictions that Texas placed on nursing homes mostly followed the CMS's rules and were updated accordingly. In mid-March 2020, the governor of Texas issued an emergency order to suspend visits in nursing homes (Harper 2021). The state began to ease restrictions for nursing facilities in early August (Harper 2021). At that time, the Texas Health and Human Services Commission (HHSC) updated the rules to allow limited visits at nursing homes and other LTC facilities (Weldon 2020). At nursing homes, public visits were restricted to only outdoor visits, but limited indoor and outdoor visiting procedures were allowed at LTC facilities, provided that there were no active cases and that infection control procedures had been met (Weldon 2020). Further, effective on September 24, 2020, the governor directed the HHSC to expand visit options and allow designated caregivers to visit and provide supportive care to residents without having to maintain physical distancing (Mann 2020). Later, per federal guidance issued by the CMS on March 10, 2021, the Texas HHSC expanded visits statewide in nursing facilities and other LTC settings (Mann 2021). The updated rules permitted all visits without time limits and personal contact during any visit for fully vaccinated residents who followed infection control protocols (Mann 2021).

As seen in Figure 10.5, Massachusetts had the sixth highest ratio of resident deaths to nursing home beds among all the states in the period of 2020 to 2022. However, it also went through a cautious step-by-step process of changing its COVID-19 policies from lockdown to opening up. On March 16, 2020, the Department of Public Health in Massachusetts restricted nursing home entry by all visitors and nonessential healthcare personnel and suspended communal dining as well as internal and external group activities (Massachusetts Executive Office of Elder Affairs [EOEA] 2020a). The reopening process began carefully during summer 2020. On July 2, Massachusetts allowed outdoor in-person visits, outdoor group activities, and communal dining, with standardized physical distance, face mask use, symptom screening, PPE use, and other staff requirements. They also provided additional guidance, such as on the length and frequency of visits and the time of day visits could occur (Massachusetts EOEA 2020b). Indoor visits were allowed beginning September 25, 2020, provided that careful evaluations occurred (Massachusetts EOEA 2020d). Indoor group activities gradually resumed starting on November 9, 2020, and in-room visits resumed on March 17, 2021 (Massachusetts EOEA 2020c; 2021b). Subsequently, on June 14, 2021, the state lifted the face mask requirement during visits for residents and visitors who were fully vaccinated (Massachusetts EOEA 2021a).

Consequences of Pandemic Restrictions for Residents

Even though restrictions on visits to and interactions among nursing home residents were imposed to protect a very vulnerable population, the resulting social isolation has been associated with a variety of adverse consequences for the health and well-being of residents. These have included decreased intake of nutrition, weight loss, reduction in activities of daily living and in cognitive ability, and increased loneliness, agitation, symptoms of depression, and mortality (Karlawish et al. 2020; Wan 2020; Hugelius et al. 2021; Li et al. 2021; Paananen et al. 2021; Stolz et al. 2021; Barnett et al., 2022; Webber et al. 2022). Given the similarity of the restrictions imposed during the first year of the pandemic in wealthy nations around the world, studies from outside the United States also provide data that can illuminate the consequences of US restrictions.

Mortality

One longitudinal study that examined how variations in state-specific social distancing restrictions in the United States from June to August 2020 affected mortality in nursing homes found opposite effects on the rates of COVID-19 and non-COVID-19 deaths. Stricter state physical distancing measures reduced COVID-19-specific cases and deaths among nursing home residents but contributed to more non-COVID-19-specific deaths among residents, which confirms that there are potentially detrimental consequences of social isolation for older adults in nursing homes (Li et al. 2021). Using 2018–2020 Medicare claims data, the Minimum Data Set, and a retrospective observational study design, another study found that the absence of COVID-19 cases at SNFs was modestly associated with lower resident mortality, while the presence of active COVID-19 cases was associated with significantly increased mortality and cognitive decline among nursing home residents (Wan 2020).

In particular, residents with AD and other dementias were disproportionately affected by nursing home restrictions and the resulting social isolation. According to a 2020 *Washington Post* analysis, social isolation contributed to 13,200 excess deaths attributable to AD and other dementias between March and August 2020 (Wan 2020). Cognitively impaired residents who were still capable of communicating expressed the feeling of being "doomed and trapped" since the stimulation of their minds that previously had been routine—such as receiving music therapy, eating meals with coresidents, and interacting with family members—was all suspended during the early phase of the pandemic (Barnett et al. 2022). Nursing home residents with dementia were hit the hardest by visit restrictions because, for them, family members not only provided routine social interactions but also covered many gaps at nursing homes that resulted from frequent insufficient staffing. Family caregivers are often the first to notice changes in residents' conditions (Karlawish et al. 2020). Therefore, keeping family members who were essential caregivers out of nursing homes amounted to an enormous threat to residents' well-being, and unsurprisingly, residents with dementia were particularly likely to experience the worst health outcomes as a result of this restriction.

Cognitive Impact

Although the evidence is mixed, it appears that the COVID-19 restrictions imposed on nursing homes may lead to steeper rate of cognitive decline among residents. On the one hand, a 2021 study in Finland, which drew on thematic interviews with nursing home residents and their family members, reported substantially deteriorated physical abilities and increased progression of memory disorders in nursing home residents because of COVID-19-related distancing measures (Paananen et al. 2021). This suggests that such restrictions come at a high price, and not imposing them could be a better policy, even though it could lead to more cases of COVID-19. On the other hand, a retrospective observational study in the United States found that the presence of active COVID-19 cases was associated with significantly increased cognitive decline among nursing home residents (Wan 2020). In contrast, a Canadian matched-population study found similarly trending cognitive decline patterns among LTC residents with or without COVID-19 outbreaks. Therefore, the researchers concluded that COVID-19-induced social isolation and restrictive measures at LTC homes were not specifically associated with increased cognitive decline among LTC residents (Webber et al. 2022).

Mental Health Impact

Using 2018–2020 Medicare claims data and the Minimum Data Set, a US study found that SNF residents generally experienced weight loss and heightened depressive symptoms during the first year of the pandemic when protective measures were most strictly executed (Wan 2020).

Focusing on the impact of a seven-week lockdown implemented during March–April 2020, an Austrian study reported substantially increased loneliness among older adults resulting from COVID-19 restrictions, with greater levels of loneliness associated with more restrictive measures (Stolz et al. 2021).

Another study in a selected sample of twenty-six nursing homes examined the impact of Dutch guidelines for cautiously reopening nursing homes for visitors after that country's complete lockdown had been relaxed. The mixed-methods cross-sectional study found good compliance with new guidelines, which included spacing visits out during the day and across the week, requiring PPE or distancing, and limiting each resident to one visitor at a time. The study found no surge of COVID-19 cases and highlighted the great value of family visits for residents' well-being. Based on results from the study, the Dutch government later decided to reopen all nursing homes using the new guidelines (Verbeek et al. 2020).

Consequences of Pandemic Restrictions for Family Members and Staff

Besides their consequences for nursing home residents, restrictions imposed in nursing homes during the pandemic also profoundly affected the psychological and emotional well-being of residents' family members. Two overarching themes emerge from studies from around the world: the importance of the caregiving role to family members' sense of self and well-being and the need for increased information and communication options for family members to sustain connections with, and to be informed about, nursing home residents (O'Caoimh et al. 2020; Wammes et al. 2020; Cooke et al. 2022; Cornally et al. 2022; Giebel et al. 2022).

One Irish study, which used surveys with open-ended questions and thematic analysis, found that the nursing home visit restrictions imposed during the COVID-19 pandemic negatively affected the emotional and mental welfare of family members. In particular, family members expressed frustration that the visitor restrictions were imposed universally and that they made no distinction between relatives who were essential caregivers and those who were casual visitors. Family members who were in essential caregiving roles reported diminished purpose and meaning in their own lives (Cornally et al. 2022). Another study in Ireland, which was based on cross-sectional surveys, suggested that the family members of cognitively impaired residents experienced an even more pronounced decrease in well-being, further highlighting the mental health toll caused by interrupted caregiving (O'Caoimh et al. 2020).

In the Netherlands, researchers asked 1997 family members and relatives of nursing home residents about their perspectives on visitation restrictions. While there was no agreement among surveyed family members about whether the restrictions' adverse effects outweighed their protective effects, they unanimously expressed a strong need for more information about—and more opportunities to communicate with—their relatives residing in nursing homes so as to sustain relational continuity (Wammes et al. 2020).

A study in the United Kingdom based on semistructured interviews with family members of nursing home residents with dementia and with staff working at care homes across the country suggested that the UK restrictions in care homes had adversely affected the mental health of staff, residents, and family members. The study found that the restrictions generated stress, burnout, frustration, and anger, and respondents reported that very little mental health support was available. The interviews also revealed the presence of severe tension between family members and nursing home staff (Giebel et al. 2022).

Opportunities for Future Research

In assessing whether the policies are consistent with the principle of proportionality, one needs to evaluate the role that ethical and medical considerations can and should play in official actions to suspend in-person visits to and interaction among residents of LTC facilities during a pandemic. The point of departure is, of course, the policies adopted in nursing homes during the COVID-19, beginning in March 2020.

A central issue here is whether the benefits provided by the restrictions mandated by the government were proportionate to the costs—not only to the government but also to those directly affected. While the immediate justification for the policies seemed clear, given the high risk of infection and death at the beginning of the pandemic for residents and the staff of LTC facilities, the harms caused by isolation and the suspension of in-person visits were not openly debated. Some of the consequences attributed to the restrictions—for example, excess deaths among the most vulnerable, such as roughly forty-two thousand more deaths from dementia during early 2020, which was an excess of 16% over the historical average (Alzheimer's Association 2021)—are measurable. However, other results, such as the negative emotional and mental health effects on family members and especially on the residents who survived, may never be quantified (Vittone and Sotomayor 2021).

It seems probable that some of the suffering that resulted from the restrictive policies in nursing homes during the COVID-19 pandemic could have been avoided. Having a better understanding of the consequences of public health measures—that is, one that is richer and more complete—will be an essential part of achieving proportionality in future emergencies. Part of this effort involves considering the intangible benefits and costs of the public health restrictions, including the ways in which they did or did not endorse, reinforce, or embody core bioethical principles. For that reason, future research should probe the effects of various interventions in ethical terms. That is, in the view of those who implemented the policies in nursing homes as well as those whose lives were shaped by them, did the policies respect human dignity, provide for voluntary informed choice, and enact beneficence as well as nonmaleficence by attending to patients' mental as well as their physical health (Ge et al. 2024)? Ultimately, the question is how such ethical values might be incorporated into decisions that are based on a utilitarian calculus, since ethical considerations—like the emotional and spiritual consequences for patients and families—are not usually identified, much less quantified. By what processes can decision-makers integrate factors that actually matter to the people involved?

Basing Decisions on Quantitative Analysis

Before getting to the problem of quantifying the ethical considerations, we must acknowledge that the dilemma for decision-makers responding to future public health emergencies begins with having to act when facts—including the unintended harms of policy choices—are unknown or perhaps even unknowable. Planning for the future, therefore, has to start with making special efforts in the wake of a public health crisis to gather data about the full range of good and bad consequences of different actions. Moreover, rather than focusing solely on mortality, the data gathered should encompass all major outcomes, such as the effects on nursing home residents' long-term physical and mental health when they are protected from viruses brought in by family members and friends but also deprived of these individuals' presence and support for weeks or months. Another limitation on accurately predicting the consequences of policies and actions is that future public health crises are likely to involve new unknowns: the nature of a novel virus, the types of risks it poses, and how it is transmitted; how well prepared facilities are to deal with those particular risks; and so forth. All of these will affect the relevance and utility of the data gathered about what occurred when particular public health policies were used in the past.

A second difficulty concerns whether such data will be extensive enough to allow public health officials to make accurate predictions about the benefits and costs entailed in their actions when the details of each situation can differ widely. For example, although the governmental guidance that was intended to protect nursing home residents was issued relatively early in the COVID-19 pandemic, at least 34% of all COVID-19 deaths between March 2020 and March 2021 occurred in LTC facilities (Curiskis et al. 2021). Does that mean the policies implemented did not meet the basic requirement of being effective? Or would the death rate have been even higher had the policies not been adopted? If the states had been left to decide what rules to adopt about residents' contact with visitors and with other residents, the effectiveness of various policies might have been discerned by comparing outcomes in different states. Since countries other than the United States enforced different restrictions on nursing homes, an alternative source would be the outcomes of these natural experiments. Yet relying on results from countries that adopted different policies is often problematic because their populations, social structure, systems for delivering and financing healthcare, and so forth diverge in other ways. In sum, we may lack reliable data on causation—or even correlation—that links outcomes to particular public health policies adopted around the world during the COVID-19 pandemic.

And the difficulties go beyond predictability. Even if benefits and costs were predictable, how would they be compared? This is a familiar challenge in all attempts to quantify actual, much less predicted, benefits and costs. The common metric for conducting benefit-cost analysis (BCA) is monetary. While measuring human lives and the pain and disabilities that result from serious illness in dollars seems almost inhuman—since money provides such an inadequate and incomplete picture of how people think about their own lives and those of the people they know—that is the way loss and inconvenience are treated. Money equivalents are used both in the judicial system (e.g., when a court awards monetary damages to an injured person) and in the regulatory system (e.g., when a government agency justifies imposing fees or restrictions on a harm-producing activity based on the value of the human lives and human health that will be protected against loss or impairment by restricting or prohibiting the activity). Although monetary measures of everything from lost lives to various degrees of morbidity may be discernible through marketplace behavior, for nonmarket goods, questionnaires or behavioral experiments must be administered to members of the public in order to produce an equivalent willingness to pay based on the public's stated or revealed preferences.

But the problems with BCA go deeper still. Assuming that the people who have to promulgate policies to deal with the next public health emergency—such as one that again threatens the well-being of nursing home residents and staff—have some basis (from data about the effects of various policies during the recent pandemic) to estimate the costs of implementing a variety of policies, is conducting a BCA the right way to proceed if their knowledge about benefits is quite incomplete? That question invites two responses. The first is, Compared to what? If the alternative to BCA is that the policies adopted reflect nothing more than the personal knowledge, experiences, and biases of the decision-makers, then a BCA is likely to lead to more-effective policies and better outcomes. But a second response would be more cautionary: If BCA leaves an impression of scientific certitude that is harder to revise, then performing a BCA could generate harms that could be avoided by being open to trying different approaches and quickly modifying policies in light of outcomes. Indeed, in the face of great therapeutic uncertainty, that is what several international consortia of physicians and scientists did—with careful research designs and data collection—in determining the best therapies for COVID-19.

BCA's Limits When Faced with Intangible Values

Modesty about the strength of the results that a particular decision-making aid can provide is also necessary because of the need to recognize that factual or evidence-based decisions are always grounded in a set of values, whether visibly so or not. Some proponents of using BCA in selecting policies to advance health do recognize that it rests on two normative elements: "that each individual is the best, or most legitimate, judge of his or her welfare" and "that the preferred policy is that which maximizes social welfare, measured by summing the effects of policy across individuals" (Robinson et al. 2019). Some theorists therefore prefer to fold BCAs into social welfare functions (SWFs)—a tool from welfare economics not yet in use by governments. A SWF describes the state of a society based on the well-being of everyone in it, which takes into account individuals' subjective sense not just of their health but also of their general welfare. SWF analysis uses an uncertainty module (appropriate for decision-making during a public health emergency) when evaluating the outcomes produced by a policy.

But even this attempt to include factors beyond the monetary value of a statistical life has trouble taking into account less tangible benefits and costs, such as those involving respect for persons' agency and the fair distribution of burdens. How can such factors even be converted into monetary units? Yet without an agreed metric, how can we know whether an action is consonant with the principle of proportionality when it not only produces physical consequences for the health and lives of the people affected but also affects the extent to which their dignity is respected and their preferences about their lives and activities are considered?

Three responses to this challenge seem possible: (a) not to investigate how the values and principles that have been developed under the banner of bioethics over the past half-century interacted with COVID-19 policies, (b) to treat the values and principles simply as side constraints on, rather than integral components of, public health policies, or (c) to recognize that the values and principles are central to individuals' well-being and should be included when calculating costs and benefits. The first approach means decision-makers would have no data to plug into the BCAs and SWFs that will guide them when responding to future public health emergencies, while the second means that the values and principles will probably be dismissed as soft ideals that must yield to evidence-based conclusions.

Given how consequential bioethical analysis has been in shaping medical practice and research over the past fifty years, we believe it is worth trying to make the third alternative work in public health policymaking. When counting the inputs—namely, the costs to the government of implementing policies—and the outputs—namely, the benefits those policies produce—we need to recognize not only that some of the benefits will be negative (e.g., the decline in nursing home residents' mental function caused by the loss of social interactions) but also that some may involve intangibles (e.g., the importance that people attach to agency, equity, and liberty). Paying attention to these values does not mean giving them a decisive role in policymaking. Nor does it mean forgetting that bioethical principles conflict with each other—as with, for example, the familiar tension between beneficence and autonomy. And the same is true of such moral considerations as *necessity* and *least infringement*, which, like *proportionality*, are justificatory conditions for exercising public health powers to prevent harm and to maximize utility when the measures taken also infringe liberty or diminishes justice (Childress et al. 2002).

Further research on the effects of the COVID-19 nursing home restrictions is needed for policymaking to be able to relate these value questions to the more practical, but obviously also very consequential, concerns about containing the spread of communicable diseases and avoiding life-threatening infections that were at the forefront of policymakers' thinking in March 2020. The aim of such studies would not be to pronounce judgment, be it favorable or unfavorable, on the nursing home policies that the CDC or the CMS promulgated. Rather, the aim would be to open the policymaking lens wider in order to bring bioethical concerns into focus, because these factors are necessary for a valid assessment of whether those policies meet the proportionality condition. It is essential that future public health decision-making be informed by a greater understanding of the extent to which the people directly affected by the COVID-19 restrictions in US nursing homes experienced gains and losses beyond whatever health improvements and physical constraints arose from those restrictions.

Acknowledgments

The authors are grateful the members of the advisory panel who provided valuable insights and suggestions when the research was being designed, and especially to Karl E. Steinberg and Michael Wasserman for their tireless support in outreach to leaders in LTC.

Competing Interests

There are no competing interests to declare.

Funding

The authors are grateful to the Greenwall Foundation, New York, NY, for supporting this research project, "Evaluating the Role of Ethical, Medical, and Economic Considerations in the Suspension of In-Person Visits to Long-Term Care Residents During a Pandemic," with a Fall 2021 Making a Difference grant.

Appendix

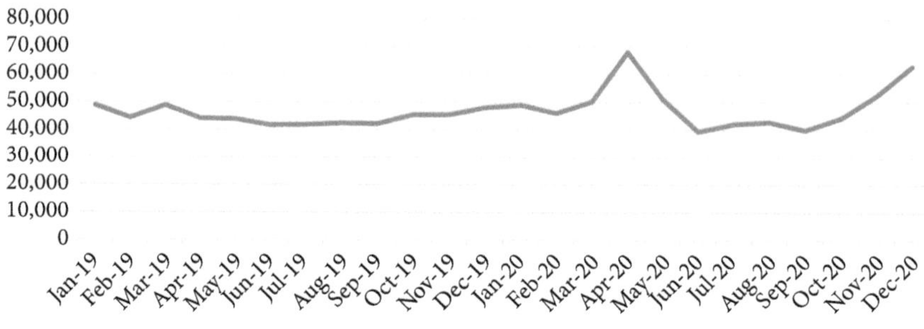

Appendix Fig. 10.A1 Total deaths in nursing home and LTC facilities, 2019–2020. Numbers are based on the death certificates of US residents, so they differ from CMS nursing home data.
Source: CDC WONDER (n.d.).

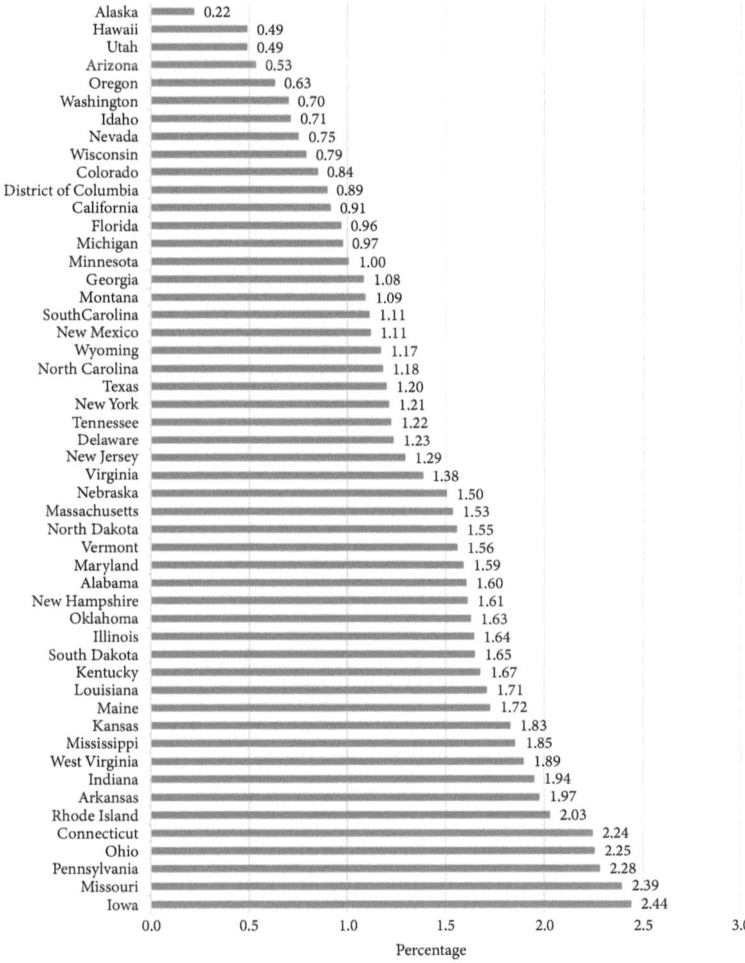

Appendix Fig. 10.A2A COVID-19 nursing home resident cases as a percentage of total cases by state, 2020–2022. The percentages are calculated based on cumulative case numbers in each state from 2020 to 2022.

Source: CMS (2022a).

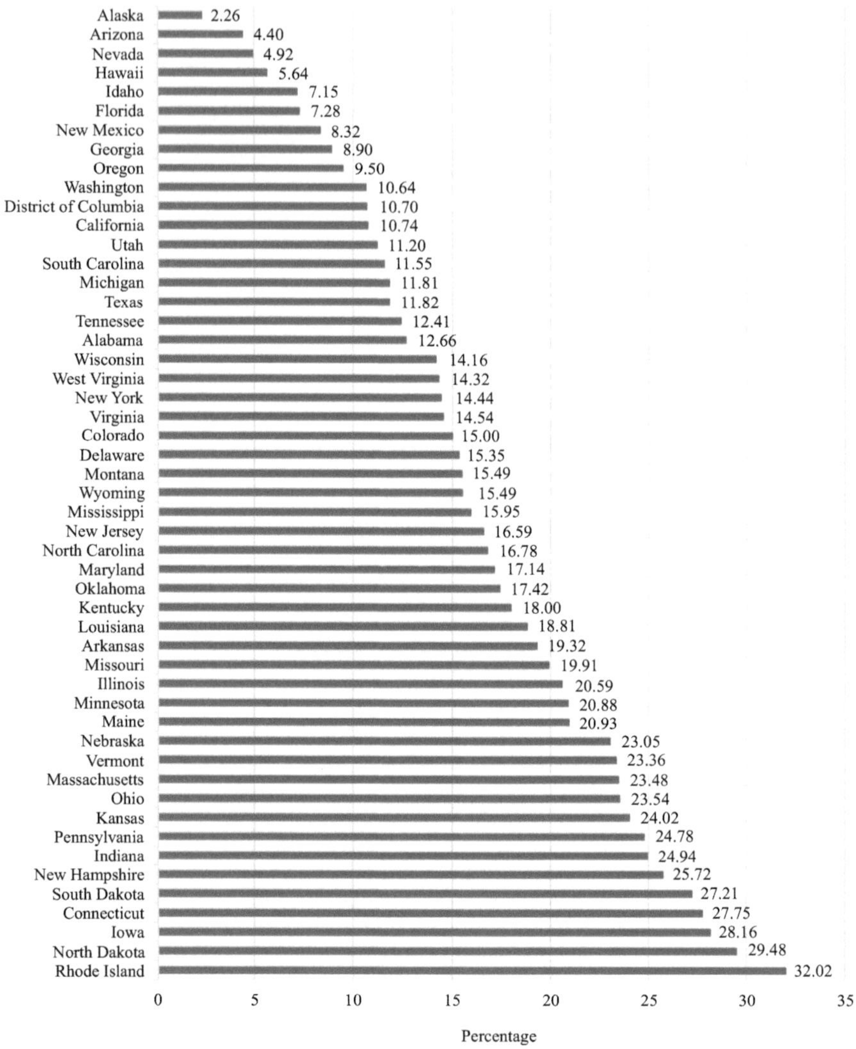

Appendix Fig. 10.A2B COVID-19 nursing home resident deaths as a percentage of total deaths by state, 2020–2022. The percentages are calculated based on cumulative death numbers in each state from 2020 to 2022.
Source: CMS (2022a).

References

AARP. 2023. "AARP Nursing Home Covid-19 Dashboard Fact Sheets," September 14. https://www.aarp.org/ppi/issues/caregiving/info-2020/nursing-home-covid-dashboard.html.

AHCA/NCAL (American Health Care Association and National Center for Assisted Living). 2021. "State of Nursing Home and Assisted Living Industry: Facing Workforce Challenges." https://www.ahcancal.org/News-and-Communications/Fact-Sheets/FactSheets/Workforce-Survey-June2020.pdf.

Alzheimer's Association. 2021. "2021 Alzheimer's Disease Facts and Figures." *Alzheimer's & Dementia* 17 (3). https://www.alz.org/media/Documents/alzheimers-facts-and-figures.pdf.

Alzheimer's Association. 2022. "2022 Alzheimer's Disease Facts and Figures." *Alzheimer's & Dementia* 18 (4): 700–789. https://doi.org/10.1002/alz.12638.

Barnett, M. L., R. J. Waken, J. Zheng, E. J. Orav, A. M. Epstein, D. C. Grabowski, and K. E. Joynt Maddox. 2022. "Changes in Health and Quality of Life in US Skilled Nursing Facilities by Covid-19 Exposure Status in 2020." *JAMA* 328 (10): 941–950. https://doi.org/10.1001/jama.2022.15071.

CDC WONDER (Centers for Disease Control and Prevention Wide-Ranging Online Data for Epidemiologic Research). n.d. "About Underlying Cause of Death, 1999–2020." CDC. https://wonder.cdc.gov/ucd-icd10.html. Accessed June 6, 2025.

CDPH (California Department of Public Health). 2020a. "Covid-19: Guidance for Skilled Nursing Facilities." https://www.cdph.ca.gov/Programs/CHCQ/HAI/CDPH%20Document%20Library/Covid.19_GuidanceFor_SNF_HAI%20WebinarFINAL_03.13.20.pdf.

CDPH. 2020b. "Guidance for Limiting the Transmission of Covid-19 in Long-Term Care Facilities." https://canhrnews.com/guidance-for-limiting-the-transmission-of-Covid-19-in-long-term-care-facilities-4/.

CDPH. 2021a. "Guidance for Limiting the Transmission of Covid-19 in Long-Term Care Facilities." https://canhrnews.com/guidance-for-limiting-the-transmission-of-Covid-19-in-long-term-care-facilities-5/.

CDPH. 2021b. "Guidance for Limiting the Transmission of Covid-19 in Long-Term Care Facilities." https://www.gccsouthgate.com/wp-content/uploads/2021/06/AFL-20-22.8-Vaccination-Group-Dining-Activity.pdf.

CDPH. 2022. "Skilled Nursing Facilities: Covid-19." Division of Communicable Disease Control, February 11. https://www.cdph.ca.gov/Programs/CID/DCDC/Pages/Covid-19/SNFsCovid_19.aspx.

Childress, J. F., R. R. Faden, R. D. Gaare et al. 2002. "Public Health Ethics: Mapping the Terrain." *Journal of Law, Medicine & Ethics* 30:170–178.

CMS (Centers for Medicare and Medicaid Services). 2020a. Suspension of Survey Activities. Ref. QSO-20-12-all (March 4). https://www.cms.gov/files/document/qso-20-12-all.pdf.

CMS. 2020b. Guidance for Infection Control and Prevention of Coronavirus Disease 2019 (Covid-19) in Nursing Homes. Centers for Medicare and Medicaid Services; Center for Clinical Standards and Quality; and Quality, Safety, and Oversight Group. Ref: QSO-20-14-NH (March 9). https://www.cms.gov/files/document/3-13-2020-nursing-home-guidance-Covid-19.pdf.

CMS. 2020c. Guidance for Infection Control and Prevention of Coronavirus Disease 2019 (Covid-19) in Nursing Homes (REVISED). Centers for Medicare and Medicaid Services; Center for Clinical Standards and Quality; and Quality, Safety, and Oversight Group. Ref: QSO-20-14-NH (March 13). https://www.cms.gov/files/document/3-13-2020-nursing-home-guidance-Covid-19.pdf.

CMS. 2021. "On March 10, 2021, CMS Released Revised Guidance for Nursing Home Visitation During the Covid-19 Public Health Emergency." Press release. https://www.cms.gov/files/document/Covid-visitation-nursing-home-residents.pdf.

CMS. 2022a. "Covid-19 Nursing Home Data." https://data.cms.gov/Covid-19/Covid-19-nursing-home-data. Accessed on September 12, 2022. https://data.cms.gov/Covid-19/Covid-19-nursing-home-data.

CMS. 2022b. "Nursing Home Visitation—Covid-19 (REVISED)." Ref: QSO-20-39-NH (March 10). https://www.cms.gov/files/document/qso-20-39-nh-revised.pdf.

Cooke, H. A., S. A. Wu, A. Bourbonnais, and J. Baumbusch. 2022. "Disruptions in Relational Continuity: The Impact of Pandemic Public Health Measures on Families in Long-Term Care." *Journal of Family Nursing* 29 (1): 6–17. https://doi.org/10.1177/10748407221102462.

Cornally, N., C. Kilty, C. Buckley et al. 2022. "The Experience of Covid-19 Visitor Restrictions Among Families of People Living in Long-Term Residential Care Facilities During the First Wave of the Pandemic in Ireland." *International Journal of Environmental Research and Public Health* 19 (11): 6559. https://doi.org/10.3390/ijerph19116559.

Curiskis, A., C. Kelly, E. Kissane, and K. Oehler. 2021. "What We Know—and What We Don't Know—About the Impact of the Pandemic on Our Most Vulnerable Community." The Covid Tracking Project at *The Atlantic*, March 31. https://covidtracking.com/analysis-updates/what-we-know-about-the-impact-of-the-pandemic-on-our-most-vulnerable-community.

Dickfoss, P. 2020. "Updated Guidance on Coronavirus Disease 2019 (Covid-19) Related to the Critical Role of Testing, Modification of Visitation Guidelines, Need for Infection Prevention and Control, and Use of Face Coverings in Adult and Senior Care Facilities." State of California Department of Social Services. https://www.cdss.ca.gov/Portals/9/CCLD/PINs/2020/ASC/PIN-20-23-ASC.pdf

Gandhi, A., H. Yu, and D. C. Grabowski. 2021. "High Nursing Staff Turnover in Nursing Homes Offers Important Quality Information." *Health Affairs* 40 (3): 384–391. https://doi.org/10.1377/hlthaff.2020.00957.

Ge, Y., S. Xu, A. M. Capron, M. S. Keller, and J. P. Hlávka. 2024. "Exploring the Impact of COVID-19 Restrictions on Nursing Home Residents', Families', and Staff's Perceptions of Bioethical Principles: Qualitative Study." *Journal of Applied Gerontology* 43 (11): 1640–1656. https://doi:10.1177/07334648241249626.

Giebel, C., K. Hanna, P. Marlow et al. 2022. "Guilt, Tears and Burnout—Impact of UK Care Home Restrictions on the Mental Well-Being of Staff, Families and Residents." *Journal of Advanced Nursing* 78 (7): 2191–2202. https://doi.org/10.1111/jan.15181.

Gilstrap, L., W. Zhou, M. Alsan, A. Nanda, and J. S. Skinner. (2022). "Trends in Mortality Rates Among Medicare Enrollees with Alzheimer Disease and Related Dementias Before and During the Early Phase of the Covid-19 Pandemic." *JAMA Neurology* 79 (4): 342–348. https://doi.org/10.1001/jamaneurol.2022.0010.

Glasbey, J., A. Ademuyiwa, A. Adisa et al. 2021. "Effect of Covid-19 Pandemic Lockdowns on Planned Cancer Surgery for 15 Tumour Types in 61 Countries: An International, Prospective, Cohort Study." *The Lancet Oncology* 22 (11): 1507–1517. https://doi.org/10.1016/s1470-2045(21)00493-9.

Hall, A. J., M. E. Wikswo, K. Pringle, L. H. Gould, and U. D. Parashar. 2014. "Vital Signs: Foodborne Norovirus Outbreaks—United States, 2009–2012." *Morbidity and Mortality Weekly Report* 63 (22): 491–495. https://www.ncbi.nlm.nih.gov/pmc/articles/PMC5779359/.

Harper, K. B. 2021. "Vaccinated Texas Nursing Home Residents Can Now Hug Their Families and Receive More Visitors After a Year of Isolation." *The Texas Tribune*, March 23. https://www.texastribune.org/2021/03/23/Texas-nursing-homes-coronavirus-visits/.

Harris-Kojetin, L., M. Sengupta, J. P. Lendon, V. Rome, R. Valverde, and C. Caffrey. 2019. *Long-Term Care Providers and Services Users in the United States, 2015–2016*. National Center for Health Statistics. https://www.cdc.gov/nchs/data/series/sr_03/sr03_43-508.pdf.

Hewitt, J., B. Carter, A. Vilches-Moraga et al. 2020. "The Effect of Frailty on Survival in Patients with Covid-19 (COPE): A Multicentre, European, Observational Cohort Study." *The Lancet Public Health* 5 (8): e444–e451. https://doi.org/10.1016/s2468-2667(20)30146-8.

Hugelius, K., N. Harada, and M. Marutani. 2021. "Consequences of Visiting Restrictions During the Covid-19 Pandemic: An Integrative Review." *International Journal of Nursing Studies* 121:104000. https://doi.org/10.1016/j.ijnurstu.2021.104000.

Karlawish, J., D. C. Grabowski, and A. K. Hoffman. 2020. "Continued Bans on Nursing Home Visitors Are Unhealthy and Unethical." *The Washington Post*, July 13. https://www.washingtonpost.com/opinions/2020/07/13/residents-good-nursing-homes-should-consider-re-allowing-visitors/.

Kaiser Family Foundation. 2022. "Total Number of Residents in Certified Nursing Facilities." https://www.kff.org/other/state-indicator/number-of-nursing-facility-residents/?currentTimeframe=0&sortModel=%7B%22colId%22:%22Number%20of%20Nursing%20Facility%20Residents%22,%22sort%22:%22desc%22%7D.

Levinson, D. R. 2014. "Adverse Events in Skilled Nursing Facilities: National Incidence Among Medicare Beneficiaries." Department of Health and Human Services Office of Inspector General (OEI-06-11-00370). https://oig.hhs.gov/oei/reports/oei-06-11-00370.pdf.

Li, Y., Z. Cheng, X. Cai, Y. Mao, and H. Temkin-Greener. 2021. "Association of State Social Distancing Restrictions with Nursing Home Covid-19 and Non-Covid-19 Outcomes." medRxiv, https://doi.org/10.1101/2021.02.08.21251382.

Li, Y., C. Harrington, H. Temkin-Greener, K. You, X. Cai, X. Cen, and D. B. Mukamel. 2015. "Deficiencies in Care at Nursing Homes and Racial/Ethnic Disparities Across Homes Fell, 2006–11." *Health Affairs* 34 (7): 1139–1146. https://doi.org/10.1377/hlthaff.2015.0094.

Mann, C. 2020. "HHSC Expands Visitation at Long-Term Care Facilities." *Texas Health and Human Services Commission*. https://web.archive.org/web/20220517003249/https://www.hhs.texas.gov/news/2020/09/hhsc-expands-visitation-long-term-care-facilities.

Mann, C. 2021. "HHSC Updates Visitation Rules for Long-Term Care Facilities." *Texas Health and Human Services Commission*. https://www.hhs.texas.gov/news/2021/03/hhsc-updates-visitation-rules-long-term-care-facilities.

Markowitz, A., and E. Paulin. 2022. "AARP Answers: Nursing Homes and the Coronavirus. The Latest on Evolving Rules, Visiting Loved Ones, Your Rights and More." *AARP*, March 16. https://www.aarp.org/caregiving/health/info-2020/nursing-homes-coronavirus-faqs.html.

Massachusetts EOEA (Executive Office of Elder Affairs). 2020a. "Covid-19 Update: Amended EOEA Guidance." Commonwealth of Massachusetts EOEA, March 16. https://www.mass-ala.org/wp-content/uploads/2020/03/COVID-19-Update-AMENDED-EOEA-Guideline.pdf.

Massachusetts EOEA. 2020b. "Guidance for Assisted Living Residences (ALRs) during the Covid-19 Outbreak." Commonwealth of Massachusetts EOEA. https://www.mass-ala.org/wp-content/uploads/2020/07/ALR-Visitation-Guidance-07-02-20.pdf

Massachusetts EOEA. 2020c. "Updated Guidance Regarding Visitors and Indoor Congregate Activities for Assisted Living Residences (ALRs) during the Covid-19 Outbreak." Commonwealth of Massachusetts EOEA. https://www.mass-ala.org/wp-content/uploads/2020/11/EOEA-Broadens-Visitation-Guidelines-Reinforces-Quarantine-Limitations.pdf.

Massachusetts EOEA. 2020d. "Updated Guidance Regarding Visitors for Assisted Living Residence (ALRs) During the Covid-19 Outbreak." Commonwealth of Massachusetts EOEA. https://mass-ala.org/wp-content/uploads/2021/03/EOEA-Updated-Visitation-Guidance_9_21_20.pdf.

Massachusetts EOEA. 2021a. "Guidance for Assisted Living Residences (ALRs) Following the Covid-19 State of Emergency." Commonwealth of Massachusetts EOEA, June 14. https://mass-ala.org/wp-content/uploads/2021/06/Guidance-for-ALRs-following-the-Covid-19-State-of-Emergency_6_14_21.pdf.

Massachusetts EOEA. 2021b. "Updated Guidance for Assisted Living Residences (ALRs) During the Covid-19 Public Health Emergency." Commonwealth of Massachusetts

EOEA. https://mass-ala.org/wp-content/uploads/2021/03/Updated-Guidances-from-EOEA_3_17_21.pdf.

Maxouris, C. 2021. "Covid-19 Exposed the Devastating Consequences of Staff Shortages in Nursing Homes: But the Problem Isn't New." *CNN*, June 27. https://www.cnn.com/2021/06/27/us/nursing-homes-staff-shortages/index.html.

McMichael, T. M., S. Clark, S. Pogosjans et al. 2020. "COVID-19 in a Long-Term Care Facility—King County, Washington, February 27–March 9, 2020." *Morbidity and Mortality Weekly Report* 69 (12): 339–342. https://www.cdc.gov/mmwr/volumes/69/wr/mm6912e1.htm.

Mor, V., J. Zinn, J. Angelelli, J. M. Teno, and S. C. Miller. 2004. "Driven to Tiers: Socioeconomic and Racial Disparities in the Quality of Nursing Home Care." *The Milbank Quarterly* 82 (2): 227–256. https://doi.org/10.1111/j.0887-378X.2004.00309.xhttps://doi.org/10.1111/j.0887-378X.2004.00309.x

Musumeci, M., E. Childress, and B. Harris. 2022. "State Actions to Address Nursing Home Staffing During Covid-19." *Kaiser Family Foundation*, May 16. https://www.kff.org/medicaid/issue-brief/state-actions-to-address-nursing-home-staffing-during-Covid-19/.

Nania, R. 2020. "What You Need to Know About the Coronavirus." *Health AARP*, September 9. https://www.aarp.org/health/conditions-treatments/info-2020/coronavirus-facts.html.

O'Caoimh, R., M. R. O'Donovan, M. P. Monahan et al. 2020. "Psychosocial Impact of Covid-19 Nursing Home Restrictions on Visitors of Residents with Cognitive Impairment: A Cross-Sectional Study as Part of the Engaging Remotely in Care (ERiC) Project." *Frontiers in Psychiatry* 11. https://doi.org/10.3389/fpsyt.2020.585373.

Paananen, J., J. Rannikko, M. Harju, and J. Pirhonen. 2021. "The Impact of Covid-19-Related Distancing on the Well-Being of Nursing Home Residents and their Family Members: A Qualitative Study. *International Journal of Nursing Studies Advances* 3:100031. https://doi.org/https://doi.org/10.1016/j.ijnsa.2021.100031.

Robinson, L. A., J. K. Hammitt, D. T. Jamison, and D. G. Walker. 2019. "Conducting Benefit-Cost Analysis in Low- and Middle-Income Countries: Introduction to the Special Issue." *J Benefit Cost Anal* 10 (S1): 1–14. https://doi.org/10.1017/bca.2019.4.

Rocard, E., P. Sillitti, and A. Llena-Nozal. 2021. "Covid-19 in Long-Term Care: Impact, Policy Responses and Challenges." OECD, October 21. https://www.oecd.org/en/publications/covid-19-in-long-term-care_b966f837-en.html.

Sepúlveda-Loyola, W., I. Rodríguez-Sánchez, P. Pérez-Rodríguez et al. 2020. "Impact of Social Isolation Due to Covid-19 on Health in Older People: Mental and Physical Effects and Recommendations." *The Journal of Nutrition, Health & Aging* 24 (9): 983–947. https://doi.org/10.1007/s12603-020-1469-2.

Stolz, E., H. Mayerl, and W. Freidl. 2021. "The Impact of Covid-19 Restriction Measures on Loneliness Among Older Adults in Austria." *European Journal of Public Health* 31 (1): 44–49. https://doi.org/10.1093/eurpub/ckaa238.

Su, Z., D. McDonnell, and Y. Li. 2021. "Why Is Covid-19 More Deadly to Nursing Home Residents?" *QJM: An International Journal of Medicine* 114 (8): 543–547. https://doi.org/10.1093/qjmed/hcaa343.

Verbeek, H., D. L. Gerritsen, R. Backhaus, B. S. de Boer, R. T. C. M. Koopmans, and J. P. H. Hamers, 2020. "Allowing Visitors Back in the Nursing Home During the Covid-19 Crisis: A Dutch National Study into First Experiences and Impact on Well-Being." *Journal of the American Medical Directors Association* 21 (7): 900–904. https://doi.org/10.1016/j.jamda.2020.06.020.

Vittone, S., and C. R. Sotomayor. 2021. "Moral Distress Entangled: Patients and Providers in the COVID-19 Era." *HEC Forum* 33:415–423. https://link.springer.com/article/10.1007/s10730-021-09450-y.

Vose, J. 2020. "Delay in Cancer Screening and Diagnosis During the Covid-19 Pandemic: What Is the Cost?" *Oncology* (3409): 343–343. https://doi.org/10.46883/onc.2020.3409.0343.
Wammes, J. D., M. D. Kolk, M. J. H. Van Den Besselaar et al. 2020. "Evaluating Perspectives of Relatives of Nursing Home Residents on the Nursing Home Visiting Restrictions During the Covid-19 Crisis: A Dutch Cross-Sectional Survey Study." *Journal of the American Medical Directors Association* 21 (12): 1746–1750. https://doi.org/10.1016/j.jamda.2020.09.031.
Wan, W. 2020. "Pandemic Isolation Has Killed Thousands of Alzheimer's Patients While Families Watch from Afar." *The Washington Post*, September 16. https://www.washingtonpost.com/health/2020/09/16/coronavirus-dementia-alzheimers-deaths/.
Webber, C., D. T. Myran, C. Milani et al. 2022. "Cognitive Decline in Long-Term Care Residents Before and During the Covid-19 Pandemic in Ontario, Canada." *JAMA*. https://doi.org/10.1001/jama.2022.17214.
Weldon, K. 2020. "HHSC to Allow Limited Visitation at Nursing Facilities and Long-Term Care Facilities." *Texas Health and Human Services Commission*. https://web.archive.org/web/20220517003252/https://www.hhs.texas.gov/news/2020/08/hhsc-allow-limited-visitation-nursing-facilities-long-term-care-facilities.
White House. 2022. "Protecting Seniors by Improving Safety and Quality of Care in the Nation's Nursing Homes." https://www.whitehouse.gov/briefing-room/statements-releases/2022/02/28/fact-sheet-protecting-seniors-and-people-with-disabilities-by-improving-safety-and-quality-of-care-in-the-nations-nursing-homes/.

11

Proportionality Behind Locked Doors

Nursing Homes, Fundamental Rights, and Visit Restrictions During the Coronavirus Pandemic

Settimio Monteverde

Introduction and Overview

In health crises caused by natural disasters, wars, or the pandemic spread of pathogens with yet unknown effects, extensive public health measures may become necessary to safeguard the bases of society's functioning. Policies and crisis standards of care may then even provide restrictions on fundamental rights. Although such measures should in principle be based on sufficient evidence to be legitimate, they may also be ordered on a precautionary basis before evidence is available, based on considerations of the currently perceived risk to vulnerable groups or society as a whole. For the present generations, the pandemic spread of the novel coronavirus starting in the first trimester of 2020 provided, almost worldwide, a striking example of the dynamics of implementing and adapting such measures through concomitant policies. Four years after the first pandemic outbreak of the novel coronavirus, the virus is tending to be more endemic, the public is better informed, infection control and prevention measures are increasingly evidence based, and vaccines are more available. Meanwhile, many countries are attempting to critically reappraise how effectively this pandemic was mastered from the outset, incorporating a broad range of perspectives such as from politics, science communication, law, healthcare, and ethics (see Sachs et al. 2022). This reappraisal also raised the question of the extent to which the restrictions on fundamental rights that are associated with many public health measures and crisis standards of care were legally and ethically justified, thereby bringing the principle of proportionality to the fore (for Switzerland, see Balthasar et al. 2022). Usually, this principle has served as a justification for such measures in that it has been used to bolster claims that situations of extraordinary risk and for which there is clear public interest in risk mitigation require extraordinary policies and

Settimio Monteverde, *Proportionality Behind Locked Doors*. In: *Proportionality*. Edited by: Nikola Biller-Andorno et al., Oxford University Press. © Oxford University Press (2026). DOI: 10.1093/9780197759370.003.0012 measures, which could restrict fundamental rights when necessary. In particular, this principle was also used to justify (more or less comprehensive) prohibitions or restrictions on nursing home residents' visits and going out, which are the subject of this chapter. Starting with the outset of the pandemic, these restrictions were in force for a long time in many places, albeit often in a weakened form. To understand the justifications put forward and discuss them from the perspective of proportionality, different considerations are necessary.

The chapter is divided into four sections. The first section elaborates on a basic understanding of the concept of proportionality by combining sources from both the legal and ethical traditions and including a clarification of the relationship between the proportionality and precautionary principles and their relevance in responding to public health threats. This basic understanding is then translated into the context of prolonged visit restrictions in nursing homes. In the second section, the example of Switzerland is used to illustrate the complex dynamics between different players in securing the proportionality of visit policies that affected the fundamental health, personal integrity, and privacy rights of residents. It describes a series of challenges faced by many nursing homes struggling to keep pace with the dynamic epidemiological situation in the first waves of the pandemic. It also highlights the lack of evidence supporting the effectiveness of restrictions in preventing viral spread and the increasing evidence of the serious harm caused by these measures. Similar to that of other countries (Szczerbińska 2020; Hall Dykgraaf et al. 2021), Switzerland's official talk about alleged dilemmas between freedom and security could not prevent the nursing home sector's structural problems, which were already known, from increasingly coming to light (Ackermann et al. 2020; Monteverde 2022a). On the basis of this example, the third section discusses the thorny question of whether the prolonged restrictions on fundamental rights that rely exclusively on the place of residence (i.e., in this chapter, those that target *specifically* the nursing home population)—which often result in disproportionate suffering, health deterioration, or even death—meet the elements of *torture and other cruel, inhuman, or degrading treatment or punishment* (hereafter abbreviated as *torture*), which signatories to the UN Convention Against Torture and Other Cruel, Inhuman or Degrading Treatment or Punishment (A/RES/39/46 [December 10, 1984]) and its subsequent Optional Protocol (A/RES/57/199 [December 18, 2002]) have committed to protect (Convention Against Torture Initiative [CTI], 2020). This question is not of a purely rhetorical or expressive nature but proves indispensable in establishing torture as the paradigmatic expression of *disproportionality* (Egli et al. 2022). The final section considers how the fundamental rights of residents can be better protected and translated into proportionate visit policies. These considerations include the continual, safe access of essential care partners, legal guardians, and professional caregivers in the privately inhabited space of residents under the same safety precautions as apply to the nursing home staff.

Proportions, Precautions, and Fundamental Rights

In both the legal and ethical traditions, proportionality has been described as a principle that becomes instrumental in the realization of justice, either by *balancing* principles or by establishing an acceptable *ratio between means and ends* when principles collide (Luterán 2014). Following an Aristotelian framework of justice (Weinrib 2012, 62), justice can be achieved both in an *arithmetic* mode by realizing an "equality of quantities" and in a *geometric* mode by realizing an "equality of proportions." The arithmetic mode is transactional and focuses on the exchange of goods and purchase of commodities in relation to their (market) value. In contrast, the geometric mode appears more dynamic and connects the just distribution of goods in accordance with other aspects such as the interests of those affected by the distribution. Needs, merits, public interest, or the (contingent) dignity of important persons can be used as criteria on the basis of which an allocation or distribution is deemed proportionate. Examples of geometric distributions include more support for (nonrepayable) scholarships for students from poor settings (not granted for students coming from wealthy settings) or the reception of heads of state in official representational events (not granted for average citizens). What appears to be the just proportion may then have two different connotations: It may both include "continuity" in the case of arithmetic exchange and "discontinuity" in the case of geometric distribution (Engle 2013, 273).

Classically, the reparation of wrongs after criminal offenses with the aim to confirm and restore the rule of law has figured among the goods that can be subject to proportionality concerns (Engle 2013; for the discussion within jurisprudence, see Chiao 2022). In the contemporary discourse on human rights, proportionality emerges as a principle explaining how prima facie incommensurable fundamental rights[1] may well be negotiated under certain conditions.

[1] Fundamental rights are understood here as the set of enforceable, sanctionable, and constitutionally guaranteed rights that derive from universal human rights and to which all inhabitants of a country—members of a constitutional community of law—are entitled. The Swiss Federal Constitution, for example, lists—among others—the following fundamental rights: respect for and protection of human dignity, equality before the law, protection against discrimination, protection against arbitrary action by state authorities, the right to life and personal freedom, the right not to be subjected to torture and other forms of cruel, inhumane, or degrading treatment, the right to assistance when in need, the right to privacy, the right to marry and to have a family, protection against deprivation of liberty (except when there is a legal basis), and the political right to form an opinion and freely express it (Swiss Federal Constitution 1999 arts. 7–10, 12–14, 31, 34). The Swiss Federal Constitution

First, the reasons for doing so must not be taken lightly. They must be *compelling*—that is, considered indispensable for achieving an important and publicly acknowledged good. Second, the extent to which basic rights may become negotiable must be *reasonable*—that is, it must indicate a positive relationship between the ends of such negotiation and the means needed to reach them. As an intermediary principle (Hermerén 2012), proportionality does not entail material statements about which goods are to be distributed or weighted in individual cases. Rather, it leads to rules that enable a comparability of actually incomparable goods—like fundamental rights, freedoms, or liberties—when extraordinary circumstances require it. Proportionality, then, makes a limitation of such per se incommensurable rights or distribution of goods appear fair, even when such a limitation or distribution imposes significant burdens and restrictions on those affected. In addition to the legal tradition of proportionality entailing aspects of both "arithmetic" (equality of quantities) and "geometrical" (equality of ratios) (Weinrib 2012, 62) considerations on justice, questions of public safety and the welfare of the community have also been debated as issues involving proportionality. Measures targeting the health of the population as a whole or specific groups likely to suffer serious harm (thus identified as *vulnerable*) require the conditions of both indispensability and reasonableness if the purpose of these measures is in the general interest (e.g., März et al. 2022).

It is intuitive to list wars, natural disasters, pandemics, or any other public health crisis as paradigmatic circumstances requiring these kinds of rules be established and translated into manageable policies (Bruchhausen and Kuhn 2021). Undoubtedly, such circumstances are out of the ordinary for those affected and threaten many constitutive aspects of daily life. Nevertheless, proportionality warrants that these measures be handled neither as exemptions *outside* or exceptions *besides* the legal and moral framework of the civil society but as (extraordinary) challenges to be dealt with *within* this framework (Rixen 2021). As will be demonstrated, by acknowledging the *extraordinariness*—but not exceptionality—of restrictions on fundamental rights for compelling reasons, proportionality ensures that these restrictions are legitimate (i.e., consistent with the applicable legal and moral frameworks) (Schorb and Schmidt-Semisch 2021).

The Nuffield Council on Bioethics (2022, 1) discusses the problem of fundamental rights becoming negotiable within state interventions in terms of *intrusiveness* when weighting measures to face public health threats like the

also describes the circumstances under which restrictions on fundamental rights are permissible: Restrictions require a sufficient legal basis (art. 36), must be in the public interest, and must be proportionate. But beyond any weighting, "the essence of fundamental rights is sacrosanct" (art. 36.3). In the root version of the law (in German), the term of the English translation "sacrosanct" is rendered as "inviolable" (*unantastbar* in German; literally, "untouchable").

pandemic spread of a novel pathogen: "Decision makers should aim for a proportionate response that takes into account the nature and degree of the harm posed, the certainty of the evidence, the intrusiveness of the intervention, and the views of those affected." Intrusion and intrusiveness are spatial categories that relate to the interface between the public and the private spheres. As a morally thick term, intrusiveness positions the integrity of the private sphere as a moral imperative that must not be put at risk lightly. In a public health crisis like a pandemic, these spheres become particularly visible in both their distinctiveness and their interdependency and also in their permeability when threats to the functioning and well-being of the community are evident. Thus, in addition to the legal tradition, *evidence* becomes an important criterion for assessing the proportionality of public health interventions that imply the negotiability of fundamental rights like curfews in pandemic hotspots, prohibitions of mass gatherings, or obligations to wear face masks in public spaces (März et al. 2022). However, if evidence is not yet sufficiently given or is still in the process of being gathered and the risk of serious and irreversible harm cannot be excluded with certainty, the *probability* of serious and irreversible harm alone is sufficient to justify these measures, which brings into play the precautionary principle (Ten Have 2022). This principle may justify *ex ante* means that may become necessary in the attempt to secure a valuable common good (e.g., saving more lives or securing the functionality of the healthcare system) but that *ex post* could be considered as disproportionate. At the beginning of the coronavirus pandemic, closures of schools and churches, prohibitions of mass gatherings, restrictions on visits in nursing homes and hospitals, and curfews have figured under these measures. They were justified on the basis of the precautionary principle and stood in the context of a novel coronavirus, whose spreading dynamics were not sufficiently known. This now stands in stark contrast to the evidence of the devastating health effects on particularly vulnerable populations, which soon became apparent. Nonetheless, two important clarifications need to be made when the precautionary principle is advocated:

1. There are limits to a crude, simplistic utilitarian calculus and to the range of means to be used on a precautionary basis, no matter how desirable the ends and how favorable the relationship between means and ends. The means, per se, must be both legitimate and not excessive in the sense that the means must be the least harmful alternative (Hermerén 2012).
2. The fact that certain measures restricting fundamental rights that are introduced on a precautionary basis may prove *ex post* (i.e., at the moment evidence is available) to be disproportionate neither implies any statements about their wrongness at the moment of their first implementation nor provides a valid basis for compensation or restoration claims when such measures prove *ex post* to be disproportionate.

In a public health crisis whose extent is currently unclear, three elements enable but simultaneously limit the power of the ordering authority (e.g., the management of the nursing home or health authorities): the *legitimacy* condition, the *nonexcessiveness* condition, and the *nonenforceability* of restrictions on fundamental rights introduced on a precautionary basis. The formal reason for this tense balance is that even extraordinary circumstances requiring extraordinary measures are to be considered as circumstances *within* the legal and moral framework of society. There cannot be such a thing as a state of emergency *outside* this framework (Rixen 2021; Ten Have 2022). Consequently, although provisions justified by the precautionary principle might be considered as extraordinary, they are still not *exceptional*: Their actuation must reflect the core content (or the *essence*; see note 1) of the moral and legal fabric of a democratically constituted society. In the event of serious risks calling for precautionary measures, *exceptionalism* builds on potentially arbitrary, nongeneralizable, and freestanding arguments. In contrast, *extraordinariness* follows a "default and challenge" rationality (Bayertz 2014) that departs from the binding nature of fundamental rights until proven otherwise, the burden of proof being borne by the one who wishes to limit those rights. This may involve difficult decisions, not even refraining from restricting fundamental rights when responding to serious, unknown threats. Table 11.1. summarizes these concepts and relates them to each other.

These specifications allow for a closer look at the proportionality of visit policies that were enacted in many nursing homes during the coronavirus pandemic. In the first wave, because of both a lack of knowledge and of protective equipment, many measures mandated by the authorities can be explained with the precautionary principle and the aim of protecting the lives of those most vulnerable from fatal courses of the COVID-19 disease. The precautionary principle challenges the assumption that the harm caused by these initial measures and motivated by this principle allows automatically for claims for compensation or redress in both legal and moral terms. This holds true even when these measures are found *ex post* to be disproportionate, partly by failing their goal in terms of effective infection prevention in nursing homes and partly because the measures themselves have had a severe impact on the health of those affected (e.g., Diamantis et al. 2020).

Over the subsequent waves, public health measures, often initiated on a precautionary basis, were increasingly replaced by more proportionate measures. As a result of the availability of vaccines, testing facilities, and knowledge about effective ways to prevent and treat infection, these measures became generally looser. Notwithstanding, many nursing homes maintained visit restrictions and bans on going out. These restrictions seemed increasingly disconnected from the coronavirus pandemic, developing a dynamic of their own and accentuating

Table 11.1 Rationale and extent of restrictions to fundamental rights—clarifications of concepts

Rationale of measures	Precautionary principle	Explains how authorities and institutions may react to sudden, previously unknown threats to public health even before reliable scientific evidence is available (ex ante) Examples: Lockdowns and closures of schools and nursing homes in the event of the emergence of new, unknown pathogens
	Proportionality principle	Explains how prima facie incommensurable fundamental rights may well be negotiated under conditions of sufficiently proven threats to public health. Calls for adaptation to new evidence and evaluation ex post. Examples: Prolonged measures and public health strategies implemented in the context of natural disasters or pandemics
Extent of measures	Extraordinariness	Explains the extent of restrictions (based on precautionary or proportionality considerations) on private and public life. Acknowledges such restrictions as *out of the ordinary* and even as threatening constitutive aspects of daily life. Examples: Curfews and restrictions of social contacts
	Nonexceptionality	Explains the necessary condition for such restrictions to be legally and morally legitimate, and explicitly refers to the rule of law and the moral foundations of society Examples: Nondiscrimination against individuals and populations, nonintrusiveness, and prevention of harm that is inherent to the restrictive measures themselves

preexisting structural problems within the nursing home sector (Dichter et al. 2020; Moerenhout 2020; Anand et al. 2021; Hardwick et al. 2022).[2] In nursing homes that upheld restrictions for structural reasons such as easier manageability, staff shortages, or problems in financing due standards of safe care, it is this shift in scope that marks the transition to *disproportionality*.

One explanation for this transition is that, as the Nuffield Council on Bioethics (2022) differentiates, only the harms caused by the pandemic itself

[2] For example, restrictions could be upheld for logistical reasons, like when visitor management becomes time consuming because of a serious staffing shortage. If the nursing home manager were risk-averse and the authorities were to grant appropriate leeway, visiting bans could be maintained, either on the basis of individual safety considerations or for the banal reason that the facility has no concept of contagion prevention (e.g., Bell et al. 2021, 24).

have been considered in assessing proportionality, which neglects the serious harms caused by the measures of infection prevention (e.g., Diamantis et al. 2020; Ó Néill 2022). These harms were either not acknowledged or dismissed even when recognized, thereby challenging or even violating the principle of nonexcessiveness. Based on an analysis of secondary sources dating from March to December 2020, Anand et al. (2021, 1) conclude that "a significant contributing factor to the scale and nature of deaths and harms is the abject disregard of older people's human rights." Furthering this argument, the Nuffield Council on Bioethics (2022, 4) suggests that fundamental proportionality considerations should not solely reside in the protection of (biological) *life* but rather the broader concept of *personal life*, which encompasses the right to privacy, freedom, and choice. Accordingly, only the joint protection of biological *and* personal life constitutes a sufficient condition for maintaining the proportionality of restrictions on fundamental rights.

In summary, there is strong evidence that the proportionality of restrictions on fundamental rights—a pillar for legal and ethical safety in any democratically constituted society—was not sufficiently ensured for residents of nursing homes in many places by the responsible governmental and institutional actors.[3] This oversight occurred both in the beginning of the pandemic, because of the limitations to the precautionary principle described earlier in this section (Anand et al. 2021), and throughout its progression, because of structural problems preventing many nursing homes from not only adequately addressing but also promptly and effectively mitigating the severe physical and psychological harm of numerous measures in place (Diamantis et al. 2020; Hardwick et al. 2022; Ó Néill 2022).

Breaking Down Proportionality from Recommendations to Practices: The Swiss Example

Compared to other high-income countries with aging societies, Switzerland faced similar challenges and took analogous measures with respect to populations that proved particularly vulnerable during the coronavirus pandemic, including nursing home residents (INFRAS 2021).[4] As provided for in the Swiss

[3] A commendable exception to this grim conclusion is, of course, the many courageous managers, nurses, general practitioners, and other individuals who, overwhelmed by the human tragedy and suffering, courageously and imaginatively defied the (sometimes harsh) orders of health authorities and the institutional management (see Garros et al. 2021).

[4] Residents (as opposed to patients) are persons living in a privately used space within a healthcare facility. The basis is a contract, usually not limited in time, that combines aspects of *housing* and *care*. Although nursing homes form both *own* and *common* households that can come into tension with

Constitution, the interaction between the Confederation and the Cantons is crucial to ensuring the health of the population, including in public health crises like pandemics.

During the coronavirus pandemic, the Federal Office of Public Health issued a series of recommendations dealing with the protection of *particularly vulnerable persons*, a group that, in the first recommendation addressing long term care facilities, dated April 2, 2020, was exclusively defined by medical criteria (Federal Office of Public Health 2020a).[5] Surprisingly and somewhat abruptly, the section "Protective Measures for Particularly Vulnerable Persons" at the end of the document states that "visits by family, friends and acquaintances to institutions such as nursing homes and facilities for people with disabilities are prohibited" (Federal Office of Public Health 2020a, 3). This clearly exceeded the character of a recommendation. In addition, whereas the list of particularly vulnerable persons at the end of the document only mentions medical conditions and not places of care, *residents* are generally among those subject to the most stringent measures, which effectively equates the status of a resident to a *medical condition*. All successive recommendations, however, refrain from a total ban on visits and, over time, replaced "prohibitions" with "restrictions" and "restrictions" with "concepts of protection." At the same time, the recommendations expressly place the competence for visit regulations in the hands of the Cantons (Federal Office of Public Health 2020b). The latest versions of the recommendations (Federal Office of Public Health 2022a; 2022b) explicitly call for ethical aspects to be taken into account when regulating visits and even refer to the documents of the National Advisory Commission on Biomedical Ethics (2020) and the clinical ethicists in Switzerland (Ackermann et al. 2020).[6] At the same time, the most recent recommendations recall the "institutional heterogeneity" whose implementation requires "a flexible approach" and the adaptation to "individual conditions and circumstances" (Federal Office of Public Health 2022b, 3). In sum, while the recommendations of the Federal Office of Public Health (2022b, 3) seem to encourage prudent practices and foster considerations of proportionality, they simultaneously make the assessment of proportionality difficult by allowing for flexible approaches.

each other in a pandemic, fundamental rights (e.g., relating to privacy, dignity, or liberty) may only be restricted under the conditions listed in note 1 (see also Petrik 2021).

[5] "Persons 65 years of age and older as well as individuals, including those under 65, who have the following conditions in particular: hypertension, chronic respiratory diseases, diabetes, diseases and therapies that weaken the immune system, cardiovascular diseases, or cancer" (Federal Office of Public Health 2020a, 1).

[6] Both documents very early on introduced proportionality considerations, called for humane visiting policies, addressed structural deficits of the nursing home sector, and advocated for ensuring continual, safe physical social contacts between particularly vulnerable persons and their essential care partners (Ackermann et al, 2020; National Advisory Commission on Biomedical Ethics 2020).

With the federal government refraining from explicitly regulating visit policies within the COVID-19-related legal framework and limiting itself to recommendations, the Cantons had the task of creating guidelines (Balthasar et al. 2022). In the first year of the pandemic, most Cantonal authorities issued more or less comprehensive bans on visits and going out (National Advisory Commission on Biomedical Ethics 2020; Zimmermann 2021). In general, Cantonal regulations tended to tighten the recommendations of the Federal Council. As a rule, Cantonal provisions regarding visits were implemented rigorously, often with erroneous reference to a federal emergency law.

At the level of internal directives, many Cantons gave nursing home management a great deal of discretion in determining closures, openings, and when exceptions could and could not be made. This practice not only de facto established the nursing home management as a gatekeeper but also promoted the risk that nursing homes would take on the characteristics of total institutions (Ayalon and Avidor 2021; Monteverde 2022a, 2022b). One characteristic of totality is the lack of any corrective or balancing mechanism between the interests of the commissioning individual (the resident) and the commissioned institution (the nursing home). These developments posed the greatest threat to proportionality, and—as the final report commissioned by the Federal of Public Health states—increased "the risk of unequal treatment, arbitrary house rules and the unnecessary isolation of people in care homes as well as a laissez-faire attitude that promoted the transmission of the disease" (Balthasar et al. 2022, 29). In addition, some Cantonal supervisory authorities reduced or even canceled routine inspection visits because of the pandemic situation.[7] The discontinuation of visits posed an even greater threat to the proportionality of prolonged fundamental rights restrictions in nursing homes (Association for the Prevention of Torture 2020; Anand et al. 2021; Hardwick et al. 2022). To better understand these dynamics, the verbatim protocols of the sessions of the Cantonal Parliaments can be useful.[8] Some of them reveal an astonishing ease with which some Cantonal Parliaments long neglected questions of proportionality in restricting the fundamental rights of one specific population—clearly going beyond possible precautionary considerations that characterized the beginning of the pandemic (Ten Have 2020). They sustain the observation that "the fundamental

[7] See, as an example, the official 2020 healthcare report of the Canton of Basel-City: "In accordance with the epidemiological course, various protective measures were recommended to the nursing homes: from compulsory masks for nurses to health checks for visitors and finally to the closure of the nursing homes to visitors. . . . For the division of long-term-care, the extraordinary situation declared by the Confederation meant, as in other areas of the Department of Health, an adjustment of daily business. For example, no supervisory visits were carried out during this time" (Department of Health of the Canton of Basel-Stadt 2020, p. 7).

[8] In terms of examples, see the Cantons of Basel-City or Solothurn (Grosser Rat des Kantons Basel-Stadt 2020; Grosser Rat des Kantons Solothurn 2020).

rights of residents in retirement and care homes institutions and of their relatives were strongly limited by the measures restricting visits and the right to leave the premises" (Balthasar et al. 2022, 98).

The question arises at this point as to how this development can be explained. Undoubtedly, health authorities together with the nursing homes faced enormous challenges in securing the safety of this particularly vulnerable sector of society (Zimmermann 2021). But the federal government's successive recommendations encouraging safe reopening policies were implemented only hesitantly in many places. Practices of careful "keeping open" were also observed in some places, regardless of existing official regulations. Moreover, rhetoric abounded regarding the alleged dilemma between freedom and security. This increasingly blurred the boundaries of the urgent structural problems in the nursing home sector, which the pandemic had exacerbated worldwide (Moerenhout 2020; National Advisory Commission on Biomedical Ethics 2020, 5–6; Petrik 2021, 44). In addition to, or perhaps as a specific aspect of, the question of proportionality, the efficacy of visit bans and restrictions also warrants examination. In Switzerland, as in other countries, these restrictions could not prevent the high death toll of persons living in nursing homes, including both COVID-19-related mortality and excess mortality (Federal Office of Public Health 2021; Balthasar et al. 2022). The evaluation report commissioned by the Federal Office of Public Health (Balthasar et al. 2022, 29) concludes that

> irrespective of their individual risk situation, the majority of retirement, nursing and care institutions have at times imposed strict bans on visiting and leaving, thus massively restricting fundamental rights. . . . Despite the measures taken, it was not possible during either the first or second wave of the pandemic to adequately protect the residents of retirement and nursing institutions. . . . According to [Federal Office of Public Health] statistics, at least 49% of all confirmed COVID-19 deaths occurred at a retirement or care institution between the start of October 2020 and the end of February 2021.

When attempting to weigh the long-lasting and intense restriction of the fundamental rights of residents—comparing their desired outcomes in terms of protecting lives with the outcomes that actually occurred in terms of morbidity, mortality, and psychological suffering (see National Advisory Commission on Biomedical Ethics 2020, 5–6; INFRAS 2021, 100–101; Balthasar et al. 2022, 29)—both proportionality and precautionary considerations come into play. Whereas the former requires a favorable ratio between means and ends, the latter requires the nonexcessiveness of measures in dealing with unknown risks (Ten Have 2022). On the basis of a study commissioned by the Federal Office of

Public Health (INFRAS 2021), both must be doubted. In analyzing in depth the effects of strict visit prohibitions on the numbers of infections in the institutions, the study authors conclude that "the effect of the strict visiting ban on the number of infected persons overall cannot be interpreted unambiguously: it is true that fewer people tended to become infected in facilities with a strict visiting ban than in facilities that never implemented a strict visiting ban. However, a trend reversal can be observed in facilities that were particularly severely affected. It is possible that the causality here goes in the other direction: because the number of cases in the facilities was high, a strict visiting ban was imposed to prevent further spread of the virus. Even with a strict curfew, the situation is not clear-cut: the facilities that imposed a strict curfew in one of the waves were more affected" (INFRAS 2021, 61–62). The authors of the study conclude that "whether or not the bans were justified from an epidemiological point of view cannot be clearly answered within the scope of the present report" (INFRAS 2021, 73). However, when it comes to prolonged restrictions of fundamental rights, precisely this type of justification is urgently needed, since evidence-informed decisions are indispensable in order to sustain or adapt public health emergency policies, even more so when they target specific populations (März et al. 2022). Beyond the lack of proof that visit restrictions prevented high mortality in nursing homes, evidence points to the harm they caused, with no data to suggest that cautious and targeted opening policies for essential care partners would result in more infections, which was also confirmed by a Dutch study by Verbeek et al. (2020; see also Hall Dykgraaf et al. 2021).

Looking back on the first three years of the pandemic in Switzerland and the complex interplay between the various protagonists in the nursing home field, a number of challenges have been described in translating proportionality from the level of general recommendations to safe, humane, and reliable practices that safeguard "the essence of fundamental rights" (Swiss Federal Constitution art. 36.3; see note 1) for a particularly vulnerable population within the pandemic crisis. Protagonists at the federal, Cantonal, health-authority, and institutional levels have transferred responsibility for the implementation of visit policies to the next level down in each case, not paying enough attention to the fact that the proof of proportionality would become more and more blurred. The excessive discretionary power "at the sharp end" of care provision (Hughes 2008) also meant that those responsible at the institutional level tended to be overburdened. Many did not feel sufficiently protected from the possible consequences of decisions to open or close nursing homes. This situation encouraged institutional inertia and the quest for maximum security, often resulting in overly restrictive policies. This, in turn, widened the gap between the human rights requirements governing restrictions on personal rights and the implementation of restrictions in Swiss nursing homes during the pandemic.

Furthermore, the underrepresentation of residents and relatives in public debates (Monteverde 2022b) also highlights the broader societal challenge of upholding proportionality. For an astonishingly long time, there was a great silence at a societal level about the situation in nursing homes, which demonstrates the social invisibility of this sector. Nursing home residents and their relatives lacked political advocacy for their interests, a point exacerbated under pandemic conditions. Relevant documents and statements by organizations and boards (e.g., see note 6) received public attention rather hesitantly or were dismissed with reference to alleged federal emergency law that was repeatedly used as a wildcard for waiving proportionality considerations (Monteverde 2022a). Some voices saw this perception as an expression of ageist thinking (Zimmermann 2021). This could explain not only the societal neglect of this particularly vulnerable societal group but also the phenomena of societal stigmatization that arose from blaming residents for necessitating "drastic" lockdowns affecting the whole society (Zimmermann 2021, 9–15; see also McDonald 2022).

In summary, the Swiss example shows that the challenges to ensuring proportionality were not only of a legal or ethical nature but also of a political, structural, and societal one. In many places, structural problems within the nursing home sector triggered a prolonged adherence to the precautionary principle and consequently prevented a timely review of restrictions. Thus, the proportionality of these measures could not be ensured, and—more seriously, in an ethical sense—avoidable suffering could not be prevented. A normative framework of law and ethics is a necessary condition for ensuring proportionality. But this framework is only sufficient if it is reliably translated to the macro level of political deliberation and becomes binding at the meso-level of the organizations that secure proportionality within the structure and in the condition of the individual resident.

Proportionality and the Tightrope Between Protection, Torture, and Degradation

Among the worst abysses of the coronavirus pandemic are the harrowing experiences of suffering that residents and their families underwent at the beginning of the pandemic in certain nursing homes around the world, which triggered indignation worldwide. These experiences were characterized by the egregious neglect of residents, sometimes resulting in death, following the initial coronavirus outbreak (e.g., Comas-Herrera et al. 2020; Rada 2020; Anand et al. 2021). It quickly became evident that such occurrences could not be dismissed as merely isolated tragedies arising from an acutely overburdened healthcare system. Instead, they must be acknowledged as symptoms of systemic deficiencies, which were present prepandemic and severely amplified by the crisis (Hardwick et al. 2022). They unveiled the pronounced vulnerability of certain care environments and, more poignantly, of the people who reside in them who face elevated risks of fatal infection outcomes attributable not only to their medical condition but also, specifically, to the place of care.

The early evidence of serious harm in terms of death and suffering from social deprivation and neglect underscored the need to adequately protect populations disproportionately at risk during the pandemic. Consequently, a "securitization" of health could be observed at a global level (Gozdecka 2021). It included issues related to healthcare and health-related fundamental rights, which soon became subject to proportionality considerations (Anand et al., 2021; Nawrot et al. 2022). As mentioned, a key driver of the discussion was the recognition that nursing homes under COVID-19 had transformed from ordinary residential care facilities into highly vulnerable spaces that could quickly become places of deprivation of liberty and render residents socially invisible through prohibitions on visits (Hardwick et al. 2022).

In this line of thinking, the European Committee for the for the Prevention of Torture and Inhuman or Degrading Treatment or Punishment (CPT) released a statement addressing "the treatment of persons deprived of their liberty in the context of the coronavirus disease (COVID-19) pandemic" (CPT 2020; see also the 1984 UN Convention Against Torture and Other Cruel, Inhuman or Degrading Treatment or Punishment and its 2002 Optional Protocol). In the preamble, the CPT explicitly lists "social care homes" as places of *deprivation of liberty* under pandemic conditions, along with other institutions like penitentiaries, immigration detention centers, psychiatric hospitals, and specific quarantine facilities (CPT 2020; Steele et al. 2020). Of greatest importance for the preservation of fundamental rights in all the facilities listed is the statement's assertion that the "nature of the prohibition of torture and inhuman or degrading treatment" is "absolute" and that, therefore, "protective measures must never result in inhuman or degrading treatment of persons deprived of their liberty" (CPT 2020). With this statement, not only does the Council of Europe present torture as the paradigmatic example of disproportionality, but it also notes that in the pandemic, nursing homes can become particularly vulnerable to this challenge for residents because of the many restrictions of fundamental rights carried out *in camera*. At an international level, the UN Convention Against Torture and Other Cruel, Inhuman or Degrading Treatment or Punishment and the Optional Protocol to that convention went in a similar direction. Both concur in highlighting the relevance of preventing actions and omissions that constitute torture by the prudent application of restraints and involuntary placements as well as by ensuring standards of due care.

At first glance, it seems easy to rebut the presumption of torture through the lack of intentionality. This is undoubtedly promising because the very accusation that torture has taken place on the premises of a nursing home seems fundamentally outrageous. But following the broad definition of the UN Torture Convention, this is more difficult in the case of acts other than outright torture that constitute *unintentional* "other [forms of] cruel, inhuman or degrading treatment." Anand et al. (2021, 5) list a series of international references describing grievances they consider evidence of cruel, inhuman, or degrading treatment such as

- dying in a facility under inhumane or degrading conditions, such as being left alone without adequate, food, water, or access to pain relief;
- being deliberately left unattended after a positive test for COVID-19;
- being left without food because staff is quarantined;
- increasing the use of antipsychotics and psychotics for persons suffering from dementia, wandering, and showing agitation or aggressive behavior;
- abandoning the dying and excluding their relatives from visits.

Whereas these observations are confined to the prohibition of torture, others pertain to the rights to life, liberty, security, privacy, family, and nondiscrimination (Anand et al. 2021, 5). Of course, when enumerating "torture *and other* cruel, inhuman or degrading treatment or punishment," extreme caution is required in order to avoid epistemic injustice toward victims of torture in the narrow sense and thereby increasing the suffering of the victims and their families. Even if these terms are mentioned together, this does not mean that there is no gradation among them. In particular, the words "and other" seem to allow for such a gradation. But at the same time, they also indicate that the difference between *torture* and *other cruel, inhuman, or degrading treatment and punishment* is not absolute but occurs on a gradual continuum. Therefore, given the broad definition of torture and its association with inhumanity and degradation, it is hard to simply dismiss the thorny question of whether nursing homes risked becoming places of torture during the early stages of the pandemic. In connection with visit bans, staff shortages, social deprivation, and frailty, substantial evidence points to disproportionate suffering, the rapid deterioration of health, and even unnecessary deaths within the nursing home population worldwide (Andrews 2020; National COVID-19 Science Task Force 2021; Ó Néill 2022). As a result, these considerations depict torture as a paradigmatic example of disproportionality. They also reveal how easily the offense of torture can be committed in vulnerable places that are hidden from public view. This makes it all the more important to monitor and secure proportionality in places where liberty can be deprived and to use all the means available under the rule of law to protect potential victims and bring to light and penalize dehumanizing practices.

Reframing Proportionality

A fundamental insight of the preceding considerations is the *vulnerability of the proportionality principle itself.* This principle is at risk when corresponding norms are not embedded in the structures and processes that ensure the respect of fundamental rights, even for those who are offline (i.e., those disconnected from mainstream societal networks).

In discussing the relationship among health, illness, and criminality, Schorb and Schmidt-Semisch (2021) introduce the construct of *health deviance* in the context of the coronavirus pandemic. They describe a punitive approach that blurred the lines between health issues and criminality that was applied not only to ill people (e.g., unvaccinated patients who contracted the coronavirus) but also to people suffering disproportionately from coronavirus-related border closures (e.g., transnational couples and families). The authors emphasize the relevance of proportionality in uncovering these dynamics and upholding the rule of law. Interestingly, Schorb and Schmidt-Semisch (2021, 534) identify the emergence of a *new penology* that maps the aforementioned increase from *extraordinariness* to *exceptionality*—and thus the loss of proportionality. According to the authors, this new penology abstains from influencing behavior through the threat of punishment. Rather, it limits itself to constructing risk groups and regulating them through risk management. Punishment is replaced by exclusion based on objective characteristics and does not even shy away from justified incarceration (Schorb and Schmidt-Semisch 2021, 534). This argument casts a critical light on the perceived vulnerability of the nursing home population, which served as the main justification for restricting this population's fundamental rights during the coronavirus pandemic (Federal Office of Public Health 2020a; Krones et al. 2020; Monteverde 2022a). In this line of thinking, a first step consists of epistemic clarifications of salient concepts that have shaped the discussion until now. These include the quest for proportionate wordings such as *essential care partner* instead of *visitor* (Kemp 2021), the analysis of vulnerability as a means of controlling people (Schorb and Schmidt-Semisch 2021), and the imperative to protect *life* in the narrow sense (invoked to justify visit bans) versus *personal life* in the broad sense (Nuffield 2022). The latter encompasses the totality of a person's existence, including the protection of their biological, social, economic, and spiritual well-being and their clearly expressed, presumed, or understood interests (Monteverde 2022b).

Together with the imperative to tackle the known structural challenges of the nursing home sector, standards of proportionality must be addressed. Proper proportionality must reliably reflect the legal and moral foundations of the civil society; address the safeguarding of life, freedom, privacy, and choice; be issued and monitored by a competent authority; and not be delegated down and left to discretionary decisions that are not subject to appeal. Given the potential of nursing homes to become sites of liberty deprivation under pandemic conditions, continual efforts are essential to prevent any form of *torture*, and *other cruel, inhuman, or degrading treatment and punishment* (CTI 2020; Anand et al. 2021). In light of the overwhelming evidence of the disproportionate suffering of residents and families, policies must guarantee the continual and safe access for *essential care partners*, *legal guardians*, and *professional caregivers* in the privately inhabited space of residents. This access should adhere to the same safety precautions that apply to the nursing home's staff and should be determined in agreement with nursing home guidelines. These measures and others like them will safeguard the ethical security of residents in care homes, honor the trust placed in them by families, and cultivate public confidence in these institutions throughout into the future.

Competing Interests

There are no competing interests to declare.

Funding

There is no funding to declare.

References

Ackermann, S., R. Baumann Hölzle, N. Biller Andorno et al. 2020. "Pandemie: Lebensschutz und Lebensqualität in der Langzeitpflege; Appell an die Verantwortungsträger aus Politik, Management, Pflege und Betreuung." *Schweizerische Ärztezeitung* 101 (2728): 843–845. https://doi.org/10.4414/saez.2020.19037.

Anand, J. C., S. Donnelly, A. Milne et al. 2021. "The COVID-19 Pandemic and Care Homes for Older People in Europe—Deaths, Damage, and Violations of Human Rights." *European Journal of Social Work* 25 (5): 804–815. https://doi.org/10.1080/13691457.2021.1954886.

Andrews J. 2020. "Irrational Restrictions." *New Scientist* 248 (3308). https://doi.org/10.1016/S0262-4079(20)32001-7.

Association for the Prevention of Torture. 2020. "Monitoring Places of Detention Through the COVID-19 Pandemic." *Guidance*. https://www.apt.ch/sites/default/files/publications/Guidance%20note_final%20version_web.pdf.

Ayalon, L., and S. Avidor. 2021. "'We Have Become Prisoners of Our Own Age': From a Continuing Care Retirement Community to a Total Institution in the Midst of the COVID-19 Outbreak." *Age and Ageing* 50 (3): 664–667. https://doi.org/10.1093/ageing/afab013.

Balthasar, A., S. Essig, T. von Stokar et al. 2022. "Evaluation of the Management of the COVID-19 Crisis up to Summer 2021." Final report for the Federal Office of Public Health, Evaluation and Research Service, Lucerne. https://www.bag.admin.ch/dam/bag/en/dokumente/e-f/evalber-mt/2022-evaluation-krisenbewaeltigung-covid-19-schlussbericht.pdf.download.pdf/2022-final-report-evaluation-management-covid19-crisis-e.pdf.

Bayertz, K. 2014. "'Die Rationalität des Amoralisten': Westfälische Wilhelms-Universität Münster. Preprints and Working Papers of the Centre for Advanced Study in Bioethics No. 2014/64. *Wissen.Leben*. https://www.uni-muenster.de/imperia/md/content/kfg-normen begruendung/intern/publikationen/bayertz/64_bayertz_-_rationalit__t_des_amora lismus.pdf.

Bell, K., K. Frodé, A. Olivares Jones et al. 2021. "A Human Rights Analysis of the Impacts of COVID-19 on Persons in Australian Residential Aged Care Facilities: Submission to the Independent Expert on the Enjoyment of all Human Rights by Older Persons." https://www.monash.edu/__data/assets/pdf_file/0018/2503431/2021-Castan-Centre-Submission-to-the-Independent_Expert-on-the-enjoyment-of-all-human-rights-by-older-persons.pdf

Bruchhausen, W., and E. Kuhn. 2021. "Menschenrechte und internationale Verpflichtungen in Pandemie-Zeiten—mehr als Gesundheitsschutz." In *Pandemien und Ethik*, edited by Andreas Reis, Martina Schmidhuber, and Andreas Frewer. Springer. https://doi.org/10.1007/978-3-662-63530-8_4.

Chiao, V. 2022. "Proportionality and Its Discontents." *Law and Philosophy* 41:193–217. https://doi.org/10.1007/s10982-021-09423-9.

Comas-Herrera, A., J. Zalakaín, E. Lemmon et al. 2020. "Mortality Associated with COVID-19 In Care Homes: Early International Evidence." LTC Responses to COVID-19: International Long Term Policy Network, April 12. https://ltccovid.org/2020/04/12/mortality-associated-with-covid-19-outbreaks-in-care-homes-early-international-evidence/.

CPT (European Committee for the Prevention of Torture and Inhuman or Degrading Treatment or Punishment). 2020. "Statement of Principles Relating to the Treatment of Persons Deprived of Their Liberty in the Context of the Coronavirus Disease (COVID-19) Pandemic." https://rm.coe.int/16809cfa4b.

CTI (Convention Against Torture Initiative). 2020. "COVID-19 and the UN Convention Against Torture." https://cti2024.org/resource/cti-covid-19-and-uncat-advice-paper/.

Department of Health of the Canton of Basel-Stadt. 2020. Health Care Report on Hospitals, Nursing Homes, Day-Care Facilities and Home Care Providers in the Canton of Basel-City. https://media.bs.ch/original_file/1b26439ffa49a984d38b19bee74062c7f1954b89/qokcp01.pdf.

Diamantis S., C. Noel, P. Tarteret et al. 2020. "Severe Acute Respiratory Syndrome Coronavirus 2 (SARS-CoV-2)-Related Deaths in French Long-Term Care Facilities: The 'Confinement Disease' Is Probably More Deleterious Than the Coronavirus Disease-2019 (COVID-19) Itself." *J Am Med Dir Assoc* 21 (7): 989–990. https://doi.org/10.1016/j.jamda.2020.04.023

Dichter, M., M. Sander, S. Seismann-Petersen, and S. Köpke. 2020. "COVID-19: It Is Time to Balance Infection Management and Person-Centered Care to Maintain Mental Health of People Living in German Nursing Homes." *International Psychogeriatrics* 32 (10): 1157–1160. https://doi.org/10.1017/S1041610220000897.

Egli, S., K. Bishop, E. M. Belser, and J. Künzli. 2022. “Grund- und Menschenrechte als Leitlinien für die Bekämpfung von Pandemien.” In *Menschenrechte in der Schweiz stärken: Neue Ideen für die Politik und Praxis*, edited by Schweizer Kompetenzzentrum für Menschenrechte. buch & netz. https://www.skmr.ch/cms/upload/pdf/2022/220816_Menschenrechte_in_der_Schweiz_staerken.pdf.

Engle, E. 2013. “The General Principle of Proportionality and Aristotle.” In *Aristotle and the Philosophy of Law: Theory, Practice, and Justice*, edited by Liesbeth Huppes-Cluysenaer and Nuno Coelho. Springer. https://doi.org/10.1007/978-94-007-6031-8_15.

Federal Office of Public Health. 2020a. “COVID-19: Informationen und Empfehlungen für Institutionen wie Alters- und Pflegeheime sowie Einrichtungen für Menschen mit Behinderungen Stand,” April 2. https://www.infodrog.ch/files/content/schadensminderung_de/2020_covid_19/PHI_200402_Factsheet_Sozialmedizinische%20Institutionen_DE.pdf.

Federal Office of Public Health 2020b. “COVID-19: Informationen und Empfehlungen für Institutionen wie Alters- und Pflegeheime sowie Einrichtungen für Menschen mit Behinderungen,” April 29. https://www.infodrog.ch/files/content/schadensminderung_de/2020_covid_19/29_04_2020_Factsheet_Sozialmedizinische_Institutionen.pdf.

Federal Office of Public Health. 2021. “Deaths Related to COVID-19 in Switzerland and Compared with Other Countries.” https://www.bag.admin.ch/dam/bag/en/dokumente/mt/k-und-i/aktuelle-ausbrueche-pandemien/2019-nCoV/bericht-todesfaelle-februar-2021.pdf.download.pdf/Report%20on%20deaths%20in%20connection%20with%20COVID-19%20in%20Switzerland%20and%20in%20international%20comparison.pdf.

Federal Office of Public Health. 2022a. “COVID-19: Informationen und Empfehlungen für sozialmedizinische Institutionen wie Alters- und Pflegeheime,” December 9. Updated February 17, 2022. https://www.bag.admin.ch/dam/bag/de/dokumente/mt/k-und-i/aktuelle-ausbrueche-pandemien/2019-nCoV/covid-19-empfehlungen-pflegeheime.pdf.download.pdf/Factsheet_Sozialmedizinische_Institutionen.pdf.

Federal Office of Public Health. 2022b. “Empfehlungen zur Infektionsprävention und -kontrolle für sozialmedizinische Institutionen und die häusliche Pflege bei SARS-CoV-2 und Influenza,” April 1. Updated October 14, 2022. https://www.bag.admin.ch/dam/bag/de/dokumente/mt/k-und-i/aktuelle-ausbrueche-pandemien/2019-nCoV/sozialmedizinische-institutionen-haeusliche-pflege.pdf.download.pdf/Informationen%20zur%20Infektionspr%C3%A4vention%20und%20-kontrolle%20f%C3%BCr%20%20sozialmedizinische%20Institutionen%20und%20f%C3%BCr%20die%20h%C3%A4usliche%20Pflege.pdf.

Garros, D, W. Austin, and P. Dodek. 2021. “How Can I Survive This? Coping During Coronavirus Disease 2019 Pandemic.” *Chest* 159 (4): 1484–1492. https://doi.org/10.1016/j.chest.2020.11.012.

Gozdecka, D. A. 2021. “Human Rights During the Pandemic: COVID-19 and Securitisation of Health.” *Nordic Journal of Human Rights* 39 (3): 205–223. https://doi.org/10.1080/18918131.2021.1965367.

Grosser Rat des Kantons Basel-Stadt. 2020. Protokoll der 8.-11.Sitzung, Amtsjahr 2020/2021. https://grosserrat.bs.ch/media/files/ratsprotokolle/vollprotokoll_2020-04-22.pdf

Grosser Rat des Kantons Solothurn. 2020. Protokoll III. Session – 6. Sitzung – 23. Juni 2020. https://so.ch/fileadmin/internet/pd/pdf/protokolle/2020/2020_Session_III_Sitzung_6.pdf

Hall Dykgraaf S., S. Matenge, J. Desborough et al. 2021. “Protecting Nursing Homes and Long-Term Care Facilities from COVID-19: A Rapid Review of International Evidence.” *Journal of the American Medical Directors Association* 22 (10): 1969–1988. https://doi.org/10.1016/j.jamda.2021.07.027.

Hardwick, N., J. Marriott, K. Mason, and M. Steinbrecher. 2022. “Human Rights and Systemic Wrongs: National Preventive Mechanisms and the Monitoring of Care Homes for

Older People." *Journal of Human Rights Practice* 14 (1): 243–266. https://doi.org/10.1093/jhuman/huab050.

Hermerén, G. 2012. "The Principle of Proportionality Revisited: Interpretations and Applications." *Medicine, Health Care, and Philosophy* 15 (4): 373–382. https://doi.org/10.1007/s11019-011-9360-x.

Hughes, R. G. 2008. "Nurses at the 'Sharp End' of Patient Care." In *Patient Safety and Quality: An Evidence-Based Handbook for Nurses*, edited by Ronda G. Hughes. Agency for Healthcare Research and Quality. https://pubmed.ncbi.nlm.nih.gov/21328771/.

INFRAS. 2021. "Corona-Krise: Analyse der Situation von älteren Menschen und von Menschen in Institutionen. Studie im Auftrag des Bundesamts für Gesundheit," July 16. https://www.infras.ch/media/filer_public/53/88/538895f9-beb3-40f2-9163-5516245e7d9b/corona_altere_menschen_schlussbericht_fin_210716.pdf.

Kemp, C. L. 2021. "#MoreThanAVisitor: Families as 'Essential' Care Partners During COVID-19." *The Gerontologist* 61 (2): 145–151. https://doi.org/10.1093/geront/gnaa161.

Krones, T., G. Meyer, and S. Monteverde. 2020. "Medicine Is a Social Science: COVID-19 and the Tragedy of Residential Care Facilities in High-Income Countries." *BMJ Global Health* 5 (8): e003172. http://dx.doi.org/10.1136/bmjgh-2020-003172.

Luterán, M. 2014. "The Lost Meaning of Proportionality." In *Proportionality and the Rule of Law: Rights, Justification, Reasoning*, edited by Grant Huscroft, Bradley W. Miller, and Grégoire Webber. Cambridge University Press. https://doi.org/10.1017/CBO9781107565272.004.

März, J. W., C. Mouton-Dorey, T. Manríquez Roa, and N. Biller-Andorno. 2022. "Proportionality and Evidence-Based Pandemic Management." *Swiss Medical Weekly* 152 (2526): w30208. https://doi.org/10.4414/smw.2022.w30208.

McDonald, T. 2022. "Lethal Ageism in the Shadow of Pandemic Response Tactics." *International Nursing Review* 69:249–254. https://doi.org/10.1111/inr.12700.

Moerenhout, T. 2020. "The Problem in Nursing Homes Is Not COVID-19—It Is Nursing Homes" (blog). *Journal of Medical Ethics*, September 11. https://blogs.bmj.com/medical-ethics/2020/09/11/the-problem-in-nursing-homes-is-not-covid-19-it-is-nursing-homes/.

Monteverde, S. 2022a. "Dying in Place: COVID-19, Pflegeheime und moralische Geografien des Sterbens." In *Kontext Sterben: Institutionen–Strukturen–Beteiligte*, edited by Corina Caduff, Minou Afzali, Francis Müller, and Eva Soom Ammann. Scheidegger & Spiess. http://dx.doi.org/10.53788/CAST0107.

Monteverde, S. 2022b. "Who Is Essential in Care? Reflections from the Pandemic's Backstage." *Nursing Ethics* 29 (5): 1096–1106. http://dx.doi.org/10.1177/09697330221113061.

National Advisory Commission on Biomedical Ethics. 2020. "Schutz der Persönlichkeit in Institutionen der Langzeitpflege." Position Paper 34/20. https://www.nek-cne.admin.ch/inhalte/Themen/Stellungnahmen/NEK_Stellungnahme_Schutz_der_Persoenlichkeit_in_Institutionen_der_Langzeitpflege_-_final.pdf.

Nawrot, O., J. Nawrot, and V. Vachev. 2022. "The Right to Healthcare During the COVID-19 Pandemic Under the European Convention on Human Rights." *The International Journal of Human Rights* 27 (5): 789–808. https://doi.org/10.1080/13642987.2022.2027760.

Nuffield Council on Bioethics. 2022. "Ethics Tools for Decision-Makers Responding to Public Health Threats." Policy briefing, May 17. https://www.nuffieldbioethics.org/publications/ethics-tools-for-decision-makers-responding-to-public-health-threats.

Ó Néill, C. 2022. "'This Is No Country for Old (Wo)men'? An Examination of the Approach Taken to Care Home Residents During the COVID-19 Pandemic." *Medical Law Review* 31 (1): 24–46. https://doi.org/10.1093/medlaw/fwac023.

Petrik, A. 2021. "Schutzpflichten der Dienstleistungserbringer." *Pflegerecht* 1:40–44. https://pflegerecht.recht.ch/de/artikel/04pf0121for/schutzpflichten-der-dienstleistungserbringer.

Rada, A. G. 2020. "COVID-19: The Precarious Position of Spain's Nursing Homes." *British Medical Journal* 369:m155. https://doi.org/10.1136/bmj.m155.

Rixen, S. 2021. "Einschränkungen von Grundrechten im Namen von Public Health. Grundrechte als Regulative verhältnismässiger Pandemie-Bewältigung." In *Pandemien und Ethik*, edited by Andreas Reis, Martina Schmidhuber, and Andreas Frewer. Springer. https://doi.org/10.1007/978-3-662-63530-8_4.

Sachs, J. D., S. S. A. Karim, L. Aknin et al. 2022. "The Lancet Commission on Lessons for the Future from the COVID-19 Pandemic." *The Lancet* 400 (10359): P1224–1280. https://doi.org/10.1016/S0140-6736(22)01585-9.

Schorb, F., and H Schmidt-Semisch. 2021. "Ausgangssperren, Bussgelder und Immunitätsausweise: Umrisse einer Punitivität im Kontext der COVID-19-Pandemie." In *Public Health / Sozialwissenschaftliche Gesundheitsforschung*, edited by Henning Schmidt-Semisch and Friedrich Schorb. Springer VS. https://doi.org/10.1007/978-3-658-30377-8_29.

Steele L., K. Swaffer, R. Carr et al. 2020. "Ending Confinement and Segregation: Barriers to Realizing Human Rights in the Everyday Lives of People Living with Dementia in Residential Aged Care." *Australian Journal of Human Rights* 26 (2): 308–328. https://doi.org/10.1080/1323238X.2020.1773671.

Szczerbińska, K. 2020. "Could We Have Done Better with COVID-19 in Nursing Homes?" *European Geriatric Medicine* 11:639–643. https://doi.org/10.1007/s41999-020-00362-7.

Ten Have H. 2022. *The Covid-19 Pandemic and Global Bioethics*. Springer. DOI: 10.1007/978-3-030-91491-2.

National COVID-19 Science Task Force. 2021. "Protecting Older Persons in Long-Term Care in the Context of the SARS-CoV-2 Pandemic While Maintaining Quality of Life." https://sciencetaskforce.ch/wp-content/uploads/2021/01/Protecting_older_persons_in_long-term_care22Jan21-EN.pdf.

Verbeek, H., D. Gerritsen, R. Backhaus et al. 2020. "Allowing Visitors Back in the Nursing Home During the COVID-19 Crisis: A Dutch National Study into First Experiences and Impact on Well-Being." *Journal of the American Medical Directors Association* 21 (7): 900–904. https://doi.org/10.1016/j.jamda.2020.06.020.

Weinrib, E. 2012. *The Idea of Private Law*. Oxford Academic. Revised edition. https://doi.org/10.1093/acprof:oso/9780199665815.003.0003.

Zimmermann, H. P. 2021. "Alters- und Pflegeheime in der Pandemie." In *Alters- und Pflegeheime in der Pandemie. Leben mit Besuchs- und Ausgangsbeschränkungen*, edited by Harm-Peer Zimmermann. Vol. 12. Institut für Sozialanthropologie und Empirische Kulturwissenschaft.

12

Mobile Vaccination Teams in Long-Term Care Homes for the Elderly in Germany During the COVID-19 Pandemic

Jonathan Hunger and Eva Kuhn

With the approval of the first COVID-19 vaccine in late December 2020, municipalities, associations of statutory health insurance physicians (*Kassenärztliche Vereinigungen*), the German Armed Forces, fire brigades, and others, assembled mobile vaccination teams. The teams' primary task was to conduct field vaccinations in long-term care homes for elderly people and people with disabilities. According to the media, the approval was "as significant as the moon landing" (Simmank 2020, our translation). Public health intervention plans were woven together hurriedly and generated significant workforce demand. Medical doctors trained in public health were a particularly scarce resource. Hence, especially early on, the mobile teams were constituted pragmatically according to who was available. The teams were made up of people with heterogeneous levels of medical qualification; with some team members even having no previous medical qualification at all. Thus, as in one instance, medical students, nurses, and volunteers from civilian relief agencies might find themselves working alongside the IT systems administrator of a bank, a member of the rescue dog unit, and a physics researcher (ASB Karlsruhe 2021), each bringing highly diverse previous experience in interprofessional collaboration.

The public excitement about the vaccination approval was also perceptible within the mobile teams. They were highly motivated to fulfill their mission: the efficient distribution of the vaccine.[1] The medical staff especially considered the assignment to be very meaningful and felt that they had a share in quickly ending the pandemic (Hunger and Schumann 2020). This feeling was reinforced by politicians publicly claiming that the vaccinated citizens "are a small first step toward end of the pandemic" (Schreiner 2021, our translation).

[1] For example, one person, on training to become a paramedic, said, "What is happening here right now is modern history! I am very pleased that we are helping people who are particularly vulnerable to the virus take a step toward normality" (Malteser Baden-Württemberg 2021, our translation).

Jonathan Hunger and Eva Kuhn, *Mobile Vaccination Teams in Long-Term Care Homes for the Elderly in Germany During the COVID-19 Pandemic.* In: *Proportionality.* Edited by: Nikola Biller-Andorno et al., Oxford University Press. DOI: 10.1093/9780197759370.003.0013

The (Lack of) Evidence—Methodological Considerations

Empirical data on the mobile teams' actions in German nursing homes is nonexistent. To our best knowledge, only two publications that can be classified as scholarly literature touch upon the topic.[2] Meyer et al. (2022) mention mobile teams as one pillar of the COVID-19 vaccination campaign but do not go beyond a superficial description of the teams' operations. Arend (2022) traces the course of the pandemic by providing insights into the nonprofit organization Kuratorium Wohnen im Alter gAG (KWA). He only mentions mobile teams in the context of administrative hurdles. As mobile teams were not organized centrally, no statement can be made regarding the number of teams deployed, their mode of vaccination (who vaccinated whom where—in the residents' rooms or in a treatment room—and with what kind of vaccine), and so on. Hence, as hardly anything is known about the actual mode of operation of the mobile teams and the residents' perception of and reaction to the intervention, this case study draws on other sources of information. These sources are mainly media coverage and government messages from the period when the mobile teams were active. All sources utilized for this chapter are listed in this chapter's appendix. Their content largely matches the firsthand experiences of the first author and his colleagues who worked inside the mobile teams. Some observations included in the following discussion are not backed up by third-party reporting and are only based on the first author's and his colleagues' experiences. The written sources available did not capture the full breadth of the teams' operations. For full disclosure, the respective information is labeled explicitly as firsthand experiences.

The Issue—Mobile Vaccination Teams in Long-Term Care Homes

Within five days (December 27–31, 2020), 206,000 individuals were vaccinated (German Federal Ministry of Health [BMG] 2022a). To achieve this, the mobile teams worked in shifts (e.g., from 6:00 a.m. to 11:00 p.m.), according to firsthand experiences. The long-term care homes in a specific region reported their vaccination readiness to an established central coordination point (e.g., at the association of statutory health insurance physicians). One of the few pieces of information in scholarly literature about the mobile teams describes their operations as follows:

[2] As of January 2024.

> The mobile vaccination teams formed themselves on a self-organized basis from the local medical practices that cater to the nursing homes following a call from the KVWL [Association of Statutory Health Insurance Physicians Westphalia-Lippe]. The teams reported the exact number of vaccinations carried out to the RKI [Robert Koch Institute] on a daily basis and via a shortened nationwide standardized route using a KBV [National Association of Statutory Health Insurance Physicians] reporting portal. The KVWL was responsible for billing the vaccinations carried out. After the vaccination centers were launched, the mobile teams were administratively linked to the vaccination center and their coordination units for the purposes of ordering the vaccine, documentation, and personnel and deployment planning. Until the final closure of the vaccination centers, outreach vaccination offers were documented in 3,078 facilities. (Meyer et al. 2022, 1268, our translation)

In total, 755,300 vaccinations were administered by mobile teams. However, the data provided is not disaggregated by operation site (nursing homes for the elderly, homes for persons with disabilities, refugee homes, etc.).

In most cases, the care homes were instructed to seek their residents' consent for vaccination prior to the arrival of the mobile team and to report the *exact* number of vaccines needed. As this happened on short notice, during the Christmas season and end of the year, it must be assumed retrospectively that obtaining informed consent did not always follow established standards. The level of involvement of the elderly population's general practitioners (e.g., providing help in decision-making, addressing aftercare when needed, attending to any specificity in the resident's medical history, and building trust towards the mobile team) remains unclear.[3] It is also unclear whether consent was sought from each resident individually and whether residents' proxies or legal guardians were duly informed. Media outlets, however, reported that care homes obtained blanket consent statements (*pauschale Einwilligungserklärungen*) from their residents (ZDF 2020). Arend (2022, 200) points out that "the fact that the residential home areas of the KWA facilities—except for Hessen—are considered a form of assisted living and were therefore initially excluded from vaccination by the mobile vaccination teams in some regions posed a major problem. Similar to the start of testing, follow-up with the relevant authorities was necessary in order to avoid placing an additional burden on residents and staff. It would have been impossible to organize external vaccination appointments for all residents in the

[3] As the concept of *resident physicians* (i.e., only one physician being in charge of a long-term care home) is not yet well established in Germany, each resident living in the nursing home stays with the general practitioner they had before moving in. This makes it very unlikely that all general practitioners were fully involved in the campaign.

residential home areas within a reasonable time frame and to arrange or support travel to the vaccination centers."

Firsthand experience during a vaccination day indicated that the mobile team had to follow an extremely strict schedule, as the vials required complex logistics, including traveling through an uninterrupted cooling chain to the appropriate processing at the point of care. According to the care home's prior notice, a precise number of injections was prepared. For vaccination, residents were either "visited" in their room or they went through certain stations. For example, stations might be set up to inquire about the resident's current health condition, take their temperature, and inject the vaccine. Because of time constraints, aftercare was not always provided by the team itself.

Firsthand experience has also shown that residents who were capable of understanding the purpose of the mobile team and their mission were generally relieved, as vaccination implied the end of strict isolation. In contrast, residents with cognitive impairments experienced the team, their way of operating, and their appearance in personal protective equipment from head to toe as a renewed threat (see also Hampton et al. 2020). They could not make sense of the ongoing bustle and might have been reminded of the diagnostic teams that regularly had taken on-site COVID-19 swab tests and effected outbreak control measurements.

The Context—Pandemic Management in Germany with a Focus on Vaccination

Mobile vaccination teams conducting field vaccination are exceptional to the German system in many regards. First, large-scale on-site public health interventions are relatively uncommon in Germany, especially among the most vulnerable groups of people. Second, the teams were faced with high public expectations regarding the efficient distribution of the vaccine and a high level of media attention (e.g., "Corona-Impfung" 2020; Ostermeier 2020). Third, as interprofessional working competencies and knowledge of interprofessional processes are hardly addressed in training for medical professionals in Germany (Spura et al. 2016), no real-life, approved template for the multiprofessional mobile vaccination teams existed.

Mobile teams were formally introduced as potential service providers in the Coronavirus Vaccination Regulation (Verordnung zum Anspruch auf Schutzimpfung gegen das Coronavirus SARS-CoV-2 [CoronaImpfV] of December 18, 2020). This legally binding regulation governed the prioritization and provision of the COVID-19 vaccine. Accordingly, residents in long-term care homes for the elderly were among those with highest priority (§ 2 CoronaImpfV). Likewise, regulations specified certain responsibilities of the mobile vaccination teams—for example, to perform short medical assessments of the residents beforehand, to provide them sufficient information about the vaccination, to advise them on preventive measures after the vaccination, and to verify their legal eligibility for vaccination (§§ 1 III, 6 IV CoronaImpfV). The regulations were of a very general and merely legal nature, partly enacted past reality (see Arend's example of assisted living). Hence, each mobile team (or at least organization unit) had to develop its own way of operating and putting the Coronavirus Vaccination Regulation into practice. Efforts were further hampered by the teams' professional composition. Most teams almost exclusively consisted of physicians, nurses, paramedics, medical assistants, and laypersons (i.e., professionals without any kind of medical or public health training). Yet the workflow of the vaccination campaign was organized by local health authorities; public health professionals were rarely present or involved in any practical sense during the implementation on-site. Thus, the mobile teams were also responsible for the on-site vaccination surveillance—namely, reporting to the RKI as the federal institute for disease control and prevention (§ 7 CoronaImpfV). The teams carried out both vaccinations that were necessary for basic immunization in 2020–2021, although it was very likely that for any given resident the same team was not responsible for both vaccinations.

Before the onset of the vaccination campaign, residents in long-term care homes faced a variety of pervasive restrictions such as visiting bans, curfews, and the reduction of physical contact (Gangnus et al. 2022; for the consequences of social isolation in the United States, see, e.g., Abbasi 2020). Nonetheless, care homes for the elderly were one of the hotspots of the pandemic in Germany. Within the first wave (spring 2020), around one-third of deaths that had happened in relation to a SARS-CoV-2 infection could be traced back to elderly care home residents. Of the deaths in these residencies, 71% were related to COVID-19 (Dullin and Hartwig 2021).

The Assessment—Proportionality of the Actual Pandemic Measure

Public Health Benefits

The prioritization of the elderly was based on the rational of providing "adequate and equitable immunization services to those exposed to biological and social risk factors that could worsen health outcomes" (Vigezzi and Odone 2022, e126)—namely, a more severe course of the disease with a high likelihood of hospital admissions and excess mortality. The public health benefits have been considered to be even more significant. The line of argumentation for the SARS-CoV-2 vaccine was comparable to arguments for other vaccines. First, high vaccination coverage results in lower mortality rates as a result of background immunity. This means that the vaccination trains the immune system to prepare for future mutations of SARS-CoV-2. This in turn also lowers the risk that there will be more lethal mutations. Second, politicians and public health experts argued at the start of the pandemic that high vaccination coverage also leads to herd immunity against COVID-19 and thus end the pandemic. This entails the indirect protection of people who are not vaccinated by preventing a disease from spreading (Bundesregierung 2020).[4] As the BMG (2022b, our translation) explained, "the more people who are vaccinated, the better protected will be those who cannot be vaccinated." The BMG had repeated this appeal regularly since the beginning of the pandemic and called upon the people's solidarity. With the implementation of mobile vaccination teams and a highly standardized vaccination procedure, the public health benefits could be achieved relatively quickly. Moreover, it was ensured that the care home residents would receive both vaccinations necessary for basic immunization. However, in the cases of residents who were hospitalized or currently infected, administering an individual vaccination was complicated to organize.

General Moral Considerations

Generally speaking, a public health campaign should take several moral principles into consideration.[5] The following list of principles and also the considerations outlined are by no means exhaustive. They particularly draw upon the seminal work by Childress et al. (2002), "Public Health Ethics: Mapping the Terrain," and a normative framework offered specifically for vaccination ethics by Schröder-Bäck and Martakis (2019). The latter pays special attention to the German context and interlaces public health considerations with individual ethics argumentation. The principles listed do not follow any hierarchical order but are mentioned in the order of appearance in these reflections:

[4] Whether herd immunity for COVID-19 is realistic or not has been subject of an ongoing scientific and public health debate since mid-2021. As the case study predates this discussion, the state of knowledge and communication at that time is central in the present contribution.

[5] Together with coauthors, the two authors of this chapter outlined the general concerns in a policy brief titled *Mobile SARS-CoV-2 Vaccination Teams in Long-Term Care Homes* that was issued at the start of the vaccination campaign (January 8, 2021). The present case study partly adopts the policy brief's structure so that interested readers can compare the anticipated moral considerations with the situation that had actually arisen in the care homes. For the policy brief, see Hunger et al. (2021).

- population benefit (background immunity and herd immunity)
- protection of privacy and confidentiality (Childress et al. 2002)
- development and maintenance of public trust (Childress et al. 2002)
- avoidance, prevention, and removal of harms (Childress et al. 2002)
- beneficence and nonmaleficence (Schröder-Bäck and Martakis 2019)
- respect for (individual) autonomy (Schröder-Bäck and Martakis 2019)
- duty of simple rescue (Schröder-Bäck and Martakis 2019)
- distributive justice (i.e., the fair distribution of burdens and benefits and the fair allocation of resources) (Schröder-Bäck et al. 2020; Childress et al. 2002)
- procedural justice (i.e., involvement of those that are or will be affected by the policy) (Childress et al. 2002)
- transparency (Childress et al. 2002)

Privacy, Development, and Maintenance of Public Trust

"Unlike a hospital, a nursing home is someone's home." Although Barnett and Grabowski (2020) have raised this obvious but often neglected point regarding challenges concerning quarantine and the comparably easy spread of the virus in long-term care homes, this observation is generalizable for living conditions in eldercare homes. In cases in which the mobile team entered the residents' rooms or, at least, living areas without any advance notice and introduction, their privacy was infringed. Regardless of the exact location where the vaccination took place (in the resident's room or in a treatment room dedicated to medical procedures), the fact that team members appeared suddenly to carry out an invasive medical procedure might have also impeded the development or maintenance of public trust in the healthcare workforce and the healthcare system. This would particularly apply to situations in which the members of the mobile team were complete strangers to the residents and were not accompanied by someone familiar (e.g., the resident's general practitioner or a nurse working in the care home). Then again, another reaction might have been that the residents' trust in health policy and healthcare was (re)established because they were given top priority for vaccination, as the vaccine was normally followed by the easing of restrictions, such as curfews.

Avoidance, Prevention, and Removal of Harms—Predominantly Addressing Public Health Agents

The vaccination led to a removal of ongoing harms—namely, nonpharmaceutical interventions such as visit bans and reductions of physical contact. Mandated for an already vulnerable population and kept up for several months, these interventions transformed social isolation and loneliness from individual concerns into public health risks (Simard and Volicer 2020). Even though it cannot be quantified, the vaccination campaign may have prevented harm from isolation and severe loneliness (e.g., the risk of alcoholism and depression). Similar harm reduction was seen in the direct effect of the vaccination: the prevention of a severe course of illness or even death from COVID-19. It was shown that the hospitalization incidence was higher for the unvaccinated population in all age groups and at all periods throughout the course of the pandemic (RKI 2022). On this basis and at a later stage in the pandemic, long after the mobile teams had been deployed, vaccination campaigns were also justified by their ability to relieve the burden on the healthcare system.[6]

Beneficence and Nonmaleficence—Predominantly Addressing the Mobile Team Members

Closely linked to considerations of harms are the normative aspects of beneficence and nonmaleficence that are put forward to those carrying out a public health measure—in this case, vaccination (Schröder-Bäck and Martakis 2019). Many residents considered the vaccination a relief; the vaccination campaign preserved the residents' health and was a stepping stone toward restoring overall public health. All of this can be considered a fulfillment of the principle of beneficence. However, residents without the cognitive capacity to understand the situation and procedure (e.g., with advanced dementia) might have experienced the presence of the mobile teams as intimidating and a threat. The staff's impaired nonverbal and verbal communication because of the use of personal protective equipment may even have worsened the situation. In cases in which the resident, as the addressee of the nonmaleficence, became agitated or stressed in another manner, the beneficence of the vaccination (i.e., immunization) and nonmaleficence (i.e., avoiding further distress about an experience perceived as potentially traumatizing) should have been weighed for each individual case to comply with professional ethical standards. However, the strict timing of the process and the focus of the parties involved (particularly the resident's caregivers and proxies) on the potential benefits of the vaccine often led to overriding such signals from cognitively impaired residents. If the vaccine was even administered using coercion (e.g., by holding the person down with the help of several team members), further harm was done (for the effect on the respect for autonomy, see the next section).

While this interference with a person's physical and psychosocial integrity should not be taken lightly, the intervention often prevented the individuals

[6] In autumn 2021 particularly, the overload of German intensive care units (ICUs) was discussed publicly (e.g., NDR Info 2021), and public health considerations (i.e., the proper functioning of the healthcare system) gained the upper hand over the individual's risk of being admitted to the hospital or ICU.

from other harms in the middle and long run—namely, ongoing isolation for an uncertain period of time.[7]

Respect for (Individual) Autonomy

The case of residents with cognitive impairments already highlights that the operation of the mobile teams was often quite paternalistic. This could be observed at several points of the intervention.

First, in cases in which the resident's proxy was not present on vaccination day and had consented beforehand on behalf of a resident who was unable to give written consent themselves, this consent was usually taken for granted, and no in-person informed consent was obtained on-site at that moment. Conflicts between prior consent and later refusal (verbally or presumed) were often resolved in favor of the immunization. Second, it must be questioned whether the proxies always decided based on what the residents themselves would have decided had they been capable of doing so or whether proxies were guided by the overall excitement of the vaccination approval and their awareness that access to the vaccination outside the program was difficult. Similar questions must be raised for residents who were capable of consenting for themselves: Truly voluntary consent might have been impeded by this same knowledge, their caregivers' expectations, or the intimidating presence of the mobile team. Third, it remains unclear what kind of information the residents and their proxies received about the vaccination beforehand. In cases of blanket consent statements or when only the information leaflet issued by RKI (2020) was distributed without further explanations from the residents' general practitioners or responsible persons from the nursing home, it is questionable whether the resident had an adequate understanding of the prioritized vaccination, its implications, and its contraindications.

Consequently, there were many occasions when even the minimum that is required for informed consent (i.e., ensuring proper information and understanding in addition to voluntariness) was not met.

Distributive and Procedural Justice, Duty of Simple Rescue, and Transparency

Distributive and procedural justice considerations were at the forefront of the public and political debate on vaccination prioritization. However, beyond the lack of the elderly's (and, in general, society's) participation in the decisions

[7] There was no guideline on how to proceed with those residents who rejected the vaccination or could not be vaccinated for any reason. Given the highly uncertain situation and past devastating experiences with SARS-CoV-2 outbreaks in long-term care homes, it was decided mainly to continue isolating unvaccinated residents. Hence, they faced ongoing measures depriving them of their freedom of movement while their vaccinated coresidents could enjoy joint activities and the like again.

about prioritizing, the strict rules of prioritization did not leave any room for legally safeguarded flexibility on-site.

As it was standard operating procedure for the teams to bring a precise, pre-announced number of injections to the long-term care home, it could happen that there were not enough vials for everyone or that vaccine doses were left over. In the latter case, the teams vaccinated other persons (e.g., family members of a resident or cleaning staff) who were much further down the prioritization list. It remains unclear whether the teams carried out ad hoc prioritizations (see Hunger et al. 2021) or vaccinated whoever was available. At times it also happened that vaccine doses were discarded. No backup was provided for residents who missed the first and/or second vaccination day (e.g., because of a hospital stay or a temporary contraindication such as an infection). They (or, in many cases, their proxies) had to organize a vaccination appointment elsewhere. As vials were scarce at the beginning of the campaign, mainly distributed to mobile teams and rationed in advance, this endeavor was very time-consuming. Hence, the way the teams operated could not always guarantee a fair distribution of benefits and burdens nor a continually fair and transparent allocation of the vaccine.

On a superordinate level that concerns the population being vaccinated, arguments about the fair distribution of costs and benefits can be taken even further. Giubilini et al. (2018, 554) elaborate upon the moral obligation of being vaccinated with reference to the duty of simple or easy rescue:

> If a collective could realise herd immunity, then this collective ought to realise herd immunity, provided that the collective cost is small and can [be] distributed in such a way that the cost borne by each individual is also small (so that the collective cost is small under any plausible understanding of 'collective' and that the collective duty is consistent with an individual duty of easy rescue).

Regarding the present case study, the collective could be considered society as a whole or the residents of a distinct care home as a group. For those residents who did not have any medical contraindications, benefits usually outweighed the burdens. On this basis and if the line of argumentation by Giubilini and colleagues is followed, the collective duty of simple rescue implies that elderly individuals without contraindications had the moral obligation to be vaccinated. However, it remains up to further debate whether this duty can justify the compulsory and, hence, unconsented, vaccination of a vulnerable group of people (Giubilini 2019; Douglas et al. 2021; März et al. 2021).

The Exploration—Some Thoughts on Proportionality

This assessment has revealed several moral principles that were infringed upon or even completely overridden by the operation of mobile vaccination teams in long-term care homes for the elderly in the year 2021. The following thoughts do not question the proportionality of the COVID-19 vaccination as such. They also do not make any statements about the idea of deploying mobile teams as such. Instead, their focus is solely on the actual planning of the field vaccination and its actual on-site implementation during the COVID-19 pandemic. Moreover, considerations are restricted to the field of ethics; widening them to legal questions and, for example, applying the principle of proportionality (*Verhältnismäßigkeitsgrundsatz*) as elaborated by the German Federal Constitutional Court to the mobile teams' operations would go beyond the scope of this case study (for an overview of the legal facets, see Lang 2020).

Most of the considerations outlined in this chapter concern questions of autonomy, to which the principle of privacy and the issues raised around nonmaleficence can be traced to a great extent. Given that vaccinating someone is more invasive than the regular COVID-19 testing that most residents experienced at least weekly, the infringement upon or breach of respect of autonomy is even more significant. Hence, the question arises as to whether the benefits of the field vaccination outweighed the costs and whether the means and ends were proportionate (for a general understanding of proportionality, see Childress et al. 2002; Hermerén 2012).

However, answering this question with a mere "yes" or "no" would miss the point. Additionally, merely referring to a (very broadly conceived) duty of simple rescue or a general justification of the actual implementation and (manner of) the mobile teams' operation with reference to "pandemic exceptionalism" would abridge the underlying question of the measure's overall proportionality. Instead of resolving the conflict in one direction or another, we propose a grid for weighing the particularities of each case in relation to the means used to achieve the overall end of high vaccination coverage and restoration or maintenance of public health (Figure 12.1).

Figure 12.2 illustrates how the grid can be applied in the case of a resident with chronic obstructive pulmonary disease (COPD) and cognitive impairment who was coerced into being vaccinated in their own room without prior notice being given to their legal guardian.

Given the circumstances of vaccination in the resident's own room through coercion and without the prior notification of their legal guardian, the moral norms of privacy, respect for autonomy and nonmaleficence are highly

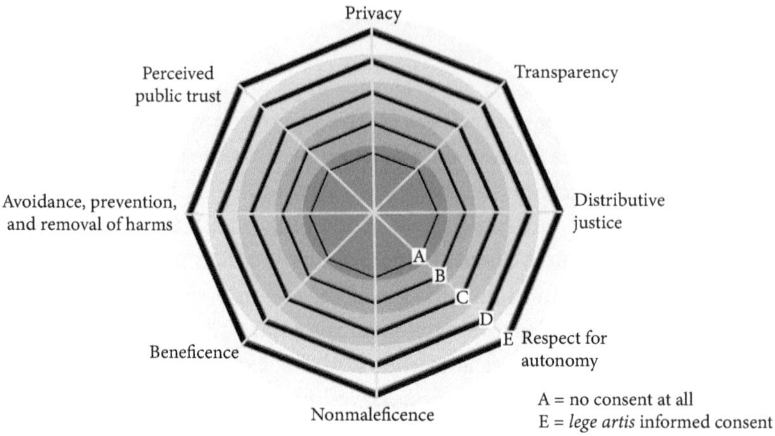

Fig. 12.1 Moral principles and their relation in assessing proportionality

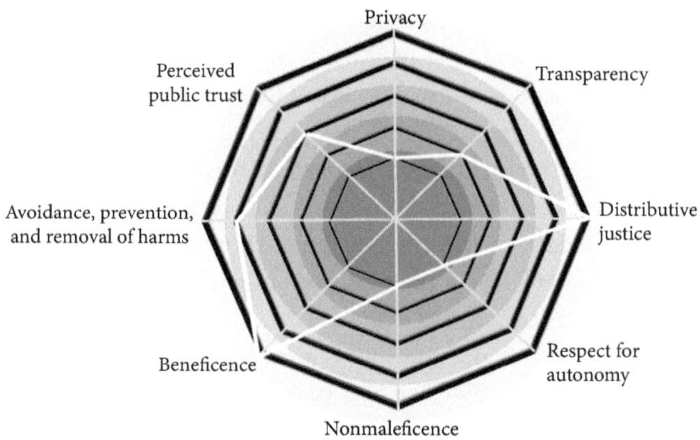

Fig. 12.2 Case example for application of the grid.

infringed. This must be weighed against the high benefit the vaccine had for a person suffering from COPD, including the avoidance of further harms and the removal of nonpharmacological interventions such as curfews that the resident might have perceived as physically and socially restricting.

Although such a grid is, by its very nature, as schematic as a list of acceptable infringements that takes into consideration the public health benefit, it shows the relatedness of and dynamic interplay between infringements. It also illustrates that infringements can occur and be acceptable in terms of the end that shall be achieved (i.e., not every infringement leads to a measure being unproportionate). Moreover, the grid emphasizes that there is no clear line between infringement and noninfringement. It can only assist in the evaluation of a certain measure in a certain moment and situation. But still, the practicability of such a grid—for example, to help mobile team members reflect on their deployment or decide in cases of dilemma—must yet be investigated.

Given the lack of empirical evidence for the COVID-19 pandemic as a public health emergency, a general assessment of past actions or even of the overall implementation of mobile vaccination teams in long-term care homes is impossible. Thus, this chapter attempts to highlight the valuable contribution of field experience to the academic discourse. At the same time, it calls upon research to develop handy tools that allow for a simple collection of empirical material in future emergency situations and, subsequently, a structured analysis of lessons learned to inform practice. Nonetheless, further reappraisal and retrospective reflection on past field vaccination efforts should be undertaken. In doing so, attention should also be paid to the theoretical and practical relation between the legal and ethical principles of proportionality.

Although the multiple legal, ethical, and professional exceptions made in 2020–2021 cannot be undone, the idea of (ethical) pandemic preparedness entails that health policy, the healthcare workforce, and the other stakeholders involved learn lessons for similar future events. This also includes looking beyond what is legally permitted or prohibited in times of emergency and paying attention to the moral dimension of a regulation's practical implementation.

Acknowledgments

We are thankful for the experiences we shared with deeply motivated people who contributed to pandemic control and the patients' valuable perspectives. We also gratefully acknowledge the effort and time devoted by the reviewers to providing in-depth feedback and helping improve our manuscript.

Competing Interests

There are no competing interests to declare.

Funding

There is no funding to declare.

Appendix

Information Sources Used in the Case Study

"12 Tage mobiles Impfen gegen das Covid-19-Virus." 2021. *Malteser Baden-Württemberg*, January 8. https://www.malteser-bw.de/unsere-standorte/karlsruhe/news-detailansicht/news/12-tage-mobiles-impfen-gegen-das-covid-19-virus.html.

ASB Karlsruhe. 2021. "ASB Karlsruhe in Mobilen Impfteams (MIT) im Einsatz." https://www.asb-ka.de/news-und-specials/asb-karlsruhe-mobilen-impfteams-im-einsatz.

"Corona-Impfung: So arbeitet ein mobiles Impfteam im Altenheim." 2020. Stuttgarter Zeitung & Stuttgarter Nachrichten, YouTube, December 30. https://www.youtube.com/watch?v=sOcOs_Tw7Uo.

"Corona-Pandemie: Freiheiten für Bewohnerinnen und Bewohner der stationären Pflegeeinrichtungen kehren zurück." 2021. *Landesregierung NRW*, June 12. https://www.land.nrw/pressemitteilung/corona-pandemie-freiheiten-fuer-bewohnerinnen-und-bewohner-der-stationaeren.

Debes, M., A. Geisler, K. Polke-Majewski, and D. Reinhard. 2021. "Wo die Impfungen stocken." *Die Zeit*, January 18. https://www.zeit.de/gesellschaft/2021-01/corona-impfungen-bundeslaender-impfstrategien-impfstoff-logistik-faq.

Dietz, J. 2021. "Wie groß ist die Erleichterung nach der Impfung?" *Die Zeit*, March 13. https://www.zeit.de/gesellschaft/2021-03/pflegeheim-seniorenheim-corona-pandemie-bewohner-pflegekraefte-impfung.

Hollmann, K. 2021. *Corona-Impfung—Impfstoff, Impfzentrum, Termine*. KV Circular No. 1/2021. *ÄrzteNetz*, January 15. https://www.aerztenetz-hamburg.de/rundschreiben-der-kv-nr-1-2021-corona-impfung-impfstoff-impfzentrum-termine/.

"Impfen gegen COVID-19—Bundeswehr leistet bundesweit Amtshilfe" 2021. *Bundeswehr*, January 18. https://www.bundeswehr.de/de/meldungen/impfen-covid-19-bundeswehr-bundesweit-amtshilfe

Ostermeier, A. 2020. "Impfteams kommen ins Altenheim." *SüddeutscheZeitung*, December 22. https://www.sueddeutsche.de/muenchen/fuerstenfeldbruck/coronakrise-impfteams-kommen-ins-altenheim-1.5156021.

Ruddat, M. 2021. "Nicht nur ein Pieks." *Taz*, January 11. https://taz.de/Impfstart-im-Seniorenheim/!5738803/.

Schnack, D. 2021. "Über 100 Corona-Impfungen am Tag—unterwegs mit 'Team Lübeck eins.'" *ÄrzteZeitung*, January 19. https://www.aerztezeitung.de/Politik/Ueber-100-Corona-Impfungen-am-Tag-unterwegs-mit-Team-Lueb eck-eins-416341.html.

Schreiner, E. 2021. "Mobile Teams impfen 1562 Personen in Pflegeheimen." https://corona.lkgi.de/presse/mobile-teams-impfen-1562-personen-in-pflegeheimen/.

ZDF. 2020. "Corona-Impfungen in Pflegeheimen: Patientenschützer warnen." https://www.zdf.de/uri/d5ea91b3-bd87-410e-b694-9b5a845e66b1.

References

"12 Tage mobiles Impfen gegen das Covid-19-Virus." 2021. *Malteser Baden-Württemberg*, January 8. https://www.malteser-bw.de/unsere-standorte/karlsruhe/news-detailansicht/news/12-tage-mobiles-impfen-gegen-das-covid-19-virus.html.

Abbasi, J. 2020. "Social Isolation—the Other COVID-19 Threat in Nursing Homes." *JAMA* 324 (7): 619–620. https://doi.org/10.1001/jama.2020.13484.

Arend, S. 2022. "Alles auf Anfang? Die deutsche Langzeitpflege in Zeiten von Corona—Erfahrungen und Perspektiven." In *Pflege in Zeiten der Pandemie: Wie sich Pflege durch Corona verändert hat*, edited by G. Bonacker and G. Geiger. Verlag Barbara Budrich.

ASB Karlsruhe. 2021. "ASB Karlsruhe in Mobilen Impfteams (MIT) im Einsatz." https://www.asb-ka.de/news-und-specials/asb-karlsruhe-mobilen-impfteams-im-einsatz.

Barnett, M. L., and D. C. Grabowski. 2020. "Nursing Homes Are Ground Zero for COVID-19 Pandemic." *JAMA Health Forum* 1 (3): e200369. https://doi.org/10.1001/jamahealthforum.2020.0369.

BMG (German Federal Ministry of Health). 2022a. "Das offizielle Dashboard zur Impfkampagne der Bundesrepublik Deutschland." https://impfdashboard.de/.

BMG. 2022b. "Gemeinschaftsschutz: Warum Solidarität in der Coronavirus-Pandemie so wichtig ist." https://www.zusammengegencorona.de/impfen/gemeinschaftsschutz-solidaritaet-in-der-coronavirus-pandemie/.

Bundesregierung. 2020. "Impfstoff-Förderung angelaufen." https://www.bundesregierung.de/breg-de/themen/forschung/corona-impfstoff-1787044.

Childress, J. F., R. R. Faden, R. D. Gaare et al. 2002. "Public Health Ethics: Mapping the Terrain." *Journal of Law, Medicine & Ethics* 30 (2): 170–178. https://doi.org/10.1111/j.1748-720X.2002.tb00384.x.

"Corona-Impfung: So arbeitet ein mobiles Impfteam im Altenheim." 2020. Stuttgarter Zeitung & Stuttgarter Nachrichten, YouTube, December 30. https://www.youtube.com/watch?v=sOcOs_Tw7Uo.

Douglas, T., L. Forsberg, and J. Pugh. 2021. "Compulsory Medical Intervention Versus External Constraint in Pandemic Control." *Journal of Medical Ethics* 47 (12): e77–e77. https://doi.org/10.1136/medethics-2020-106435.

Dullin, M., and S. Hartwig. 2021. "Projekt COVID-Heim. Lehren aus der Corona-Pandemie für Strukturentwicklungen im Versorgungssetting Pflegeheim. Ergebnisreport Nr. 4—Covid-19 assoziierte Todesfälle von Heimbewohner:innen im Spiegel der Rechtsmedizin." https://www.gkvspitzenverband.de/media/dokumente/pflegeversicherung/forschung/projekte_unterseiten/covid_heim/CovidHeim_ErgebnisReport4_210630.pdf.

Gangnus, A., C. Hering., R. Kohl et al. 2022. "Covid-19-Schutzmaßnahmen und Einschränkungen des sozialen Lebens in Pflegeheimen." *Pflege* 35 (3): 133–142. https://doi.org/10.1024/1012-5302/a000854.

Giubilini, A. 2019. *The Ethics of Vaccination*. Springer International. https://doi.org/10.1007/978-3-030-02068-2.

Giubilini, A., T. Douglas, and J. Savulescu. 2018. "The Moral Obligation to Be Vaccinated: Utilitarianism, Contractualism, and Collective Easy Rescue." *Medicine, Health Care and Philosophy* 21 (4): 547–560. https://doi.org/10.1007/s11019-018-9829-y.

Hampton, T., R. Crunkhorn, N. Lowe et al. 2020. "The Negative Impact of Wearing Personal Protective Equipment on Communication During Coronavirus Disease 2019." *The Journal of Laryngology and Otology* 134 (7): 1–5. https://doi.org/10.1017/S0022215120001437.

Hermerén, G. 2012. "The Principle of Proportionality Revisited: Interpretations and Applications." *Medicine, Health Care and Philosophy* 15 (4): 373–382. https://doi.org/10.1007/s11019-011-9360-x.

Hunger, J., and H. Schumann. 2020. "How to Achieve Quality Assurance, Shared Ethics and Efficient Teambuilding? Lessons Learned from Interprofessional Collaboration During the COVID-19 Pandemic." *GMS Journal for Medical Education* 37 (7). https://doi.org/10.3205/zma001372.

Hunger, J., E. Kuhn, J. Stratil et al. 2021. *Ethical Recommendations for Mobile SARS-CoV-2 Vaccination Teams in Long-Term Care Homes.* https://www.public-health-covid19.de/images/2021/Ergebnisse/Mobile_Vaccination_2021_01_08_v1.pdf.

Lang, A. 2020. "Proportionality Analysis by the German Federal Constitutional Court. " In *Proportionality in Action: Comparative and Empirical Perspectives on the Judicial Practice*, edited by M. Kremnitzer, T. Steiner, and A. Lang. Cambridge University Press.

März, J. W., S. Holm, and M. Schlander. 2021. "Resource Allocation in the Covid-19 Health Crisis: Are Covid-19 Preventive Measures Consistent with the Rule of Rescue?" *Medicine, Health Care and Philosophy* 24 (4): 487–492. https://doi.org/10.1007/s11019-021-10045-0.

Meyer, F., C. Schwenzer, and D. Spelmeyer. 2022. "Umsetzung der COVID-19-Impfkampagne: Erfahrungen und Perspektiven aus Sicht der Kassenärztlichen Vereinigung Westfalen-Lippe (KVWL)." *Bundesgesundheitsblatt—Gesundheitsforschung—Gesundheitsschutz* 65 (12): 1262–1271. https://doi.org/10.1007/s00103-022-03619-7.

NDR Info. 2021. "Coronavirus-Update Sonderfolge: Intensivmediziner im Gespräch." https://www.ndr.de/nachrichten/info/Coronavirus-Update-Sonderfolge-Intensivmediziner-im-Gespraech,podcastcoronavirus348.html.

Ostermeier, A. 2020. "Impfteams kommen ins Altenheim." *SüddeutscheZeitung*, December 22. https://www.sueddeutsche.de/muenchen/fuerstenfeldbruck/coronakrise-impfteams-kommen-ins-altenheim-1.5156021.

RKI. 2020. "Aufklärungsmerkblatt zur Schutzimpfung gegen COVID-19 (Corona Virus Disease 2019)—mit mRNA-Impfstoff." https://www.rki.de/DE/Content/Infekt/Impfen/Materialien/Downloads-COVID-19/Aufklaerungsbogen-de.pdf;jsessionid=898D537CE80C3C449DCE07E503FA4CD6.internet062?__blob=publicationFile.

RKI. 2022. "Wöchentlicher Lagebericht des RKI zur Coronavirus-Krankheit-2019 (COVID-19) vom 13.01.2022." https://www.rki.de/DE/Content/InfAZ/N/Neuartiges_Coronavirus/Situationsberichte/Wochenbericht/Wochenbericht_2022-01-13.pdf?__blob=publicationFile.

Schreiner, E. 2021. "Mobile Teams impfen 1562 Personen in Pflegeheimen." https://corona.lkgi.de/presse/mobile-teams-impfen-1562-personen-in-pflegeheimen/.

Schröder-Bäck, P., and K. Martakis. 2019. "Impfethik—eine Skizze moralischer Herausforderungen und ethischer Kriterien." *Bundesgesundheitsblatt Gesundheitsforschung—Gesundheitsschutz* 62 (4): 472–478. https://doi.org/10.1007/s00103-019-02915-z.

Schröder-Bäck P., V. Wild, J.-C. Heilinger et al. 2020. "Vaccination Policy. Ethical Perspectives on a Future Vaccination Program Against COVID-19 in Germany." Policy brief. https://www.public-health-covid19.de/images/2020/Ergebnisse/PolicyBrief_vaccination_2020_final-1.pdf.

Simard, J., and L. Volicer. 2020. "Loneliness and Isolation in Long-term Care and the COVID-19 Pandemic." *Journal of the American Medical Directors Association* 21 (7): 966–967. https://doi.org/10.1016/j.jamda.2020.05.006.

Simmank, J. 2020. "Corona-Impfstoff: So bedeutend wie die Mondlandung" *Die Zeit*, December 21. https://www.zeit.de/wissen/gesundheit/2020-12/corona-impfung-erste-zulassung-biontech-pfizer-impfstoff.

Spura A., K. Werwick, A. Feißel et al. 2016. "Preparation Courses for Medical Clerkships and the Final Clinical Internship in Medical Education—the Magdeburg Curriculum for Healthcare Competence." *GMS J Med Educ* 33 (3): Doc40. https://doi.org/10.3205/zma001039.

Vigezzi, G. P., and A. Odone. 2022. "COVID-19 Immunisation in Older People." *The Lancet Healthy Longevity* 3 (3): e126–e127. https://doi.org/10.1016/S2666-7568(22)00036-8.

ZDF. 2020. "Corona-Impfungen in Pflegeheimen: Patientenschützer warnen." https://www.zdf.de/uri/d5ea91b3-bd87-410e-b694-9b5a845e66b1.

13

Proportionality of the COVID-19 Measures

The European Court of Human Rights' Approach

Helen Keller and Viktoriya Gurash

Introduction

The COVID-19 pandemic triggered a broad range of human rights challenges and highlighted existing cracks in our societies. As Damian Barr (2020) put it so aptly, "We are not in the same boat. We are in the same storm. Some are on superyachts. Some have just the one oar." Many national debates centered on the proportionality of restrictive COVID-19 measures adopted by governments and their effects on individual autonomy on one end of the spectrum and public health and solidarity on the other (Gerards 2023b, 376). As a consequence, domestic courts were called on to determine the proportionality of the restrictions concerning constitutional and human rights (Tribunal Administratif de Strasbourg 2020; King et al. 2022; Chapter 14, this volume). This chapter's analysis will focus on the case law of the European Court of Human Rights (ECtHR or Court) and examine how its decisions and judgments could potentially guide Member States in their obligations to respect human rights in the context of the COVID-19 pandemic.

The chapter is organized as follows: After this introduction, the second section will summarize the elements of the proportionality test used by the Court and explore whether this test corresponds to the classical proportionality principle. Afterward, the chapter will emphasize the unique normative strength of human rights in relation to public interest and clarify how the ECtHR determines the breadth of the margin of appreciation granted to states and the link between this margin and the degree of the proportionality analysis used by the Court. The third section will consider how states derogating from their obligations under Article 15 of the European Convention on Human Rights (ECHR or Convention) influences the Court's evaluation of COVID-19 measures. Subsequently the chapter will provide an overview of the cases related to COVID-19 measures brought before the ECtHR and discuss the Court's deferential approach in these

Helen Keller and Viktoriya Gurash, *Proportionality of the COVID-19 Measures*. In: *Proportionality*.
Edited by: Nikola Biller-Andorno et al., Oxford University Press. © Oxford University Press (2026).
DOI: 10.1093/9780197759370.003.0014

cases when applying the proportionality analysis. The conclusion will emphasize the likelihood that COVID-19 measures are shielded from the Court's rigorous review since states were urged to take rapid measures in the face of an imminent threat to public health amid considerable scientific uncertainty.

The ECtHR's Conception of Proportionality

Formula Used by the ECtHR

Proportionality analysis is one of the ECtHR's fundamental interpretative principles in qualifying human rights. However, the Court's use of proportionality analysis is not immune to criticism, as it centers on the lack of clarity about the standards used in ECtHR case law and the fact that it is not entirely in line with the classic proportionality test (Gerards 2013, 467–468). This test consists of three stages that aim to answer different questions: (a) suitability (whether the rights-restricting measure is able to realize the measure pursued), (b) necessity (whether the measure is strictly necessary to realize the aim and whether there are less restrictive measures to accomplish the same end), and (c) balancing sensu stricto (whether the measure, relative to its objective, has disproportionate effects on the exercise of the right) (Stone et al. 2008, 98–112; Chapter 14, this volume).

As confirmed by the Court, "a search for a fair balance" between the general interest of the community and the protection of individual rights is integral to the whole of the Convention system.[1] The proportionality analysis of a state's interference with an applicant's Convention rights is instrumental in determining whether a fair balance has been achieved. The ECtHR has applied the proportionality test across the vast majority of Convention rights (Mowbray 2010, 294–308). Furthermore, the qualified structure of certain ECHR Articles—namely, Articles 8–11 and Article 1 of Protocol No. 1[2]—justifies the Court's application of the proportionality principle (Mowbray 2010, 315). The ECtHR applies a "necessary in a democratic society" formula to address whether a measure interfering with these rights fulfills a "pressing social need." In addition, the Court assesses whether the reasons presented by national authorities to

[1] *Soering v. The United Kingdom*, ECtHR, App. No. 14038/88, July 7, 1989, (89); see also *Sporrong and Lönnroth*, ECtHR, App. Nos. 7151/75–7152/75, September 23, 1982, (69).

[2] Qualified rights are rights that may be interfered with in order to protect the rights of another or the wider public interest, as opposed to unqualified rights, which cannot be balanced against the needs of other individuals or against any general public interest. They may be subject to specific exceptions (e.g., the right not to be deprived of liberty; Art. 5) or to none at all, when they are called absolute rights (e.g., freedom from torture; Art. 3). See Council of Europe. 2023a. Definitions. Accessed January 10, 2024. https://www.coe.int/en/web/echr-toolkit/definitions.

justify the measure are "relevant and sufficient" and whether it is proportionate to the legitimate objective being pursued.[3] It should be noted that, according to the Court's case law, a pressing social need is not synonymous with the measure being "indispensable," nor does it possess the flexibility of terms such as "admissible," "ordinary," "useful," "reasonable," or "desirable."[4] The pressing social need requirement expressed in the formula appears to concern the weight and importance of the objectives being pursued (Gerards 2013, 467). For all intents and purposes, determining the relevance and sufficiency of measures that restrict rights is equivalent to determining their suitability (Smet 2017, 32). The formula's proportionality requirement appears to align with the final stage of balancing sensu stricto. Nevertheless, the necessity subtest is not explicitly included in the proportionality review formula used by the ECtHR. The Court simultaneously makes use of a "less restrictive measure" test in many cases (Brems and Lavrysen 2015, 154–168).

Although classical elements of proportionality review could be read into the formula, the Court is accused of inconsistently using the formula in its judgments (Gerards 2013, 467–468). Moreover, some commentators argue that the Court has shifted away from applying an open ad hoc balancing review toward providing strongly precedent-based and analogy-driven reasoning that primarily relies on case comparison and on developing and using tests and standards (Gerards 2023b, 368). Another objection is that substantive balancing review is often augmented or even replaced by forms of procedural review (Gerards 2023b, 371).[5] This criticism underscores the Court's lack of clarity regarding the scope and intensity of its approach to proportionality review.

Special Normative Force of Human Rights

A measure should have a legitimate aim. The proportionality analysis requires the identification of interests, the assignment of values to these interests, and ultimately a determination of which interest outweighs the others in yielding a net benefit (Calí 2007, 259). When analyzing the balance of interests in a human rights context, a distinction should be made between two scenarios: (a) conflicts between human rights and a public interest and (b) a conflict between several human rights (Smet 2017, 30). Under the ECHR, human rights hold special

[3] See, e.g., *Dubská and Krejzová v. the Czech Republic* (GC), ECtHR, App. Nos. 28859/11 and 28473/12, November 15, 2016, (174).

[4] See, e.g., *The Sunday Times v. the United Kingdom (No. 1)*, ECtHR, App. No. 6538/74, April 26, 1979, (59).

[5] Procedural review means that the Court will not look into the actual substantive interests involved in a case but will only check if the infringement of a fundamental right has been accompanied by sufficient procedural safeguards at the national level (Gerards 2023b, 371).

normative force over non-rights considerations, since human rights protect the fundamental interests of individuals against the abuse of power by states or majorities within states (Smet 2017, 30). As argued by Smet (2017, 30), if human rights are not hierarchically superior to the public interest, "simple aggregation of the preferences and interests of the many will always threaten to outweigh the human rights of the few." In case of conflict with non-rights considerations, priority should be given to the protection of human rights owing to their special normative force. Accurately categorizing these conflicting values affects the strength and relevance of the reasons justifying interferences with human rights.

The Court adopts a deferential approach when assessing whether an objective is legitimate (Dzehtsiarou 2020, 369) and follows this approach when deciding public health cases. For example, in *Vavřička and Others v. the Czech Republic*,[6] it adhered to the government's arguments and the findings of the domestic courts that the vaccination requirement corresponded to the objectives of protecting public health and the rights of others. It is questionable whether *Vavřička* (310) involved a conflict between several human rights rather than situations in which human rights conflicted with a collective goal "to guard against major disruptions to society caused by serious disease." Some commentators argue that states are under more stringent obligations to protect the lives of concrete individuals in actual danger than to protect statistical and anonymous persons (Dworkin 2011, 279). There was no indication in *Vavřička* that if the vaccination of the applicants' children were not performed, this would present the likelihood of a violation of, for example, the right to life of concrete individuals. Therefore, the states' positive obligation to protect the life and health of those within their jurisdiction is not immediately relevant to the present case. Similarly, in *Dubská and Krejzová v. the Czech Republic*, the Court accepted the government's argument that the state's policy of encouraging hospital births served the legitimate aim of the protection of the rights of others, since such policy "was designed to protect the health and safety of the mother and the child during and after delivery" (*Dubská and Krejzová* [n. 3], [182]–[184]). However, the facts in Ms. Dubská's and Ms. Krejzová's cases show that no risks or complications associated with the applicants' pregnancies demanded that they should give birth in a hospital (*Dubská and Krejzová* [n. 3], [8]–[23]).[7] At the same time, the rights of other concrete mothers and children were not at stake in these cases. Instead, the policy in question concerned the public interest of safety.

[6] *Vavřička and Others v. the Czech Republic* (GC), ECtHR, App. Nos. 47621/13 and 5 others, April 8, 2021 (196).

[7] See also arguments in joint dissenting opinion of Judges Sajó, Karakaş, Nicolaou, Laffranque, and Keller in *Dubská and Krejzová* ([n. 3], [31]–[34]).

Intensity of Proportionality Review

The proportionality review involves difficult decisions, and an international court may not be properly equipped to appreciate national sensitivities or discern the problems that were considered by the national decision-making bodies (Gerards 2023b, 467). These considerations are often discussed in terms of judicial deference covered by the concept of the margin of appreciation in the ECtHR's case law (Brems and Lavrysen, 2015, 142; Shany 2018, 183). Acknowledging the subsidiary role of the Convention system, the ECtHR recognizes that states must, in principle, be allowed to determine the most suitable means of reconciling competing interests (*Dubská and Krejzová* [176]). Nevertheless, even if the margin of appreciation is wide, the Court "can and will police the borders of the exercise of national discretion" by making the final evaluation in the case (Gerards 2023a, 8; see also *Dubská and Krejzová* ([n7], [177]).

The standard of proportionality review applied by the Court is closely linked to the margin of appreciation retained by national authorities. To determine the scope of margin, the Court uses different factors, including the nature of the right under consideration,[8] the extent of European consensus on the significance of the interest at stake or the best means of protecting it,[9] the level of uncertainty surrounding the subject,[10] and the availability of adequate procedural safeguards at the domestic level.[11] Critics point to the lack of clarity in the Court's approach to the interplay of different factors and how it proceeds when they pull in different directions (Chagas 2022, 7). The general point for the Court in healthcare policy is that these matters "are in principle within the margin of appreciation of the domestic authorities, who are best placed to assess priorities, use of resources and social needs."[12] However, it is argued in this chapter that subject matter should not be decisive as regards the breadth of the margin. The Court's approach to the margin of appreciation should be nuanced and evaluated on a case-by-case basis and take all relevant considerations into account.

[8] *S.A.S. v. France* (GC), ECtHR, App. No. 43835/11, July 1, 2014, (129).

[9] *Hämäläinen v. Finland* (GC), ECtHR, App. No. 37359/09, July 16, 2014, (67); *Fadeyeva v. Russia*, ECtHR, App. No. 55723/00, June 9, 2005, (102); *Pavlov and Others v. Russia*, ECtHR, App. No. 31612/09, October 11, 2022, (75).

[10] *Hristozov and Others v. Bulgaria*, ECtHR, App. Nos. 47039/11 and 358/12, November 13, 2012, (119)–(120).

[11] *Animal Defenders International v. the United Kingdom*, ECtHR, App. No. 48876/08, April 22, 2013, (108).

[12] For example, as regards access to experimental treatment whose quality, safety, and efficacy have not been subjected to comprehensive testing, the Court afforded a wide margin of appreciation to the state. See *Hristozov* ([n. 10], [119]).

For example, in *Dubská and Krejzová*, the Court afforded a wide margin of appreciation to the Czech state's policy of encouraging hospital births because of the absence of a consensus among Member States on home births and the complexity of the issue, which "requir[ed] an assessment by the national authorities of expert and scientific data concerning the risks of hospital and home births" (*Dubská and Krejzová* [n. 3], [182]–[184]). There is some disagreement within the Court as to the relevance of a European consensus in this case.[13] In addition, Burke and Molitorisová (2019, 248–249) aptly argue that state policies should converge "if scientific evidence supporting a policy measure stands on country non-specific grounds." It is questionable whether the domestic authorities were better placed than the ECtHR to assess the risks of hospital and home births, as such assessments typically rely on evidence that is not specific to a country. The broad margin of appreciation in *Dubská and Krejzová* limited the Court's capacity to evaluate the scientific evidence and fully justify the choice of the health policy measure adopted in the Czech Republic. The Court should have conducted a more careful analysis of the specific circumstances of the applicants' cases, which presented no pregnancy-related risks or complications that necessitated giving birth in a hospital.

Furthermore, in *Vavřička*, concerning the standard and routine vaccination of children against diseases well-known to medical science, the ECtHR defined the scope of the margin of appreciation by balancing several factors. First, the Court acknowledged that compulsory medical intervention impinges on an individual's intimate rights—namely, a person's bodily integrity, which is the most intimate aspect of one's private life. Nonetheless, the Court deemed this interference less significant since domestic law does not require this duty to be imposed by force (*Vavřička* [n. 6], [276]). The Court defined broad discretion for the state in view of the wide range of policies on the compulsory vaccination of children among Member States (*Vavřička* [n. 6], [276]–[280]). In addition, in defining the state margin of appreciation, the ECtHR accepted "the general consensus over the vital importance of these means [vaccination] of protecting populations against diseases that may have severe effects on individual health, and that, in the case of serious outbreaks, may cause disruption to society" (*Vavřička* [n. 6], [300]). Narrowing the Court's scrutiny to a very general assumption about the effectiveness of vaccination seems problematic. In particular, the Court did not consider the scientific

[13] Specifically, in this case, the dissenting judges interpreted the review of the national legislation as evidence of a consensus that home births are not be prohibited. See the Joint dissenting opinion of Judges András Sajó, Işıl Karakaş, George Nicolaou, Julia Laffranque, and Helen Keller in *Dubská and Krejzová* ([n. 3], [28]).

evidence concerning the effectiveness and necessity of vaccination for the diseases in question (poliomyelitis, hepatitis B, tetanus, measles, mumps, rubella, etc.).

Having allowed the state a wide margin of appreciation in *Vavřička*, the Court proceeded with a relatively deferential proportionality assessment. Although the applicants argued that less restrictive alternatives were available,[14] the Court explicitly rejected the relevance of this test and emphasized that the question to be determined was whether, in striking this particular balance, the authorities remained within their wide margin of appreciation in this area (*Vavřička* [n. 6], [310]). Overall, the Court did not examine the details of the justifications for the vaccination policy, deferring instead to state decisions. The judgment makes numerous passing references to expertise, scientific authority, and the institutional status of the Czech health advisories, without examining the content of those decisions or the general scientific basis on which they rest (McWhirter and Clark 2023, 1041). In addition, the ECtHR placed considerable emphasis on the procedural safeguards provided for in domestic law, such as the availability of administrative appeals and judicial remedies, and on the transparency of the domestic system (*Vavřička* [n. 6], [295], [297]–[299]).

In the context of COVID-19, the Court must consider numerous factors to determine the appropriate scope of the margin of appreciation for restrictive measures. Public health is inherently political, and the human rights approach to this issue is a relatively recent development that emerged during the global response to the AIDS crisis (McWhirter and Clark 2023, 1045). National authorities faced numerous decision-making challenges when implementing measures in response to COVID-19. These challenges included scientific uncertainty surrounding the nature and management of health threats and difficult ethical dilemmas about whether to prioritize the protection of human life or to minimize disruption to the economy. The acknowledgment of these challenges is reflected in the broad discretion granted to national authorities and the limited judicial review of these measures by international human rights courts (Tzevelekos 2020).

While the unprecedented uncertainty and imminent threat posed by the novel coronavirus would point to a broad margin of appreciation for governments to develop their pandemic response, the impact of a specific restrictive measure on a concrete human right will determine the scope of the margin of appreciation in each case. The Court may find compelling reasons to conduct an intense review of particularly intrusive measures that challenge the most fundamental

[14] Specifically, the applicants claimed that the aim of protecting the health of other children could be achieved by the exclusion of unvaccinated children from educational establishments only in the event of a threatened or actual outbreak of one of the diseases. See *Vavřička* ([n. 6], [184]).

human rights. For example, a threat posed to one's life and health by compulsory vaccination (Krasser 2021, 209)[15] could weigh against the broad margin of appreciation to introduce such an obligation. Furthermore, if compulsory vaccination is litigated only under Article 8 of the ECHR, then since the Court has held that "a person's bodily integrity concerns the most intimate aspects of one's private life ... that compulsory medical intervention, even if it is of a minor importance, constitutes an interference with this right."[16] Therefore, even in the challenging context of COVID-19, there remains an important role for the ECtHR to play. If it were merely to accept the government's own assessments, it would fail to provide adequate protection against majoritarian abuses (Brems and Lavrysen 2015, 142).

Proportionality in Times of Pandemic

Derogations

In situations of extreme crisis, the ECHR provides states with the power to derogate from certain Convention obligations (Art. 15 ECHR). Specifically, under Article 15 § 1 of the ECHR, states must satisfy three requirements for a derogation to be valid: (a) the crisis must occur during wartime or in another public emergency that threatens the life of the nation, (b) the measures must not exceed the strict exigencies required of the situation, and (c) the measures must not be inconsistent with the state's other international law obligations. Furthermore, there are certain rights from which states can never derogate that represent the most fundamental values of democratic societies.[17] Overall, the purpose of these derogations is to grant governments flexibility in addressing crises by permitting measures that would otherwise breach the Convention.

During the COVID-19 crisis, ten states derogated from the ECHR after notifying the secretary general of the Council of Europe under Article 15 of the ECHR of the emergency situation.[18] The majority of the Member States, however, decided that such derogation was unnecessary. While there is no doubt

[15] It seems appropriate to define any vaccination system that enforces sanctions for refusing to carry out a vaccination as *compulsory vaccination* subject to justification, as these consequences can influence one's decision to be vaccinated. However, compulsory does not mean that a vaccination would be applied under duress Krasser (2021), 209.

[16] *Solomakhin v. Ukraine*, ECtHR, App. No. 24429/03, March 15, 2012, (33).

[17] Specifically, according to Art. 15 § 2 ECHR, "no derogation from Article 2, except in respect of deaths resulting from lawful acts of war, or from Articles 3, 4 (§ 1) and 7 shall be made under this provision."

[18] Council of Europe. 2023b. "Derogations Covid-19." January 2. https://www.coe.int/en/web/conventions/derogations-covid-19.

that the pandemic fell within the definition of a public emergency,[19] there are different opinions as to whether derogations were needed. Some have argued that the pandemic required exceptional measures and that the failure to use Article 15 of the ECHR risks normalizing extraordinary domestic powers and will lead to a permanent weakening of human rights protections (Greene 2020). Others, however, caution that with Article 15 derogations the Court will provide a wide degree of deference to states (Dzehtsiarou 2020, 370; Molloy 2020; Zysset 2022, 286).

States that declared a state of emergency under Article 15 of the ECHR may only take measures derogating from the Convention to the extent "strictly required by the exigencies of the situation" (Art. 15 § 1 ECHR). The Court can scrutinize derogation measures to ensure their strict necessity. In any case, when an applicant complains that their Convention rights were violated during a period of derogation, the Court will first examine whether the measures taken can be justified under the substantive articles of the Convention. Only if a measure cannot be justified in this manner will the Court proceed to evaluate the validity of the derogation itself.[20]

For example, Romania derogated from Article 2 of Protocol No. 4 and Article 8 of the ECHR (See note 18). In *Terheş v. Romania*, the applicant's complaint concerning the general lockdown invoked Article 5 § 1 of the ECHR, which was declared inadmissible on the ground of *ratione materiae*.[21] However, since the applicant did not invoke Article 2 of Protocol No. 4 to the ECHR, the Court did not examine the situation under the purview of Article 15 (*Terheş* [46]). The validity of the derogation was not under scrutiny in *Piperea v. Romania*, in which the applicant's complaints concerned social distancing, the duty to wear a mask, and self-isolation. These complaints were declared inadmissible, since the applicants failed to comply with the requirements for victim status.[22]

Drawing on the Court's case law in relation to Article 15, the ECtHR allows states a wide margin of appreciation regarding how they choose to respond to emergency situations.[23] Given the relatively unprecedented nature of COVID-19, the often conflicting medical evidence guiding government

[19] "Public emergency threatening the life of the nation" refers to "an exceptional situation of crisis of emergency which affects the whole population and constitutes a threat to the organised life of the community of which the State is composed." See *Lawless v. Ireland (No. 3)*, ECtHR, App. No. 332/57, July 1, 1961, (28).

[20] *A. and Others v. the United Kingdom* (GC), ECtHR, App. No. 3455/05, February 19, 2009, (161).

[21] *Terheş v. Romania* (dec.), ECtHR, App. No. 49933/20, April 13, 2021, (30), (43)–(45).

[22] *Gheorghe Piperea v. Romania* (dec.), ECtHR, App. No. 24183/21, July 5, 2022.

[23] For example, the Court held that "by reason of their direct and continuous contact with the pressing needs of the moment, the national authorities are in principle in a better position than the international judge to decide both on the presence of . . . an emergency and on the nature and scope of derogations necessary to avert it." See *Ireland v. the United Kingdom*, ECtHR, App. No. 5310/71, January 18, 1978 (207).

responses, and the different impacts and rates of infection across different countries, it is likely that the Court will apply a wide degree of deference to states in this context (Molloy 2020). The emergency declaration and subsequent derogations will justify an even broader margin given to states. Specifically, Article 15 of the ECHR can significantly influence the final stage of the proportionality test—namely, the assessment of necessity and proportionality sensu stricto (Dzehtsiarou 2020, 370). Overall, the proportionality assessment under the derogation clause is relatively superficial and not concerned with scrutinizing, for example, less restrictive measures available to the government or whether "and how all individuals and groups share the burden of pursuing the legitimate aim equitably" (Zysset 2020, 295).

In an era characterized by extreme inequality, the COVID-19 pandemic was a particularly inequitable event in that its effects were most damaging for certain segments of the population, including children, whose right to education was interrupted (UN Sustainable Development Group 2020b); marginalized and vulnerable members of society, who could not work from home and lived at subsistence levels; older people, who were isolated and without access to essential services or who were exposed to poor treatment in care institutions; and migrants, refugees, and internally displaced people, who were pushed back or deported to dangerous environments (UN Sustainable Development Group 2020a). In the context of COVID-19, rigorous proportionality assessments using the limitation clauses (Arts. 8–11 ECHR) would have ensured better human rights protection, as opposed to assessments made through the narrow lens of the derogation clause (Art. 15 ECHR). However, it remains to be seen what standard of judicial scrutiny the ECtHR will apply in pending cases concerning Article 15 derogations in the context of COVID-19 health crisis.[24]

Cases Before the ECtHR

Numerous ECtHR judgments feature references to the COVID-19 pandemic in their texts. Nonetheless, in many of the ECtHR's judgments, mention of the COVID-19 situation was related to procedural adaptations and did not have a clear impact on the outcome of the cases (Gerards 2023b, 365).[25] In contrast, the Court took the COVID-19 crisis into account as a factual circumstance in other cases when analyzing the length of proceedings before the domestic courts.[26]

[24] See, e.g., *E.B. v. Serbia* and *A.A. v. Serbia*, ECtHR, App. Nos. 50086/20 and 50898/20, communicated to the government on November 5, 2021.

[25] See, e.g., *Tunikova and Others v. Russia*, ECtHR, App. No. 55974/16, December 14, 2021, (150); *Buş v. Romania* (dec.), ECtHR, App. No. 46160/19, October 19, 2021, (39).

[26] See, e.g., *G.K. v. Cyprus*, ECtHR, App. No. 16205/21, February 21, 2023, (20); *Adamčo v. Slovakia*, ECtHR, App. No. 25436/21, February 9, 2023, (22).

To date, the Court has handed down several inadmissibility decisions relating to measures implemented in response to COVID-19. These cases have concerned, for example, "health passes,"[27] declarations of a state of alert, restrictions on the freedom of movement (*Piperea* [n. 22]), the duty to wear masks in certain places,[28] lockdowns (*Terheş* [n. 21]), full bans on public gatherings to prevent the spread of the virus,[29] legislation mandating vaccination and the possibility of criminal prosecution for noncompliance,[30] vaccination requirements imposed on workers in certain occupations,[31] and general measures allegedly affecting lawyers to prevent the spread of COVID-19 in courts and prisons.[32] Furthermore, the Court has ruled on certain restrictions of national rights within the framework of the ECHR under Articles 3,[33] 5,[34] and 6.[35] Among the reasons for these cases having been declared inadmissible is the applicants' failure to prove that they had been individually affected by the contested COVID-19 measure. For example, in *Árus v. Romania*, the Court held that the obligation to wear masks in certain public places was directed at the entire population in response to what the competent national authorities had determined to be a serious public health situation (*Árus* [n. 28], [10]–[11]). Since the applicant provided little information about his individual circumstances (*Árus* [n. 28], [12]), the Court held that there was no evidence that he had suffered any consequences or prejudice from missed opportunities or events.[36] Likewise, the applicant's claim in *Piperea* that the obligation to complete a certificate detailing the purpose, destination, and duration of his journey had infringed his privacy and liberty of movement was rejected because of insufficient evidence to demonstrate the effects of this measure on the applicant's individual situation (*Piperea* [n. 22], [13]). It follows from these examples that applicants are expected to provide detailed explanations regarding how the contested measure had particularly adversely affected their rights in comparison to the broader population also affected by these measures. In addition, these pronouncements highlight the Court's strict view regarding the impact's severity relative to the rest of the population.

[27] *Zambrano v. France* (dec.), ECtHR, App. No. 41994/21, September 21, 2021.

[28] *Árus v. Romania* (dec.), ECtHR, App. No. 39647/21, May 30, 2023.

[29] *Communauté Genevoise d'Action Syndicale (CGAS) v. Switzerland* (GC), ECtHR, App. No. 21881/20, November 27, 2023.

[30] *Mittendorfer v. Austria* (dec.), ECtHR, App. No. 32467/22, July 4, 2023.

[31] *Thevenon v. France* (dec.), ECtHR, App. No. 46061/21, September 13, 2022.

[32] *Pernechele and Others v. Italy* (dec.), ECtHR, App. No. 7222/22, October 31, 2023.

[33] See, e.g., *Feilazoo v. Malta*, ECtHR, App. No. 6865/19, March 11, 2021; *Fenech v. Malta*, ECtHR, App. No. 19090/20, March 1, 2022.

[34] See, e.g., *Khokhlov v. Cyprus*, ECtHR, App. No. 53114/20, June 13, 2023.

[35] See, e.g., *Makovetskyy v. Ukraine* (dec.), ECtHR, App. No. 50824/21, May 19, 2022.

[36] In particular, the applicant did not argue that he had to go to public places covered by the obligation to wear masks for professional, personal, or other reasons on a regular basis or for prolonged periods (*Árus* [n. 28], [14]).

A number of communicated (but still pending at the time of writing in September 2023) cases related to restrictive COVID-19 measures concern the respect of proportionality.[37] For example, in *Pasquinelli and Others v. San Marino*, twenty-six health care and social health workers complained about the vaccination obligation imposed by law on their professional sector.[38] The Court asked the parties whether the applicants had suffered a violation of their right to private life and whether they had been subjected to discrimination (*Pasquinelli*). Similarly, *M.C.K. and M.H.K.-B. v. Germany* raised potentially interesting proportionality questions. In this case, the applicants challenged restrictions on and the prohibition of in-class lessons, alleging an infringement on their right to education.[39] Furthermore, in *Scheffer and Others v. Slovakia*, the Court may examine whether the temporary closure of the applicants' businesses or limitations on the maximum number of guests or customers allowed at one time disproportionately interfered with their property rights.[40] The Court is also presented with the opportunity to rule on the proportionality of bans on public worship during COVID-19 in *Figel' v. Slovakia* (n. 37), *Mégard v. France* (n. 37), *Chirilă v. Romania*,[41] and *Association of Ecclesiastical Orthodoxy v. Greece* (n. 37). While the Court's application of a proportionality review in these cases remains to be seen, it has so far handed down only one judgment applying proportionality assessments to COVID-19-related measures.

In particular, *Constantin-Lucian Spînu v. Romania* concerned a refusal by national authorities, on the grounds of measures taken during the COVID-19 pandemic, to authorize a prisoner to attend religious services outside the prison.[42] In *Spînu*, the ECtHR decided to allow a wide margin of appreciation to the state because of the consideration that the national authorities were better placed to pronounce on the matter (the right to manifest one's religion) on which profound differences may reasonably exist between societies (*Spînu*

[37] See, e.g., *Avagyan v. Russia*, ECtHR, App. No. 36911/20, communicated to the government on November 4, 2020; *Association of Orthodox Ecclesiastical Obedience v. Greece*, ECtHR, App. No. 52104/20, communicated to the government on February 25, 2021; *Guhn v. Poland*, ECtHR, App. No. 45519/20, communicated to the government on November 17, 2021; *Mégard v. France*, ECtHR, App. No. 32647/22, communicated to the government on September 19, 2022; *Figel' v. Slovakia*, ECtHR, App. No. 12131/21, communicated to the government on December 12, 2022; *Petrova v. Bulgaria*, ECtHR, App. No. 938/21, communicated to the government on August 26, 2022.

[38] *Pasquinelli and Others v. San Marino*, ECtHR, App. No. 24622/22, communicated to the government on December 12, 2022.

[39] *M.C.K. and M.H.K.-B. and Others v. Germany*, ECtHR, App. No. 26657/22, communicated to the government on December 20, 2022.

[40] *Scheffer and Others v. Slovakia*, ECtHR, App. No. 16627/21 and 47 Others, communicated to the government on January 24, 2023.

[41] *Chirilă v. Romania*, ECtHR, App. No. 5610/21, communicated to the government on March 20, 2023.

[42] The derogation made by Romania under Art. 15 of the ECHR was no longer applicable to the complaint brought by the applicant. Therefore, the Court considered only the provisions of Art. 9 of the ECHR. *Constantin-Lucian Spînu v. Romania*, App. No. 29443/20, October 11, 2022, (48)–(49).

[n. 42], [53]). Moreover, the Court attached significant weight to the "principle of social solidarity" and the uncertainty surrounding the development of the health situation, which presented so many challenges that the authorities could not envisage reacting promptly to the applicant's situation, let alone immediately after the sudden changes imposed by COVID-19 (*Spînu* [n. 42], [68]).

In this case, the Court considered that the church's activities were affected by the health crisis, since access to religious services was subject to conditions and even suspended for all members of the applicant's religious community, including religious representatives (*Spînu* [n. 42], [68]). The Court took into account the applicant's particular circumstances, such as the introduction of videoconferencing in the prison to enable worship and the fact that his complaint was a unique situation (*Spînu* [n. 42], [69]–[70]). However, the proportionality review conducted in *Spînu* was relatively lenient. The Court did not conduct a comprehensive analysis of the evidence justifying the measures pursued by the domestic authorities to curb the spread of COVID-19. Additionally, it did not analyze whether these measures disproportionately affected the applicant, who remained particularly vulnerable as a prisoner.

Concluding Remarks

The Court's proportionality test typically aligns with a classical model, although the ECtHR's variable application of the proportionality assessment can be attributed to its concern for the principle of subsidiarity. This principle means it is primarily up to the Member States to secure the Convention rights within their domestic legal orders. The ECtHR only becomes involved as a last resort, thereby allowing States some flexibility in implementing the Convention, which is often expressed in terms of the margin of appreciation granted to them (Gerards 2023a, 8). The Court's subsidiary role is then to check whether a state has overstepped its margin of appreciation. There is a correlation between the margin of appreciation afforded to national authorities and the intensity of the Court's proportionality review. The ECtHR's recent pronouncements demonstrate its judicial self-restraint by according a wide margin of appreciation to national authorities in tackling the pandemic. After all, governments were urged to act in the face of an imminent threat to the whole community in a context of scarce scientific knowledge and complete uncertainty as to the possible evolution of the pandemic. As a consequence, the Court applied a low-intensity proportionality review and neither engaged with scientific evidence nor questioned the governments' justifications for their COVID-19 measures.

Even in the context of COVID-19, the ECtHR should not lose sight of the specific circumstances of each individual case. When a right of fundamental importance is threatened by a particularly intrusive quarantine measure, the Court should provide well-considered analysis and good reasons for the breadth of the margin of appreciation afforded to the government. Respect for human rights requires careful attention to the unique situation of every applicant.

COVID-19 was a challenge that called for collective measures. Yet the collective response often came at the expense of individual rights. As the world readies itself to address potential future public health crises, the legal system must also prepare itself against potential encroachments on individual human rights that may arise. Safeguarding individual rights also protects society's collective rights, even when confronting crises such as COVID-19. The ECtHR can play an essential role in championing this cause by carefully reviewing each case and ensuring the individuals' voice is heard when their rights are endangered.

Undoubtedly, we have yet to reach the end of our wisdom in proportionality analysis. This is also true for the ECtHR. Above all, the COVID-19 pandemic has highlighted existing limits of courts in general and the ECtHR in particular. It is crucial that science accompany this process and that court decisions concerning the question of proportionality be questioned critically. This is the only way to guarantee the effective protection of fundamental rights, even in times of crisis.

Competing Interests

There are no competing interests to declare.

Funding

This work was supported by the Swiss National Science Foundation (SNSF) under grant number IZSEZ0_216766.

References

Barr, D. (@Damian_Barr Barr). 2020. https://www.damianbarr.com/latest/https/we-are-not-all-in-the-same-boat.

Brems, E., and L. Lavrysen. 2015. "'Don't Use a Sledgehammer to Crack a Nut': Less Restrictive Means in the Case Law of the European Court of Human Rights." *Human Rights Law Review* 15 (1): 154–168.

Burke, C., and A. Molitorisová. 2019. "(Not) Proving the Public Good: Scientific Evidence and the Margin of Appreciation." *The Law and Practice of International Courts and Tribunals* 18:248–249.

Calí, B. 2007. "Balancing Human Rights? Methodological Problems with Weights, Scales and Proportions." *Human Rights Quarterly* 29 (1): 251–270.
Chagas, C. A. 2022. "Balancing Competences and the Margin of Appreciation: Structuring Deference at the ECtHR." *Vienna Journal on International Constitutional Law* 16 (1): 1–26.
Dworkin, R. 2011. *Justice for Hedgehogs*. Harvard University Press.
Dzehtsiarou, K. 2020. "Article 15 Derogations: Are They Really Necessary During the Covid-19 Pandemic?" *European Human Rights Law Review* 4: 359–371.
Gerards, J. 2013. "How to Improve the Necessity Test of the European Court of Human Rights." *International Journal of Constitutional Law* 11 (2): 369–373.
Gerards, J. 2023a. *General Principles of the European Convention on Human Rights*. 2nd edition. Cambridge University Press.
Gerards, J. 2023b. "Moving Away from Open Judicial Balancing Review: The European Court of Human Rights' Approach as Illustrated by Its Case Law Relevant to the Covid-19 Pandemic." *The Law and Practice of International Courts and Tribunals* 22 (2): 365–383.
Greene, A. 2020. "States Should Declare a State of Emergency Using Article 15 ECHR to Confront the Coronavirus Pandemic." Strasbourg Observers, April 1. https://strasbourgobservers.com/2020/04/01/states-should-declare-a-state-of-emergency-using-article-15-echr-to-confront-the-coronavirus-pandemic/.
King, J., O. L. M. Ferraz, and A. Jones. 2022. "Mandatory COVID-19 Vaccination and Human Rights." *The Lancet* 399 (10321): 220–222.
Krasser, A. 2021. "Compulsory Vaccination in a Fundamental Rights Perspective: Lessons from the ECtHR." *Vienna Journal on International Constitutional Law* 15 (2): 207–233.
McWhirter, R., and M. Clark. 2023. "Expertise, Public Health and the European Convention on Human Rights: Vavřička v Czech Republic." *The Modern Law Review* 86 (4): 1035–1048.
Molloy, S. 2020. "Covid-19 and Derogations Before the European Court of Human Rights" (blog). VerfBlog, April 10. https://verfassungsblog.de/covid-19-and-derogations-before-the-european-court-of-human-rights/.
Mowbray, A. 2010. "A Study of the Principle of Fair Balance in the Jurisprudence of the European Court of Human Rights." *Human Rights Law Review* 10 (2): 294–308.
Shany, Y. 2018. "All Roads Lead to Strasbourg? Application of the Margin of Appreciation Doctrine by the European Court of Human Rights and the UN Human Rights Committee." *Journal of International Dispute Settlement* 9 (2): 180–198.
Smet, S. 2017. *Resolving Conflicts Between Human Rights: The Judge's Dilemma*. Routledge.
Stone Sweet, A., and J. Mathews. 2008. "Proportionality Balancing and Global Constitutionalism." *Columbia Journal of Transnational Law* 47:98–112.
Tribunal Administratif de Strasbourg, N. 2003058, Ordonnance du 25 Mai 2020. Accessed September 5, 2023. http://strasbourg.tribunal-administratif.fr/content/download/171091/1705849/version/1/file/2003058-1.pdf.
Tzevelekos, V. P. 2020. "Herd Immunity and Lockdown: The Legitimacy of National Policies Against the Pandemic and Judicial Self-Restraint by the ECtHR." Strasbourg Observers, May 11. https://strasbourgobservers.com/2020/05/11/herd-immunity-and-lockdown-the-legitimacy-of-national-policies-against-the-pandemic-and-judicial-self-restraint-by-the-ecthr/.
UN Sustainable Development Group. 2020a. "Covid-19 and Human Rights: We Are All in This Together," April. https://unsdg.un.org/sites/default/files/2020-04/COVID-19-and-Human-Rights.pdf.
UN Sustainable Development Group. 2020b. "Policy Brief: The Impact of Covid-19 on Children," April 15. https://unsdg.un.org/sites/default/files/2020-04/160420_Covid_Children_Policy_Brief.pdf.
Zysset, A. 2022. "To Derogate or to Restrict? The COVID-19 Pandemic, Proportionality and the Justificatory Gap in European Human Rights Law." *Jus Cogens* 4:285–301.

14

Proportionality and the Swiss Courts

Helen Keller and Violetta Sefkow-Werner

Introduction

The COVID-19 pandemic put a spotlight on the legal principle of proportionality in the public health law discourse. How are health and proportionality connected? Health and life are rights protected by law. In Switzerland, they are part of the fundamental rights of every individual. The state is obliged to protect these rights (e.g., against pandemic risks and by providing the necessary health infrastructure). At the same time, fundamental rights shield the individual's liberty from state restrictions. Proportionality then serves as a crucial framework for balancing the need to protect public health in ways that respect individual rights and freedoms in times of crisis. The states' responses to the COVID-19 pandemic illustrate this process, as they were taken within a complex situation of conflicting interests.

This chapter seeks to explore the delicate equilibrium between government intervention and individual freedoms by examining how the principle of proportionality has shaped decision-making processes and the measures implemented to combat the pandemic. It will focus on Swiss law because the Federal Constitution of the Swiss Confederation (April 18, 1999, SR 101; *Bundesverfassung*, BV) enshrines the proportionality principle,[1] and it therefore offers a rich foundation of legal scholarship and case law that can be used to illustrate its content and meaning. The chapter begins in the next section with an explanation of the proportionality principle, taking into account the context of the pandemic and pointing out some of the main legal issues it has raised. It then introduces the proportionality test's criteria and discusses how they have been applied and deployed in the context of pandemic measures. The chapter also explains, in the fifth section, how emergency law has shaped and challenged pandemic decisions before concluding with a summary and some remarks on long-term legal responses to health issues.

[1] The BV thus places itself in a broader Western European context, in which the principle of proportionality plays a central role in all constitutional orders; see, for example, Germany, France, Italy, and Austria.

Helen Keller and Violetta Sefkow-Werner, *Proportionality and the Swiss Courts*. In: *Proportionality*.
Edited by: Nikola Biller-Andorno et al., Oxford University Press.
DOI: 10.1093/9780197759370.003.0015

Proportionality During the Pandemic

Proportionality as a Legal Principle

In a literal sense, *proportionality* refers to the relationship between multiple positions without specifying which positions, goods, or interests serve as a point of reference (Rütsche 2020, para. 1). Before finding its way into the Constitution, the concept of proportionality was already paraphrased by the Swiss Federal Supreme Court (FSC) in 1926 (BGE 52 I 222, E. 5)[2] and mentioned explicitly for the first time in 1939 (BGE 65 I 65, E. 3c). Until 1999, the proportionality principle was applied only as a general unwritten rule in administrative law and later also as a requirement for restrictions of fundamental rights (Engi 2017 regarding the use of the term "principle" versus "rule" and the respective implications on the applicability and normative content; Rütsche 2020, para. 9; Schweizer and Krebs 2023, para. 52). Today, it is enshrined in the Swiss Constitution in Article 5[2] as a general principle of the rule of law, which means that all state action (e.g., when the state provides social aid, acts entrepreneurial, or for legal enactment, see Schindler 2023, para. 57) must serve a public interest in a reasonable manner and, per Article 36[3], when the state restricts fundamental rights (Epiney 2015, para. 67; Schindler 2023, para. 54). This is remarkable from a comparative legal perspective, as other constitutions—for example, those of Germany (Rütsche 2020, para. 4),[3] France, Italy, Austria, and the United States—do not specify proportionality as a stand-alone, written principle; the European Convention on Human Rights only mentions it specifically in the context of individual single human rights (Rütsche 2020, para. 9; Chapter 13, this volume). The Swiss FSC, building upon German doctrine of fundamental rights (Schindler 2023, para. 56), has refined the *contours* of this principle through a legal test to give it more clarity and practicability. According to this well-established case law, the principle of proportionality requires that a measure be suitable and necessary for attaining an objective that lies in public or private interest and that it prove reasonable for the persons concerned, given the severity of the restriction of fundamental rights. In short, there must be a reasonable relationship between the ends and the means (BGE 147 I 450, E. 3.2.3, with further references).

The principle of proportionality applies to all state bodies. This means that the legislator must respect it, as must the executive when it adopts certain measures (e.g., during a pandemic). Then, the courts are required to assess measures that restrict fundamental rights in terms of whether they are proportionate (Macheret 2002, 190–191; Rütsche 2020, para. 34). While the first two organs

[2] BGE refers to the Recueil officiel where major decisions by the FSC are published. All decisions by the FSC are available here: https://search.bger.ch/ext/eurospider/live/fr/php/clir/http/index_atf.php?lang=fr.

[3] Historically, however, the idea of proportionality has roots in German eighteenth-century law.

often shortchange proportionality out of political expediency considerations, it is up to the courts to closely examine the proportionality of a measure based on constitutional requirements.

The purpose of the proportionality principle is to prevent the abuse or overuse of state power and to ensure individual justice (Macheret 2002, 188; Rütsche 2020, paras. 17–18). It plays a central role in weighing public and private interests and community versus individual interests. However, the proportionality principle does not itself prescribe where the line between conflicting interests must be drawn; it only sets the framework and outer limits for this (political) balancing process. For the courts, proportionality then constitutes a yardstick for the assessment of whether the solutions found or measures adopted are appropriate and can be regarded as just (Rütsche 2020, para. 19).

Collision of Rights During the COVID-19 Pandemic

The COVID-19 pandemic was a situation in which states' responses (or lack thereof) necessarily entailed a clash of fundamental rights between multiple stakeholders. Broadly speaking, there was a conflict between the individual's right to self-determination and personal freedom and the state's duty to protect its population. The state's duty relates to a sum of individual rights (e.g., life and health) and a public interest (public health and the healthcare system). Almost all pandemic measures in Switzerland based on the COVID-19 regulations touched on fundamental rights: personal liberty (Art. 10[2] BV), privacy (Art. 13 BV), freedom of assembly (Art. 22 BV), freedom of religion/faith (Art. 15 BV), the right to primary education (Art. 19 BV), and economic freedom (Art. 27 BV) (Häner and Kneissler 2020, 849; Märkli 2020, 62; Zünd and Errass 2020, 75).

When referring to the protection of health, it should be noted that under Swiss law, there is no direct and actionable right to health as such. The Constitution does not feature an explicit right to health, and the FSC does not consider Article 12 of the International Covenant on Economic, Social, and Cultural Rights (ICESCR)[4] actionable.[5] Nonetheless, a right to access existing health services can be derived from other fundamental rights—in particular, the rights to life and physical integrity (Art. 10 BV) (Poledna and Rütsche 2023, para. 5). Moreover, the BV contains a general health protection mandate (Arts. 41(1)(b) and 118 BV) as a constitutional goal and public interest and stipulates a duty for the

[4] ICESCR (adopted December 16, 1966, entered into force January 3, 1976) 993 UNTS 3.

[5] See BGE 120 Ia 1, E. 5c; 126 I 240, E. 2c. Switzerland has not signed the Optional Protocol to the ISESCR that allows individual complaints to the UN Committee on Economic, Social and Cultural Rights.

Confederation and the Cantons to guarantee basic healthcare (Art. 117a BV) (Seitz 2018; Poledna and Rütsche 2023, para. 8).

This conflict between personal liberty and protection is resolved by balancing the individual and community rights and interests involved (*praktische Konkordanz*); the principle of proportionality comes into play as a methodological framework for this balancing (Flückiger 2020, 146). As put by the Swiss FSC,

> The principle of proportionality is of particular importance for the harmonizing concretization of conflicting constitutional principles, such as the protection of life and health on the one hand and the restrictions of fundamental rights imposed for this purpose on the other hand . . . . In accordance with the principle of proportionality, the acceptable risk must be asked for, and a weighing of the interests involved must be carried out. (BGE 147 I 450, E. 3.2.3, our translation; see also BGE 147 I 393, E. 5.3.1)

On the one hand, there is no abstract hierarchy among the fundamental rights (Tschentscher 2020a, para. 13; BGE 137 I 167, E. 3.7). The protection of the lives of its citizens does not provide the state a *carte blanche* to implement restrictive pandemic measures. In the words of the FSC, the state's duty to protect against health hazards, which is based on fundamental rights, does not allow for any strict measure to prevent all transmission of diseases to be taken (BGE 147 I 450, E. 3.2.3). Moreover, the state's protective duties do not go so far as to require the elimination of every technical or human-made risk (BGE 147 I 450, E. 3.2.3); an individual can also choose to take on a certain risk and thereby dispose of their individual liberties (Tschentscher 2020b, paras. 28–29). On the other hand, courts have attached great importance to common goods, such as the life and health of the population and a functioning healthcare system, and the level of threat (Rhein-Fischer and Nussberger 2022, 194 with reference to BGE 147 I 450, E. 3.3.4). Taken to an extreme, this approach would make it almost impossible for a potential measure to be considered disproportionate, which reveals a structural limit to the proportionality test for highly important common goods (Rhein-Fischer and Nussberger 2022, 194).

The Judicial Review of Proportionality

Preliminary Remark

The principle of proportionality applies to all state bodies at all levels, including, for example, the executive of a municipality or the federal legislature (Art. 5[2] BV) (Epiney 2015, para. 67). The most prominent statements on proportionality come from the courts—in particular, the FSC—when examining the conformity of a measure with fundamental rights. Any restriction of fundamental rights must meet the requirements of Article 36 of the BV: It must have a legal basis (Art. 36[1] BV), serve a public interest or the protection of fundamental rights of others (Art. 36[2] BV), and be proportionate (Art. 36[3] BV). In many fundamental rights cases, the proportionality test—that is, the suitability, necessity, and appropriateness of the measure in question—provides the main argument against the constitutionality of a measure. This is the reason why we focus mainly on the Swiss FSC's case law in the following discussion.

Public Interest

The concept of public interest will be addressed here first, as its consideration necessarily precedes the proportionality analysis. Identifying the public interest that a measure is intended to protect sets the point of reference that serves as the basis of an assessment of its proportionality (BGE 140 II 194, E. 5.8.2; Uhlmann and Bukovac 2019, 36; Leisner-Espenberger 2021). This is because the appropriateness test involves weighing the public interest against private interests, so the decision on the proportionality of a measure presupposes the existence of a legitimate public interest (Uhlmann and Bukovac 2019, 35). There is no conclusive positive list of recognized public interests, although it is possible to name inadmissible (i.e., unconstitutional) interests. Owing to the changeability (BGE 138 I 378, E. 8.3) and variety of admissible public interests, this criterion is usually rather unproblematic.[6]

According to the FSC, it was undisputed that the pandemic measures served "a public interest" (see, e.g., BGE 147 I 450, E. 3.3.1). In some judgments, it specified that the public interest was combating the pandemic by containing the spread of the novel coronavirus (BGE 148 I 33, E. 6.5; 148 I 19, E. 5.4), disease control (Swiss FSC, Judgment of September 22, 2021, 2C_369/2021, E. 6), or the protection of public health by preventing infections, hospitalizations, and deaths (BGE 147 I 393, E. 5.2). Additionally, in legal scholarship, protecting the population against transmissible diseases and pandemics (Zünd and Errass 2020, 77)—or, simply public health (Zumsteg 2020, 806)—is regarded as an accepted interest that may justify the restriction of fundamental rights. Some authors criticize the lack of clarity about the pursued aim (e.g., in the case of school closures), which may have resulted from the absence of a formal legal duty for lawmakers to give reasons for a particular law (Glaser 2021, 50).

While the aim(s) of the pandemic measures—protecting public health and maintaining a functioning healthcare system—may seem obvious at first,

[6] Swiss FSC, Judgment of May 2, 2023, 2C_852/2022, E. 7.4.2, in which the Court even speaks of "not too great importance."

pinpointing a specific purpose proves more difficult and raises the question of how narrowly the aim of a measure needs to be defined before its proportionality can be analyzed. This question is important for both the legislator and the courts (Leisner-Espenberger 2021, 914). The more broadly the objective is defined, the more possible it is to identify milder measures for achieving the objective. This means that a general objective can lead to many restrictive measures being seen as unnecessary and therefore disproportionate (Leisner-Espenberger 2021, 917). When multiple aims serve as a reference point, the selection of the least severe measure becomes more random or even arbitrary (Leisner-Espenberger 2021, 922). For example, in a ruling on a testing mandate, the FSC referred to the "intermediate aim" of increasing the vaccination rate of healthcare workers without clarifying its relationship to the direct aim of the protection of public health (Swiss FSC, Judgment of December 12, 2022, 2C_886/2021, E. 4.4.4.1). When views differ as to what exactly the aim of a pandemic measures was, or when an aim (e.g., preserving a functioning healthcare system) is not clearly distinct from the means to achieve it (e.g., contact restrictions), the function of this legal criterion in structuring the proportionality test may be undermined (Leisner-Espenberger 2021, 917).

A restriction of fundamental rights may also be justified by the protection of the fundamental rights of others (Art. 36[2] BV). Whereas most judgments refer to public health as the legitimizing public interest (see, e.g., BGE 147 I 393, E. 5.2., 148 I 19, E. 5.4; Swiss FSC, Judgment of September 22, 2021, 2C_369/2021, E. 6), three later judgments specifically addressed the protection of others: In one case, the FSC emphasized that a testing mandate for unvaccinated health workers particularly protects the most vulnerable in their respective facilities (BGE 149 I 105, E. 4.4.4.1); in two others, it stated that safety measures at schools are in the interest of the other students, whose right under Article 19 of the BV requires that school operations with face-to-face teaching be maintained.[7] As will be discussed later, this special consideration of vulnerable groups was lost in the subsequent proportionality analysis, which raises the question of whether their interests were sufficiently factored in when measures were implemented to combat the pandemic.

Suitability

The first requirement of the proportionality test is that the pandemic measure must be suitable to achieve its aim. Concrete suitability is always based on a prognosis and therefore involves probabilities and an element of uncertainty.

[7] BGE 149 I 191, E. 6.4; Swiss FSC, Judgment of May 2, 2023, 2C_852/2022, E. 7.4.4. See also BGE 149 I 191, E. 5, in which where the Court decided that online teaching was not an equivalent substitute.

How elaborated the factual basis must be and what degree of probability is sufficient is a matter of discretion (Rütsche 2020, para. 12). Case law shows that this element is rarely the reason why a court considers a measure to be disproportionate. This may be due to the wide latitude that the courts grant to the legislator (Macheret 2002, 195).

The FSC, for example, has held that restrictions for public events or gatherings are, in principle, a suitable measure, as this limits human contact, which, according to the current state of research, hinders the spread of the virus (BGE 148 I 19, E. 6.2.2; 148 I 33, E. 7.5). In another case, it deemed it "plausible" that the storage of contact data improves the effectiveness of contact tracing, and therefore the data storage was a suitable measure (Swiss FSC, Judgment of September 22, 2021, 2C_369/2021, E. 6.4). Concerning face masks, the Court referred to the World Health Organization's recommendations and the current state of knowledge and held that it was not "completely obvious" that a mask mandate was unsuitable (BGE 147 I 393, E. 5.3.3). It suffices that wearing a face mask, in principle, helps prevent infections, even if it remains unclear to what extent exactly it lowers the risk of infection (BGE 148 I 89, E. 6.5). Regarding the efficacy of COVID-19 tests, it considered "significant plausibility" to be sufficient and stated that specific proof was usually nearly impossible to find (Swiss FSC, Judgment of May 2, 2023, 2C_852/2022, E. 7.5.2).

Accordingly, the Court based its review on a rather loose standard, requiring only plausibility and limiting unsuitability to obvious cases. This reveals a reluctance in judicial review, wherein a wide breadth of deference is given to legislative or executive decision-making power, which may rely on the current state of knowledge. As the preventive measures always entail some element of uncertainty as to their consequences and effects, the FSC may consider them suitable even if the effectiveness is not fully scientifically proven (see, e.g., BGE 147 I 450, E. 3.2.6; 147 I 393, E. 5.3.2). The FSC thus lowers the bar for the required degree of certainty without completely abandoning it (Flückiger 2020, 151). However, the standard of proving *suitability* may be stricter at a later stage if the measure subsequently proves to be unsuitable in light of new contradictory scientific evidence. The proportionality principle can thus be understood as requiring an ongoing obligation to observe and review (Uhlmann and Bukovac 2019, 42; see also BGE 147 I 393, E. 5.3.2, 147 I 450, E. 3.2.7).

Necessity

The second requirement is that a measure must be necessary. This means it may only be imposed if there is no other measure that is less severe but equally effective (Rütsche 2020, para. 13). For instance, conditions or incentives are preferable to prohibitions.[8] Moreover, caution must be exercised regarding general restrictions when individual measures based on a concrete threat are also possible (Glaser 2021, 52).

Again, the FSC referred to the executive authorities' "relatively significant margin of appreciation" (Swiss FSC, Judgment of September 22, 2021, 2C_369/2021, E. 6.5; BGE 147 I 450, E. 3.3.2–3.3.6, 149 I 191, E. 7.5) and relied on a rather low standard of certainty regarding the effectiveness of a measure (substantial plausibility, see BGE 148 I 19, E. 6.3.1). The most reluctant version of this approach is the FSC confining itself to the statement that milder measures were neither apparent nor sufficiently substantiated by the applicant, and thus the collection of contact data was deemed necessary (Swiss FSC, Judgment of September 22, 2021, 2C_369/2021, E. 6.5). In other judgments, it did consider alternative measures but discarded them as either not equally effective[9] or not less invasive.[10] In two cases, the Court addressed the importance of differentiation: Whereas it accepted mandatory testing only for certain unvaccinated health workers as necessary (BGE 149 I 105, E. 4.4.5.3), it rejected the general prohibition of gatherings, because every gathering is already subject to authorization, which allows for individual case decisions (BGE 148 I 33, E. 7.7.3). Furthermore, it explained that even when milder measures are possible, a stricter measure may be admissible in order to prevent even heavier restrictions at a later stage (e.g., mask mandates instead of closing schools or shops, see BGE 148 I 89, E. 7.3; 147 I 393, E. 5.3; see also BGE 147 I 450, E. 3.2.7; 149 I 191, E. 7.3).

The FSC does not always reveal which criteria it used to conclude that a measure is less severe or more effective. Some inconsistencies may be explained by rapidly changing knowledge (e.g., regarding the infection routes of new variants or the efficacy of masks, testing, and vaccines). To some extent, however, the FSC's elusiveness diminishes the transparency of public action and the substance of its judicial review.

Appropriateness

At the heart of the proportionality analysis lies the question of whether a measure's effects are appropriate for its objectives. Hence, measures for limiting human contact—such as the closure of shops, restaurants, and recreational facilities along with mandates for masks or vaccinations—must be carefully

[8] See Glaser 2021, 51; Swiss FSC, Judgment of December 12, 2022, 2C_886/2021, E. 4.4.4.3; cf. for a more nuanced approach Uhlmann and Bukovac 2019, 43–44.

[9] BGE 148 I 19, E. 6.3.4 (allowing a larger number of participants to gatherings while requiring a mask and distancing); Swiss FSC, Judgment of May 2, 2023, 2C_852/2022, E. 7.5.3 (distance and hygiene rules instead of testing).

[10] BGE 149 I 191, E. 7.5 (reducing the size of university classes instead of requiring a COVID-19 certificate).

weighed against their intended effects of limiting the spread of the virus and maintaining a functioning healthcare system. Determining and weighing the interests involved is partly empirical and partly discretionary. Prioritizing these interests in the balancing process requires a value judgment that introduces a large political element into the criterion of appropriateness. This underscores the purpose and limits of the proportionality principle: It provides methodological guidance but does not establish an abstract hierarchy of values and goods (Rütsche 2020, paras. 14–15).

The FSC therefore primarily considers it the task of the legislative and executive power to determine and balance the interests involved and thereby to define the *acceptable risk* (BGE 147 I 450, E. 3.2.5; 147 I 393, E. 5.3.2). The Court also based its judicial restraint on deference to the Cantons' discretion and their superior knowledge of local conditions, which shapes their risk assessment (BGE 147 I 450, E. 3.2.5, 148 I 33, E. 7.4; Swiss FSC, Judgment of September 22, 2021, 2C_369/2021, E. 5.4.4). It approved of a measure as proportionate if the Canton had provided a reasonable justification, given the uncertainty at the time about the threat posed by new variants and the Canton's margin of appreciation (BGE 148 I 89, E. 7.4; Swiss FSC, Judgment of September 22, 2021, 2C_369/2021, E. 5.4.6). Furthermore, it justified its approach by implicitly referring to the precautionary principle and (limited) scientific knowledge (see "Risk Prevention and Dealing with Uncertainty," in this chapter).

For example, the Court accepted restrictions on the number of people for political (BGE 148 I 19, E. 6.4) or private gatherings (BGE 147 I 450, E. 3.3) but drew a line where this number was to be reduced to fifteen persons for public demonstrations, as this would de facto undermine the freedom of assembly (BGE 148 I 33, E. 7). Regarding COVID-19 tests, the FSC held that compulsory testing for health and social workers without vaccination was proportionate because it had little impact on their ability to pursue their job, involved no costs, and took due account of their higher responsibility as health staff and the vulnerability of other people (BGE 149 I 105, E. 4.4.5). However, it dismissed a similar duty for university students because the regulation failed to include provisions for covering the testing costs, which might have placed undue hardship on the students (BGE 149 I 191, E. 5 and 7).

The FSC's approach shows the fine line between providing a sound judicial proportionality analysis while respecting the discretion of the legislative and executive bodies and, thus, the separation of powers. This may come with some vagueness as to what factors the authorities and/or the courts take into account when deciding on the proportionality of a measure and leaves some questions unanswered. For example, to what extent are short-term and long-term effects relevant? Which individuals or groups are deemed affected and in what manner? How much weight was given to the measure's quantitative and qualitative effects?

One aspect that the FSC clarified, however, was the importance of limiting the temporal scope of a measure, especially in the face of acute threats that require rapid responses. As already mentioned in the context of the necessity requirement, severe restrictions may be justified in an uncertain situation to prevent an uncontrollable development and even more severe restrictions thereafter. In such cases, a measure that potentially overshoots or is excessive may be lawful in the short term (BGE 147 I 393, E. 5.3.2; 148 I 89, E. 7.4; 149 I 191, E. 7.3). Accordingly, time limits can make a very restrictive measure proportionate (see, e.g., BGE 148 I 19, E. 6.5). But the longer the period of validity, the harder it is to justify, and the foundation for the measure must be constantly re-evaluated (see the earlier section "Necessity," in this chapter).

Important Findings Regarding the Pandemic Measures

Density of Judicial Review

The first striking aspect of the FSC's reaction to the pandemic measures is the low level of judicial scrutiny with which it assessed the proportionality of the measures. This raises the question of whether the proportionality principle effectively served as a corrective to the governmental crisis mode.

On the one hand, the FSC emphasized the importance of the proportionality requirement, since the legal basis for pandemic measures was relatively broad. According to the FSC, the vaguer the legal basis of the measure is, the stricter its assessment of proportionality will be (BGE 147 I 450, E. 3.2.1; 147 I 478, E. 3.2.1; 147 I 393, E. 5.1.1).

On the other hand, the FSC granted the executive authorities considerable leeway in terms of both factual and legal assessments.[11] This means that the balancing of interests and, consequently, the determination of the acceptable risk were largely left to the executive power, and the Court exercised great caution when reviewing this balancing process (see, e.g., BGE 147 I 450, E. 3.2.5; 147 I 393, E. 5.3.2). Moreover, it accepted that measures needed to be taken on the basis of incomplete knowledge available at the time (BGE 147 I 478, E. 3.7.2). The Court mainly required "significant plausibility," instead of scientific certainty,

[11] See also Rhein-Fischer and Nussberger 2022, 191, who consider this as remarkable from a comparative law perspective. Other European constitutional courts only accepted a margin regarding specific elements of the proportionality test or only the factual basis but not legal determinations. In contrast, the Swiss FSC largely accepted the lawmakers' assessment as to causes, consequences, and appropriate countermeasures and generally all measures of discretion that cantonal authorities are more familiar with than the Court.

with respect to the causes, consequences, and effects of the pandemic measures (BGE 147 I 450, E. 3.2.6 and 3.3.4). In doing so, the FSC gave the authorities a wide margin of discretion in making various decisions (e.g., about how serious the threat situation is, whether an instrument is suitable or necessary, and whether a given matter is it not a case of shooting at sparrows with cannons). It seems that the more acute the crisis, the less likely it is—although it cannot be completely ruled out—that the FSC will declare a specific pandemic measure disproportionate. The Court's restraint also shows a certain respect for the extraordinary pandemic situation and the authorities' will to solve the problem.

Additionally, the FSC confined itself to an isolated review of each pandemic measure in question, which means that it did not take other pandemic measures currently in place into account when assessing the proportionality of a single measure. Disregarding the interaction of several pandemic measures both in terms of their negative impacts and their positive effects on combating the virus may have reduced the effectiveness of the proportionality test and, consequently, the level of protection of fundamental rights (Rhein-Fischer and Nussberger 2022, 194 with reference to BGE 147 I 450, E. 3.3.5, and 195).

Risk Prevention and Dealing with Uncertainty

One of the characteristics of the pandemic was the need to act despite being faced with uncertainty or having incomplete knowledge regarding numerous risks. Most pandemic measures were of a preventive nature to avert further harm. In that context, the proportionality principle required that the pandemic measures be proportionate to the risks caused by the virus (BGE 147 I 393, E. 5.3.1; 147 I 450, E. 3.2.4).

The first practical and methodological challenge was grasping the relevant risk. The FSC responded with the following: As far as possible, the risks shall be quantified. A risk assessment shall not be based on the worst-case scenario but take into account the probability of occurrence along with the gravity of the effects, the suitability of countermeasures, and adverse socioeconomic effects. The Court further held that the risk does not necessarily have to be reduced to zero and that a policy seeking the reduction of the risk to a tolerable level suffices (BGE 147 I 393 E. 5.3.1; 149 I 191, E. 7.2–3; 147 I 450, E. 3.2.3–4). Absent a law that draws the line between an acceptable and unacceptable risk, it is up to the executive body to do so based on current scientific knowledge.[12] Initially, this

[12] Swiss FSC, Judgment of December 12, 2022, 2C_886/2021, E. 4.4.5.1; BGE 147 I 393, E. 5.3.2; 147 I 450, E. 3.2.4.

gives the government more flexibility to respond. However, the proportionality principle mandates continual reassessment and, at a later stage, if necessary, the adaptation of pandemic measures in light of new insights.[13] This also illustrates the temporal component of the proportionality test. The measures ordered must not last longer than is necessary to prevent the spread of a communicable disease, and the review becomes stricter the longer they last (BGE 147 I 393, E. 5.3.1 and 2).

Uncertainty is likely to exist with respect to not only the risk posed by the virus but also the effectiveness of the envisaged countermeasures. This uncertainty modified the yardstick for the proportionality review, as shown by the FSC's requiring significant plausibility without full scientific proof. This strategy is commonly applied in environmental law and reflects the precautionary principle. The FSC's approach may be viewed as an application of this principle to the proportionality analysis in the context of pandemic risks (Flückiger 2020, 151; Poledna and Rütsche 2023, para. 17).

The debate on a vaccination mandate shows the tension produced by the different uncertainties (Langer 2017; Keller 2023). The FSC emphasized the high degree of uncertainty that the emergence of new infectious diseases and the choice of appropriate measures entailed and concluded that "a measure cannot be considered inadmissible simply because it does not appear to be optimal in retrospect, with the benefit of hindsight and better knowledge" (BGE 147 I 393, E. 5.3.2; our translation). Its ex post review hence applied a generous ex ante standard that may even allow the state "to take rigorous measures immediately before serious negative effects occur in order to avoid having to take even more restrictive measures afterward" (BGE 147 I 393, E. 5.3.2, our translation). Although the Court stated that the appropriate measures cannot be provided for in advance in a law and must be decided on the spot (BGE 147 I 393, E. 5.3.2), it missed the opportunity to clarify the legal framework, conditions, and parameters for such preventive action. While the Court did propose to elevate the requirements for the risk assessment relative to the duration of the restrictions on liberty with a corresponding duty to adjust the measures (BGE 147 I 393, E. 5.3.2), the practical implementation and enforcement of this adaptive risk assessment remain unclear. This again shows that the FSC is hesitant to limit the executive's margin of appreciation in its prognosis, which makes the proportionality test less effective in pandemic cases.

[13] BGE 147 I 393, E. 5.3.2; 149 I 191, E. 7.3; Flückiger 2020, 151; Thurnherr 2020, para. 104.

Duty to Protect as a Justification for Liberty Restrictions and Vulnerability

The bundle of pandemic measures also raised the question of how to best protect vulnerable groups (on vulnerability, see Rittossa 2021; Zimmermann 2022). As mentioned, the restrictive measures were motivated by the aim to protect the lives and health of the population. The state thus invoked its duty to protect. The Court referred to vulnerability, to the extent that it does, only in the context of the legitimizing aim (Swiss FSC, Judgment of May 2, 2023, 2C_852/2022, E. 7.4.3) but barely within the subsequent proportionality analysis.[14] This neglects the fact that, on an individual level, safety measures may backfire and eventually hit the most vulnerable among those they intended to protect. The question thus arises whether certain vulnerable groups (e.g., children and the elderly) that were especially affected by the pandemic measures were in fact sufficiently considered in the crisis management (Ehni and Wahl 2021).

There is no clear definition of a vulnerable group (Schweizer and Spenlé 2023, paras. 54–58). In the context of the pandemic, one may consider not only persons with a greater risk of exposure to be vulnerable (e.g., teachers, health staff) but also the elderly and children because of their innate physiological characteristics, among other reasons.

For the elderly, their rights to self-determination, health, and basic medical care demand consideration. Restrictive pandemic measures, while intended to protect, disproportionately affected this group. For instance, isolation-induced depression and dementia were exacerbated by provisions tailored to the elderly. These measures show that greater weight was given to the element of public interest (Kaufmann and Senn 2021, 181). Paradoxically, while the elderly were particularly susceptible to the virus' dangers, they were particularly affected by the protective measures. Despite their vulnerability, the elderly's voices were marginalized in the public and political discourse surrounding the pandemic's ramifications (Kaufmann and Senn 2021, 182).

Likewise, pandemic measures deeply affected children's rights. This was especially evident in cases of school closures. Article 19 of the BV accords special protection to the right to primary education, which encompasses not only academic instruction but also social integration and equal opportunities. However, widespread closures significantly impaired these facets and particularly harmed children with specialized educational needs (Glaser 2021, 50).

[14] "Solidarity" and "protection of the weakest" are mentioned in BGE 149 I 105, E. 4.4.4.3 regarding the necessity of a testing requirement for unvaccinated health workers. In BGE 148 I 89, E. 7.3, the Court briefly mentions that a mask mandate at schools is necessary, as it also protects teachers, who might be persons at particular risk.

Additional ancillary effects included increased domestic violence and compromised social interaction. Article 11[1] of the BV avows special safeguards for children, yet these safeguards received little attention during the pandemic, which has led to potentially lasting consequences for children. After all, the FSC, on two occasions, emphasized the importance of face-to-face teaching (BGE 148 I 89; 149 I 191).

These considerations for the elderly and children, and the multifaceted implications of pandemic measures, underscore the intricate balance required in crises. Juggling the public interest, the rights of vulnerable groups, and broader societal concerns necessitates nuanced legal frameworks. The proportionality principle provides a starting point yet still needs to be refined for these types of situations.

Emergency Law

While the fundamental rights set a framework that applies generally, specific federal law on emergencies or crises, such as the Swiss Epidemics Act (Federal Act on Controlling Communicable Human Diseases of September 28, 2012, SR 818.101; *Epidemiegesetz*, EpG), becomes relevant for how to respond to public health threats. The EpG sets an organizational and procedural minimum framework for state authorities. It also specifies the proportionality requirements with respect to measures against the spread of contagious diseases and stipulates a range of measures to be taken vis-à-vis individual persons (Arts. 30–39 EpG) or the population (Art. 40 EpG) (Zünd and Errass 2020, 84).

Article 7 of the EpG reiterates the Federal Council's (*Bundesrat*) constitutional competence to issue emergency decrees (Art. 185[3] BV).[15] The use of that competence resulted in a comprehensive regulatory framework that affected almost every branch of law. In addition to introducing primary measures for preventing the spread of the virus, Switzerland's COVID-19 regulations also addressed the socioeconomic repercussions of such measures. This is where proportionality comes into play: When protecting the public health requires extraordinarily disruptive measures to be effective, the principle of proportionality requires that secondary compensatory measures be simultaneously implemented to attenuate the hardship (Brunner et al. 2020, 695; Flückiger 2020, 144–145).[16]

[15] There was, however, controversy in legal scholarship about whether the pandemic measures were based on Art. 7 EpG or Art. 185 (3) BV; see, e.g., Häner and Kneissler 2020, 60.

[16] For example, one regulation foresaw compensation for loss of earnings for self-employed persons because of pandemic measures; it was challenged—unsuccessfully—before the Swiss FSC for equality reasons (BGE 147 V 423).

The application of emergency law typically entails a power shift toward the executive. As opposed to the often-slow lawmaking procedures in parliament, regulation by the executive is best suited to quickly respond to acute threats. To ensure the flexibility and leeway necessary for action, and because a crisis cannot be anticipated in its concrete form, emergency laws are often broadly formulated. As (an institutional) counterbalance and to reflect the proportionality requirement, the measures should be made subject to time limits (Märkli 2020, 63, 65–66) and should include a duty to frequently re-evaluate restrictive measures during their application period (Flückiger 2020, 146–147).

A constitutional challenge that affected the applicability of the proportionality principle as such was the blurred distinction between emergency decrees for extraordinary situations (Art. 185[3] BV) and state of emergency laws. Unlike state of emergency laws, emergency decrees for extraordinary situations have to remain within the constitutional limits (Flückiger 2020, 146; on derogations from human rights in a state of emergency, see Chapter 13, this volume). Article 185[3] of the BV only dispenses with the requirement of a formal law for severe restrictions of fundamental rights (Märkli 2020, 63), but the proportionality principle must still be respected (Zünd and Errass 2020, 89). Many of the decrees, however, pushed the limits of the Constitution (Trümpler and Uhlmann 2020, 574; Brunner et al. 2020, 695–697), and established a gray zone between intra- and extraconstitutional emergency law (Flückiger 2020, 146).

Concluding Remarks

The principle of proportionality is a key constitutional concept that is both binding on state bodies and enforceable by individuals in courts. However, the COVID-19 pandemic has exposed the limitations of this theoretical concept. In the extraordinary situation, governments had to quickly take measures while a multitude of parameters and facts surrounding the virus and effective responses were unclear. This made the application of the proportionality test by the deciding authority ex ante difficult. However, the ex post examination by the FSC also proved to be largely toothless. This is because the FSC grants the deciding authorities a wide margin of discretion. In the case of situations marked by uncertain information, the FSC often refers to the assessment of the authority and does not want to substitute its discretion for that of the deciding authority. The FSC also takes an overtly adversarial approach in its scrutiny when carrying out the proportionality test by stating that the complainants have not shown in a substantial way that there are also milder measures. Perhaps the only straightforward criterion is the temporal component of proportionality: By requiring a periodic review of measures, the FSC makes it clear that a measure, once ordered, can also become disproportionate over time if, for example, the data situation changes.

The FSC's noticeably reluctant approach can be explained by the exceptional situation and a particular respect for the state organs that were under unusual pressure because of the emergency situation. The FSC seldom questions the serious and honest will of the executive to do the best for the country in such situations. This trust in the government's ability to find solutions, even outside of emergency situations, is undoubtedly a characteristic of the Swiss understanding of the state and a sentiment that is shared by broad segments of the population.

If, however, the principle of proportionality in its concrete application only leads to the courts assessing the measures as constitutional ex post, a weighty element in the protection of fundamental rights is quite obviously missing. There is a great danger that the most vulnerable groups, in particular, will be ignored in the balancing of interests. This can be seen in the concrete example of the COVID-19 pandemic with the very elderly on the one hand and children and young people on the other. Both groups were hit hard by various measures, but this was not given due weight in the proportionality assessment, and consequently, the concept fell short in protecting them. There is a need for action here both by the deciding authority and by the FSC. Both organs must take better account of the interests of the most vulnerable groups. This is the only way to live up to what the preamble of the Swiss Federal Constitution states so eloquently: The strength of a people is measured by the well-being of its weakest members.

Competing Interests

There are no competing interests to declare.

Funding

There is no funding to declare.

References

Decisions by the FSC:

- BGE 52 I 222.
- BGE 65 I 65, E. 3c.

- BGE 120 Ia 1.
- BGE 126 I 240.
- BGE 137 I 167.
- BGE 147 I 450.
- BGE 120 Ia 1.
- BGE 126 I 240.
- BGE 147 I 393.
- BGE 138 I 378.
- BGE 148 I 33.
- BGE 148 I 19.
- BGE 149 I 105.
- BGE 149 I 191.
- BGE 148 I 89.
- BGE 147 I 478.
- BGE 147 V 423.
- Swiss FSC, Judgment of September22, 2021, 2C_369/2021.
- Swiss FSC, Judgment of May 2, 2023, 2C_852/2022.
- Swiss FSC, Judgment of December 12, 2022, 2C_886/2021.

Brunner, F., N. Wilhelm, and F. Uhlmann. 2020. "Das Coronavirus und die Grenzen des Notrechts." *Aktuelle Juristische Praxis (AJP)* 6:685–701.

Ehni, H. J., and H. W. Wahl. 2021. "Ethik und Alter in der Covid-19-Pandemie." In *Pandemien und Ethik*, edited by Andreas Reis, Martina Schmidhuber, and Andreas Frewer. Springer. https://doi.org/10.1007/978-3-662-63530-8_14.

Engi, L. 2017. "Zum Prinzipienbegriff im öffentlichen Recht." *Schweizerisches Zentralblatt für Staats- und Verwaltungsrecht (ZBl)* 118:59–67.

Epiney, A. 2015. "Art. 5." In *Basler Kommentar Bundesverfassung*, edited by B. Waldmann, E. M. Belser, and A. Epiney. Schulthess.

Flückiger, A. 2020. "Le droit expérimental." *Sicherheit & Recht (S&R)* 3:142–158.

Glaser, A. 2021. "Das Verbot von Präsenzunterricht an Schulen als Massnahme zur Pandemiebekämpfung?" *S&R* 2:47–55.

Häner, I., and K. Lanz Kneissler. 2020. "Verfahrensfragen." In *COVID-19: Ein Panorama der Rechtsfragen zur Corona-Krise*, edited by H. Lichtenhahn. Helbing Lichtenhahn.

Kaufmann, C., and M. Senn. 2021. "Menschenrechte im Alter." *Pflegerecht*: 177–182.

Keller, H. 2023. "Selbstbestimmung und Fremdbestimmung in der liberalen Demokratie." *VVDStRL* 82: 67–107.

Langer, L. 2017. "Impfung und Impfzwang zwischen persönlicher Freiheit und Schutz der öffentlichen Gesundheit." *Zeitschrift für Schweizerisches Recht (ZSR)* 136:87–114.

Leisner-Espenberger, A. 2021. "Der legitime Zweck als Bezugspunkt der Verhältnismässigkeit." *Juristenzeitung (JZ)* 76:913–924.

Macheret, A. 2002. "La proportionnalité des actes étatiques: une appréciation difficile." *Revue fribourgeoise de jurisprudence I (Cahier spécial)* 187–202.

Märkli, B. 2020. "Notrecht in der Anwendungsprobe—Grundlegendes am Beispiel der COVID-19-Verordnungen." *S&R* 2:59–67.

Poledna, T., and B. Rütsche. 2023. "Art. 118." In *Bundesverfassung St. Galler Kommentar*, edited by B. Ehrenzeller, P. Egli, P. Hettich, et al. 4th edition. Dike/Schulthess.

Rhein-Fischer, P., and A. Nussberger. 2022. "Die Rückkehr des Politischen in der Krise." *Europäische Grundrechtszeitschrift (EuGRZ)*, 184–198.
Rütsche, B. 2020. "Verhältnismässigkeit." In *Droit constitutionnel Suisse*, edited by O. Diggelmann, M. Hertig Randall, and B. Schindler. Vol. 2. Schulthess.
Rittossa, D. 2021. "The Institute of Vulnerability in the Time of Covid-19 Pandemic." *EU and Comparative Law Issues Series (ECLIC)* 5:820–852. https://doi.org/10.25234/eclic/18354.
Schindler, B. 2023. "Art. 5." In *Bundesverfassung St. Galler Kommentar*, edited by B. Ehrenzeller, P. Egli, P. Hettich, et al. 4th edition. Dike/Schulthess.
Schweizer, R., and A. Krebs. 2023. "Art. 36." In *Bundesverfassung St. Galler Kommentar*, edited by B. Ehrenzeller, P. Egli, P. Hettich, et al. 4th edition. Dike/Schulthess.
Schweizer, R., and C. Spenlé. 2023. "Art. 7." In *Bundesverfassung St. Galler Kommentar*, edited by B. Ehrenzeller, P. Egli, P. Hettich, et al. 4th edition. Dike/Schulthess.
Seitz, C. 2018. "Gesundheitsschutz im internationalen Recht und die Ausgestaltung durch Bund und Kantone." *Asyl* 4:3–7.
Tschentscher, A. 2020a. "Grundrechtskonflikte." In *Droit constitutionnel suisse*, edited by O. Diggelmann, M. Hertig Randall, and B. Schindler. Vol. 2. Schulthess.
Tschentscher, A. 2020b. "Schutzpflichten." In *Droit constitutionnel suisse*, edited by O. Diggelmann, M. Hertig Randall, and B. Schindler. Vol. 2. Schulthess.
Uhlmann, F., and J. Bukovac. 2019. "Das Verhältnismässigkeitsprinzip aus dem Blickwinkel der Rechtssetzungslehre." *Zentrum für Rechtssetzungslehre (ZfR)* 9:33–56.
Thurnherr, D. 2020. "Vorsorgeprinzip. Verpflichtungen und Grenzen für die Verwaltung und weitere staatliche Akteure." Legal opinion commissioned by the Swiss Federal Office for the Environment, Bale, May 6, available at https://www.bafu.admin.ch/dam/bafu/de/dokumente/recht/rechtsgutachten/Gutachten_Vorsorgeprinzip_2020_05_06.pdf.download.pdf/Gutachten_Vorsorgeprinzip_2020_05_06.pdf.
Trümpler, R., and F. Uhlmann. 2020. "Problemstellungen und Lehren aus der Corona-Krise aus staats- und verwaltungsrechtlicher Sicht." In *COVID-19: Ein Panorama der Rechtsfragen zur Corona-Krise*, edited by H. Lichtenhahn. Helbing Lichtenhahn.
Zimmermann, N. 2022. *La notion de vulnérabilité dans la jurisprudence de la Cour européenne des droits de l'homme*. Schulthess.
Zünd, A., and C. Errass. 2020. "Pandemie—Justiz—Menschenrechte, Pandemie und Recht." *ZSR Special Edition*:69–91.
Zumsteg, P. M. 2020. "Weitere Bereiche des öffentlichen Rechts im Zusammenhang mit der COVID-19-Regulierung." In *COVID-19: Ein Panorama der Rechtsfragen zur Corona-Krise*, edited by H. Lichtenhahn. Helbing Lichtenhahn.

15

The Right to Privacy, Contact Tracing, and Public Health During the COVID-19 Pandemic

The Israeli Case

Maya Peled-Raz, Shelly Kamin-Friedman, and Nadav Davidovitch

Introduction

The present chapter seeks to discuss the legitimacy of using the Israeli Security Agency (ISA)'s capabilities for contact tracing. The ISA's mandate, as set in Article 7 of the General Security Service Law of 2002, is to use its powers "for the maintenance of the security of the state, the order of the democratic regime and its institutions, against threats of terrorism, sabotage, subversion, espionage and disclosure of state secrets." It may also "operate to maintain and promote other essential state interests for the national security of the country, all as determined by the government and subject to all laws."

Given that COVID-19 contact tracing lies beyond the conventional purview of the ISA, this chapter undertakes an examination of the debate that took place within Israel concerning the potential extension of the ISA's overarching authority to encompass this realm. Nonetheless, the principal emphasis of this chapter pertains not to the inquiry of feasibility of such authorization but rather to that of ethical imperatives of public health.

Specifically, we will deliberate the right to privacy within the framework of Israeli law, the constitutional equilibrium in Israel between individual rights and public interests, and the judgments of the Israeli High Court of Justice (HCJ) that limited the authorization of the ISA, offering commentary thereon.

Maya Peled-Raz, Shelly Kamin-Friedman, and Nadav Davidovitch, *The Right to Privacy, Contact Tracing, and Public Health During the COVID-19 Pandemic*. In: *Proportionality*. Edited by: Nikola Biller-Andorno et al., Oxford University Press. © Oxford University Press (2026). DOI: 10.1093/9780197759370.003.0016

Background

Israel's first positive COVID-19 case, identified on February 27, 2020, was followed by an exponential increase in the number of confirmed cases (Ministry of Health [MoH] 2020).

With a view to reducing transmission and flattening the epidemiological curve, the Israeli government was relatively quick to implement nonmedical measures ranging from closing borders, instituting social distancing and an obligation to wear masks, limiting gatherings, and closing school closures to lockdowns. Confirmed COVID-19 cases and those who came in close contact with them were required to isolate.

An epidemiological investigation aimed at locating the aforementioned close contacts was initially carried out by public health personnel.[1] On March 17, 2020, as the number of confirmed cases rose, the Israeli government resolved to authorize the ISA to assist the MoH in tracing individuals who were in the vicinity of confirmed COVID-19 cases.[2]

On March 22, 2020, the MoH called on the public to download a voluntary contact tracing application (the Shield app), which made use of proximity data provided by smartphones. However, as people realized that ISA tracking made the voluntary app unnecessary, the level of public cooperation with this measure was low.[3]

The authorization given to the ISA was first implemented via emergency regulations, and subsequently by implementing Section 7(b)(6) of the Israeli Security Agency Law of 2002 (ISA Law), which, as mentioned, allows the ISA to operate to "safeguard and promote State interests vital to the national security of the State").[4]

Specific legislation, distinct from the broad authorization outlined in the ISA Law, was subsequently passed on July 1, 2020, granting the ISA the authority to

[1] The duty to report an infection is provided by Section 12 of the Public Health Ordinance 1940, which was translated from the Palestine Gazette Extraordinary No. 1065 of December 20, 1940—Supplement No. 1 and was carried over into Israeli law in 1948.

[2] According to the Emergency Regulations—ISA Authorization to Assist in the National Effort to Reduce COVID-19 cases growth, for the purpose of assisting the MoH in conducting an epidemiological investigation to reduce and prevent the spread of the new coronavirus, the ISA was authorized to receive, collect, and process technological information for carrying out an examination during the fourteen-day period before a patient's diagnosis, which can be used to identify the patient's location data, his whereabouts, and those who had contact with him. In addition, the ISA is authorized to transmit information to the MoH. (https://www.gov.il/BlobFolder/legalinfo/kor06/he/files_legislation_corona_kor06.pdf).

[3] By July 28, 2020, only 1.6 million people (of almost ten million Israelis) had downloaded the first version of the app, and 88% of those have taken it off soon after. Fewer than forty-four thousand downloaded the second version, which has been available since July 2020 (https://www.globes.co.il/news/article.aspx?did=1001343009).

[4] All Israeli laws and regulations henceforth are our translations. Available unofficial translations will be offered in the references section.

support the MoH in conducting contact tracing during the pandemic. Section 5 of this newly enacted law delineated the permissible actions for the ISA, such as acquiring information from the MoH about individuals testing positive for COVID-19, tracking their movements and contacts, and subsequently relaying this information to the MoH.

The ISA's specific modus operandi in this respect was as follows: Subsequent to an individual being positively diagnosed with COVID-19, the MoH would initiate contact with the ISA to ascertain the individual's movements within the fourteen days preceding the diagnosis date. The objective was to identify individuals who spent more than fifteen minutes close to the diagnosed individual during this specified period. To this end, the ISA would be provided with the positive individual's name, National Identification Certificate number, mobile phone number, and date of diagnosis. At this point, a text message would be sent to the positive individual to inform her or him that her or his details were provided to the ISA. After processing the required information, the ISA was to provide the MoH with the individual's movements in the fourteen days prior to diagnosis and with details regarding relevant contacts. These details included the names of those who were in close contact with the diagnosed individual, their National Identification Certificate numbers, their phone numbers, their dates of birth, and the date and location of exposure. A text message would then be sent to each of the people whose details had been transferred to the MoH as having come into close contact with a diagnosed individual, and they would be asked to stay in home isolation for fourteen days and to report their isolation on the MoH website (*Ben Meir and Others v. the Prime Minister and Others* 2020).

The ISA's legal authorization was temporary and expired on July 6, 2021.[5]

On November 28, 2021, and following another increase in COVID-19 cases in Israel (because of the spread of the Omicron variant), the Israeli government renewed the ISA's previous authorization via emergency regulations for a short, five-day period.

Rapid contact tracing is the cornerstone of an effective public health response in the case of infectious disease outbreaks (Parker et al. 2020). Several countries used contact tracing schemes, either voluntary[6] or mandatory (Weiwei et al. 2020; Akinbi et al. 2021), with a view to breaking COVID-19 chains of infection.

[5] The law was initially valid for six months and was set to expire on January 20, 2021. Because of an election cycle, all temporary laws were extended by six months, so the law was scheduled to expire on July 6, 2021. In its March 1, 2021, ruling, the High Court held that the government must formulate objective criteria for the ISA's future authorization. However, following a decrease in COVID-19 morbidity, the ISA's assistance was halted. With that said, the law only expired officially on July 6, 2021.

[6] See, for example, the Australian Department of Health and Aged Care's COVIDSafe app (https://www.health.gov.au/resources/apps-and-tools/covidsafe-app) and the Government of Singapore's TraceTogether platform (https://www.tracetogether.gov.sg).

Israel, however, was the only democracy that used its security services to reduce morbidity via a nonvoluntary digital tracing tool.

This should have been—and indeed was—challenged on the grounds of both its epidemiological added value as well as its compliance with human rights and public health ethics.

The Right to Privacy Under Israeli Law

Privacy is a fundamental right in a liberal democracy, and violating privacy is perceived as a violation of autonomy and human dignity.[7]

Israel's legal system guarantees privacy as a constitutional right. The right to privacy is enshrined in Article 7 of the Israeli Basic Law: Human Dignity and Liberty (adopted in 1992), which states that "all persons have the right to privacy."[8] Furthermore, privacy has been defined by the HCJ as "one of the freedoms that shape the nature of the regime in Israel as a democratic nation" (*Ben Meir* 2020) and as "one of the most important of rights" (*Gottesman Architecture Ltd. and Others v. Vardi* 2013).

The right to privacy is also protected under the Protection of Privacy Law of 1981, which forbids the infringement of privacy (Art. 1). Specifically, spying on or trailing others is considered an infringement of privacy under the provisions of this law (Art. 2; see also Birnhack 2022).

In addition to these laws, the 1996 Israeli Patient's Rights Law (Art. 10[a]) states, with respect to medical information, that "a caregiver, any person under the caregiver's supervision, and any other healthcare institution employee shall maintain a patient's dignity and privacy during all stages of medical care." According to Section 2 of the same law, "medical information" that must be kept confidential is "information that bears a direct relation to a patient's state of physical or mental health or to the medical care said patient is receiving," and "medical care" includes medical diagnosis and preventive medical care.

[7] International Covenant on Civil and Political Rights (ICCPR) 1976 Art. 17; UN General Assembly, Resolution 217A (III); Universal Declaration of Human Rights, A/RES/217(III) (December 10, 1948).

[8] The State of Israel does not have a constitution. Up to 1992, its Public Law framework has been based on the English model of parliamentary sovereignty, mostly drawn in common law. It underwent a constitutional metamorphosis in 1992, with the enactment of Basic Law: Human Dignity and Liberty, and Basic Law: Freedom of Occupation. These two Basic Laws, are located at the apex of the Kelsian pyramid of norm, intended to limit the Knesset's powers as the legislative authority. For an in-depth analysis of the Israeli constitutional framework and the legal statues of Israeli Basic Laws, please see Navot (2007, 35–50).

Privacy and Public Health

Within public health practice, the question of privacy has been constantly considered with respect to the increasingly common practice of reporting the names of people with diseases to health authorities in order to control infectious disease transmission and, in recent decades, more broadly with respect to the creation of disease registries related to such chronic conditions as cancer and diabetes. While these practices are crucial for promoting public health, they also raise questions about the interplay between the imperative to control threats to public health, on one hand, and legal and ethical concerns about privacy, on the other hand. Furthermore, many of these practices were instituted at the turn of the twentieth century, long before the introduction of modern bioethics or recognition of human rights (Fairchild et al. 2007).[9]

It should also be emphasized that public health ethics emerged in recent decades in an attempt to frame ethical questions that are more relevant to public health practices and to focus on prevention at the community level (Parasidis and Fairchild 2022). The issue of privacy within the context of contact tracing during an outbreak of an infectious disease or even a pandemic should thus be based on an understanding of the values of public health and its development.

The Israeli Constitutional Balancing Scheme

Both the ICCPR and the International Covenant on Economic, Social, and Cultural Rights (ICESCR) state that the rights protected therein may be justifiably limited under certain conditions[10] "to the extent strictly required by the exigencies of the situation" (ICCPR 1976 Pt. II, Arts. 4–1) and "so far as the limitation is compatible with the nature of these rights and solely for the purpose of promoting the general welfare in a democratic society" (ICESCR 1976 Pt. II, Art. 4).

Accordingly, almost every national constitutional guarantee of fundamental rights attaches limitations to the breadth of those rights in an effort to balance

[9] See Fairchild et al. (2007) for the development of surveillance practices in public health and the legal and ethical challenges they raised in the past 150 years. Note, however, that the analysis offered by this source is largely limited to the US context.

[10] Exceptions include the rights to life (Art. 6); the right to freedom from torture and from cruel, inhuman, or degrading treatment or punishment (Art. 7); the right to recognition as a person before the law (Art. 16); and the right to freedom of thought, conscience, and religion (Art.18), which the ICCPR has proscribed any derogation of.

the interests of the individual against those of the community when certain conditions arise.

The Israeli constitutional limitation clause, set forth in Section 8 of the Basic Law: Human Dignity and Liberty,[11] has been interpreted as consisting of three main stages for examining the legitimacy of infringing individual rights. Specifically, the first stage examines the question of whether a constitutional right has been restricted by a subconstitutional norm. The second stage, in turn, examines the question of whether this restriction is justified, and the third stage relates to the constitutional remedy in the case of a constitutional right's restriction (Barak 2018).

This balancing scheme, allowing the weighing of state powers and discretions against individual human rights—also known as the *limitation clause*—states that "there shall be no violation of rights under this Basic Law except by a law befitting the values of the State of Israel, enacted for a proper purpose, and to an extent no greater than is required" (Basic Law: Human dignity and Liberty 1992).

The provision "no greater than is required," which justifies an intervention despite its potentially restricting a basic individual right, relates to three subconditions: the expected effectiveness of the intervention (the rational connection between the intervention and its objective), its being the least-infringing intervention among possible effective interventions, and the affirmation of proportionality between the intervention's expected benefits and the concomitant infringement of human rights.[12]

Legitimacy of the ISA Contact Tracing: Balancing the Right to Privacy and the Public Interest in the HCJ's Decisions

As a whole, the justification and legality of the ISA contact tracing scheme was deliberated in three HCJ decisions: *Ben Meir* (April 2020), *Association for Civil Rights in Israel and Others v. The Knesset and Others* HJC 6732/20 (March 2021), and *Association for Civil Rights in Israel and Others v. The Knesset and Others* HJC 8196/21 (December 2021).

In the first case (*Ben Meir*), the court held that the authorization via the ISA law was legitimate, given the rare emergency circumstances in which it

[11] Its equivalent resides in Section 4 of the Basic Law: Freedom of Occupation.

[12] The idea of proportionality first appeared in Israeli law in the late 1980s in the context of administrative law followed by constitutional settings of conflicting rights and was anchored in the 1992 Basic Law: Human Dignity and Liberty. In this respect it should be noted that the European Court of Human Rights and its use of proportionality for scrutinizing actions that restrict the European Convention on Human Rights was a direct inspiration for the drafters of the 1992 Israeli Basic Law with respect to the issue of proportionality (Barak 2007).

was granted. Moreover, the decision focused on the legality of the authorization under the ISA law in lieu of engaging in a proportionality analysis. In an *obiter dictum*, the Honorable Chief Justice Esther Hayut asserted that the infringements on privacy were notably substantial, given the character of the security entity conducting the surveillance, coupled with the nontransparent and nonvoluntary nature of the measures implemented. Nevertheless, the court accepted that the authorization granted to the ISA facilitated the prompt identification of individuals close to those testing positive for COVID-19, thereby contributing to the preservation of lives and public health. Notably, Chief Justice Hayut concluded that any additional engagement of the ISA for this purpose should rely on appropriate designated primary legislation.

The second ruling (*Association for Civil Rights v. The Knesset* HCJ 6732/20), dated March 2021, pertained to the legitimacy of the dedicated law, authorizing the ISA to aid in contact tracing, enacted on July 1, 2020. Notably, this case involved a panel of seven judges, an expansion from the typical three-justice composition, which conducted a thorough proportionality analysis. According to the justices, the statutory provision in question represented a severe infringement on the right to privacy. In this respect, they determined that the disclosure of an individual's presence at a specified locale contravenes the notion of privacy as "the right to be left alone" and, furthermore, challenges the paradigm of privacy as the entitlement to exercise authority over one's personal information. In this context, the mere compilation of data pertaining to an individual's location engenders an immediate forfeiture of dominion over information concerning one's life. Furthermore, the aggregation of location data bears the potential to expose intimate facets of an individual's private domain, including but not limited to sexual orientation, religious affiliation, and political inclinations.

The HCJ further opined that a violation of privacy by the state is more destructive than a violation of privacy at the interpersonal or consumer level and that the severity of this violation is intensified by the use of ISA tools intended for protection against enemies of the state rather than against law-abiding citizens. Other dimensions of privacy infringement according to the HCJ were the lack of transparency in the ISA's actions and the risk of data leaks.

Aside from the violation of the right to privacy, the justices also noted the violation of the right to liberty, given the inability to act freely under the government's watchful gaze. They also further noted that the public's trust in the government had been diminished. Specifically, the forced gathering of data conveys a sense of distrust to the public and undermines its willingness to cooperate with government directives aimed at controlling the pandemic.

Notwithstanding, six out of the seven justices constituting the panel ruled that the limitation of rights was proportionate. The principal rationale underpinning this determination was grounded on the constraints, which were incorporated into the dedicated authorization law, which included prerequisites for the exploration of alternative courses of action and the utilization of less-restrictive measures prior to resorting to such limitations. A further justification for the ISA's authorization arose from the precautionary principle. This principle posits that the government is warranted in implementing measures designed to avert a potential catastrophe while dealing with the pandemic's substantial potential harms.

A minority opinion ruled that the ISA authorization law was not proportionate because of the improved human epidemiological investigations that had been conducted and the more effective vaccinations available at the time the HCJ reached its decision. Moreover, the minority judge made note of the fact that the ISA's tools were found to be less effective than expected, given that they wrongly detected many contacts.

The HCJ's final decision held, in accordance with the majority opinion, that the ISA's authorization to detect contacts was legitimate. However, the court also ruled that the ISA's assistance could only serve as a supplementary tool and that its use should be restricted to cases in which an individual does not cooperate with an epidemiological investigation.

In November 2021, the Israeli government renewed the ISA's authorization via emergency regulations for a third time, and the HCJ once again found this authorization legitimate (*Association for Civil Rights v. The Knesset*, HCJ 8196/21). This time around, the restriction of the right to privacy was justified by concerns that existing COVID-19 vaccines could not protect people from the Omicron variant and by the assumption that the ISA could effectively break the chain of Omicron infections. The HCJ nonetheless emphasized that the emergency regulations (which governed the ISA's authorization at this point) limited its intervention to locating contacts who were Omicron variant carriers only. Furthermore, these emergency regulations were to expire within five days.

An In-Depth Discussion of the Legitimacy of the ISA's Authorization

As evidenced, the ISA's authorization to assist in locating the contacts of those diagnosed with COVID-19 was repeatedly confirmed by the Israeli HCJ, which held that the concomitant limitation of individual rights, especially the right to privacy, was proportionate.

Although we may have reservations about the evidential foundation underpinning these judgments, our principal area of concern revolves around the necessity to scrutinize the legitimacy and proportionality of the authorization conferred upon the ISA, within the context of upholding public health values.

Health, according to the WHO, is a state of complete physical, mental, and social well-being and not merely the absence of disease or infirmity.

The authorization of the ISA to conduct contact tracing, which entails a breach of privacy, concurrently compromises the broader dimensions of social well-being and health.

In this respect, it is worth quoting the late Jonathan Mann, who once stated that "the proposal that promoting and protecting human rights is inextricably linked to the challenge of promoting and protecting health derives in part from [a] recognition that health and human rights are complementary approaches to the central problem of defining and advancing human well-being" (Mann et al. 1994, 19).

Moreover, maintaining public trust is a crucial component of public health ethics (Cullen and Reilly 2008). A decrease in public trust may reduce the public's willingness to comply with health authorities' guidelines, including directives to get tested and report illnesses (Myers et al. 2008) and recommendations to be vaccinated (Gilles et al. 2011; Siegrist and Zingg 2014; Ozawa et al. 2016).

Several HCJ justices addressed the implications of the ISA authorization on public trust alongside its benefit in reducing infections. The Honorable Justice Anat Baron, for example, stated that forced surveillance using covert technology erodes trust between the government and citizens, and "when citizens' private sphere is significantly reduced, it is unsurprising that they will reduce their social participation." The Honorable Justice Itzhak Amit asserted that the perception of being constantly monitored undermines the public's willingness to cooperate. The Honorable Justice Dafna Barak-Erez emphasized that fostering public trust is imperative for successfully combating the COVID-19 pandemic.[13]

Within Israeli legal frameworks, proportionality assessments concentrate on weighing the encroachment upon individual rights against public interest. These evaluations scrutinize whether a selected strategy aligns with the public interest while minimizing the infringement upon individual rights. The legitimacy of the ISA authorization should be appraised in light of public health ethics, considerations of well-being, and trust, in conjunction with assessments regarding privacy violations and infection reduction.

Conclusions

In order to break the chain of COVID-19 infection in Israel, the ISA was authorized to assist the MoH in obtaining the location data of those Israelis who were found to be COVID-19 positive and those who were in close contact with them.

[13] For a further discussion of the effect of nonvoluntary contact tracing measures on public trust, see Toch and Ayalon (2023). Different strata of society possess different levels of trust. In a study examining public trust in the ISA's proper use of location data (for infection prevention only), 63% of Jewish respondents stated they trust the ISA, while only 38% of Arabs responded in the affirmative. See Duke (2021).

In evaluating the legitimacy of the ISA's authorization, due consideration should have been given to its impact on the well-being of individuals, crucial to health in its comprehensive sense. This assessment should be conducted in tandem with an examination of the repercussions of privacy infringement on autonomy and democracy. Additionally, it would be pertinent to contemplate the effects that the ISA authorization might have on public trust in policymakers and to recognize the pivotal role that trust plays in fostering public compliance with governmental recommendations, particularly in times of a pandemic.

It is also crucial to acknowledge the diverse methods available for gathering information about individuals and communities. Resorting to the extreme measures represented by the ISA's technological tools, which were primarily designed for national security objectives and particularly within the clandestine realm of counterterrorism, poses a perilous scenario. This goes beyond merely encroaching on privacy and extends into the realms of militarization and the securitization of public health. Therefore, exploring alternative avenues for contact tracing—involving collaboration with various communities to comprehend their apprehensions rather than adopting a predominantly authoritative, top-down military approach—would foster greater public cooperation.

All in all, taking these considerations into account would evince a profound understanding of the values and foundations of public health and establish a public health policy that is grounded in trust and respect for human rights, on the one hand, and that bypasses the need to use extreme measures such as those used in the Israeli case, on the other hand.

Competing Interests

There are no competing interests to declare.

Funding

There is no funding to declare.

References

Akinbi, A., M. Forshaw, and V. Blinkhorn. 2021. "Contact Tracing Apps for the COVID-19 Pandemic: A Systematic Literature Review of Challenges and Future Directions for Neo-Liberal Societies." *Health Information Science and Systems* 9 (18): 1–15.

Barak, A. 2007. "Proportional Effect: The Israeli Experience." *The University of Toronto Law Journal* 57 (2): 369–382.

Barak, A. 2018. "The Constitutional Right and Its Infringement: The Three-Stage Theory." [In Hebrew]. *Law and Government* 19:119–185.

Birnhack, M. 2022. “Constitutional Privacy in Israeli Law.” In *Oxford Handbook on the Israeli Constitution*, edited by Aharon Barak, Barak, Medina, and Yaniv Roznai. Oxford University Press. http://dx.doi.org/10.2139/ssrn.4082324.

Cullen, R., and P. Reilly. 2008. “Information Privacy and Trust in Government: A Citizen-Based Perspective from New Zealand.” *Journal of Information Technology and Politics* 4 (3): 61–80.

Duke, S. A. 2021. “Nontargets: Understanding the Apathy Towards the Israeli Security Agency's COVID-19 Surveillance.” *Surveillance and Society* 19 (1): 114–129.

Fairchild, A., R. Bayer, and J. Colgrove. 2007. *Searching Eyes: Privacy, the State and Disease Surveillance in America*. University of California Press.

Gilles, I., A. Bangerter, A. Clémence et al. 2011. “Trust in Medical Organizations Predicts Pandemic (H1N1) 2009 Vaccination Behavior and Perceived Efficacy of Protection Measures in the Swiss Public.” *European Journal of Epidemiology* 26 (3): 203–210.

Mann, J. M., L. Gostin, S. Gruskin, T. Brennan, Z. Lazzarini, and H. M. Fineber. 1994. “Health and Human Rights.” *Health and Human Rights* 1 (1): 6–23.

MoH (Ministry of Health). 2020. “Coronavirus Update 25–27/2/20.” Press release. Gov.il, February 27. https://www.gov.il/en/pages/25022020_2.

Myers, J., T. R. Frieden, K. M. Bherwani, and K. J. Henning. 2008. “Ethics in Public Health Research: Privacy and Public Health at Risk; Public Health Confidentiality in the Digital Age.” *American Journal of Public Health* 98 (5): 793–801.

Navot, S. 2007. *The Constitutional Law of Israel*. Kluwer Law.

Ozawa, S., L. Paina, and M. Qiu. 2016. “Exploring Pathways for Building Trust in Vaccination and Strengthening Health System Resilience.” *BMC Health Services Research* 16 (Suppl. 7): 131–141.

Parasidis, E., and A. Fairchild. L. 2022. “Closing the Public Health Ethics Gap.” *New England Journal of Medicine* 387 (11): 961–963.

Parker, M. J., C. Fraser, L. Abeler-Dörner, and D. Bonsall. 2020. “Ethics of Instantaneous Contact Tracing Using Mobile Phone Apps in the Control of the COVID-19 Pandemic.” *Journal of Medical Ethics* 46 (7): 427–431.

Siegrist, M., and A. Zingg. 2014. “The Role of Public Trust During Pandemics: Implications for Crisis Communication.” *European Psychologist* 19 (1): 23–32.

Toch, E., and O. Ayalon. 2023. “How Mass Surveillance Can Crowd Out Installations of COVID-19 Contact Tracing Apps.” *Proceedings of the ACM on Human-Computer Interaction* 7 (CSCW1): 58. https://doi.org/10.1145/3579491

Weiwei, X., J. Wu, and L. Cao. 2020. “COVID-19 Pandemic in China: Context, Experience, and Lessons.” *Health Policy and Technology* 9 (4): 639–648.

Laws, Regulations, and Covenants

Basic Law: Human Dignity and Liberty. Book of Laws for the Year 1991–1992 (published March 25, 1992). Updated till May 13, 2020. https://main.knesset.gov.il/Activity/Legislation/Documents/yesod3.pdf [In Hebrew]. English translation available at https://m.knesset.gov.il/EN/activity/documents/BasicLawsPDF/BasicLawLiberty.pdf.

Israeli Security Agency Law 2002. https://fs.knesset.gov.il//15/law/15_lsr_300465.pdf [In Hebrew].

Emergency Regulations (Authorization of the General Security Service to Assist in the National Effort to Reduce the Spread of the Novel Coronavirus) 2020. https://www.gov.il/he/departments/policies/dec4899_2020 [In Hebrew].

ISA Authorization to Assist in the National Effort to Reduce the Spread of the Novel Coronavirus [COVID-19] and to Promote the Use of Civilian Technology to Locate Those Who Had Been in Close Contact with Patients Law (Temporary Order) 2020. https://fs.knesset.gov.il//23/law/23_lsr_575397.pdf [In Hebrew].

Emergency Regulations (Authorization of the General Security Service to Assist in the National Effort to Reduce the Spread of the Omicron Variant of the Novel Coronavirus) 2021. https://www.gov.il/he/departments/policies/dec_714_2021 [In Hebrew].
Patient's Rights Law 1996. https://fs.knesset.gov.il/13/law/13_lsr_211755.PDF [In Hebrew].
Protection of Privacy Law 5741-1981. Book of Laws 1011, P. 128 (November 3, 1981). https://fs.knesset.gov.il/9/law/9_lsr_208332.PDF [In Hebrew]. An unofficial English translation is available at https://www.gov.il/BlobFolder/legalinfo/legislation/en/ProtectionofPrivacyLaw57411981unofficialtranslatio.pdf.
UN General Assembly, Resolution 217A (III), Universal Declaration of Human Rights, A/RES/217(III) (December 10, 1948). https://undocs.org/en/A/RES/217(III).
UN Office of the High Commissioner for Human Rights, International Covenant on Civil and Political Rights [ICCPR]; (updated March 23, 1976). https://www.ohchr.org/en/instruments-mechanisms/instruments/international-covenant-civil-and-political-rights.
UN Office of the High Commissioner for Human Rights, International Covenant on Economic, Social and Cultural Rights [ICESCR]; updated January 3, 1976. https://www.ohchr.org/en/instruments-mechanisms/instruments/international-covenant-economic-social-and-cultural-rights.

Court Cases

High Court of Justice case 2109/20, Ben Meir and Others v. the Prime Minister and Others (2020). https://supremedecisions.court.gov.il/Home/Download?path=HebrewVerdicts/20/090/021/v43&fileName=20021090.V43&type=2 [In Hebrew]. An unofficial translation is available at https://versa.cardozo.yu.edu/opinions/ben-meir-v-prime-minister-0.
High Court of Justice case 6732/20, Association for Civil Rights in Israel and Others v. The Knesset and Others (Decision published March 1, 2021). https://supremedecisions.court.gov.il/Home/Download?path=HebrewVerdicts/20/320/067/v19&fileName=20067320.V19&type=2 [In Hebrew].
High Court of Justice case 8196/21, Association for Civil Rights in Israel and Others v. The Knesset and Others (Decision published December 2, 2021). https://supremedecisions.court.gov.il/Home/Download?path=HebrewVerdicts%5C21%5C960%5C081%5Cz04&fileName=21081960.Z04&type=2 [In Hebrew].
Civil Appeal (Supreme Court) 1697/11, Gottesman Architecture Ltd. and Others v. Vardi (Decision published January 23, 2013). https://www.nevo.co.il/search/Highlighter2.aspx?id=6f112acd-12bc-44b1-85eb-8d8e259f7f6b#0 [In Hebrew]. An unofficial English translation is available at https://versa.cardozo.yu.edu/sites/default/files/upload/opinions/Gottesman%20v.%20Vardi.pdf.

16

The Principle of Proportionality and the Digitalization of Epidemic Countermeasures in Hong Kong Special Administrative Regions

Calvin Wai-Loon Ho

Introduction

In the early stages of the COVID-19 pandemic, digital tools were quickly developed and deployed across China, including its Special Administrative Region (SAR) of Hong Kong, to support the self-management of chronic disease in the community in order to protect these otherwise healthy individuals from contracting the virus and to prevent healthcare facilities from being overwhelmed. Regardless of whether mandated shelter-in-place or voluntary work-from-home arrangements were adopted as pandemic countermeasures, the use of digital tools greatly intensified to sustain many aspects of professional and social life. While the use of digital technology is not new, digitalization as a social phenomenon has arguably been rendered mainstream in the context of public health and has since crept further into other spheres of social life. The widespread and intensified use of digital technologies and the immense volume of data amassed are likely to have a crucial role in shaping the postpandemic world. By *digitalized* and *digitalization*, I refer to the added value of applying digital technologies to interventions directed at meeting healthcare, public health, and, even more broadly, social goals (Ho et al. 2020, 657).

This chapter examines how, in the context of Hong Kong SAR, the digitalization of two COVID-19 countermeasures relates to a *formalistic* reading and application of the proportionality principle. This formalistic interpretation enabled the design and use of contact tracing and proximity tracking software applications (apps) for the prevention and control of infectious diseases by putting the focus on personal data protection and thereby sidestepping

Calvin Wai-Loon Ho, *The Principle of Proportionality and the Digitalization of Epidemic Countermeasures in Hong Kong Special Administrative Regions*. In: *Proportionality*. Edited by: Nikola Biller-Andorno et al., Oxford University Press. © Oxford University Press (2026). DOI: 10.1093/9780197759370.003.0017 concerns over the effectiveness of these apps and surveillance for nonpublic health purposes. Similarly, it legitimized the "vaccine pass" public health (and, essentially, digital) intervention that was in operation for almost a year amid controversy as to whether a "dynamic zero" COVID-19 strategy would be sustainable in the territory (Master 2022).[1] As a general common law requirement, public authorities in Hong Kong SAR must ensure that any discretionary powers exercised by them must not be irrational (otherwise known as *Wednesbury unreasonable*), in the sense that no sensible person could have properly made the decision in questionit (*Associated Provincial Picture Houses v. Wednesbury Corporation* [1948] 1 KB 223 Bill of Rights Ordinance [BRO]). Where the fundamental rights of individuals are affected, the proportionality principle requires a critical assessment (in judicial review, for instance) of the relative weight attributed to competing interests and considerations about the means chosen to achieve the intended goals, over and above the consideration of whether those means are within the range of rational or reasonable decisions (*Soering v. United Kingdom* [1989] 11 EHRR 439). These considerations have been set out methodically by Göran Hermerén as (a) the importance of the objective or intended goal to which the means relate, (b) the relevance of those means to the objective or goal, (c) the assurance that the chosen means are the most favorable (or least risky or controversial), and (d) the nonexcessive nature of the means such as achieving a reasonable balance between societal benefits and the restriction of individual rights (Hermerén 2012).

As we shall see, the principle of proportionality as applied in Hong Kong SAR continues to reflect the characteristics accorded to it in the doctrinal jurisprudence of the German administrative courts to assess the relations between rights-based means and particular ends (Cohen-Eliya and Porat 2010). As an important aspect of the *Rechtsstaat* (Thorburn 2016), the principle operates within a conception of law that not only limits the powers of the state (commonly attributed to the common law tradition) but also to empower the state to advance values that are associated with the liberal state and the social welfare state—at least in the context of continental Europe. Whether a state action (typically in the form of a law, regulation, or public measure) that limits a specific fundamental freedom is justifiable will depend on the hypothetical relationship between the intended infringement and the intended goals to be achieved by it. Appreciably, there may be significant variability in the assessment of what state actions are proportionate, particularly in a time when the survival of the state (whether actual or perceived) is at stake. Arguably, the formalistic application of the proportionality principle in Hong Kong reflects the traditional deferential

[1] The dynamic zero strategy involved stamping out infection with strict and harsh countermeasures (e.g., lockdowns) as opposed to a "Live with COVID" strategy, which relied on high vaccination rates and more moderate countermeasures (e.g., mask wearing).

disposition of English law (as applied by English courts) toward the actions of the executive (Wagstaff 2014). Consequential compromise to the rule of law is accepted if expanded state power is strictly required by the exigencies of the situation (Green and Adams 2003).[2] As a descriptive principle, proportionality has not been devised to advance the normative evaluation of state action or the critical assessment of its outcome in the way that optimizing principles like justice do. This is perhaps its weakness and its strength.

Digitalization of Public Health Countermeasures

Contact tracing is a standard countermeasure for infectious outbreaks that has been digitally augmented in a number of health systems (World Health Organization [WHO] 2020; WHO 2022; WHO 2024). Conventional contact tracing is labor intensive when a large number of suspect cases needs to be tested in a timely manner and monitored. Digital technologies enhance public health surveillance by alleviating demands on already overtaxed public health workers during an infectious disease outbreak and by facilitating rapid reporting, data collection, and analyses. Digital tracking technologies for contact tracing vary in purpose, features, and complexity but commonly involve the use of devices like smartphones or electronic wristbands (Kahn and Hopkins Project on Ethics and Governance of Digital Contact Tracing Technologies 2020). These digital tools have been used to disseminate information, enforce isolation or quarantine measures by establishing virtual boundaries, and track users according to where they access the Internet or GPS. Digital devices may also be used to detect signals from similar devices that are nearby and to maintain a record of them. This record allows other users who have been in close contact with an infected user to be notified and to take precautionary measures, including undergoing testing and self-isolation. Data collected by these devices have in some jurisdictions been used to support epidemiological modeling, public health research aimed at controlling transmission of the disease, or the prevention of a disease's resurgence. However, the collection of such data to identify whom users have been in frequent contact with, places they have often visited, and social activities they have commonly engaged in has raised concerns about the loss of privacy and unwarranted population surveillance (by a public authorities) or commercial exploitation (by for-profit entities).

[2] From a jurisprudential standpoint, the positivistic conception of the English legal system by H. L. A. Hart and Joseph Raz famously put forward the proposition that there is no conceptual relationship between law and morality. A "thin" conception of the rule of law may thus be sustained, so that a government could pass laws that are legitimate in satisfying the principle of legality but morally wrong or in violation of human rights for serious curtailment of individual rights.

In Hong Kong SAR, the Centre for Health Protection (CHP) of the Department of Health was responsible for carrying out epidemiological investigations of confirmed COVID-19 cases and tracing close contacts of those diagnosed with the disease. The Director of Health has the legal authority to appoint public officers to assist in conducting contact tracing work in response to a surge in the number of confirmed COVID-19 infection cases (Prevention and Control of Disease Ordinance [Cap. 599]). Digital technologies have been applied to support infection control and contact tracing since the early stages of the COVID-19 outbreak in Hong Kong. A geofencing mechanism was developed to enforce a mandated quarantine (of up to twenty-one days, depending on the country of embarkation and the severity of the domestic outbreak) for travelers arriving in Hong Kong. Travelers were required to install the StayHomeSafe (SHS) app on their smartphone and then pair it with an individual-specific wristband by scanning the QR code on it. The wristband served to verify location by enabling signals in the surrounding area to be analyzed to determine, using Bluetooth and geofencing technologies, whether the user was inside or outside of the quarantine premises.

During the quarantine period, the Bluetooth, Wi-Fi, and location services of the smartphone were to be constantly active. The SHS app was linked to a significant amount of personal data collected and tied to the wristband and, thus, posed some privacy risks but fewer than were posed by apps that apply GPS location tracking. The government provided public assurance of information security, as data were stored on its private cloud (Government of the Hong Kong SAR 2020). As far as I am aware, it is unclear whether data collected are still retained. Personal data could only be used by the Department of Health or relevant department(s) for pandemic prevention and control, and arrangements for handling personal data were required to be in compliance with legal requirements on personal data protection. Authorized public health officers were empowered through regulation to require any person to provide or disclose information—such as travel history, places visited, and close contacts—that was relevant to the identification and tracking of persons who might have been at risk of contracting the disease (Prevention and Control of Disease [Disclosure of Information] Regulation [Cap. 599D]). Failure to comply with the requirement of providing information to an authorized officer or the provision of any false or misleading information was a legal offense. The maximum penalties for such offenses were a fine and imprisonment for six months (Government of the Hong Kong SAR 2021d).

On November 16, 2020, a voluntary LeaveHomeSafe (LHS) app was launched by the Hong Kong government.[3] This app enabled users to record the date

[3] The LHS app had been downloaded about 7.19 million times as of December 2021. See Government of Hong Kong SAR News (2021).

and time they visited different venues by scanning the QR code of participating venues on arrival and to indicate departure by clicking the Leave button (Government of Hong Kong SAR 2021b). If a confirmed COVID-19 case were discovered at a participating venue, the LHS app would notify users of who had been at the same venue and time and offer health advice. It also allowed users who had been diagnosed with COVID-19 to voluntarily upload the encrypted visit records to the CHP for epidemiological investigations. A one-time password would be provided for this purpose. Similar to the SHS app, the LHS app did not use positioning services or any other data on the user's mobile phone. Location data were encrypted and stored only in the user's mobile phone. Venue check-in data saved on the user's phone were deleted automatically after thirty-one days. Matching a user's venue data and issuing health alerts would only be carried out within the LHS app. Members of the public were also required to scan the LHS QR code with their mobile phones before they were allowed to enter certain public places (e.g., restaurants, sports venues, public buildings) (Prevention and Control of Disease [Requirements and Directions] [Business and Premises] Regulation [Cap. 599F]). If individuals did not have the LHS app, then before they would be permitted entry, the venue managers would complete a paper registration with the individual's name and contact number and the date and time of the visit (Food and Environmental Hygiene Department 2021). The records were to be retained for thirty-one days for contact tracing purposes, if required. As it turned out, use of the LHS app provided greater privacy security than when individuals provided their personal data on paper registration forms to the managers of different venues.[4]

Whereas some jurisdictions initially pushed for the use of digital contact tracing and/or proximity tracking apps or devices but subsequently placed less emphasis on them (Selby 2021),[5] these apps and devices have been in continuous use in Hong Kong from the time they were introduced until December 14, 2022 (Government of the Hong Kong SAR 2022a). This was in spite of the lack of clear evidence as to the effectiveness of these apps (Juneau et al. 2023) and the low level of public trust that could in part explain the often mixed results of pandemic countermeasures that were introduced to encourage vaccine uptake—for instance, among adolescents (Communications and Public Relations Office

[4] About a year after the launch of the LHS app, at least forty-nine complaints were lodged with the PCPD on the mishandling of registration data by venues such as restaurants, commercial buildings, clinics, private clubs, and recreational venues. The Office of the PCPD indicated that fifteen complaints from among the thirty-eight completed investigations were found to be substantiated, and all of them related to restaurants mishandling their customers' registration data (Office of the PCPD 2021b).

[5] In Australia, the COVIDSafe app has a design that is similar to Singapore's digital contact tracing app. While it remains part of the Australian government's COVID-19 pandemic response strategy, as of June 2021, the COVIDSafe app no longer had a significant role in fighting the pandemic, including the more recent Delta strain viral outbreak in Sydney. The focus has instead been on requiring the public to use QR-code-based registration at venues.

of the Chinese University of Hong Kong 2021; Chung et al. 2022). Reasons for the low level of public trust are well documented elsewhere (Hartley and Jarvis 2020; Chan 2021), and the indirect enforcement of contact tracing measures did not help improve public trust (Kwan 2022). In the following section, I consider how state actors have been able to rely on the proportionality principle to legitimize the development and use of the LHS app by focusing on privacy in the form of personal data protection. This could have helped draw public attention away from significant concerns over the effectiveness of these apps and from their potential use for wider surveillance purposes that did not relate to public health (Li 2021).

Proportionality in Digital Proximity Tracking Tools

Concern over the loss of privacy was reportedly the main reason for the low uptake of the LHS app when it was initially introduced ("Over Half" 2021). Consequently, state actors took great pains to reassure the public that the SHS and LHS apps had undergone security and privacy assessments and audits for compliance with requirements under the personal data protection law before they were launched ("Clarification" 2022). The privacy commissioner for personal data (PCPD) has indicated in a statement that the LHS app was in compliance with personal data protection requirements (Personal Data [Privacy] Ordinance [Cap. 486]). In order to alleviate the public's concern about privacy, the privacy commissioner added that an independent third party was engaged by the government to conduct a Privacy Impact Assessment to ensure that the LHS app complies with statutory requirements. The following findings were noted in particular:[6]

1. The LHS app did not have a location tracking function, and it did not collect users' GPS data or have any function of tracking users' movements;
2. The downloading of the LHS app did not involve registering users' personal data, and no personal data were collected during the process of download;

[6] Repeated assurance from the government that the LHS app applies the least privacy-intrusive design for which data-protection authorities advocated internationally has not prevented complaints from being made to the privacy commissioner about the LHS app allegedly having a location tracking function and about the fact that the access permissions required for the app to function were excessive. These complaints were found to be unsubstantiated after investigation by the Office of the PCPD. See Office of the PCPD (2021a).

3. Visit records were kept on users' mobile phones only and not in any government systems. Personal data were also not transferred to government's systems or venue managers for retention. This decentralized approach was observed to be more privacy friendly and consistent with the data minimization principle (European Data Protection Board [EDPB] 2020);
4. Visit records would be automatically erased after thirty-one days; and
5. Only a user who had been diagnosed with COVID-19 would be legally required to upload the relevant visit records and provide her or his name and contact telephone number to assist CHP in contact tracking (Prevention and Control of Disease [Disclosure of Information] Regulation [Cap. 599D]).

Owing to personal data protection considerations, there was no direct link between personal data collected by the LHS app and the user's health data. The purposes for which such personal data could be collected and used were also limited to those directly linked to the COVID-19 pandemic.

In its assessment, the PCPD referred to the EDPB (2020) *Guidelines*, which is important for the purposes of this chapter. The EDPB was among the first regulatory entities to emphasize that data protection is indispensable for building trust and creating conditions for the social acceptability of the data-driven solutions that were being considered or otherwise adopted by governments and private actors as part of the response to the COVID-19 pandemic. With reference to the General Data Protection Regulation (2016/679/EU)—on protecting natural persons with regard to the processing of personal data and on the free movement of such data—and the Privacy and Electronic Communications Directive (2002/58/EC), or ePrivacy Directive, the EDPB states that the principle of proportionality (along with the principles of effectiveness and necessity) should be applied to guide measures that involve processing personal data to combat COVID-19. In this vein, the EDPB's (2020) *Guidelines* clarified the conditions and principles for the proportionate use of location data and contact tracing tools.[7] In essence, these guidelines highlight (a) the need to use anonymized location data in monitoring and containing the spread of the SARS-CoV-2 virus and (b) the voluntary nature of the contact tracing apps, which should rely not on tracing individual movements but on proximity information regarding users. Implicit in these recommendations is the recognition that the conditions under which such apps could contribute effectively to the management of the pandemic

[7] EDPB (2020n30). Anticipated data applications are identified as (a) using location data to support the response to the pandemic by modeling the spread of the virus in order to assess the overall effectiveness of confinement measures and (b) contact tracing to break infection chains as early as possible.

would need to be established prior to their deployment (EDPB 2020, 11). Additionally, deployment should be accompanied by an evaluation protocol, so that the effectiveness of the app may be validated in terms of public health (EDPB 2020, 14).

Where processing of anonymized data is concerned, the EDPB explains that *anonymization* refers to the use of a set of techniques used to remove the ability to link the data with an identified or identifiable natural persona against any reasonable effort. This reasonability test must take into account both the objective aspects (e.g., time and technical means) and the contextual elements (EDPB 2020, 5). Evaluating the robustness of anonymization relies on singling out or identifying an individual in a large group using data, linkability, and inferences. Given the complexity of anonymization processes, the EDPB strongly encouraged transparency on anonymization methodology. In relation to contact tracing apps, the EDPB points out that "systematic and large scale monitoring of location and/or contacts between natural persons is a grave intrusion into their privacy" (EDPB 2020, 7). To address these concerns, its recommendations include avoiding disproportionate data retention and carrying out a data protection impact assessment before implementing the app. The recommendations of the EDPB were largely affirmed by the Working Group on COVID-19-Related Privacy and Data Protection Issues of the Global Privacy Assembly (GPA) in a *Compendium of Best Practices* that also considered the experiences and best practices of thirty-two of its members (including Hong Kong SAR) with contact tracing and location tracking in response to COVID-19 (GPA 2020).

Where clear laws and regulations exist, the proportionality principle helped ensure that important values (e.g., privacy, harm minimization, autonomy, and stewardship) were observed in policy and practice, whether mediated by digital technology or not. However, this narrow focus on one set of concerns drew attention away from hardships faced by the territory's especially vulnerable and marginalized groups, particularly homeless individuals, individuals without job security, and migrant domestic workers (Ho 2021; Au 2021; Chan and Piper 2022). Nevertheless, these assurances of privacy safeguards—along with the relatively low COVID-19 transmission rate in the population throughout much of 2021 until the devastating fifth wave of the COVID-19 outbreak in 2022 (Hinson et al. 2022)—did appear to legitimize the use of the LHS app. The next section considers a stepped-up version of the LHS app that operated as a vaccine pass. The proportionality principle underscored this essentially digital COVID-19 countermeasure that was in operation for almost a year and was invoked by the judiciary when an applicant sought leave from the court to challenge the constitutionality of the underpinning regulation and the announcements and decisions associated with the regulation.

Proportionality in Vaccine Pass Requirements

On June 1, 2021, the Office of the Hong Kong Government Chief Information Officer announced the addition of an Electronic Vaccination and Testing Record function to an updated version of the LHS app to enable users to store their vaccination and testing records by scanning the QR codes on these paper or electronic records ("App Update" 2021). Separately, iPhone users of the iAM Smart App were able to save the QR codes of electronic vaccination records into Apple Wallet. QR codes on vaccination records applied digital signature technology for authentication and to prevent tampering. To ensure data privacy, biometric or password authentication would be required to access the records in the app. As with the users' check-in data, electronic vaccination records saved in the LHS app would be uploaded or transferred to government systems. In addition, users could replace or remove the electronic vaccination or testing records from the app at any time.

The use of the LHS app gradually expanded in force and scope as the outbreak of COVID-19 intensified from the end of 2021 to mid-2022 owing to vaccination hesitancy, particularly among the most vulnerable in the territory. From November 1, 2021, use of the LHS app was mandated for access to all government buildings and venues and the premises of the Department of Health, which included clinics and health centers (Government of the Hong Kong SAR 2021b; see also Government of the Hong Kong SAR 2021c). With the emergence of the Omicron variant of COVID-19, the requirement to use the LHS app was extended to all premises regulated under the Prevention and Control of Disease ([Requirements and Directions] [Business and Premises) Regulation from December 9, 2021]) (Government of the Hong Kong SAR 2021a). All catering business venues that offered dine-in services, bars or pubs, fitness centers, places of amusement or public entertainment, sports and event venues, and hotels and guesthouses were added to the list. Users of these premises had to scan the venue QR code using the LHS app before entering the premises. However, paper-based registration continued to apply to three categories of persons exempted from this requirement: (a) persons aged sixty-five or older and aged fifteen years or younger, (b) persons with disability, and (c) other persons recognized by the government or organization(s) authorized by the government. In response to concerns about vulnerable persons who could be omitted and left without assistance or recourse (SCMP Editorial 2021), various (notably social welfare) organizations were authorized to issue exemption certificates so that holders could continue to have access to public facilities and services (see, e.g., Food and Environmental Hygiene Department 2021).

In January 2022, a new version of the LHS app was introduced under the Prevention and Control of Disease (Vaccine Pass) Regulation (VP Regulation) to function as a vaccine pass including the expressed goal of promoting the uptake of vaccination.[8] Under this legal framework, the Secretary of Food and Health could make a vaccine pass regulatory direction in relation to any type of venue to disallow a person to enter or remain at any specified venues unless the person had been vaccinated in a specific manner or otherwise medically exempted.[9] Legal sanctions could also be imposed on those who failed to display individual-specific QR codes for their electronic vaccination records or medical exemption certificates on their smartphones when entering specified venues, which included restaurants and bars, government premises and gyms, houses of worship, shopping malls and departmental stores, markets, supermarkets, theme parks, and salons (Westbrook 2022).[10]

In March 2022, an applicant sought leave from the High Court of the Hong Kong SAR to apply for judicial review to challenge the legality of the VP Regulation (Cap. 599L [n. 46]) and announcements and decisions made by the chief executive (who is the political head of Hong Kong SAR) and the SFH made under this legal framework.[11] This application was made at a time when the COVID-19 outbreak was at its most intense; hence, pandemic countermeasures that included the vaccine pass requirements were also correspondingly stringent. According to the applicant, the requirements of vaccine pass restricted (a) her right to apply for and sit for property agent license exams, thereby causing a loss of job opportunity, (b) her access to wet markets, supermarkets, or restaurants, thereby denying her easy access to, among other things, affordable food and daily necessities, and (c) her access to the courts as an unrepresented litigant. Ultimately, leave for the applicant to apply for judicial review was denied by the court on essentially technical grounds, but for the purposes of this chapter, the most relevant aspects of the judgment are the pronouncements on whether the fundamental rights of the applicant had been violated and whether the requirements of the vaccine pass satisfied the proportionality test.

[8] The Prevention and Control of Disease (Vaccine Pass) Regulation, Cap. 599L, was introduced under section 8 of the Prevention and Control of Disease Ordinance, Cap. 599. On February 21, 2022, a vaccine pass direction was issued by the Secretary of Food and Health Under Vaccine Pass Regulation (Cap. 599L) to specify the venues that were subject to the requirements of the vaccine pass, in addition to those already specified under the Prevention and Control of Disease (Requirements and Directions) (Business and Premises) Regulation, Cap. 599F(n. 13).

[9] An overview of vaccine pass requirements from their initial implementation to dispensation may be gleaned from the press releases published between February 17, 2022, to December 13, 2022. See Government of the Hong Kong SAR (2022b).

[10] The new version of the LHS app also has an inbuilt timer to prevent anyone from using a screenshot to gain entry into these specified venues.

[11] *Law Yee Mei v. Chief Executive of Hong Kong SAR, Secretary of Food and Health, and Secretary for Innovation and Technology* (2022) HKCFI 688. Although the application was dismissed for lack of merit, the applicant was not ordered to pay its cost, as the proceedings were considered to qualify as public interest litigation.

Residents of Hong Kong have rights and freedoms guaranteed under the Basic Law and the BRO. The Basic Law is the constitutional document of Hong Kong, and it was enacted by the National People's Congress in accordance with Article 31 of the Constitution of the People's Republic of China. It took effect on July 1, 1997, following the establishment of Hong Kong SAR and maintains laws previously in force (including the common law and rules of equity), except when they contravene the Basic Law and are subject to amendment by the Hong Kong SAR legislature. National laws of the People's Republic of China do not apply in Hong Kong, except for laws that relate to defense, foreign affairs, and other matters that are listed in Annex III of the Basic Law. The rights and freedoms guaranteed under the Basic Law include the right to equality before the law; freedom of speech, of the press, and of publication; freedom of association, of assembly, of procession, and of demonstration; and the right and freedom to form and join trade unions and strike; freedom of movement; freedom of conscience; and freedom of religious belief. In addition, the provisions of the International Covenant on Civil and Political Rights (ICCPR), the International Covenant of Economic, Social and Cultural Rights (ICESCR), and the international labor conventions that applied in Hong Kong remain in force under the Basic Law (Art. 39).

To enhance the justiciability of fundamental rights, key provisions of the ICCPR are encapsulated in twenty-three articles under Part II of the BRO, but not those of the ICESCR, as they were not considered to be easily enforceable in the courts. Similar to the ICCPR,[12] Section 5 of the BRO states that certain rights and freedoms may be restricted by measures introduced in response to a public emergency but only to the extent strictly required by the exigencies of the situation, and the measures should not involve discrimination on the grounds of race, color, sex, language, religion, or social origin. The rights and freedoms that cannot be restricted are the right to life (Art. 2 BRO), the prohibition of torture and inhuman treatment (Art. 3 BRO), the prohibition of slavery and servitude (Art. 4[1] and [2] BRO), the prohibition of imprisonment for breach of contract (Art. 7 BRO), the prohibition of retrospectively criminalizing something that, at the time, was legal (Art. 12 BRO), the right to be recognized as a person with legal rights (Art. 13 BRO), and freedom of thought, conscience, and religion (Art. 15 BRO). Even when fundamental rights and freedoms may be restricted in response to a public emergency, such restriction must be prescribed by law, not be arbitrary, and be justifiable under a four-step proportionality test that

[12] ICCPR (Art. 4[1]) states that "in time of public emergency, which threatens the life of the nation and the existence of which is officially proclaimed, the States Parties to the present Covenant may take measures derogating from their obligations under the present Covenant to the extent strictly required by the exigencies of the situation, provided that such measures are not inconsistent with their other obligations under international law and do not involve discrimination solely on the grounds of race, color, sex, language, religion or social origin."

has been devised by the Hong Kong Court of Final Appeal, which is the highest court of the Hong Kong SAR.

Because the court found that the pandemic countermeasures were taken in response to a public emergency, the standard of review was set at the less stringent "manifestly without reasonable foundation" rather than the more onerous standard of "no more than reasonably necessary" (*Law Yee Mei*, para. 63). This standard was similarly applied by the court in two preceding cases wherein the applicants sought (unsuccessfully) to challenge the legality of policies that mandated quarantine in a designated facility rather than at home for air passengers arriving from designated countries (*Syed Agha Raza Shah v. Director of Health* [2020] HKCFI 770; *Horsfield v. Chief Executive of the HKSAR* [2020] HKCFI 903). As noted earlier, the court found that the three fundamental rights that the applicant sought to premise her claims on were either without basis or misplaced for the following reasons:

1. No breach of the liberty of movement under Article 8 or the right to private life under Article 14 of the BRO was found, as the restrictions that the vaccine pass requirements gave rise to were prescribed by law were not arbitrary and could be justified (*Law Yee Mei*, para. 62); and
2. A violation of Article 3 of the BOR that prohibits torture or inhuman treatment was not established, as the applicant failed to show that human dignity was degraded or that the requirements of the vaccine pass caused her to suffer cruel and inhumane treatment (*Law Yee Mei*, para. 67).

The court then explained why the vaccine pass requirements satisfied all four limbs of the proportionality test (*Hysan Development Co. Ltd. v. Town Planning Board* [2016] 19 HKCFAR 372, at Secs. 134–135):

1. The first limb requires any restriction or limitation on fundamental rights to pursue a legitimate aim. For reasons that it would subsequently explain, the court accepted that the aims of the vaccine pass requirements formally satisfied this limb of the test as they were prescribed by law (i.e., backed by subsidiary legislation properly issued under the Prevention and Control of Disease Ordinance (Cap. 599) (*Law Yee Mei*, para. 72).
2. The second limb requires the restriction or limitation to be rationally connected to that legitimate aim. The court accepted that the vaccine pass requirements were "obviously pursuing" the legitimate aim of protecting public health and were rationally connected with the advancement of that aim. In his judgment, the Honorable Justice Russell Adam Coleman observed that the public health value of vaccination was clear, as the unvaccinated disproportionately suffered from the worst effects of a

COVID-19 infection. He also noted that certain scientific literature was considered in the domestic context when the vaccine pass requirements were considered by the legislature. While the applicant sought to argue that the waning effectiveness of the vaccine was justification for not being vaccinated, the court did not find this to be persuasive. The court noted that the rational connection had been clearly set out in the VP Regulation, which provides that the SFH could "make a vaccine pass [regulatory] direction in relation to any category of premises having regard to (a) the extent and pattern, whether general or specific, of the spread of the specified disease in Hong Kong or anywhere else in the world; (b) the uses and effects of vaccination on reducing the health risks of persons contracting the specified disease; and (c) the need to alleviate the effects of the specified disease on the social or economic activities in Hong Kong" (*Law Yee Mei*, para. 76). Even then, it emphasized that the applicant retained her right to decide on whether to get vaccinated or not (*Law Yee Mei*, paras. 73–75).

3. The third limb of the test requires the restriction or limitation to be no more than necessary to accomplish that legitimate aim. In applying the third and fourth limbs of the test, the court indicated that a wide margin of discretion should be accorded to the government in assessing the legality of COVID-19 measures, as it observed that the subsidiary legislations (specifically Caps. 599F and 599L) were not "manifestly without reasonable foundation in the light of prevailing circumstances" (*Law Yee Mei*, para. 77).
4. Finally, the fourth limb requires a reasonable balance to have been struck between the societal benefits of the encroachment and the inroads made into the constitutionally protected rights, asking in particular whether pursuit of the societal interest resulted in an unacceptable or excessively hard burden on the individual. In this contestation, the court found that the impugned measures did strike a reasonable balance between the societal benefits (i.e., protection of public health in Hong Kong) and the restriction of the applicant's individual rights (*Law Yee Mei*, para. 78). The court highlighted a number of considerations to be especially important: (a) the size, population density and urban setting of Hong Kong, (b) the fact that Hong Kong residents remained highly mobile within the city in spite of the vaccine pass requirements, (c) the limited number of specified venues where the vaccine pass requirements were applied (i.e., mainly in places with considerable human traffic, often inside and at close quarters, where a higher risk of COVID-19 transmission may be expected), (d) the fact that activities and services affected by the vaccine pass requirements were not of absolute necessity, and many alternatives were often available, even

> if not always at the same cost, (e) the existence of exemptions to meet the crucial needs of residents and to limit some of the inconveniences, (f) the understanding that vaccine pass requirements had a clear expiration date, were subject to regular review, and could be revoked, and (g) that residents were not legally required to get vaccinated (*Law Yee Mei*, para. 79).

The applicant also sought to rely on Article 11 of the ICESCR, which requires state parties to recognize the right of everyone to an adequate standard of living, including adequate food, but the court held that the ICESCR does not have the force of law in Hong Kong, as its provisions have not been incorporated into domestic law. However, the court observed that, even if the ICESCR were to have legal force in Hong Kong, the applicant would have failed to establish on a reasonable basis that the requirements of the vaccine pass removed her (or other unvaccinated persons') physical and economic access at all times to adequate food or the means to procure it (*Law Yee Mei*, para. 68).

Conclusion

From the experiences of Hong Kong SAR, we see that the proportionality principle has been applied to shape software architecture (Lessig 2006, 67–80), legitimize novel pandemic countermeasures in the form of digital proximity tracking apps and vaccine passes, and improve transparency and accountability by making explicit the relationship between a specific infringement and its concrete purpose. The proportionality of a law, regulation, action, or measure that infringes on one or more fundamental freedoms is determined by the objective suitability of that law, regulation, action, or measure; its necessity; and its reasonableness (or *proportionality*, in its narrow sense). As an intermediary (or descriptive) principle, however, it does not prescribe normative standards for state actors and actions, identify the ends (such as social justice) that should be optimized or secured during a public health emergency, or set out an ideal conception of the state. Arguably, the strength of the proportionality principle is its empowerment of public authorities to act within a constitutional context. However, its narrow focus and/or application within a narrow conception of the rule of law is a limitation, particularly under conditions of great uncertainty and/or existential crisis (Sanchez Barroso 2023).

Social distancing imposed a heavier burden on individuals in lower socioeconomic groups (particularly in urban settings), as they often had to work closely to their colleagues and relied more on public facilities and transportation. They were also less able to afford personal protective equipment. These conditions rendered them more susceptible to the virus, and when they did, they were less likely to have paid sick leave, more likely to have worse health outcomes because of the high prevalence of comorbidities, and more likely to pass the virus on to others who lived nearby. For these reasons, outbreaks of COVID-19 and its variants have tended to be more serious in poorer neighborhoods comprising densely built-up and small rental public housing units. As a public health countermeasure against the COVID-19 pandemic, the development and use of digital technologies for contact tracing and/or proximity tracking have been at best reactive and, hence, largely lacking in consistency or coherence when considered in relation to the overall and long-term pandemic response. As noted in this chapter, digitalization has also reached into other aspects of public health practice, including quarantine monitoring, self-testing of symptoms through online symptom checks, providing public health information, and accessing public health interventions (e.g., checking the availability of vaccines and booking vaccination appointments) and public venues or facilities. Moving forward, there is a need to consider how the principle of proportionality could better support a substantial conception of the rule of law. One possibility may be to strengthen the link between human rights and the rule of law. By this approach, a state action may undergo substantive evaluation as to whether the desired ends are consistent with human rights while also being fair and just.

Acknowledgments

The author is grateful for the comments from two anonymous reviewers and from Professor Stéphanie Dagron. All errors are his own.

Competing Interests

There are no competing interests to declare.

Funding

This research is in part funded by a grant from the WHO (Ethics of Public Health Emergency and Response HEG 2020/1081451-0).

References

"App Update Aids Jab Record Retrieval." 2021. Government of Hong Kong News, June 1. https://www.news.gov.hk/eng/2021/06/20210601/20210601_141555_875.html.

Au, A. 2021. "Why the 'Leave Home Safe' App Won't Leave Hong Kong Safe." *South China Morning Post,* March 2. https://www.scmp.com/comment/opinion/article/3123565/why-leave-home-safe-app-wont-leave-hong-kong-safer. Accessed January 22, 2024.

Chan, R. K. H. 2021. "Tacking COVID-19 Risk in Hong Kong: Examining Distrust, Compliance and Risk Management." *Current Sociology* 69 (4): 547–565. https://doi.org/10.1177/0011392121990026.

Chan, Y.-W., and N. Piper. 2022. "Sanitized Boundaries, Sanitized Homes: COVID-19 and the Sporadic Hyper-Precarity of Migrant Domestic Workers in Hong Kong." *Asian and Pacific Migration Journal* 31 (3): 270–291. https://doi.org/10.1177/01171968221124346.

Cheung, P.-H. H., C.-P. Chan, and D.-Y. Jin. 2022. "Lessons Learned from the Fifth Wave of COVID-19 in Hong Kong in Early 2022." *Emerging Microbes & Infections* 11 (1): 1072–1078. https://doi.org/10.1080/22221751.2022.2060137.

Chung, G. K.-K., Y.-H. Chan, S.-M. Chan, J.-K. Chen, H. Wong, and R. Y.-N. Chung. 2022. "The Impact of Trust in Government on Pandemic Management on the Compliance with Voluntary COVID-19 Vaccination Policy Among Adolescents After Social Unrest in Hong Kong." *Frontiers in Public Health* 10:992895. https://doi.org/10.3389/fpubh.2022.992895.

"Clarification on LeaveHomeSafe App." 2022. News.gov.hk, May 3. https://www.news.gov.hk/eng/2022/05/20220503/20220503_212249_062.html?type=category&name=covid19&tl=t.

Cohen-Eliya, M., and I. Porat. 2010. "American Balancing and German Proportionality: The Historical Origins." *International Journal of Constitutional Law* 8 (2): 263–286.

Communications and Public Relations Office of the Chinese University of Hong Kong. 2021. "Press Release: Survey Findings on Views About the Use of Mobile App 'LeaveHomeSafe' Launched by the Hong Kong SAR Government." Chinese University of Hong Kong, April 1. https://www.cpr.cuhk.edu.hk/en/press/survey-findings-on-views-about-the-use-of-mobile-app-leavehomesafe-launched-by-the-hong-kong-sar-government/

EDPB (European Data Protection Board). 2020. *Guidelines 04/2020 on the Use of Location Data and Contact Tracing Tools in the Context of the COVID-19 Outbreak,* April 21. https://www.edpb.europa.eu/sites/default/files/files/file1/edpb_guidelines_20200420_contact_tracing_covid_with_annex_en.pdf.

Food and Environmental Hygiene Department. 2021. "Specified Persons Allowed to Adopt Alternative Measure Under the LeaveHomeSafe Requirement and Warm Reminders Relating to the Air Change Requirement." Government of Hong Kong SAR (Special Administrative Region), December 10. https://www.fehd.gov.hk/english/events/covid19/LeaveHomeSafe_Requirement_and_Warm_Reminders_20211210.html.

GPA (Global Privacy Assembly). 2020. *Compendium of Best Practice in Response to COVID-19,* October 27. https://globalprivacyassembly.org/wp-content/uploads/2020/10/Compendium-of-Best-Practices-in-Response-to-COVID-19-final-27-Oct-2020.pdf

Government of the Hong Kong SAR (Special Administrative Region). 2020. "Quarantine Data Secure." News.gov.hk, March 27, 2020. https://www.news.gov.hk/eng/2020/03/20200327/20200327_104909_454.html (accessed January 22, 2024).

Government of Hong Kong SAR. 2021a. "Government Announces 'LeaveHomeSafe' Mobile Application Arrangements in Cap. 599F Premises and Adjustment to Catering Business Modes of Operation." December 6. https://www.info.gov.hk/gia/general/202112/06/P2021120600679.htm.

Government of Hong Kong SAR. 2021b. "Strict Enforcement of Requirement of Using 'LeaveHomeSafe' Mobile Application When Entering Government Buildings or Offices." Press release, October 21. https://www.info.gov.hk/gia/general/202110/21/P2021102100647.htm.

Government of Hong Kong SAR. 2021c. "Use of 'LeaveHomeSafe' Mobile App Required on Entering DH's Offices and Venues Starting November 1." October 30. https://www.info.gov.hk/gia/general/202110/30/P2021103000587.htm.

Government of the Hong Kong SAR. 2021d. "Woman Sentenced for Violating Prevention and Control of Disease Regulation." December 21. https://www.info.gov.hk/gia/general/202112/21/P2021122100723.htm.

Government of the Hong Kong SAR. 2022a. "Government Adjusts Five Anti-Epidemic Measures." Press release, December 13. https://www.info.gov.hk/gia/general/202212/13/P2022121300859.htm.

Government of the Hong Kong SAR. 2022b. "Vaccine Pass." Last modified December 29, 2022. https://www.coronavirus.gov.hk/eng/vaccine-pass.html.

Government of Hong Kong SAR News. 2021. "LeaveHomeSafe App to Be Enhanced," December 17. https://www.news.gov.hk/eng/2021/12/20211217/20211217_165030_310.html.

Green, L., and Adams, T. 2003. "Legal Positivism." In *The Stanford Encyclopedia of Philosophy*, edited by E. N. Zalta. January 3. Last substantive revision December 17, 2019. https://plato.stanford.edu/archives/win2019/entries/legal-positivism/.

Hartley, K., and D. S. L. Jarvis. 2020. "Policymaking in a Low-Trust State: Legitimacy, State Capacity, and Responses to COVID-19 in Hong Kong." *Policy and Society* 39 (3): 403–423. https://doi.org/10.1080/14494035.2020.1783791.

Hermerén, G. 2012. "The Principle of Proportionality Revisited: Interpretation and Application." *Medicine, Health Care and Philosophy* 15:373–382. https://doi.org/10.1007/s11019-011-9360-x.

Hinson, J. S., E. Klein, A. Smith, et al. 2022. "Multisite Implementation of a Workflow-Integrated Machine Learning System to Optimize COVID-19 Hospital Admission Decisions." *NPJ Digital Medicine* 5 (1): 94. https://doi.org/10.1038/s41746-022-00646-1.

Ho, C. W. L., K. Caals, and H. Zhang. 2020. "Heralding the Digitalization of Life in Post-Pandemic East Asian Societies." *Journal of Bioethical Inquiry* 17 (4): 657–661. https://doi.org/10.1007/s11673-020-10050-7.

Ho, K. 2021. "COVID-19: How Hong Kong's Homeless Are Struggling to Adapt to New Smartphone Contact-Tracing Rules." *Hong Kong Free Press*, November 2. https://hongkongfp.com/2021/11/02/covid-19-how-hong-kongs-homeless-are-struggling-to-ada pt-to-new-smartphone-contact-tracing-rules/.

Juneau, C.-E., A.-S. Briand, P. Collazzo, U. Siebert, and T. Pueyo. 2023. "Effective Contact Tracing for COVID-19: A Systematic Review." *Global Epidemiology* 5:100103. https://doi.org/10.1016/j.gloepi.2023.100103.

Kahn, J., and Johns Hopkins Project on Ethics and Governance of Digital Contact Tracing Technologies, eds. 2020. *Digital Contact Tracing for Pandemic Response: Ethics and Governance Guidance*. Johns Hopkins University Press.

Kwan, T.-H. 2022. "Enforcement of the Use of Digital Contact-Tracing Apps in a Common Law Jurisdiction." *Healthcare* (Basel) 10 (9): 1613. https://doi.org/10.3390/healthcare10091613.

Lessig, L. 2006. *Code: Version 2.0*. Basic Books.

Li, Y.-T. 2021. "Accounting for 'The Social' in Contact Tracing Applications: The Paradox Between Public Health Governance and Mistrust of Government's Data Use." *Big Data & Society* 8 (2). https://doi.org/10.1177/20539517211054277.

Master, F. 2022. "China Says Hong Kong Must Stick to 'Dynamic Zero' COVID Strategy." *Reuters*, March 8. https://www.reuters.com/world/china/china-says-hong-kongs-priority-is-cut-covid-infections-deaths-2022-03-08/.

Office of the Privacy Commissioner for Personal Data (PCPD). 2021a. "'LeaveHomeSafe' Mobile App in Compliance with the Requirements of the Privacy Law," February 19 February. https://www.pcpd.org.hk/english/news_events/media_statements/press_20210219.html

Office of the PCPD. 2021b. "Privacy Commissioner Received Nearly 50 Complaint Cases About the Handling of Registration Data of Visitors," November 24.
"Over Half of Adult[s] Don't Use LeaveHomeSafe: Survey." 2021. *The Standard*, May 16. https://www.thestandard.com.hk/breaking-news/section/4/172342/Over-half-of-adult-don%E2%80%99t-use-LeaveHomeSafe:-survey.
Sanchez Barroso, B. 2023. "Beyond the Principle of Proportionality: Controlling the Restriction of Rights Under Factual Uncertainty." *Oslo Law Review* 9 (2): 74–91. https://doi.org/10.18261/olr.9.2.1.
Selby, J. 2021. "The Efficacy, Equity and Externalities of Australia's COVIDSAFE App as a Policy Intervention During the COVID-19 Pandemic: Was It Sunscreen or Tanning Lotion?" *University of New South Wales Law Journal* 44 (4): 1584–1618.
SCMP Editorial. 2021. "Clarity Needed on the Mandatory Use of Contact Tracing App." *South China Morning Post* (Hong Kong), October 22. https://www.scmp.com/comment/opinion/article/3153371/clarity-needed-mandatory-use-contact-tracing-app.
Thorburn, M. 2016. "Proportionality." In *Philosophical Foundations of Constitutional Law*, edited by D. Dyzenhaus and M. Thorburn. Oxford University Press. https://doi.org/10.1093/acprof:oso/9780198754527.003.0016.
Wagstaff, R. H. 2014. "Judicial Deference." *Terror Detentions and the Rule of Law: US and UK Perspectives, Terrorism and Global Justice Series*. Oxford University Press. https://doi.org/10.1093/acprof:oso/9780199301553.003.0010.
Westbrook, L. 2022. "Hong Kong Has Updated Its 'Leave Home Safe' COVID-19 App: Here's What You Need to Know." *South China Morning Post* (Hong Kong), January 29. https://www.scmp.com/news/hong-kong/hong-kong-economy/article/3165190/hong-kong-has-updated-its-leave-home-safe-covid-19?module=storypackage&pgtype=homepage.
World Health Organization. 2020. *Digital Tools for COVID-19 Contact Tracing*, June 4. https://www.who.int/publications/i/item/WHO-2019-nCoV-Contact_Tracing-Tools_Annex-2020.1.
World Health Organization. 2022. *Contact Tracing and Quarantine in the Context of COVID-19: Interim Guidance*, July 6. https://www.who.int/publications/i/item/WHO-2019-nCoV-Contact_tracing_and_quarantine-2022.1.
World Health Organization. 2024. *WHO Guideline on Contact Tracing*. December. https://iris.who.int/bitstream/handle/10665/380060/9789240102965-eng.pdf?sequence=1.

17

Proportionality, Epidemiological Research, and Data Protection in a Pandemic

Fruzsina Molnár-Gábor

The Need for Data Sharing

The novel coronavirus, SARS-CoV-2, has been rapidly spreading around the world, causing the disease COVID-19. Until effective therapeutics or vaccines were developed, nonpharmaceutical interventions such as social distancing, travel restrictions, and the closure of public institutions and businesses were the most effective instruments used to contain the pandemic. Many of these instruments had significant socioeconomic consequences.

To avoid the overapplication of such measures and reduce their impact, it is essential to obtain timely information about the pathogen, such as the characteristics of the virus, risk factors influencing disease prognosis, and data enabling drug response predictions (World Health Organization [WHO] 2020). In order to obtain data sets that are large and detailed enough to generate the required evidence, it is necessary for partners from various jurisdictions to engage in data sharing and conduct scientific research (Peek et al. 2020).[1]

Health-related data are personal and often sensitive; their processing falls within the scope of the EU General Data Protection Regulation (GDPR).[2] For international data transfers, the GDPR prescribes a two-step compatibility test: First, it must be determined whether the data have been processed lawfully; second, the available legal transfer mechanisms can be determined

[1] The importance of cross-border data sharing during a pandemic has also been emphasized by the Global Research Collaboration for Infectious Disease Preparedness (GloPID-R 2019; see also Modjarrad et al. 2016).

[2] It should be briefly noted here that the concept of different data categories is now very flexible because of the decontextualization and recontextualization resulting from the emergence of big data and the use of machine learning and the expansion of data sets by the data subjects themselves through real-world data. This gives rise to a need for further investigation into data quality and data integrity. Furthermore, there is reason to think about the terminology for data categories. Accordingly, the term *health-related data* is often used instead of health data.

Fruzsina Molnár-Gábor, *Proportionality, Epidemiological Research, and Data Protection in a Pandemic*.
In: *Proportionality*. Edited by: Nikola Biller-Andorno et al., Oxford University Press.
© Oxford University Press (2026). DOI: 10.1093/9780197759370.003.0018

(Wybitul et al. 2017). To support a common European response to cross-border health threats and to strengthen Europe's contribution to the global effort of pandemic containment (Research Data Alliance [RDA] COVID-19 Working Group 2020), the key issue must be to foster the lawful sharing of personal health-related data pursuant to the GDPR (i.e., to implement the first step of the compatibility test).

It is therefore crucial to decide whether the planned data processing falls within the scope of the GDPR. If yes, then a legal basis must be identified to justify the processing. These steps present a significant hurdle for researchers aiming to process personal data for scientific purposes.

The Scope of Application of the GDPR

The material scope of application of the GDPR (Art. 2[1]) includes the processing of personal data. *Personal data* is defined in the GDPR (Art. 4[1]) as any information relating to an identified or identifiable natural person. If the data cannot be related to a person, they are considered anonymous.

Anonymous Data

According to Recital 26 sentence 3 GDPR, identifiability depends on whether the reference to a person can be established by the controller responsible for the data processing or by another person. Here, all means that are reasonably likely to be used to identify an individual must be considered. In determining whether means are reasonably likely to be used, Recital 26 sentence 4 of the GDPR requires that all objective factors be considered. These include the costs, time, and level of technology required for identification. However, factors only then deserve consideration if they can be "reasonably" used to establish the reference to a person (Patrick Breyer v. Bundesrepublik Deutschland). The classification of data as anonymous thus depends on the effort required to establish a personal reference, which must not be disproportionate. The mere fact that measures exist that in themselves can enable the establishment of a personal link does not mean that they can be used for this purpose with a proportionate effort (Mourby et al. 2018). To assess the effort needed, both the inherent factors of those potentially processing the data, such as their knowledge, and the means to establish attribution that they could apply need to be considered (Roßnagel 2021). In practice, this assessment boils down to a risk prediction of the likelihood of identification, whereby a maximum level of risk is assumed and the probability of its occurrence is based on an assessment of all objective factors according to general discretion (Molnár-Gábor 2023).

In order to avoid the legal hurdles of having to apply data protection law to pandemic data sharing, anonymization has been implemented in various pandemic research projects. While anonymization can reduce the degree of identifiability of data below the critical threshold of the material scope of application of the GDPR, such efforts must be performed on a context-specific basis, which means there are no one-size-fits-all solutions for anonymization methods (El Emam et al. 2015), which need to reflect the particular context of data processing. It might easily happen that, owing to a quickly changing pandemic situation, answers to research questions that are based on potentially anonymous data become revealing if there are, for example, low case numbers in a specific region. That data set may then become subject to data protection law. Hence, an approach based on the continuous anonymity of health-related research data can only be used for some types of analyses, in most cases meta-analyses that combine anonymous intermediate results. Altogether, this can lead to significant limitations regarding whether the initial research questions have influenced the knowledge and evidence that can be generated (DG Health and Food Safety, 2020b; Molnár-Gábor et al. 2022). Other data-sharing initiatives might only use nonpersonal data, such as viral sequences, expression, and protein profiles or literature.[3]

Overall, the broad interpretation of personal data based on the GDPR, the contextual assessment of anonymity, the rapidly changing situation of data processing in a pandemic, and unforeseen needs to actively change the processing context to answer research questions—for example, by resorting to further data—lead to an increasingly fluid scope of application of data protection law.

Making a Case—Presentation of the Facts

It can be valuable to establish a case study in order to explore the issues at stake. Take as an example the following: A research institute, perhaps a public university, receives raw virus sequence data generated by public and private institutions as part of the surveillance of SARS-CoV-2 infections. These raw sequence data can be obtained from samples that tested positive for SARS-CoV-2 at COVID-19 test sites and sequenced by the responsible laboratories. During a research project, the university may collect these raw sequence data, which are linked to an identifier by the sequencing laboratories, under which the sample is also listed in the respective database of a public authority. The data are anonymized by the university and undergo scientific evaluation by its researchers and are

[3] Examples include the Virus Outbreak Data Network Implementation Network (https://www.go-fair.org/implementation-networks/overview/vodan/) and the European COVID-19 Data Platform (https://www.covid19dataportal.org/).

then also made available to external researchers in anonymized form. Besides raw virus data, clinical-epidemiological data, including the sampling date and the first digits (regularly five) of the official municipality code of the place where the case was reported, can also be collected, and laboratory parameters can be determined during a polymerase chain reaction examination of the samples to estimate the virus concentration therein. Additionally, technical case data such as the sequencing platform, the name of the device used by the laboratory for sequencing and the amplification kit, the name of the product used by the laboratory to enrich SARS-CoV-2-specific genetic material broaden the types of data collected. Different IDs may be generated during data collection. Besides the ID created by the laboratories for reporting the sample to the public authorities, automatically generated unique identifiers for the transmitted case data will also be generated by the university, together with IDs related to the submission, user, user groups, and the recording time of case data.

Research with this data can contribute to the development of new methods of analyzing viral genome sequencing data and characterizing, for example, mutation patterns in the viral genome, in particular to detect a nondominant quasi-species at an early stage and to explore the mutation behavior of SARS-CoV-2. It enables the analysis and visualization of the viral types circulating in a region and identification of spike and immune escape variants and thus observation of the regional distribution of certain viral types. Through anonymization and providing access for external researchers, it contributes to making data available to the scientific community for research purposes. Last but not least, it contributes to fostering research on methods of virus genome analysis through the development and application of uniformly standardized procedures (pipelines) for genome assembly that can validate the previously determined genome sequence and thus determine the reliability of so-called consensus sequences (National Library of Medicine 1991).

Within the scope of such a project, personal data are processed pursuant to Recital 26 in conjunction with Art. 4 No. 1 GDPR. This includes, in particular, ID numbers and location data but also physiological or genetic characteristics and health information. With the ID submitted to the public authority, each case record receives an ID number. This refers to the test person from whom the sample was taken and who was given a positive COVID-19 at a specific time at a specific location. This allows conclusions to be drawn about the disease state of the person when the sample was taken. In addition, the raw sequence data are mostly individual data sets, which in very exceptional cases can also identify particular mutations that occurred exclusively in one test person. This allows conclusions to be drawn about the SARS-CoV-2 mutations occurring in the individual and thus also about health effects, which are to be classified as health data according to Art. 4 No. 15 GDPR and hence as a special category of personal data according to Art. 9(1) GDPR. Additionally, the process of anonymization also falls within the scope of the GDPR (Hornung and Wagner 2020).

Exceptions from the Ban on Processing Sensitive Data

To process personal data, public research institutions can regularly rely on the legal basis of Art. 6 (1)(e) GDPR combined with provisions in national laws (DG Health and Food Safety 2020a). With the public interest including everything that is a recognized[4] objective in the general interest in the EU (Kotschy 2020), it can be demonstrated that the research is in the public interest (Art. 6 [1][e] GDPR). Article 13 Charter of Fundamental Rights of the European Union (CFREU) and Article 179 Treaty on the Functioning of the European Union (TFEU) protect the freedom of research as the exercise of the researcher's subjective right and the research's contribution to the development of society as a whole (Weichert 2020).[5] Member State laws regulating the tasks of public research institutions within the area of science can be understood as specifying tasks in the public interest in the research sector.[6]

An exemption from the general ban on processing such data needs to be identified according to Art. 9 (2) GDPR in order to use special data categories such as health-related data.

Explicit Consent

Using consent is generally not ideal for sharing data at the rapid pace required in a pandemic. Obtaining explicit consent from the data subjects would only be possible with disproportionate effort because of the high number of patients who would be involved at many distributed sites. Depending on the place of data collection, consent would also not be feasible in practice. Informed consent is not possible at walk-in or drive-in test centers and would require a time commitment that would not be commensurate with the speed of testing. Additionally, sample

[4] Recognition shall be by EU law or in the law of the Member State to which the controller is subject (Frenzel, 2021a).

[5] The German Basic Law protects the freedom of research in Art. 5(3).

[6] Under German law, the Baden-Württemberg State Data Protection Act § 6(1) No. 1 permits the transmission of personal data for purposes other than collection if it is necessary for the fulfilment of a task incumbent upon the transmitting or the receiving public body. In addition, the Baden-Württemberg State Higher Educational Institutions Act § 2(1) No. 1 defines that universities are responsible for the cultivation and development of science in the combination of research, teaching, study, and further education.

collectors and diagnostic laboratories operate independently, which creates further difficulties for obtaining informed consent. Attempting to obtain consent after testing would run counter to the speedy provision and publication of the data, as it would require contacting the respective laboratories first and then the testing sites. This would entail extensive communication and the need to pass contact details across several entities. Additionally, challenges regarding the inclusion of data about children and unconscious patients would arise.

The Exception to Process Data for Scientific Research Purposes

The additional provision of having to draw on an exception to process specific data types is due to their sensitivity and the fact that their processing may lead to a higher risk for the data subjects (Buchner 2020). At the same time, the exceptions according to Article 9(2) of the GDPR respect the interests of those pursuing data usage and are introduced only for certain processing operations that pursue specific purposes (Frenzel 2021b).

For the processing of (special categories of) personal data for scientific research purposes, Article 9(2)(j) of the GDPR requires that those purposes cannot be achieved by other means or can only be achieved with disproportionate effort and that the interests in carrying out the research outweigh the interests of the data subject in not having the processing carried out. Furthermore, the processing must be based on EU or Member State law. Most Member States have implemented this provision following the wording of the GDPR (DG Health and Food Safety 2020b).

Scientific research purposes are not legally defined in the GDPR. However, according to Recital 159 GDPR, *scientific research purposes* are to be understood broadly as any activity whose aim is to gain new knowledge in a methodical, systematic, and verifiable manner (Jarass 2021). The collection and analysis of data as an essential step toward developing a better understanding of SARS-CoV-2, allowing the pandemic to be observed and interpreted, and making predictions about its further course is an endeavor that thus falls within the category of fundamental and applied scientific research.

Necessity and Proportionality

Necessity

The necessity of research needs to be demonstrated in order to prove that its purposes cannot be achieved by other means or can only be alternatively achieved with disproportionate effort (see the wording of Art. 9(2)(j) GDPR).

Accordingly, the purpose of processing and the processing itself must be interdependent, with processing limited to what is "absolutely necessary" in line with the principle of data minimization (Heberlein 2018). It will not normally be overly challenging to demonstrate in the course of a pandemic that the data collected for a research project are unique in their need for completeness in order to answer the scientific questions posed because knowledge about the pathogen will usually be limited. Referring to the case example, an in-depth analysis of the complete virus sequence data must be performed in order to detect new non-dominant virus variants at an early stage. The combination of sequencing and geographical and temporal information can provide important insights into the spread of certain variants and helps develop an understanding of variants of concern and correlate them with the overall frequency of infection. The provision of the ID by the laboratories is necessary for the quality assurance of the research data, including avoiding duplicate results that could then falsify the results with regard to the distribution of certain mutations. Furthermore, linking the case data transmitted to the university with public databases might enable further data linkages such as with clinical-epidemiological case data, but it may also help assess the quality of the viral consensus sequences used by public health authorities as a basis for decision-making.

Proportionality

Proportionality in General

The investigation of proportionality can be done by weighing the conflicting legal positions (Wienbracke 2013; Martini 2021a; Kingreen 2022)—that is, the legally described positions of relevant actors involved in data processing. For example, the legal position of patients is determined by their general right to protection of personality and the researcher's legal position by the freedom of research. Additionally, individual health and health as a public interest need due respect in the weighing. This assessment may vary depending on the specifics of the individual case; different cases may involve different health care systems and exposure to the COVID-19 pandemic, particular legal systems' weighing traditions, and legal cultures.[7]

Proportionality in the Pandemic Setting

In order to draw on Article 9(2)(j) of the GDPR, it needs to be demonstrated that the interests of researchers engaged in data processing as part of a research project outweigh the interests of the data subject.

[7] See further on the topic of the principle of proportionality as a boundary for administrative discretionary powers in German administrative law (Marsch and Tünsmeyer 2015).

Interests of Data Subjects Relevant to the Weighing Process

The data subject's interests primarily arise from their data protection and data security rights. The interests are not to be examined on the basis of their justification; rather, the term is to be understood broadly and can therefore refer to personal, legal, economic, or factual interests (Art. 29 Data Protection Working Party 2017; Piltz 2018).

With regard to data protection, particular attention must be paid to the interest in providing special protection for sensitive information. The protection of personal data is guaranteed in Article 8 of the CFREU in conjunction with the protection of privacy in Article 7 of the CFREU, and secondary law in Article 13–22 of the GDPR. The interest in protecting sensitive information and privacy depends on the risk arising from the processing.

It should be borne in mind that the assignment of a positive test result for a COVID-19 infection to a test person, the time and place of the test are health (-related) data of the data subject. These are particularly protected as personal data of a special category according to Article 9(1) of the GDPR, and any interference accordingly requires special justification. It should be noted that an infection with a disease can result in social stigmatization, which can have significant consequences for the person concerned. For example, especially at the beginning of the pandemic, an infected person might be blamed for having not been conscientious enough—perhaps for not wearing protective masks, not maintaining social distance, or disregarding hygiene rules. Such stigmatization, however, has largely disappeared as the virus spread through wider population groups.

The value of information should be weighed against the likelihood of identification and the associated risks to the data subject. For example, information about a virus variant allows researchers to draw conclusions about the possible course of the disease and the symptoms of the affected person. A COVID-19 infection can lead to a reduction in an infected person's ability to perform in the short, medium, or long term, so that the affected person will have an interest in avoiding economic consequences resulting from the fact that they are considered less capable because of the effects of the disease. The value of this information is somewhat limited, though. Without information on the exact process of the disease, whether immunization through vaccination has taken place, or about specific symptoms and affiliation with particular risk groups, no further insights about the affected person can be gained. That should be weighed alongside the fact that identification and stigmatization from tracking the disease variant is only likely in very exceptional cases (e.g., in the case of a so-called patient zero) (Carinci 2020).

In addition to interests in the protection of data, other, converse interests of the data subject can also be identified, such as in data processing. These interests must be taken into account and can (further) shift the balance in favor of data processing. A partial waiver of fundamental rights cannot, however, be regularly assumed and included in the weighing without consent.

Technical-Organizational Measures to Ensure a High Level of Data Protection and Data Security

Any impairment of the fundamental rights of Article 8 of the CFREU in conjunction with Article 7 of the CFREU needs to be limited and minimized throughout processing.

A risk assessment when processing sensitive data, regularly conducted in the form of a data protection impact assessment, serves to determine the specific interests of data subjects in not conducting the data processing. Here, risk scenarios are identified and evaluated with regard to the severity and probability of the occurrence of damage; then a strategy is developed to mitigate the risks by using appropriate technical-organizational measures (TOMs) (Martini 2021b). Risks need not be reduced to zero but merely to a tolerable and reasonable—that is, proportionate—level. Article 32(1)–(2) of the GDPR serves as a guarantee for risk minimization by requiring controllers and processors to establish technical and organizational measures that provide a level of data protection appropriate to the risk, whereby the risk is determined on the basis of the type and manner of processing, the processing context, and the degree of threat to the data subject.

Pseudonymization represents an important TOM in any research project, including the case example.[8] Researchers processing pseudonymized data are not aware of the identities of data subjects and they normally have no access to the pseudonymization logic held by data-providing institutions. Therefore, they cannot assign the pseudonymized data to a specific data subject without additional information. IDs, which the data subject can obtain from, for example, the competent health authority can be used to process inquiries about data subjects' rights at the research institutions. In order to do so, the identity of the data subject needs to be established based on further information not collected for the research purposes, such as name or birth date. This data may only be processed to manage the data subject request according to specific TOMs and must be deleted after this purpose has been fulfilled.

An important TOM is the implementation of deletion periods for the various processed data in order to comply with the requirements of Article 17 of the GDPR. Further TOMs include data secrecy under contractual and labor law as well as confidentiality and secrecy obligations under criminal law based on laws of the respective Member States. The data-providing laboratories will regularly bear responsibility for the data transfer to the research institutes and thus be obliged to inform the data subjects about the processing operations in accordance with Article 13 of the GDPR. The institution receiving data can comply

[8] For the definition of *pseudonymisation*, see Art. 4 No. 5 GDPR.

with transparency and information obligations pursuant to Article 14(1)–(4) of the GDPR by providing information about the scientific research conducted with the data on their website.

In case of public research institutes, the data subject's right to object pursuant to Article 21(6) of the GDPR can be limited based on overriding public interest in the research. With regard to the case study, an overriding interest can be demonstrated if individual objections to the data processing distort the research result—for example, with regard to the distribution of variants in the population.

Researchers' Interests

For research institutions, the most important purpose is to gain knowledge based on scientific analysis. This knowledge can be used to determine with which virus variant the sample donor was infected. By analyzing numerous virus genome data, statistical conclusions can be drawn about the current incidence of infection within a territory. Additionally, an interest in promoting research by other institutions can be constituted and fulfilled by providing as much analyzed viral genome data as possible. Last but not least, it is possible to claim significant public interest in the research purpose of pandemic containment.

Evaluation and Weighing

When evaluating the different interests, it needs to be demonstrated that the interests of the researchers outweigh the interests of the data subjects by considering the risks for data protection and the TOMs implemented.

In research projects, the identification of a person can be made particularly difficult by not disclosing the pseudonymization key to the data recipient researcher or research institute. In addition, access by unauthorized third parties can be impeded by access controls. Further concrete risk reduction measures can be established through purpose limitation, data quality measures, confidentiality, and data minimization and by increasing the transparency and integrity of the processing operations and limiting the storage period. Within the case example, the recipient organization's anonymization of data before distributing it to external researchers can also be considered a TOM.

Stigmatization of COVID-19 patients is essentially no longer to be expected at this stage of the pandemic. This is especially true since there have already been widespread infections. The risk of economic disadvantages for the person concerned about whether their identity is revealed is also low.

The research interest in conducting the scientific analysis will regularly weigh heavily in the balancing process. This is related to the benefits of the research for the general public and for the affected persons. As demonstrated by the case example, the scientific analysis of viral sequences can yield information about the pathogen and possible viral variants—for example, with regard to spike and immune escape variants and thus the observation of the regional distribution of certain viral types. These data are of great value for managing the pandemic through vaccination, therapeutic options, and nonpharmaceutical interventions. Furthermore, they can also become the basis for future research projects of other research institutes, which in turn contribute to the management of the pandemic. The public interest in this purpose must be classified as considerable: first, in view of the massive impact on public health; second, with regard to the significant mortality rate and possible late effects of an infection and an associated impairment of the right to life under Article 2(1) of the CFREU and the right to physical integrity under Article 3(1) of the CFREU; and third, considering the necessity and intensity of the impairment of fundamental rights by nonpharmaceutical measures, should there be no scientific knowledge about the pathogen to guide containment measures.

In the weighing process, it must generally be considered that the data subject can also have an interest in the research if they are ill and could directly benefit from making sequenced viral genomes available related to their interest in individual health care. Not only diagnosis but therapy and long-term treatment for the residual effects of an infection will be guided by knowledge about the virus and its ability to interact with and damage the human body.

The guarantee of a European Research Area pursuant to Article 179 of the TFEU is a general interest within the European Union, which must also benefit individuals. This applies in particular to research on infectious diseases, whereby nonpharmaceutical interventions or treatment options based on research data can have considerable impact on the incidence of infections and treatment options to benefit affected persons both directly and indirectly.

Outlook

The risks and benefits of data sharing in a pandemic context are strongly related to the technical realization of data sharing. Examples include the degree of the identifiability of types of data relevant for studying a specific pathogen and the effectiveness of technical and organizational data protection measures at different healthcare organizations. It also includes the usefulness of specific processing methods for performing different types of scientific analyses.

When interpreting proportionality, one of the main lessons learned is that a better understanding of the inherent interdependencies between the legal requirements and the technical aspects of data protection can inform the administrative practice of applying the law. Technical and organizational measures can influence the context of data processing that creates the risks for data subjects. By reducing risks, the interest of data subjects in protection can be mitigated and can lead to a different assessment of their interests in the balancing process. The protection of data subjects' interests is accounted for by, in particular, minimizing identifiability, and with that the need to protect the rights and freedoms of the data subjects against those of the researchers will lose significance in the proportionality test. Putting it simply, the manner in which data are processed is a technicality, but the technical features must be designed so as to prepare for the balancing of competing interest positions. However, the option is retained to draw on TOMs to react to the results of the proportionality test.

In this context, the risk of (re)establishing a personal link and the risk of the processing for the rights and freedoms of the data subjects are to be regarded as interdependent prognoses that can be combined into a single data processing impact assessment. Implementing TOMs that can both react to the personal nature of the data being processed and reflect its proportionality in a context-based manner to a pandemic situation will help define the transitions between data processing that is relevant and nonrelevant. The assessment of adequacy would thus be based on the level of data protection in the country outside of the EU/EEA compared to that of the CFREU and its concretization in secondary law by the GDPR. The design of the transfer is thus also based on appropriate safeguards for the rights of the data subjects, which must be measured against the principle of proportionality. Over time, standardizing the legal assessment of risks in scientific data processing related to a pandemic, their impact on interest positions, and the balancing of competing interests that results in differences in technical implementations can contribute to removing hurdles related to cross-border data sharing and fuel the rapid containment of future pandemics.

The development of the European Health Data Space (EHDS) (Regulation (EU) 2025/327 on the European Health Data Space) deserves focus in this context. Embedded in the European Data Strategy, which aims to create a single European market for data, the EHDS pursues the goal of enabling the use of electronic health data for healthcare purposes and to promote research, innovation, and policymaking, while complying with data protection regulations (European Health Data Space [EHDS] 2025, Art. 1 para. 3). In order to prevent the fragmentation of the EHDS because of the existing variety of national rules on the processing of health-related data, the regulatory project is to be based on the GDPR, which enables the processing of health-related data based on EU law. In view of the fact that data processing is to be limited to the technical infrastructure of the EHDS, which does not allow users to download or otherwise reproduce the data concerned, it can be assumed that there will be a reduced risk of harm to the rights and freedoms of data subjects. The processing of data in such a technical infrastructure could, therefore, help ensure that the balance between protection and processing interests can be decided in favor of the latter when fulfilling legal compliance (Molnár-Gábor et al. 2022), especially if this is supported by important public interests. Data-protection-compliant standardization of the technical processing environment can provide a suitable empirical basis for the normative relief of trade-offs through the legal balancing of competing interest positions and thus for its further approximation across cases marked by a particular public interest.

Acknowledgments

This case example is inspired by the SARS-CoV-2 Genomics Data Platform (CoGDat), established at the University of Tübingen, Germany. For more information, see https://cogdat.de/. For the purposes of this case study, the characteristics of the case have been adjusted and do not reflect the real scenario and the characteristics of data processing in their entirety. Although the facts and circumstances of the case analyzed here are based on facts taken from the real CoGDat study, they are also enriched with additional and fictitious details to make possible legal challenges related to data sharing in the COVID-19 pandemic clearer. For the results of the case analyses presented here, it is not important which facts and/or circumstances of the case are based on the real example and which are fictitious. Special thanks go to Leon Kuchenbecker, Oliver Kohlbacher, Adam Dampc, and Lisa Kaldowski for fruitful discussions about applying the proportionality test to the real scenario of data processing.

Competing Interests

There are no competing interests to declare.

Funding

The work has been funded by the German Research Foundation (DFG)—NFDI 1/1 "GHGA—German Human Genome Phenome Archive."

References

Article 29 Data Protection Working Party. 2017. "Guidelines on Data Protection Impact Assessment (DPIA) and Determining Whether Processing Is 'Likely to Result in a High Risk' for the Purposes of Regulation 2016/679," April 4, recital 43-49.Last revised on October 4, 2017. 17/ENWP 248 rev.01, 6.

Buchner, B. 2020. "Art. 1." In *Datenschutz-Grundverordnung, BDSG*, edited by Jürgen Kühling and Benedikt Buchner. 3rd edition, recital 16. C. H. Beck.

Carinci, F. 2020. "COVID-19: Preparedness, Decentralisation, and the Hunt for Patient Zero." *BMJ* 368. https://doi.org/10.1136/bmj.m799.

Patrick Breyer v. Bundesrepublik Deutschland. C-582/14, EU:C:2016:779, recital 43 et seq.

DG Health and Food Safety. 2020a. *Assessment of the EU Member States' Rules on Health Data in the Light of GDPR.* 25. European Commission. https://health.ec.europa.eu/system/files/2021-02/ms_rules_health-data_en_0.pdf.

DG Health and Food Safety. 2020b. *Assessment of the EU Member States' rules on health data in the light of GDPR.* 60. European Commission. https://health.ec.europa.eu/system/files/2021-02/ms_rules_health-data_en_0.pdf.

EHDS (European Health Data Space). Regulation (EU) 2025/327 of the European Parliament and of the Council of 11 February 2025 on the European Health Data Space and amending Directive 2011/24/EU and Regulation (EU) 2024/2847 (Text with EEA relevance), PE/76/2024/REV/1, OJ L, 2025/327, 5.3.2025.

El Emam, K., S. Rodgers, and B. Malin. 2015. "Anonymising and Sharing Individual Patient Data." *BMJ* 350. https://doi.org/10.1136/bmj.h1139.

Frenzel, E. M. 2021a. "Art. 6." In *Datenschutz-Grundverordnung: Bundesdatenschutzgesetz*, edited by Boris Paal and Daniel Pauly. 3rd edition, recital 24. C. H. Beck.

Frenzel, E. M. 2021b. "Art. 9." In *Datenschutz-Grundverordnung: Bundesdatenschutzgesetz*, edited by Boris Paal and Daniel Pauly. 3rd edition, recital 6. C. H. Beck.

GloPID-R. 2019. "Roadmap for Data Sharing in Public Health Emergencies:" https://www.glopid-r.org/wp-content/uploads/2019/06/glopid-r-roadmap-for-data-sharing.pdf.

Heberlein, H. 2018. "Art. 5." In *Datenschutz-Grundverordnung*, edited by Eugen Ehmann and Martin Selmayr. 2nd edition, recital 13. C. H. Beck.

Hornung, G., and B. Wagner. 2020. "Anonymisierung als datenschutzrelevante Verarbeitung? Rechtliche Anforderungen und Grenzen für die Anonymisierung personenbezogener Daten." *Zeitschrift für Datenschutz* 5:223–228.

Jarass, H. D. 2021. "Art. 13." In *Charta der Grundrechte der Europäischen Union*, edited by Hans D. Jarass. 4th edition, recital 8. C. H. Beck.

Kingreen, T. 2022. "Art. 52." In *EUV/AEUV. Das Verfassungsrecht der Europäischen Union mit Europäischer Grundrechtecharta*, edited by Christian Calliess and Matthias Ruffert. 6th edition, recital 65. C. H. Beck.

Kotschy, W. 2020. "Article 6." In *The EU General Data Protection Regulation: A Commentary*, edited by Christopher Kuner, Lee A. Bygrave, and Christopher Docksey. Oxford University Press.

Marsch, M., and V. Tünsmeyer. 2015. "The Principle of Proportionality in German Administrative Law." In *The Judge and the Proportionate Use of Discretion. A Comparative Study*, edited by Sofia Ranchordas and Waard de Boudewijn. Routledge.

Martini, M. 2021. "Art. 32." In *Datenschutz-Grundverordnung: Bundesdatenschutzgesetz*, edited by Boris Paal and Daniel Pauly. 3rd edition, recital 25. C. H. Beck.

Martini, M. 2021. "Art. 32." In *Datenschutz-Grundverordnung: Bundesdatenschutzgesetz*, edited by Boris Paal and Daniel Pauly. 3rd edition, recital 48. C. H. Beck.

Modjarrad, K., V. S. Moorthy, P. Millett, P. S. Gsell, C. Roth, and M. P. Kieny. 2016. "Developing Global Norms for Sharing Data and Results During Public Health Emergencies." *PLoS Med* 13 (1): e1001935. https://doi.org/10.1371/journal.pmed.1001935.

Molnár-Gábor, F. 2023. "Schutz der Rechte und Freiheiten von Personen bei der Datenverarbeitung im Gesundheitsbereich: Der Risikoansatz der EU-Datenschutz-Grundverordnung (DGSVO). "*Bundesgesundheitsblatt*66:143–153. https://doi.org/10.1007/s00103-022-03652-6.

Molnár-Gábor, F., M. J. S. Beauvais, A. Bernier, M. P. N. Jimenez, M. Recuero, and B. M. Knoppers. 2022. "Bridging the European Data Sharing Divide in Genomic Science." *J Med Internet Res* 24 (10): e37236. https://doi.org/10.2196/37236.

Mourby, M., E. Mackey, M. Elliot et al. 2018. "Are 'Pseudonymised' Data Always Personal Data? Implications of the GDPR for Administrative Data Research in the UK." *Computer Law & Security Review* 34 (2): 222–233. https://doi.org/10.1016/j.clsr.2018.01.002.

National Library of Medicine. 1991. "Consensus Sequence." https://www.ncbi.nlm.nih.gov/mesh?Db=mesh&Cmd=DetailsSearch&Term=%22Consensus+Sequence%22%5BmeSH+Terms%5D.

Peek, N., M. Sujan, and P. Scott. 2020. "Digital Health and Care in Pandemic Times: Impact of COVID-19." *BMJ Health & Care Informatics* 27:e100166. https://doi.org/10.1136/bmjhci-2020-100166.

Piltz, C. 2018. "Art. 32." In *Datenschutz-Grundverordnung: Bundesdatenschutzgesetz*, edited by Peter Gola and Dirk Heckmann. 2nd edition, recital 22. C. H. Beck.

RDA (Research Data Alliance) COVID-19 Working Group. 2020. *RDA COVID-19: Recommendations and Guidelines on Data Sharing*, June 30. https://doi.org/10.15497/rda00052.

Roßnagel, A. 2021. "Datenlöschung und Anonymisierung." *Zeitschrift für Datenschutz* 4: 188–192.

Weichert, T. 2020. "Das Forschungsprivileg in der DS-GVO." *Zeitschrift für Datenschutz* 1:18–24.

WHO (World Health Organization). 2020. "Coronavirus Disease (COVID-19)—Events as They Happen." https://www.who.int/emergencies/diseases/novel-coronavirus-2019/events-as-they-happen.

Wybitul, T., L. Ströbel, and M. Ruess. 2017. "Übermittlung personenbezogener Daten in Drittländer." *Zeitschrift für Datenschutz* 11:503–509.

Wienbracke, M. 2013. "Der Verhältnismäßigkeitsgrundsatz." *Zeitschrift für das Juristische Studium* 2:148–155.

18

(Dis)proportionate Abortion Care Regulation and the COVID-19 Pandemic in Great Britain

Jordan A. Parsons and Elizabeth Chloe Romanis

Introduction[1]

Questions of proportionality have long been raised in relation to the regulation of abortion. Abortion has historically been considered a contentious matter of policy rather than one of individual healthcare, leading to extensive (and generally restrictive) regulation. Even more liberal governments tend to avoid making changes to abortion law, preferring not to rock the boat (Creasy and Sanquest 2021), which means that abortion policy often does not move forward in tandem with medical developments and evidence (Lohr et al. 2020). Consequently, abortion policy often lags behind clinical reality and social climate (Sheldon and Wellings 2020). Abortion is often subject to arguably excessive regulation, and Great Britain is no exception to this rule (Romanis et al. 2022). In this chapter, we explore how the excessive regulation of telemedical abortion is disproportionate and has affected access.

In Great Britain, the most recent shift in abortion policy, which has been accompanied by significant debate, was about the implementation of telemedical care pathways for the provision of early medical abortion (EMA). While there had been calls for telemedicine in abortion care for many years beforehand, the conditions created by the COVID-19 pandemic brought the policy to fruition through changes to the law—albeit in a fraught and confusing manner. It is these developments that we concern ourselves with in this chapter. We argue that abortion regulation in Great Britain has historically been significantly

[1] The contents of this chapter were correct and up-to-date at the time of writing. Due to a long production timeline, we recognise that there have been further developments in the interim that are of relevance to our discussion. We hope readers will forgive us the absence of engagement with such things.

Jordan A. Parsons and Elizabeth Chloe Romanis, *(Dis)proportionate Abortion Care Regulation and the COVID-19 Pandemic in Great Britain*. In: *Proportionality*. Edited by: Nikola Biller-Andorno et al., Oxford University Press.
 DOI: 10.1093/9780197759370.003.0019

disproportionate and that this remains the case. While there was a glimmer of hope in the COVID-19 response and subsequent introduction of progressive, evidence-based abortion policy, the fine-tuning of such policy demonstrates the presence of abortion exceptionalism—that is, the setting apart of abortion from other aspects of healthcare for increased and exceptional oversight (Borgmann 2014). This is inherently disproportionate.

Hemerén (2012) describes proportionality in terms of the relationship between the ends and means being appropriate. He provides four conditions for assessing whether a given policy or regulatory intervention is proportionate:

(1) the importance of the intended goal
(2) the relevance of the means to achieving that goal
(3) those means being the most favorable (i.e., no less controversial alternative is available)
(4) nonexcessiveness

In many ways, the final condition—nonexcessiveness—speaks to colloquial understandings of proportionality. People tend to use the term conversationally to convey notions of reasonableness and an avoidance of overkill. This condition will prove central to our discussion as we highlight how the extent to which abortion is regulated in Great Britain is excessive (Parsons and Romanis 2021; Romanis et al. 2022).

We will take as the intended goal a situation wherein pregnant people are able to access abortion care safely and without undue burden. We take it that a regulatory system, no matter how permissive of abortion it may seem, is only as good as the access it ensures for abortion-seekers in practice (Rebouché 2014; Romanis 2023a). Access to abortion is a crucial component of comprehensive reproductive and sexual health services. It preserves the physical and mental health of people with the relevant physiology (United Nations 1995, para. 7.2) and, more broadly, their social and economic rights. It is also claimed as the goal of many who support the imposition of regulations that we will argue shortly are disproportionate to achieving this goal.

In this chapter, we will take a chronological approach to examining the extent to which abortion regulation in Great Britain can be considered proportionate, though with a specific focus on the period of the COVID-19 pandemic. We ultimately argue that, while more recent developments may represent movement in the right direction, there is an underlying disproportionate regulation of abortion care in Great Britain that is rooted in abortion exceptionalism. This exceptionalism continues to limit the evolution of services that best ensure access for abortion-seekers, as the law is such that few changes can be made to service provision without regulatory change. As long as this view of abortion as distinct rather than routine healthcare continues, its regulation is likely to remain disproportionate.

EMA

Our focus in this chapter is on EMA; we are not talking about surgical abortion and medical abortion taking place later in pregnancy. As will be discussed shortly, we take EMA to refer to the use of medical methods of abortion during the first ten weeks of pregnancy. While we do consider there to be important questions of proportionality to explore in wider abortion regulation, in this chapter we concern ourselves only with EMA because this has been the focus of regulatory change and policy debate in Great Britain during the COVID-19 pandemic.

EMA is relatively straightforward and routine for most patients. It requires the individual to take two drugs—mifepristone and misoprostol—between twenty-four and forty-eight hours apart. Mifepristone first acts to inhibit the hormone progesterone, thereby causing the breakdown of the uterine lining and, consequently, the discontinuation of the pregnancy. Misoprostol then triggers uterine contractions, causing the expulsion of the products of conception. For the patient, this process can be similar to what occurs during spontaneous miscarriage in early pregnancy.

There are alternative drugs and regimens that can be safely and effectively used for EMA. Some have become necessary practice in parts of the world because of the infeasibility of other forms of abortion, whether that is due to availability of particular drugs or the practicalities of treatment timing (i.e., attending multiple clinic appointments). For example, someone may take both mifepristone and misoprostol simultaneously if they are unable to attend a clinic on two consecutive days (assuming a not-uncommon requirement that they be taken in a clinic).[2] Nonetheless, EMA hereafter refers to the mifepristone-misoprostol regimen described earlier. This is due to its being the most common method and endorsed by the World Health Organization (WHO 2022, 68).

To be considered an *early* medical abortion, this treatment must ordinarily be carried out within the first ten weeks of pregnancy. While there is no official classification, this is generally the accepted gestational cutoff.[3] For example, regulations in England and Wales stipulate a gestational limit of nine weeks and six days for treatment deemed EMA (Department of Health and Social Care

[2] This is still an effective regimen, though it is likely to result in more significant side effects (Creinin et al. 2007).

[3] However, there is movement toward twelve weeks as a more recognized limit (WHO 2022, 68). This is in light of evidence concerning safety and effectiveness that we will highlight shortly.

2018; Welsh Government 2018; Department of Health and Social Care 2020; Welsh Government 2020).[4] This is, in part, due to a lesser evidence base for certain aspects of later medical abortions.[5]

EMA is recognized as a safe and effective treatment, and the WHO (2022, 68) strongly recommends it for use up to a higher limit of twelve weeks' gestation. The WHO (2012, 3) had previously strongly recommended up to nine weeks' gestation, with a weak recommendation for up to twelve weeks. This was increased in its 2022 guidance because of more recent research findings. It may be, then, that twelve weeks will soon be recognized as the cutoff for EMA, but for now we will proceed with referring to EMA as up to ten weeks. This safety and effectiveness has been consistently demonstrated across several studies in varying geographical locations (Raymond et al. 2013; Chen and Creinin 2015). It is for this reason that in many parts of the world—such as Great Britain—it has become the most common method of abortion (Office for Health Improvement and Disparities 2022).

Further, EMA has consistently been found to be highly acceptable to patients—something we consider as important as the treatment's clinical credentials (Parsons and Romanis 2021). This is true of EMA provided in a clinical setting and through telemedicine; a recent study finds the two care pathways to be comparable (Aiken et al. 2021). Some patients may be affected by some unpleasant side effects—for example, between 1.9% and 61.2% across several studies experienced diarrhea (Chen and Creinin 2015, 18–19). However, importantly, the common side effects of EMA (e.g., nausea, diarrhea, and dizziness) are easily managed by the patient and are unlikely to require further intervention beyond over-the-counter painkillers.

A History of Disproportionate Regulation

Abortion remains a crime in Great Britain by virtue of the Offences Against the Person Act 1861 in England and Wales and the common law in Scotland. Exceptions are carved out, however, in the Abortion Act 1967; abortion is lawful when strict criteria are followed about where, when, and how abortion is carried out and for what reason (Romanis et al. 2022). However, when individuals—whether pregnant people themselves or healthcare professionals—act outside the scope of the Abortion Act's permitted conditions for abortion, they face up to life imprisonment. This potential sentence is one of the most

[4] Of note, Scotland has, in more recent guidance, departed from the rest of Great Britain in introducing a limit of eleven weeks and six days for similar regulations (Calderwood 2020).

[5] Medical abortion is safe and effective later in pregnancy, but the increased risk of side effects and complications means that reduced clinical supervision is often dismissed as an option beyond ten weeks.

punitive worldwide. There are very few examples since the 1961 Act's inception of prosecutions sought against medical professionals. However, in 2022, we saw increasing examples of prosecutions sought against people who ended their pregnancies in England outside the strict terms of the Abortion Act (Sheldon and Lord 2023; Romanis 2023b). While many of these prosecutions have since been dropped, one resulted in a successful and high-profile conviction that will have been alarming for abortion-seekers (Romanis 2023b). Abortion remaining a matter of the criminal law stigmatizes the treatment in labeling it as "elective" and in need of heavy regulation (Cook 2014; Parsons and Romanis 2021). However, considering the prosecutions currently underway, the use of the criminal law is no longer just a cause of stigmatization and control; it is a matter of people's liberty.

That abortion is the only form of healthcare that is deemed criminal is a function of abortion exceptionalism that sets abortion apart "from other areas of healthcare for exceptional and considerable oversight" (Parsons and Romanis 2021, 13). As detailed earlier in this chapter, EMA is safe. Indeed, the standard regimen is safer than commonplace antibiotics (Lohr et al. 2020). Abortion is also common, with 214,256 carried out in England and Wales in 2021 (Office for Health Improvement and Disparities 2022). Abortion-seekers themselves consider the treatment essential for their personal well-being (Janiak and Goldberg 2016). When all of this is taken to account, the exceptionalism of the legal framework can only be described as excessive and thus disproportionate.

Beyond the exceptionalism innate in the designation of abortion as criminal activity, the legal framework in Great Britain further exceptionalizes abortion in how it medicalizes the procedure. Section 1 of the Abortion Act stipulates that abortion is lawful when two medical practitioners (who must be doctors) form the opinion in good faith that the pregnancy has not exceeded the twenty-fourth week and that terminating the pregnancy poses a lesser risk to the pregnant person's mental and physical health (or that of any existing children) than continuing the pregnancy does. In making this decision, medical practitioners should consider the pregnant person's "actual and reasonably foreseeable" circumstances (Abortion Act 1967 s. 1(2)). There are further grounds under which termination is lawful *after* twenty-four weeks (Abortion Act 1967 ss. 1(1)(b)–(d)) but, given our focus on EMA, we will not detail these here.

Commentators have observed that, given the safety of EMA (Endler et al. 2019; Aiken et al. 2021), it is easy to establish that continuing a pregnancy and birth are riskier for a pregnant person (Romanis et al. 2022). This de facto makes every early pregnancy "legally terminable" (Jackson 2000). Even though EMA is easily legally justifiable within the current legal framework, the fact remains that the law is "incredibly prescriptive" about when abortion medications can be prescribed, and thus it "significantly interferes with clinical discretion by specifying" when treatment is appropriate—something that is without comparison for other treatments about which patients have decision-making capacity (Romanis et al. 2021, 12). That it must be doctors who certify an abortion is wholly unnecessary; empirical evidence illustrates that outcomes are comparable when nurses prescribe abortion medications (Kopp Kallner et al. 2014) and, consequently, the WHO recommends that nurses are able to manage abortion procedures (WHO 2022, 69). Recently, in regulating abortion in Northern Ireland, Westminster approved nurses' ability to prescribe EMA, demonstrating some recognition of the excessiveness (and, thus, disproportionate nature) of the two-doctor requirement in Great Britain. However, there is no sign of change to this requirement in the immediate future and so it continues to act as an impediment to abortion providers (Romanis et al. 2022) without demonstrably mitigating any known risk.

Further, as mentioned earlier, the law even dictates *where* abortion medications can be administered in Great Britain. Until 2017–2018, both mifepristone and misoprostol had to be administered in a clinic. After changes to the law in Scotland (Calderwood 2017), Wales (Welsh Government 2018), and England (Department of Health and Social Care 2018)—in that order—it became lawful for individuals to administer misoprostol themselves at home under instruction (Parsons 2020). Mifepristone, however, still had to be swallowed in a clinic, under supervision, in all three jurisdictions until 2020. Since 2020, while it has become lawful for abortion medications to be administered in places outside of abortion clinics, the law is still proscriptive about where abortion medications can be administered. In England and Wales, this is the abortion-seeker's usual place of residence, a clinic or hospital, or any other place approved by the Secretary of State for Health and Social Care (Abortion Act 1967 s. 1(3D), as asserted by the Health and Care Act 2022 s. 178(4)). In Scotland, abortion medications can be administered at the abortion-seeker's "usual place of residence in Scotland" (Calderwood 2020), licensed clinics and hospitals, or places approved by the Scottish Minister for Public Health and Sport and Wellbeing. Such regulation raises some puzzling questions in light of the safety of the drugs used: "Why should the self-administration of abortion medications that would be perfectly lawful in one location be unlawful in another location?" (Romanis 2023b, 611). The law interfering as it does to dictate how doctors must prescribe EMA and even where abortion medications may be administered shows how heavily regulated abortion is as a procedure.

Is such regulation necessary? We ought to consider the legal framework disproportionate if its scheme and conditions "bear no connection to or undermine its aims, however legitimate" (Erdman and Cook 2020, 14). The reality is that the

Abortion Act was enacted over fifty-five years ago and has only been amended twice since. It was amended over thirty years ago, in 1990 (Sheldon et al. 2019), and then more recently in 2022. The framework underlying provision remains much the same, with neither amendment having liberalized the grounds on which abortion is permitted.

The procedure of abortion was considerably different in 1967 (abortion medications were not available until the 1980s) and the objective of the Abortion Act was explicitly to keep women safe from the harm that resulted from clandestine abortions performed by unqualified persons (Jackson 2000; Sheldon 2014, 2016). The availability of EMA—and the large body of evidence that demonstrates the safety of abortion medications use even when their administration is self-managed outside the formal healthcare setting (Gomperts et al. 2008; Aiken et al. 2017)—illustrates that the requirements of the Abortion Act must be thought of as arbitrary because they are no longer protecting people. In fact, they may be actively harming people, since the onerous requirements can increase waiting times and prevent abortion providers from adapting their service provision to emerging evidence about best practice (Lohr et al. 2020). While the 2022 amendments have (to some extent) sought to respond to that evidence by changing where abortion medications can be administered, they do not fully embrace available evidence (such as that regarding the gestational limit for Telemedical early medical abortion [TEMA]). That the Abortion Act has only been directly amended twice in such a long time means that it is unsurprisingly outdated, and this lack of updating actively prevents the implementation of changes that would make policy more commensurate with the available evidence (Parsons and Romanis 2021).

There is a long-standing campaign by abortion providers for the decriminalization of abortion (and, with it, changes to the regulatory framework for abortion). Despite the fact that all attempts to change the law have fallen flat in recent years (most recently in 2021), there is a trend toward (partial) decriminalization in other countries. For example, New Zealand (following the enactment of the Abortion Legislation Act 2020) and all jurisdictions in Australia (following the enactment of the Termination of Pregnancy Regulations 2022 in South Australia[6]). There is some optimism that the move toward telemedicine might be the catalyst for a reform of abortion law, since the shift spotlighted the Abortion Act and the fact that its requirements are no longer necessary to meet the stated aims of abortion regulation and thus must be considered disproportionate. It has been argued that telemedicine exemplifies the urgency of decriminalizing abortion

[6] Abortion had previously been decriminalized in parts of Australia, and this act brought the remaining parts of the country in line.

because there is an increased likelihood of abortion-seekers inadvertently running afoul of the criminal law in circumstances in which the criminal law is not serving the objective of improving safety (Romanis 2023b). Further, there is another attempt to decriminalize abortion, led by Diana Johnson MP, anticipated in the House of Commons (Mason 2024).

COVID-19 and EMA

Like most healthcare provision, abortion care was immediately affected by government responses to COVID-19 globally (Parsons and Romanis 2021, 117–125). This was primarily owing to public health measures to reduce infection through in-person contact, such as national lockdowns. With the requirement that abortion care be provided in person, those seeking such care were faced with a decision between trying to go to a clinic and thereby introducing a risk of infection or continuing their pregnancy and hoping that pandemic restrictions would ease before it was too late to access abortion care. Incidentally, this hope would unfortunately prove misplaced, as lockdowns continued far longer than many initially anticipated.

For some, the decision about whether and how to travel was not one they could make. It was made for some by socioeconomic factors preventing their visiting a clinic at a time when many people were working from home, children were not in school, and public transport was operating at reduced levels. Thus, the many existing barriers to accessing abortion care were, for many, exacerbated (Nandagiri et al. 2020; Romanis et al. 2020a).

In practical terms, then, the initial, wider government response to the COVID-19 pandemic made abortion care entirely inaccessible for some people who needed it (Romanis et al. 2020a; Parsons and Romanis 2021). Further, it was not something only of relevance to a handful of individuals. Early in the pandemic, forty-four thousand people in Great Britain were estimated to have needed an abortion in the period April–June 2020 (British Pregnancy Advisory Service 2020a).

We are in no way criticizing the public health measures introduced by governments in Great Britain—much like those in many other jurisdictions—to reduce the spread of the virus. Particularly prior to the development of effective vaccines, such measures were essential. Rather, we are highlighting how the long-standing and disproportionate regulation of abortion care created a situation in which these necessary public health measures had an immediate and serious negative impact on access. In fact, the situation was so problematic that it prompted these governments to revisit abortion regulations, which they are ordinarily reluctant to do.

A Short-Term Proportionate Response

When the COVID-19 pandemic was first declared in March 2020, the focus in healthcare swiftly shifted to altering care pathways to remove what were considered nonessential in-person interactions. However, despite then–Secretary of State for Health and Social Care Matt Hancock's evangelizing more generally about a move to "a principle of 'digital first,'" such that "all consultations should be done by telemedicine" (HC Deb March 11, 2020, vol. 673, col. 383), on the question of abortion care he was, at first, clear that the government had "no proposals to change any abortion rules as part of the COVID-19 response" (HC Deb March 24, 2020, vol. 674, col. 244). Hancock did add a caveat to his telemedicine prioritization about there being exceptions in instances of clinical and practical reasons, but no such reasons can reasonably be said to exist in the case of abortion care (as we will illustrate).

At the time, there were calls from various medical bodies and organizations for the introduction of telemedicine in abortion care as part of the pandemic response (Regan et al. 2020). An initial announcement to permit telemedicine for abortion in England was published on the website of the Department of Health and Social Care on March 23, 2020, though this was removed within twenty-four hours and replaced with a message indicating that it had been published in error (Romanis et al. 2020b) One week later, on March 30, 2020, an almost identical approval order was published (Department of Health and Social Care 2020),[7] and this one remained in place. The following day, similar approvals were issued in both Wales (Welsh Government 2020) and Scotland (Calderwood 2020).

Despite this initial period of uncertainty, which in itself was significantly problematic, given the time-sensitive nature of abortion care and resultant distress caused to providers and abortion-seekers alike, the governments of Great Britain did, then, make the decision to include abortion care in the telemedical shift. This removed many—though, it is important to note, not all—of the access barriers to abortion care that were exacerbated by the COVID-19 pandemic and responses to it. Abortion-seekers were, for the most part, able to access care during national lockdowns without having to introduce unnecessary infection risk for themselves, those they live with, and the healthcare professionals involved. It is true that the nature of the regulatory change was such that not all were able to benefit. For example, the chosen definition of *home* seemingly excludes students

[7] The only difference between the two approval orders was that the latter—meaning that which remained in place—included a sunset clause. This clause stipulated that the approval would automatically expire either in two years or with the expiration of the Coronavirus Act 2020, whichever came first.

and anyone who may have chosen to spend lockdown with a friend or family member (Parsons and Romanis 2021). Nonetheless, there was recognition by the governments of Great Britain in a time of crisis that, at least to some extent, access to abortion care is essential.

That EMA was eventually permitted to be provided remotely was not only a victory for public health but an arguably rare example of a proportionate policy change in this area. As outlined earlier in this chapter, abortion regulation has a complicated history that is largely characterized by disproportionate regulation and a shunning of evidence-based care. That it took the overwhelming disruption of society caused by a pandemic to even introduce the possibility of (temporarily) improving care is itself a serious concern. Nonetheless, the changes brought about in March 2020 were proportionate—as much as opponents may try to suggest otherwise.

A key reason for this is the time-sensitive nature of abortion care. As much as it is nonideal and potentially even harmful to delay certain medical procedures to reduce the risk of COVID-19 infection, this was an option for some. Certain elective surgeries, for example, were able to be delayed, even if those delays were in some ways detrimental to the patient. With abortion, the window for possible delays is very limited—both medically and legally. At later gestations, abortion is generally provided surgically. When an abortion is to be provided surgically, there is, of course, no option for providing that treatment remotely. It is important, then, that those in need of abortion care be able to access treatment as early as possible, so that they are not prevented from seeking the option[8] of medical abortion and, thereby, remote care. Further, there is an unavoidable time limit in that the person will eventually give birth if they are unable to access abortion care in time.

From the legal perspective, abortion is more readily lawful at earlier gestations, purely because of the grounds on which abortion is permissible by law (though abortion is still subject to the strict conditions of where, when, and how it is undertaken and who must approve it). As already noted, telemedicine was only permitted up to nine weeks and six days in England and Wales (and eleven weeks and six days in Scotland). It was a similar story when home use of misoprostol was permitted a few years earlier (Parsons 2020). While there is certainly a very good argument to be made for extending these limits—at the very least for England and Wales to move into line with Scotland—there are good reasons for there being *some* cutoff for at-home care. Medical abortion in the second

[8] We do stress that it ought to be an option, as the choice of surgical abortion is important to some individuals. There are various reasons why a surgical procedure would be preferred, even early in pregnancy, such as the avoidance of certain side effects that come with a medical abortion. Though we do recognize that certain structural barriers have in fact pushed medical abortion into favor at the expense of access to surgical abortion (Footman 2023).

trimester comes with a higher risk of complications and may prove less effective (Grossman et al. 2008). Requiring greater medical oversight of abortions at later gestations (within reason, by which we mean proportionately) is therefore understandable. Such oversight, we note, could be achieved with regulation or clinical guidelines that do not have the force of criminal law. Moreover, risks associated with medical abortion later in pregnancy only increase the urgency of access to abortion care, to ensure that those in need can access it as early in their pregnancy as possible to avoid the justifiable need for in-clinic care.

There is also the issue of gestational limits on access to any kind of abortion care. As outlined earlier, the Abortion Act imposes a twenty-four-week limit with few exceptions. Apart from the telemedicine question, it is important to recognize that some people may have been pushed beyond this limit by COVID-19 regulations and the initial disruption caused by the pandemic. Should they still wish to terminate a pregnancy, such individuals would have been forced to explore clandestine options that, although often safe, may prove *less* safe (because buying medications on the internet does not guarantee that the abortion-seeker will receive the medications as described). For some abortion-seekers, assistance from healthcare professionals, or knowing they can contact healthcare professionals if needed, will be an important part of their feeling safe. There may, then, be a question as to whether a temporary extension of that limit would have been a proportionate response because it would have enabled continued access to abortion care for all affected by the unusual circumstances rather than just those early in pregnancy.

It would be remiss of us not to acknowledge that the shift to providing abortion care remotely does come with certain risks. Indeed, the introduction of telemedicine in all areas of healthcare entails a change in the way things are done and, thus, some risk, which must be balanced against the benefits. In remote abortion care, the primary concern is that an ectopic pregnancy will not be identified. When care is provided in a clinic following an ultrasound scan, this is easily identified. Through telemedicine, the risk of an ectopic pregnancy is assessed through questions. There is, then, an increased chance that such pregnancies will be missed. However, this is negligible, not least because healthcare professionals retain the ability to require that a patient come into the clinic should they have any concerns; if they feel unable to reasonably rule out an ectopic pregnancy, they can invite the patient to the clinic for an ultrasound scan and blood tests. Further, ectopic pregnancies are uncommon, and patients often present with symptoms (Duncan et al. 2022) that would flag to a professional providing care remotely that the patient should come to the clinic. Moreover, in-person care does not always involve a person having an ultrasound before abortion medications are prescribed. Given the significant benefit of increased access to care for those in need, the possibility that a small number of ectopic pregnancies will not be identified that otherwise would have been clearly constitutes a proportionate harm. The alternative is the clear harms to those unable to access care or to those who are forced to access care later in pregnancy—a less favorable option, to return to Hemerén's (2012) definition.

Overall, then, the responses of governments in Great Britain to the challenges COVID-19 presented for abortion care can, in some ways, be considered (surprisingly) proportionate. Continuation of care provision for those in need of time-sensitive treatment was largely able to continue in ways that introduced minimal possibilities for harm. It should be noted, however, that since there was already a large body of evidence establishing the safety of EMA by telemedicine prior to 2020 from other jurisdictions, introducing the regulations in a temporary manner[9] was not an evidenced-based approach (Parsons and Romanis 2021, 132). Arguably, then, it might have been more proportionate to introduce the changes without the time lapse and instead a commitment to reviewing evidence collected over a period of time. Assuming that the use of telemedicine is *only* proportionate amid the disruption of the pandemic is a clear policy failure.

The wider debate over telemedicine in abortion care has continued since its initial approval, in part because the approvals were not permanent. The disproportionate regulation of abortion care seems likely to continue through more specific aspects of the telemedicine policy.

A Future of (Dis)Proportionate Control

Despite the experience of the past five years, the future of telemedicine in providing EMA in Great Britain is uncertain. In August 2022, following a public consultation, the government announced that telemedicine is here to stay in England (Department of Health and Social Care 2022). This followed earlier announcements in February 2022 and May 2022 that telemedicine for EMA would remain in Wales (Morgan 2022) and Scotland (Scottish Government 2022), respectively. These changes became law following the enactment of the Health and Care Act 2022 (s. 178).

At first, the announcement in England appeared to be positive for securing access to care in a proportionate way, in line with our earlier discussion and the prior decisions of the other nations. However, it is in the details that an apparent

[9] In England and Wales, the approvals contained sunset clauses that would see them expire after two years or with the expiration of the Coronavirus Act 2020. Scotland did not go as far as to include such a clause but did, at the time of the approval, note that it was intended as a temporary measure.

return to disproportionate regulation becomes noticeable in England (and, as we will detail shortly, Wales).[10]

Behind the distracting headline of telemedicine's permanence are detailed guidelines on delivery that ultimately limit the continuation of high-quality care for certain people who may benefit significantly from remote provision of healthcare for myriad reasons. For example, the strict definition of *home* in the legislation continues to prevent certain groups from accessing care in private personal spaces, such as those without a permanent address in England and Wales (Parsons and Romanis 2021). A person technically risks life imprisonment—prosecution is at the discretion of the Crown Prosecution Service—if they self-administer abortion medications obtained lawfully in spaces other than their home address (Romanis 2020b). This would affect marginalized people who may feel that their homes are not the ideal place for a comfortable abortion. For example, someone worried about violence at home who may wish to go through with the procedure at the home of a trusted friend.

Safeguarding is one key area of focus in the continued overregulation of TEMA. Throughout Great Britain, healthcare professionals all have a statutory duty to safeguard their patients.[11] In addition to its reference to providing appropriate care in response to a patient's presentation, safeguarding is about "protecting an adult's right to live in safety, free from abuse and neglect" (Department of Health 2014). It is a more holistic approach to care, encompassing more than just responding to a medical complaint. Safeguarding is a very broad consideration and can encompass anything from financial abuse to honor-based violence.

Early in the move to telemedicine for abortion care, concerns were raised about the ability of healthcare professionals to carry out this safeguarding duty when providing abortion care without an in-person consultation (Parsons and Romanis 2022). Examples were commonly raised about the risk of coerced abortion when patients are not required to attend a clinic—that is, about a perceived inability to ensure that a patient is alone and able to talk freely during a remote consultation (Society for the Protection of Unborn Children 2020; Christian Concern 2021). The organization Christian Action Research and Education (2020) cited increases in domestic abuse reports during the pandemic as an additional safeguarding challenge that they felt TEMA overlooked. The focus on coerced abortion was interesting, since there is also significant evidence to suggest that victims of domestic violence are likely to be coerced into *continuing* a pregnancy—specifically, into not having an abortion (Grace and

[10] New guidance will also be released in Scotland that may also reintroduce disproportionate aspects of regulation, but this remains to be seen.

[11] This is formalized—albeit with slightly different framing—in separate legislation for each of the three nations: for England, the Care Act 2014; for Scotland, the Adult Support and Protection (Scotland) Act 2007; for Wales, the Social Services and Well-Being (Wales) Act 2014.

Anderson 2018). Using safeguarding as a reason to consider limiting TEMA even though it improves access—which can be lifesaving for some vulnerable people who are under threat of violence (Romanis et al. 2021)—is thus disproportionate in failing to capture the nuances of the matter.

When TEMA was made permanent, however, policy guidelines came to limit its availability to some marginalized groups. The Royal College of Paediatrics and Child Health, for example, published guidance that advised that providers "should aim for all CYP [children and young people] to be given an appointment for an in-person consultation at some point in the EMA care pathway unless there is a compelling indication to do otherwise" (Royal College of Paediatrics and Child Health 2022, para. 8.2). Such recommendations, however, assume that in-person care is the gold standard for safeguarding young people. Research suggests, however, that for many young people, TEMA resulted in improved safeguarding opportunities; for many, it also meant that accessing abortion through formal channels was an option (Romanis and Parsons 2023).

While remote safeguarding needs consideration (consistent with other areas of healthcare), it continues to be discussed as a concern, despite emerging evidence that effective safeguarding is taking place satisfactorily through remote care (Romanis et al. 2021; Parsons and Romanis 2022). There was a clear focus on the importance of safeguarding in how providers adapted their services to deliver TEMA; the British Pregnancy Advisory Service (2020b) reported a 12% increase in clients undergoing an enhanced safeguarding risk assessment. It is not clear from the reporting whether this was the result of an increase in safeguarding instances (which were effectively identified) or an example of caution in referring more clients than would later prove necessary. Nonetheless, whichever it is—or whether it is a combination of the two—it shows that providers are conscious of the concern and are adapting to effectively execute their safeguarding duties within the new care pathways. There has also been considerable academic discussion of some of the factors in favor of remote safeguarding, which criticisms seem to neglect. One example of such factors is the fact that people may feel more comfortable disclosing concerns about their own safety when in a place of their choosing rather than an intimidating clinical environment (Romanis et al. 2021; Parsons and Romanis 2022). Others may be unable to attend a clinic because of a violent partner (Aiken et al. 2018) and thus are more likely to have some interaction with a healthcare provider, which gives them more control over the interaction (Romanis et al. 2021; Parsons and Romanis 2022).

Regardless of the effectiveness of remote safeguarding, that it is being centered in the debate over telemedicine for abortion care is a further example of disproportionate control. All healthcare professionals in Great Britain have a safeguarding duty, but it was not a point of contention when primary care shifted to using telemedicine (nor was it when primary care was becoming increasingly remote before the pandemic). When it comes to abortion care, there seems to be an assumption made by certain groups that there is a greater duty on abortion care providers. This, we suggest, is a significantly disproportionate expectation for this group of healthcare professionals that is rooted in the abortion exceptionalism we see at the heart of abortion regulation in Great Britain more broadly.

It is true that some individuals accessing abortion care will have safeguarding needs. Indeed, some types of safeguarding concern—such as sexual violence—may create the need for an individual to access abortion care. It may also be the only form of healthcare that an abuser allows their victim to access. This does not, however, mean that such circumstances represent the majority. For many, the decision to terminate a pregnancy is made purely on the basis that they do not wish to have a child at that point in their life. It is important that efforts are made to identify the instances in which there is a safeguarding concern, but it is problematic to start from a position of assuming there to be a safeguarding concern purely because someone is seeking abortion services (Romanis et al. 2021), not least because this is somewhat specific to abortion care. There seems to be an insistence from critics that a precautionary approach be pursued in abortion care.

Conclusion

Abortion care has a long history of strict regulation. This is, at least in part, down to a failure of policymakers to revise regulations to align with evolving clinical evidence and a changing social climate. As a result, the gap between abortion regulation and best clinical practice has widened over time in Great Britain, such that this regulation has become increasingly disproportionate.

At the start of the COVID-19 pandemic, wider public health measures further highlighted the extent to which abortion is exceptionalized in how the law treats it. The excessive regulation that had long created barriers to accessing abortion care by way of requirements for in-person treatment was at odds with the sudden new way of living—that is, in lockdown. Such rare circumstances were sufficient for the governments of Great Britain to lift some regulations as something of an emergency response to enable telemedical care pathways, though initially only temporarily. As such, while the new regulations were more proportionate than the previous state of affairs, that they were initially temporary highlighted the underlying desire on the part of policymakers to return to a disproportionate regulatory landscape in the near future. While telemedicine as a permanent fixture has now been secured, this has come with a barrage of guidelines that continue to restrict healthcare professionals from exercising their clinical judgment, just in different ways than before. What has been widely hailed as a silver lining of the pandemic has, then, been limited by the finer details of the new system maintaining the status of abortion care as disproportionately regulated.

Regardless of how things ultimately settle on the question of telemedicine in abortion care, there will likely always be some policy questions concerning abortion in which proportionality is central (if tacit). Perhaps most recently, discussion of so-called buffer zones around abortion clinics has sparked such questions in the United Kingdom; Ottley (2022) has argued that the introduction of buffer zones does not infringe on would-be protestors' rights under the European Convention on Human Rights.

Ultimately, there remains a need for the decriminalization of abortion in Great Britain (Sheldon and Wellings 2020). It is the criminalization of what is routine healthcare that is at the root of its disproportionate treatment in the policy sphere. That is not to say that decriminalizing abortion would be a quick fix for strongly embedded abortion exceptionalism and excess medicalization, but it would be a significant step in the right direction and, at the very least, significantly symbolic in recognizing that the termination of pregnancy is a private matter of reproductive healthcare rather than a public matter of an offence against the state.

Competing Interests

There are no competing interests to declare.

Funding

There is no funding to declare.

References

Aiken, A. R. A, I. Digol, J. Trussell, and R. Gromperts. 2017. "Self-Reported Outcomes and Adverse Events After Medical Abortion Through Online Telemedicine: Population-Based Study in the Republic of Ireland and Northern Ireland." *British Medical Journal* 357;j2011.

Aiken, A. R. A, K. A. Guthrie, M. Schellekens, J. Trussell, and R. Gomperts. 2018. "Barriers to Accessing Abortion Services and Perspectives on Using Mifepristone and Misoprostol at Home in Great Britain." *Contraception* 97 (2):177–183.

Aiken, A. R. A, P. A. Lohr, J. Lord, N. Ghosh, and J. Starling. 2021. Effectiveness, Safety and Acceptability of No-Test Medical Abortion (Termination of Pregnancy) Provided via

Telemedicine: A National Cohort Study. *British Journal of Obstetrics and Gynaecology* 128 (9): 1464–1474.
Borgmann, C. E. 2014. "Abortion Exceptionalism and Undue Burden Pre-Emption." *Washington and Lee Law Review* 71 (2):1047–1087.
British Pregnancy Advisory Service. 2020a. "Healthcare Professionals Call on Boris Johnson to Intervene to Protect Women's Health—Reckless Failure to Listen to Scientific Advice Is Putting Vulnerable Women at Severe Risk." Press release. https://www.bpas.org/about-our-charity/press-office/press-releases/healthcare-professionals-call-on-boris-johnson-to-intervene-to-protect-women-s-health-reckless-failure-to-listen-to-scientific-advice-is-putting-vulnerable-women-at-severe-risk/.
British Pregnancy Advisory Service. 2020b. "Pills by Post: Telemedical Abortion at the British Pregnancy Advisory Service (BPAS)." https://www.bpas.org/media/3385/bpas-pills-by-post-service.pdf.
Calderwood, C. 2020. "Abortion—Covid-19—Approval for Mifepristone to Be Taken at Home and Other Contingency Measures" (SGHD/CMO [2020]9). Chief Medical Officer Directorate, Scottish Government, March 31. https://www.sehd.scot.nhs.uk/cmo/CMO(2020)09.pdf.
Calderwood, C. 2017. "Abortion—Improvement to Existing Services—Approval for Misoprostol to Be Taken at Home" (SGHD/CMO[2017]14). Chief Medical Officer Directorate, Scottish Government, October 26. https://www.sehd.scot.nhs.uk/cmo/CMO(2017)14.pdf.
Chen, M. J., and M. D. Creinin. 2015. "Mifepristone with Buccal Misoprostol for Medical Abortion: A Systematic Review." *Obstetrics & Gynecology* 126 (1):12–21.
Christian Action Research and Education. 2020. "Response to Call for Submissions on Women's and Girls' Sexual and Reproductive Health and Rights in Situations of Crisis," August 28. https://www.ohchr.org/sites/default/files/Documents/Issues/Women/WG/ReproductiveHealthRights/CSOs/christianactionforresearchandeducation/christianaction.pdf.
Christian Concern. 2021. "Tell the Government Not to Extend DIY Abortion Policy." https://christianconcern.com/action/tell-the-government-not-to-extend-diy-abortion-policy/.
Creasy, S., and C. Sanquest. 2021. "Working Within Westminster." In *Decriminalizing Abortion in Northern Ireland*, edited by Fiona Bloomer and Emma Campbell. Bloomsbury.
Creinin, M. D., C. A. Schreiber, P. Bednarek et al. 2007. "Mifepristone and Misoprostol Administered Simultaneously Versus 24 Hours Apart for Abortion." *Obstetrics & Gynecology* 109 (4): 885–894.
Cook, R. J. 2014. "Stigmatized Meanings of Criminal Abortion Law." In *Abortion Law in Transnational Perspective: Cases and Controversies*, edited by Rebecca J. Cook, Joanna N. Erdman, and Bernard M. Dickens. University of Pennsylvania Press.
Department of Health. 2014. Care and *Support Statutory Guidance*. https://assets.publishing.service.gov.uk/government/uploads/system/uploads/attachment_data/file/506202/23902777_Care_Act_Book.pdf.
Department of Health and Social Care. 2018. The Abortion Act 1967—Approval of a Class of Places. https://assets.publishing.service.gov.uk/government/uploads/system/uploads/attachment_data/file/768059/Approval_of_home_use_for_the_second_stage_of_early_medical_abortion.pdf.
Department of Health and Social Care. 2020. The Abortion Act 1967—Approval of a Class of Places. https://assets.publishing.service.gov.uk/government/uploads/system/uploads/attachment_data/file/876740/30032020_The_Abortion_Act_1967_-_Approval_of_a_Class_of_Places.pdf.
Department of Health and Social Care. 2022. "At Home Early Medical Abortions Made Permanent in England and Wales." Press release, August 23. https://www.gov.uk/government/news/at-home-early-medical-abortions-made-permanent-in-england-and-wales.

Duncan, C. I., J.J. Reynolds-Wright, and S. T. Cameron. 2022. "Utility of a Routine Ultrasound for Detection of Ectopic Pregnancies Among Women Requesting Abortion: A Retrospective Review." *BMJ Sexual & Reproductive Health* 48 (1): 22–27.

Endler, M., A. Lavelanet, A. Cleeve, B. Ganatra, R. Gomperts, and K. Gemzell-Danielsson. 2019. "Telemedicine for Medical Abortion: A Systematic Review." *British Journal of Obstetrics and Gynaecology* 126 (9): 1094–1102.

Erdman, J. N., and R. J. Cook. 2020. "Decriminalization of Abortion—a Human Rights Imperative." *Best Practice & Research Clinical Obstetrics & Gynaecology* 62:11–24.

Footman K. 2023. "Structural Barriers or Patient Preference? A Mixed Methods Appraisal of Medical Abortion Use in England and Wales." *Health Policy* 132:104799.

Gomperts, R. J., K. Jelinska, S. Davies, K. Gemzell-Danielsson, and G. Kleiverda. 2008. "Using Telemedicine for Termination of Pregnancy with Mifepristone and Misoprostol in Settings Where There Is No Access to Safe Services." *British Journal of Obstetrics and Gynaecology* 115 (9): 1171–1178.

Grace, K. T., and J. C. Anderson. 2018. "Reproductive Coercion: A Systematic Review." *Trauma, Violence, & Abuse* 19 (4): 371–390.

Grossman, D., K. Blanchard, and P. Blumenthal. 2008. "Complications After Second Trimester Surgical and Medical Abortion." *Reproductive Health Matters* 16 (31 Suppl.): 173–182.

Hemerén, G. 2012. "The Principle of Proportionality Revisited: Interpretations and Applications." *Medicine, Health Care and Philosophy* 15 (4): 373–382.

Jackson, E. 2000. "Abortion, Autonomy and Prenatal Diagnosis." *Social & Legal Studies* 9 (4): 467–494.

Janiak, E., and A. B. Goldberg. 2016. "Eliminating the Phrase 'Elective Abortion': Why Language Matters." *Contraception* 93 (2): 89–92.

Kopp Kallner, H., R. Gomperts, E. Salomonsson et al. 2014. "The Efficacy, Safety and Acceptability of Medical Termination of Pregnancy Provided by Standard Care by Doctors or by Nurse-Midwives: A Randomised Controlled Equivalence Trial." *British Journal of Obstetrics and Gynaecology* 122 (4): 510–517.

Lohr, P. A., J. Lord, and S. Rowlands. 2020. "How Would Decriminalisation Affect Women's Health?" In *Decriminalising Abortion in the UK*, edited by Sally Sheldon and Kaye Wellings. Policy Press.

Mason, R. 2024. "MPs to Get Free Vote on Decriminalising Abortion in England and Wales." *The Guardian*, February 23. https://amp.theguardian.com/world/2024/feb/23/mps-to-get-free-vote-on-decriminalising-abortion-in-england-and-wales.

Morgan, E. 2022. "Written Statement: Arrangements for Early Medical Abortion at Home." Cabinet statement. Welsh Government, February 24. https://gov.wales/written-statement-arrangements-early-medical-abortion-home.

Nandagiri, R., E. Coast, and J. Strong. 2020. "COVID-19 and Abortion: Making Structural Violence Visible." *International Perspectives on Sexual and Reproductive Health* 46 (S1): 83–89.

Office for Health Improvement and Disparities. 2022. "Abortion Statistics, England and Wales: 2021." https://www.gov.uk/government/statistics/abortion-statistics-for-england-and-wales-2021/abortion-statistics-england-and-wales-2021.

Ottley, E. 2022. "Fixed Buffer Zone Legislation: A Proportionate Response to Demonstrations Outside Abortion Clinics in England and Wales?" *Medical Law Review*30(3): 509–533. .

Parsons, J. A. 2020. "2017–19 Governmental Decisions to Allow Home Use of Misoprostol for Early Medical Abortion in the UK." *Health Policy* 124 (7): 679–683.

Parsons, J. A., and E. C. Romanis. 2021. *Early Medical Abortion, Equality of Access, and the Telemedical Imperative.* Oxford University Press.

Parsons, J. A., and E. C. Romanis. 2022. "The Case for Telemedical Early Medical Abortion in England: Dispelling Adult Safeguarding Concerns." *Health Care Analysis* 30:73–96.

Raymond, E. G., C. Shannon, M. A. Weaver, and B. Winikoff. 2013. "First-Trimester Medical Abortion with Mifepristone 200mg and Misoprostol: A Systematic Review." *Contraception* 87 (1): 26–37.
Rebouché, R. 2014. "A Functionalist Approach to Comparative Abortion Law." In *Abortion Law in Transnational Perspective: Cases and Controversies*, edited by Rebecca J. Cook, Joanna N. Erdman, and Bernard M. Dickens. University of Pennsylvania Press.
Regan, D. L., E. Morris, A. Kasliwal et al. 2020. "Re: Two Doctors' Signatures to Certify Abortion During Covid-19." Open letter, March 22. https://www.bpas.org/media/3325/open-letter-to-matt-hancock-230320.pdf.
Romanis, E. C. 2023a. "Abortion Access and the Benefits and Limitations of Abortion-*Permissive* Legal Frameworks: Lessons from the United Kingdom." *Cambridge Quarterly of Healthcare Ethics* 32 (3): 378–390.
Romanis, E. C. 2023b. "*R v Foster*: Exemplifying the Urgency of the Decriminalisation of Abortion." *Medical Law Review* 31 (4): 606–614.
Romanis, E. C., and J. A. Parsons. 2023. "Early Telemedical Abortion, Safeguarding, and Under 18s: A Qualitative Study with Care Providers in England and Wales." *BMJ Sexual and Reproductive Health* 49 (4): 238–244.
Romanis, E. C., J. A. Parsons, and N. Hodson. 2020a. "COVID-19 and Reproductive Justice in Great Britain and the United States: Ensuring Access to Abortion Care During a Pandemic." *Journal of Law and the Biosciences* 7 (1): lsaa027.
Romanis. E. C., J. Parsons, and N. Hodson. 2020b. "COVID-19 and Abortion Care Update: Department of Health and Social Care 'Error'" (blog). BMJ Sexual & Reproductive Health, March 24. https://blogs.bmj.com/bmjsrh/2020/03/24/covid-19-abortion-3/.
Romanis, E. C., J. A. Parsons, I. Salter, and T. Hampton. 2021. "Safeguarding and Teleconsultation for Abortion." *Lancet* 398 (10299): 555–558.
Romanis, E. C., A. Mullock, and J. A. Parsons. 2022. "The Excessive Regulation of Early Abortion Medication in the UK: The Case for Reform." *Medical Law Review* 30 (1):4–32.
Royal College of Paediatrics and Child Health. 2022. "Safeguarding Guidance for Children and Young People Under 18 Accessing Early Medical Abortion Services." https://childprotection.rcpch.ac.uk/resources/safeguarding-guidance-for-children-and-young-people-under-18-accessing-early-medical-abortion-services/.
Scottish Government. 2022. "Early Medical Abortion at Home." Press release, May 12. https://www.gov.scot/news/early-medical-abortion-at-home-1/.
Sheldon, S. 2014. "The Medical Framework and Early Abortion in the UK: How Can a State Control Swallowing?" In *Abortion Law in Transnational Perspective: Cases and Controversies*, edited by Rebecca J. Cook, Joanna N. Erdman, and Bernard M. Dickens. University of Pennsylvania Press.
Sheldon, S. 2016. "The Decriminalisation of Abortion: An Argument for Modernisation." *Oxford Journal of Legal Studies* 36 (2):334–365.
Sheldon, S., G. Davis, J. O'Neill, and C. Parker. 2019. "The Abortion Act (1967): A Biography." *Legal Studies* 39 (1):18–35.
Sheldon, S., and J. Lord. 2023. "Guest Editorial: Care Not Criminalisation; Reform of British Abortion Law Is Long Overdue." *Journal of Medical Ethics* 49 (8): 523–524.
Sheldon, S., and K. Wellings. 2020. *Decriminalising Abortion: What Would It Mean*. Policy Press.
Society for the Protection of Unborn Children. 2020. "New Deadly 'Phone for an Abortion' Condemned by SPUC." https://www.spuc.org.uk/ArticleHandler/ArticleType/ArticleView/ArticleID/384363.
United Nations. 1995. *Report of the International Conference on Population and Development*. https://www.un.org/development/desa/pd/sites/www.un.org.development.desa.pd/files/icpd_en.pdf.

Welsh Government. 2018. The Abortion Act 1967 (Approval of Place for Treatment for the Termination of Pregnancy) (Wales) 2018. https://gov.wales/sites/default/files/publications/2019-07/the-abortion-act-1967-approval-of-place-for-treatment-for-the-termination-of-pregnancy-wales-2018-2018-no-56.pdf.

Welsh Government. 2020. The Abortion Act 1967—Approval of a Class of Place for Treatment for the Termination of Pregnancy (Wales) 2020. https://gov.wales/sites/default/files/publications/2020-04/approval-of-a-class-of-place-for-treatment-for-the-termination-of-pregnancy-wales-2020.pdf.

WHO (World Health Organization). 2012. *Safe Abortion: Technical and Policy Guidance for Health Systems.* https://apps.who.int/iris/bitstream/handle/10665/70914/9789241548434_eng.pdf.

WHO. 2022. *Abortion Care Guideline.* https://www.who.int/publications/i/item/9789240039483.

19

A Proportional Response?

Abortion Exceptionalism, Telemedicine, and the COVID-19 Pandemic in Great Britain

Lucía Berro Pizzarossa and Rishita Nandagiri

Introduction

Abortion, almost always exceptionalized in law and medicine (Yamin and Bergallo 2017), contends with a range of barriers related to access, availability, cost, information and knowledge, and stigma, among others. This exceptionalism shapes laws (e.g., the number of laws or regulations governing abortion) and medicine (e.g., limitations to or requirements for access to care) and reproduces abortion stigma (Berro Pizzarossa 2019). Sometimes framed as elective care, it can lead to a hierarchy of abortion needs (i.e., emergency vs. elective), affecting care provision and shaping the conditions and kind of care offered (Janiak and Goldberg 2016; Watson 2018). The COVID-19 pandemic heightened many of these barriers and was underpinned, in many contexts, by abortion exceptionalism within the law and in care provision (Joffe and Schroeder 2021).

The first waves of the COVID-19 pandemic (2020) implemented stay-at-home orders that made exceptions for essential services. In addition to national and local lockdowns and movement restrictions, quarantine requirements also prevented and deterred people from visiting healthcare facilities. Healthcare workers' time and focus, along with healthcare resources, were diverted to tackling COVID-19 (Riley et al. 2020). These shifts, at the social and governance levels and within health systems, exacerbated existing gendered, racialized, classed, and other inequities that shape access to services like sexual and reproductive health (SRH). Abortion, a key element of SRH, became increasingly difficult to access under COVID-19 conditions in many parts of the world (Todd-Gher and Shah 2020).

Lucía Berro Pizzarossa and Rishita Nandagiri share joint first authorship, having equally drafted, contributed to, and reviewed this article.

Lucía Berro Pizzarossa and Rishita Nandagiri, *A Proportional Response?*. In: *Proportionality*.
Edited by: Nikola Biller-Andorno et al., Oxford University Press.
DOI: 10.1093/9780197759370.003.0020

The United Kingdom[1] announced its first lockdown on March 23, 2020, and it legally came into force on March 26, 2020 (Institute for Government 2022). On March 30, 2020, after a brief U-turn, England, Wales, and Scotland implemented temporary measures to allow medical abortion (i.e., inducing abortion by using pills—mifepristone and misoprostol—taken orally) at home (Rough 2022) as an essential service (Bayefsky et al. 2020; World Health Organization [WHO] 2020). This did not include Northern Ireland, where, despite decriminalization, services had not yet been commissioned, and the law required that mifepristone must be taken on National Health Service (NHS) premises (Kirk et al. 2021).

In keeping with other case studies in this volume, we draw on Childress et al.'s (2002, 173) framing of proportionality, whereby "the probable public health benefits outweigh the infringed general moral considerations .... All of the positive features and benefits must be balanced against the negative features and effects." As Erdman (2017, 32) argues, "Proportionality is the logic of most contemporary abortion laws, but also the logic of many human rights challenges to and justifications for these laws."

Locating our approach within this understanding of abortion and proportionality, we build on Erdman (2017) to highlight how this balance is achieved through a constant (re)calibration and (re)assessment of the moral weights assigned to abortion-seekers, their needs, and their autonomies, against that of current laws and regulations. In this case study, we focus specifically on abortion regulation and exceptionalism in Great Britain, the introduction of telemedicine for early medical abortion care as a temporary pandemic measure, and its impact on current abortion regulations. Arguing against continued abortion exceptionalism and challenging continued criminalization of abortion, we offer a third possible alternative that affirms human rights and gender justice—self-managed abortion (SMA).

In the following sections, we first present our approach to proportionality and telemedicine for early medical abortion care in the context of the COVID-19 pandemic. We then briefly explore the abortion laws and exceptions in Great Britain and the introduction of telemedicine as a COVID-19 measure, followed by reflections on its implications for progressing abortion access and meeting the needs of abortion-seekers. We end by reflecting on the potential of telemedicine and whether it balances public health and moral considerations in the test of proportionality.

[1] The United Kingdom is the political union that includes England, Scotland, Wales, and Northern Ireland. Great Britain is the political union that includes England, Scotland, and Wales only. In this case study, we largely focus on abortion legislation pertaining to Great Britain but specify individual nations when relevant.

Proportionality and Telemedicine

Discussions surrounding telemedicine have largely been dominated by the medico-legal paradigm, including by focusing on whether the adoption of telemedicine is a proportional measure in light of the barriers posed by the COVID-19 pandemic (Boydell et al. 2021; Reynolds-Wright et al. 2021; Romanis et al. 2021). Following Childress et al.'s (2002) definition of proportionality, we argue that in balancing public health and moral considerations, the introduction of telemedicine for early medical abortion care represents a step forward in securing bodily autonomies and realizing gender justice but still exists within institutionalized health systems and, therefore, falls short of a truly proportional response.

The COVID-19 pandemic undoubtedly disrupted and constrained abortion access and service provision, but instead of creating new issues, it exacerbated and "exposed existing fractures and fissures" (Nandagiri et al. 2020, 83). Focusing on telemedicine as a proportional response to the *pandemic* makes invisible the long-standing fault lines surrounding abortion care in *nonpandemic conditions* that gave rise to and heightened these barriers.

We argue that this misplaced focus obscures the fact that while telemedicine for early medical abortion care is a step in the right direction toward simpler, less medicalized models of accessing abortion, it falls well short of a proportional response, as it fails to address the biomedical model that underpins abortion regulation and leaves untouched the laws that continue to restrict and/or criminalize abortion. It then risks contributing to the false exceptionalizing of abortion in law, medicine, health, and policy. Rather than focusing on whether telemedicine is a proportional response to the constraints exacerbated by the pandemic, we argue that an analysis of proportionality first requires engaging with whether existing abortion regulations comply with the test of proportionality or not.

Abortion in Great Britain: An Overview

In the United Kingdom, abortion is governed by a number of statutes and common law provisions. The law differs significantly between England and Wales, Scotland, and Northern Ireland (Sheldon and Wellings 2020). In Great Britain, abortion is regulated by the 1967 Abortion Act. In Northern Ireland, the Abortion Regulations (2020) apply.

Abortion in Great Britain remains tied to the draconian 1861 Offences Against the Person Act (OAPA). Under the OAPA, abortion remains a criminal offense in England and Wales. In Scotland, it remains criminal under common law (Sheldon and Wellings 2020). The 1967 Abortion Act offers exceptions to the

OAPA, making abortion legal only when carried out under conditions of strict medical control. To avoid a criminal offense, three conditions must be met: (a) two doctors must certify, in good faith, that abortion is justified on the basis of one or more of the four broad grounds set out under the Act, (b) the abortion must be performed by a registered medical practitioner, and (c) it must be performed on NHS premises or another approved "class of places" (Sheldon and Wellings 2020, 8). The Abortion Act thus exempts those who conform to these requirements from prosecution, while potentially criminalizing any abortion-seekers and providers who do not.

Abortion Telemedicine and the COVID-19 Pandemic

To respond to the additional constraints posed by the COVID-19 pandemic, exceptions to the Abortion Act were proposed in Great Britain. This did not include Northern Ireland. The reforms all involved a formal regulatory act—namely, the temporary approval of the "home" as a class of place for abortion care under the Abortion Act (Rough 2022).

After a series of U-turns, the Secretary of State for Health and Social Care finally approved the home as such a class of place where medical practitioners may prescribe, and patients may take, abortion pills (Department of Health and Social Care 2020a; Wenham et al. 2020). The home is defined as the place where either person has their permanent address or usually resides, and it is the place to which pills can now be delivered by mail (BPAS 2020; MSI Reproductive Choices 2020).

Medication abortion was already an option prior to the pandemic; however, pregnant people were required to make an in-person visit to their healthcare provider for an ultrasound scan and to take the first of two pills, mifepristone. Since 2018, they could take the second pill, misoprostol, at home (Parsons 2020). At-home management of abortion was a subject of discussion before the pandemic, but it was effected in 2020 as an exceptional measure to limit the transmission of coronavirus (COVID-19) and maximize health resources, ensuring continued access abortion services (Department of Health and Social Care 2020b). The UK government continually emphasized that the measures were temporary and limited to two years or until the end of the pandemic—whichever was earlier (Department of Health and Social Care 2020b).

The shift in policy has already generated significant evidence confirming the benefits of simpler, less medicalized models of accessing abortion. Based on a sample size of 52,142 people, researchers found that no-test (i.e., without an ultrasound) telemedicine abortion model is just as safe and effective as the traditional in-person medication abortion model (Aiken et al. 2021; Glasier and

Regan 2021). Telemedicine abortion was in fact superior to in-clinic care in several respects. For example, patients received treatment more quickly. Whereas the average wait time for in-clinic medication abortion was 10.7 days, the average wait time for patients using the new no-test telemedicine model was only 6.5 days, and 40% of abortions were provided at six weeks' gestation or less (Aiken et al. 2021). Patients reported high satisfaction with the privacy, convenience, and ease of this pathway (Porter Erlank et al. 2021). Positive experiences with at-home abortion also included reduced stigma and respect for one's autonomy (Lohr et al. 2022). This evidence contributed to the calls to retain the extraordinary measures permanently, reflecting those made by many abortion rights advocates well before the pandemic (Jelinska and Yanow 2018; Assis and Larrea 2020; Nandagiri et al. 2020; Tongue 2022).

Telemedicine for abortion care, first expected to end in March 2022, was extended to August 2022. After a consultation (November 2020–February 2021) that received over eighteen thousand responses (Department of Health and Social Care 2022b), the government announced it would be ending abortion telemedicine in England and Wales at the end of August 2022 (Department of Health and Social Care 2022a). This was met with immediate condemnation from abortion providers, researchers, and advocates. In March 2022, an amendment was passed in the House of Lords and then voted on in the House of Commons to make telemedicine for early medical abortion care permanent in England and Wales from August 30, 2022 (Royal College of Obstetricians and Gynaecologists 2022a). Scotland continues to provide abortion telemedicine as part of an ongoing evaluation (Scottish Government 2022).

Abortion's Medico-Legal Frameworks and Proportionality

Criminalization of Abortion

The Abortion Act's requirements that two doctors certify the need for an abortion and that abortions be performed by registered medical practitioners are examples of medically approved autonomy, whereby access is subject to a doctor's approval (Ginsburg 1985). This links to Halliday's (2016, 172) description of a "gate-keeping" role: Medical personnel control access to abortion and hold significant influence in determining access to medical treatment during pregnancy/birth based on social, medical, or embryopathic concerns. Indeed, autonomy has never been articulated as the official justification for abortion law in the United Kingdom; rather, medical control has been the predominant rationale (Sheldon 1995; 1997) and has placed "great social responsibility . . . upon the shoulders of the medical profession" (Halliday 2016, 172).

Although considered to be "obsolete" (Law Commission 2015), the law is—and remains, after the adoption of telemedicine—in full force, and pregnant people and those who assist them still face criminalization for managing abortions outside of the limited conditions set by the law (Das 2022). Police investigations into "illegal abortions" continue, with at least one woman serving a two-year prison sentence (Al-Othman 2022). As of July 2022, two women were facing criminal charges for abortion (Hampson 2022). Detailing the harms of abortion criminalization exceeds the purpose of this chapter, but it has long been established that the criminalization of abortion does not deter people from needing and seeking abortions or enable safer access to abortion services but instead causes disproportionate harm and is a form of gender-based discrimination (Erdman 2012; Erdman and Cook 2020). Medical professionals, abortion providers, researchers, and activists continue to call for the full decriminalization of abortion (Royal College of Obstetricians and Gynaecologists 2022b).

Medicalization of Abortion

Abortion telemedicine, while enabling abortion access, is a measure firmly situated within the medico-legal paradigm, and the new policy shifts still fall within that rationale. In abortion telemedicine, abortion is constructed as a *medical* event, which reinforces the authority and power of medical personnel. This underpins theorizations and constructions of safety and risk in abortion, pregnancy, and childbirth and locates knowledge and authority within medico-legal institutions, thereby making women's bodies a site for medical practice and (non)intervention (Lock and Kaufert 1997).

Medically supervised abortion—even if now simplified by telemedical means—is still seen as the ideal model for access and, as such, the only model worthy of legal recognition and, therefore, decriminalization. The adoption of telemedicine facilitates access under the strict conditions set in the Abortion Act yet does not challenge the law itself or the medicalization model but instead reinforces it. In extending medical infrastructure and technology to the home, it increases both the social responsibility and the gate-keeping power of medical personnel in determining abortion access. While evidence shows that safeguarding concerns around abortion telemedicine in England are unwarranted (Parsons and Romanis 2022), it also underscores the social responsibility roles that abortion providers are tasked with. In addition, it points to the continued exceptionalization of abortion within these dominant medico-legal frameworks.

Calls for the demedicalization of abortion are not new. Almost forty years ago, activists pointed out that the Abortion Act handed "the abortion decision to the medical profession. The next stage is to hand this very personal decision to the woman herself" (Simms 1985, 94). Telemedicine, rather than enabling demedicalization of abortion and the long-awaited handover to abortion-seekers, further entrenches the authority of medical professionals.

Telemedicine, Telehealth, and (Self-Managed) Abortion

As countries increasingly adopt models of telemedicine similar to the ones long used by activists and feminist networks globally, the maintenance of abortion as a crime becomes even more confusing. The interplay between partial demedicalization but continuous criminalization, as in Great Britain, further exposes and exacerbates the cacophony of laws that surround abortion (Berro Pizzarossa and Nandagiri 2021).

The discussion around proportionality is further complicated by SMA (i.e., when an individual terminates their pregnancy without clinical supervision or outside of institutional systems of medical care). The advent of telemedicine is preceded by decades of practice and experiential knowledge developed by people self-managing and those who support them (Berro Pizzarossa and Nandagiri 2021). While SMA is not a new practice, advances in medical technology—that is, medical abortion pills (misoprostol and mifepristone)—have significantly increased the safety and effectiveness over the last fifty years (Gerdts et al. 2018; Zurbriggen et al. 2018; Moseson et al. 2020; Berro Pizzarossa and Skuster 2021). There are many reasons why pregnant people may prefer to self-manage their abortions: wait times, distance to available clinics, concerns around immigration status, a lack of eligibility for free NHS services, and prior negative experiences of abortion care, including a lack of confidentiality (Astbury-Ward 2015; Aiken et al. 2018).

Under the new regulations, those requiring abortion care can access a telemedicine consultation with a registered medical practitioner, receive SMA pills by mail, and use them at home. This process—the active involvement of the pregnant person, the medicine, the protocols for their use—is not fundamentally different[2] from the telehealth care that informal networks and other feminist groups have been providing for decades.[3] In fact, protocols and counseling scripts from groups such as Women Help Women that support self-management

[2] We acknowledge here the fundamental differences in terms of the philosophy, power dynamics, and models of care underpinning the work of activists and feminist networks (different from the medical model).

[3] We define *telehealth* broadly as encompassing the use of technology or other means (by institutionalized systems of care *and* autonomous health movements) to support, accompany, or provide health services remotely, while *telemedicine* refers exclusively to the remote provision of clinical services through formal systems.

have been adopted by formal abortion providers, and it is knowledge advanced by feminist groups and shared with formal systems that underpins the advance of telemedicine (Moseson et al. 2020). Importantly, while governments—including in England, Scotland, and Wales—were still debating whether abortion could be provided via telemedicine, feminist networks were developing demedicalized practices that have spread across the world (Braine 2020). The work of these actors outside of institutionalized health systems has paved the way for further autonomous models of abortion provision.

However, the legal risks that these feminist groups or autonomous networks face and are exposed to are significantly different from those functioning within formal spaces, and the introduction of telemedicine did not alter the fact that abortion regulation remains "rooted in the punitive, conservative values of the mid-Victorian era" (Sheldon 2016, 334). Thus, the introduction of telemedicine further exposes the cacophony of laws (Berro Pizzarossa and Nandagiri 2021) surrounding the current abortion framework, and prompts the question, Why is telemedicine treated differently under the law while other forms of telehealth—which have run for decades prior and set the science and practices underpinning telemedicine—continue to fall under the most onerous and draconian of state powers? The key difference between the two is that the impetus for telemedicine was to address the barriers to receiving care in the clinic in person, while the impetus for SMA is to enable care that meets the needs of the abortion-seeker, irrespective of location.

This differentiation demands that we question the proportionality of telemedicine with regard to the state's response, depending on whether abortion is accessed via telemedicine or is self-managed outside of the strict conditions set by the Abortion Act. This is particularly stark when global evidence shows that the quality of medical care in informal spaces is on par with—if not superior to—standard formal systems (Moseson et al. 2022). It also calls into question the gate-keeping of abortion within formal medical systems, when it is the work of activist networks that has transformed the discourse and science behind the telemedicine model (Berro Pizzarossa and Nandagiri 2021).

Models like the one proposed by the Socorristas[4]—whereby *acompañantes* (companions) have taught doctors about the use of misoprostol, refer women to friendly providers, and are also referred by providers and women—highlight the importance of sharing different frameworks and approaches and giving

[4] Socorristas en Red (Feminists and Transfeminists who abort) is a network of abortion support volunteers that was formed in Argentina in 2012. Today, it unites 40 feminist collectives across the country that provide information on the safe use of medication and offer abortion accompaniment. https://petrieflom.law.harvard.edu/2024/10/12/when-the-right-to-abortion-is-more-than-a-law-accompaniment-and-cultural-transformations-in-the-political-activism-of-argentinas-socorristas-en-red/.

pregnant people the array of options of access to care and methods that they need and deserve (Yanow et al. 2021).

Regarding the imperative to demedicalize and decriminalize abortion, the 2022 WHO *Abortion Care Guideline* states that SMA with medicines is not just a measure of last resort but an alternative care model that many people find works better for them for myriad reasons (Moseson et al. 2020). The WHO (2022, 22) recognizes that criminal laws and criminal frameworks regarding abortion often lead to people experiencing "significant barriers in accessing abortion and post-abortion care." As a result, the WHO (2022, 102) advises the full decriminalization of abortion, including self-management. Specifically, in relation to self-management of abortion care, the WHO (2022, 98) makes clear that this includes the "self-administration of abortion medicines outside of a healthcare facility and without the direct supervision of a trained health worker, and management of the abortion process." Yet despite evidence and increasing consensus on the importance of these models in care provision, policies and policy change continue to privilege medico-legal paradigms.

Moral Considerations and Public Health Benefits

Childress et al.'s (2002) framework demands that we interrogate whether the use of criminal law and the overmedicalization of abortion meet the standards of proportionality. Weighing the positive and negative features of this policy change necessitates that we identify what the *public health benefits* and *moral considerations* at play are. While an exhaustive discussion of the wide ranging moral considerations here are beyond the remit of this chapter, our aim is to provide further nuance about the analysis of proportionality in relation to telemedicine by attending to some of these key aspects.

We contend that the arguments that, it is typically claimed, are the motivation behind the legal restrictions and the current criminal laws—namely, the protection of women and the prevention and condemnation of the intentional destruction of fetal life—no longer hold (if they ever did).[5] It is difficult to argue that a law that is a product of the moral climate and clinical realities of the 1960s is a proportional measure, especially in face of the extensive public health evidence available today. As Undurraga (2014) notes, the fierce defense of unborn life would only be consistent if at the same time it could be

[5] We refer here to the most common arguments used in the parliamentary debates around the Abortion Act 1967. However, abortion restrictions have also been shown to fit into a larger pattern of control of female sexuality and reproduction as a population control mechanism that is built around demographic goals and as a mechanism of social control of the adequate performance of gender and a legacy of colonialism.

shown that the criminalization of abortion results in fewer abortions. There is broad consensus today that legal restrictions do not reduce the number of abortions but rather that restrictive abortion laws (nationally and internationally) are associated with a high incidence of unsafe abortions and corresponding health consequences (Guttmacher Institute 2012). Additionally, these restrictions were also the moral considerations of the parliamentarians of the time and were more concerned with (re)producing the medicalized framing of abortion as a response to unsafe abortion than in discussing the gendered, racialized, or socioeconomic inequalities that impact trajectories to abortion care (Coast et al. 2018).

Telemedicine, too, despite its widespread support and the evidence of its positive public health impact, is mired in moral considerations. Some of these moral considerations are evident in the government's public consultation[6] on telemedicine in England (Department of Health and Social Care 2022b). The majority of responses were against telemedicine, arguing that it had a negative impact on women accessing abortion service provision, and they included many safeguarding and safety concerns. Curiously, the submissions as well as the research and data on people who actually accessed abortion via telemedicine showed stark contradictions. For example, in the policy consultation, 69% of respondents stated that the temporary measure had a negative impact, while 83% of women who responded to the policy consultation and who had used both pills for early medication abortion said that the temporary approval had a positive impact on their safety (Department of Health and Social Care 2022b). The second set of respondents confirms the findings of rigorous scientific research and evidence on the topic (Aiken et al. 2021; Glasier and Regan 2021). In fact, as research shows, those who accessed abortion telemedicine said they would prefer it even if COVID-19 were not a factor and rated home use highly (Porter Erlank et al. 2021).

The policy consultation received 181,834 responses, of which 18,659 were by individuals and 175 by organizations. Nearly half of the individual responses (9,109) were affiliated with campaigns, and the majority (8,424) were associated with one campaign that was linked to a stock campaign template (Department of Health and Social Care 2022b). These are suspected to be linked to antiabortion campaigns. Such antiabortion responses are not representative of general public opinion on abortion in Great Britain (Taylor 2017; Gray and Wellings 2020).

Despite the wealth of public health evidence on telemedicine, its effectiveness, the satisfaction of service users, and the ample evidence on attitudes

[6] In public consultations (or policy consultations), the government elicits expert knowledge and public opinion on new or changing policies or laws. Affected or interested parties can, during a defined time period, submit their responses on a specific policy, law, or consultation paper. Government departments take these responses into consideration before making decisions.

about abortion, the government initially planned to end telemedicine services. It was sustained pushback from activists and intervention of scientific and medical groups that led to making telemedicine permanent (Royal College of Obstetricians and Gynaecologists 2022a).

The evidence from abortion-users highlights that moral considerations radically shift when centering on the voices of those who need and use the service. When reflecting on moral considerations, it is essential to consider *whose* voices are centered and how much weight they are assigned in decision-making. About the initial government response to the policy consultation, one might conclude that service users (who had a positive experience) and medical professionals and researchers (whose evidence and research underscored the public health impact of telemedicine) were treated as equal to a singular campaign effort (which suggested that telemedicine had a negative impact). Similarly, in considering public health impacts, it is important to consider *who* benefits (or is harmed) by policies and laws. The criminalization and overmedicalization of abortion, on balance and as evidence shows, do not serve public health needs. Engaging with the *who* and *whose* highlights that policy and law are linked to not just public health and moral considerations but political considerations, too. As Sheldon (2016) argues, it is essential to remain very vigilant of political ideology masquerading as scientific fact.

Conclusion

Whether abortion telemedicine balances moral and public health considerations in the test of proportionality is difficult to answer without acknowledging the constant exceptionalizing of abortion. The constant U-turns that telemedicine had to contend with—at the start of the pandemic and, later, in making it a permanent measure—are indicative of its exceptionalizing. This is despite the rigorous and extensive body of scientific evidence on abortion and on telemedicine. Thus, it pushes us to ask, When abortion is so exceptionalized, what does proportionality look like? How does one balance moral and public health considerations in abortion care when it begins from a skewed position?

Telemedicine, while addressing *where* an abortion can occur, does not fundamentally shift the criminalization and overmedicalization of abortion. It reinforces the existing law and focus on medical authority without championing the autonomies and agencies of abortion-seekers. A proportional response to the barriers posed by the pandemic would necessitate first acknowledging that these barriers are not new but tied to the social and structural conditions that surround abortion including laws and policies (Nandagiri et al. 2020). The decriminalization of abortion, including self-management, would balance both public health and moral considerations. This is supported by evidence, international standards, and the needs and voices of abortion-seekers. Second, permanently removing unnecessary restrictions imposed by formal systems of law, medicine, and market would no longer impede timely access to essential medicines like mifepristone and misoprostol both in communities and within healthcare systems, thereby enabling a range of abortion services, including telemedicine, that cater to pregnant people's needs (Yanow et al. 2021).

Locating the introduction of telemedicine in Great Britain within broader considerations of how abortion care is constructed and who is centered, and engaging with feminist forms of care provision via telemedicine or telehealth broadens both the public health and the moral considerations of proportionality. It demands that the frameworks that surround the overmedicalization and exceptionalizing of abortion be accounted for. While telemedicine in Great Britain is a welcome step forward, it falls short of achieving a balance between moral considerations and public health benefits, as it does not fundamentally challenge the criminalization of abortion or the exceptionalizing model of the current abortion framework and instead risks entrenching it further.

Competing Interests

The authors have no competing interests to declare.

Funding

Berro Pizzarossa's work on this piece was funded by a Rubicon Grant awarded by the Dutch Research Council (NWO).

References

Aiken, A., P. A. Lohr, J. Lord, N. Ghosh, and J. Starling. 2021. "Effectiveness, Safety and Acceptability of No-Test Medical Abortion Provided Via Telemedicine: A National Cohort Study." *BJOG: An International Journal of Obstetrics & Gynaecology* 128 (9): 1471–0528.16668. https://doi.org/10.1111/1471-0528.16668.

Aiken, A. R. A., K. A. Guthrie, M. Schellekens, J. Trussell, and R. Gomperts. 2018. "Barriers to Accessing Abortion Services and Perspectives on Using Mifepristone and Misoprostol at Home in Great Britain." *Contraception* 97 (2): 177–183. https://doi.org/10.1016/j.contraception.2017.09.003.

Al-Othman, H. 2022. "Laura's Story: Jailed for Having an Abortion in Britain." *The Sunday Times*, August 6.

Assis, M. P., and S. Larrea. 2020. "Why Self-Managed Abortion Is So Much More Than a Provisional Solution for Times of Pandemic." *Sexual and Reproductive Health Matters* 28 (1): 1779633. https://doi.org/10.1080/26410397.2020.1779633.

Astbury-Ward, E. 2015. "Abortion 'on the NHS': The National Health Service and Abortion Stigma." *Journal of Family Planning and Reproductive Health Care* 41 (3): 168–169. https://doi.org/10.1136/jfprhc-2014-101104.

Bayefsky, M. J., D. Bartz, and K. L. Watson. 2020. "Abortion During the Covid-19 Pandemic—Ensuring Access to an Essential Health Service." *New England Journal of Medicine* 382 (19): e47. https://doi.org/10.1056/NEJMp2008006.

Berro Pizzarossa, L. 2019. "Abortion, Health and Gender Stereotypes: A Critical Analysis of the Uruguayan and South African Abortion Laws Through the Lens of Human Rights." PhD Thesis, University of Groningen. https://research.rug.nl/en/publications/abortion-health-and-gender-stereotypes-a-critical-analysis-of-the.

Berro Pizzarossa, L., and R. Nandagiri. 2021. "Self-Managed Abortion: A Constellation of Actors, a Cacophony of Laws?" *Sexual and Reproductive Health Matters* 29 (1): 1899764. https://doi.org/10.1080/26410397.2021.1899764.

Berro Pizzarossa, L., and P. Skuster. 2021. "Toward Human Rights and Evidence-Based Legal Frameworks for (Self-Managed) Abortion: A Review of the Last Decade of Legal Reform." *Health and Human Rights Journal* 23 (1): 199–212.

Boydell, N., J. J. Reynolds-Wright, S. T. Cameron, and J. Harden. 2021. "Women's experiences of a telemedicine abortion service (up to 12 weeks) implemented during the coronavirus (COVID-19) pandemic: a qualitative evaluation." BJOG: *An International Journal of Obstetrics & Gynaecology* 128 (11): 1752–1761. https://doi.org/10.1111/1471-0528.16813.

BPAS (British Pregnancy Advisory Service). 2020. *Pills by Post: Telemedical abortion at the British Pregnancy Advisory Service (BPAS)*. https://www.bpas.org/media/inejqvz2/bpas-pills-by-post-service.pdf.

Braine, N. 2020. "Autonomous Health Movements: Criminalization, De-Medicalization, and Community-Based Direct Action." *Health and Human Rights* 22 (2): 85–97.

Childress, J. F., R. R. Raden, R. D. Gaare et al. 2002. "Public Health Ethics: Mapping the Terrain." *Journal of Law, Medicine & Ethics* 30 (2): 170–178. https://doi.org/10.1111/j.1748-720X.2002.tb00384.x.

Coast, E., A. H. Norris, A. M. Moore, and E. Freeman. 2018. "Trajectories of Women's Abortion-Related Care: A Conceptual Framework." *Social Science & Medicine* 200:199–210. https://doi.org/10.1016/j.socscimed.2018.01.035.

Das, S. 2022. "Women Accused of Illegal Abortions in England and Wales After Miscarriages and Stillbirths." *The Guardian*, July 2.

Department of Health and Social Care. 2020a. "Temporary Approval of Home Use for Both Stages of Early Medical Abortion." https://www.gov.uk/government/publications/temporary-approval-of-home-use-for-both-stages-of-early-medical-abortion–2.

Department of Health and Social Care. 2020b. The Abortion Act 1967—Approval of a Class of Places.

Department of Health and Social Care. 2022a. "England to Return to Pre-Pandemic System for Early Abortions." https://www.gov.uk/government/news/england-to-return-to-pre-pandemic-system-for-early-abortions.

Department of Health and Social Care. 2022b. "Home Use of Both Pills for Early Medical Abortion (EMA) Up to 10 Weeks Gestation: Summary of Consultation Responses." https://www.gov.uk/government/consultations/home-use-of-both-pills-for-early-medical-abortion/outcome/home-use-of-both-pills-for-early-medical-abortion-ema-up-to-10-weeks-gestation-summary-of-consultation-responses.

Erdman, J. N. 2012. "Harm Reduction, Human Rights, and Access to Information on Safer Abortion." *International Journal of Gynecology & Obstetrics* 118 (1): 83–86. https://doi.org/10.1016/j.ijgo.2012.04.002.

Erdman, J. N. 2017. "Theorizing Time in Abortion Law and Human Rights." *Health and Human Rights Journal* 29:29–40.

Erdman, J. N., and R. J. Cook. 2020. "Decriminalization of Abortion—a Human Rights Imperative." *Best Practice & Research Clinical Obstetrics & Gynaecology* 62:11–24. https://doi.org/10.1016/j.bpobgyn.2019.05.004.

Gerdts, C., R. T. Jayaweera, S. E. Baum, and I. Hudaya. 2018. "Second-Trimester Medication Abortion Outside the Clinic Setting: An Analysis of Electronic Client Records from a Safe Abortion Hotline in Indonesia." *BMJ Sexual & Reproductive Health* 44 (4): 286–291. https://doi.org/10.1136/bmjsrh-2018-200102.

Ginsburg, R. B. 1985. "Some Thoughts on Autonomy and Equality in Relation to 'Roe v. Wade.'" *North Carolina Law Review* 63 (2): 375–386.

Glasier, A., and L. Regan. 2021. "Induced Abortion via Telemedicine Should Become the Norm: A Commentary." *BJOG: An International Journal of Obstetrics & Gynaecology* 128 (9): 1475–1476. https://doi.org/10.1111/1471-0528.16740.

Gray, A. M., and K. Wellings. 2020. "Is Public Opinion in Support of Decriminalisation?" In *Decriminalising Abortion in the UK*, edited by Sally Sheldon and Kaye Wellings. Policy Press.

Guttmacher Institute. 2012. *Making Abortion Services Accessible in the Wake of Legal Reforms: A Framework and Six Case Studies*, April. https://www.guttmacher.org/report/making-abortion-services-accessible-wake-legal-reforms-framework-and-six-case-studies.

Halliday, S. 2016. *Autonomy and Pregnancy: A Comparative Analysis of Compelled Obstetric Intervention*. Routledge.

Hampson, L. 2022. "What We Know About the Two British Women Facing Life Sentences for Abortion in the UK." *The Independent*, August 11.

Institute for Government. 2022. "Timeline of UK Government Coronavirus Lockdowns and Restrictions," December 9. https://www.instituteforgovernment.org.uk/data-visualisation/timeline-coronavirus-lockdowns.

Janiak, E., and A. B. Goldberg. 2016. "Eliminating the Phrase 'Elective Abortion': Why Language Matters." *Contraception* 93 (2): 89–92. https://doi.org/10.1016/j.contraception.2015.10.008.

Jelinska, K., and S. Yanow. 2018. "Putting Abortion Pills into Women's Hands: Realizing the Full Potential of Medical Abortion." *Contraception* 97 (2): 86–89. https://doi.org/10.1016/j.contraception.2017.05.019.

Joffe, C., and R. Schroeder. 2021. "COVID-19, Health Care, and Abortion Exceptionalism in the United States." *Perspectives on Sexual and Reproductive Health* 53 (1–2): 5–12. https://doi.org/10.1363/psrh.12182.

Kirk, S., L. Morgan, S. McDermott, L. McLaughlin, C. Hunter, and T. Farrington. 2021. "Introduction of the National Health Service Early Medical Abortion Service in Northern Ireland—an Emergency Response to the COVID-19 Pandemic." *BMJ Sexual & Reproductive Health* 47 (4): 293–295. https://doi.org/10.1136/bmjsrh-2020-200920.

Law Commission. 2015. "Offences Against the Person," November 3. https://lawcom.gov.uk/project/offences-against-the-person/.

Lock, M., and P. Kaufert. 1997. "Introduction" in *Pragmatic Women and Body Politics*, edited by Margaret Lock and Patricia A. Kaufert. Cambridge University Press.

Lohr, P. A., M. Lewandowska, R. Meiksin et al. 2022. "Should COVID-Specific Arrangements for Abortion Continue? The Views of Women Experiencing Abortion in Britain During the pandemic." *BMJ Sexual & Reproductive Health* 48 (4): bmjsrh-2022-201502. https://doi.org/10.1136/bmjsrh-2022-201502.

Moseson, H., K. A. Bullard, C. Cisternas, B. Grosso, V. Vera, and C. Gerdts. 2020. "Effectiveness of Self-Managed Medication Abortion Between 13 and 24 Weeks Gestation: A Retrospective

Review of Case Records from Accompaniment Groups in Argentina, Chile, and Ecuador." *Contraception* 102 (2): 91–98. https://doi.org/10.1016/j.contraception.2020.04.015.

Moseson, H., S. Herold, S. Filippa, J. Barr-Walker, S. E. Baum, and C. Gerdts. 2020. "Self-Managed Abortion: A Systematic Scoping Review." *Best Practice and Research: Clinical Obstetrics and Gynaecology* 63:87–110. https://doi.org/10.1016/j.bpobgyn.2019.08.002.

Moseson, H., R. Jayaweera, S. Raifman et al. 2020. "Self-Managed Medication Abortion Outcomes: Results from a Prospective Pilot Study." *Reproductive Health* 17 (1): 164. https://doi.org/10.1186/s12978-020-01016-4.

Moseson, H., R. Jayaweera, I. Egwuatu et al. 2022. "Effectiveness of Self-Managed Medication Abortion with Accompaniment Support in Argentina and Nigeria (SAFE): A Prospective, Observational Cohort Study and Non-Inferiority Analysis with Historical Controls." *The Lancet Global Health* 10 (1): E105–E113. https://doi.org/10.1016/S2214-109X(21)00461-7.

MSI Reproductive Choices. 2020. "Abortion Pill Online (Telemedicine)." https://www.msichoices.org.uk/abortion-services/online-medical-abortion/.

Nandagiri, R., E. Coast, and J. Strong. 2020. "COVID-19 and Abortion: Making Structural Violence Visible." *International Perspectives on Sexual and Reproductive Health* 46 (Suppl. 1): 83–89. https://doi.org/10.1363/46e1320.

Parsons, J. A. 2020. "2017–19 Governmental Decisions To Allow Home Use of Misoprostol for Early Medical Abortion in the UK." *Health Policy* 124 (7): 679–683. https://doi.org/10.1016/j.healthpol.2020.04.014.

Parsons, J. A., and E. C. Romanis. 2022. "The Case for Telemedical Early Medical Abortion in England: Dispelling Adult Safeguarding Concerns." *Health Care Analysis* 30 (1): 73–96. https://doi.org/10.1007/s10728-021-00439-9.

Porter Erlank, C., J. Lord, and K. Church. 2021. "Acceptability of No-Test Medical Abortion Provided via Telemedicine: Analysis of Patient-Reported Outcomes." *BMJ Sexual & Reproductive Health* 47 (4): bmjsrh-2020-200954. https://doi.org/10.1136/bmjsrh-2020-200954.

Reynolds-Wright, J. J., A. Johnstone, K. McCabe, E. Evans, and S. Cameron. 2021. "Telemedicine Medical Abortion at Home Under 12 Weeks' Gestation: A Prospective Observational Cohort Study During the COVID-19 pandemic." *BMJ Sexual & Reproductive Health* 47 (4): bmjsrh-2020-200976. https://doi.org/10.1136/bmjsrh-2020-200976.

Riley, T., E. Sully, Z. Ahmed, and A. Biddlecom. 2020. "Estimates of the Potential Impact of the COVID-19 Pandemic on Sexual and Reproductive Health in Low- and Middle-Income Countries." *International Perspectives on Sexual and Reproductive Health* 46:73–76. https://doi.org/10.1363/46e9020.

Romanis, E. C., J. A. Parsons, I. Salter, and T. Hampton. 2021. "Safeguarding and Teleconsultation for Abortion." *The Lancet* 398 (10299): 555–558. https://doi.org/10.1016/s0140-6736(21)01062-x.

Rough, E. 2022. *Early Medical Abortion at Home During and After the Pandemic.* Research Briefing No. CBP9496. House of Commons Library. https://researchbriefings.files.parliament.uk/documents/CBP-9496/CBP-9496.pdf.

Royal College of Obstetricians and Gynaecologists. 2022a. "Parliament Votes to Make Telemedicine for Early Medical Abortion Permanent in England." https://www.rcog.org.uk/news/parliament-votes-to-make-telemedicine-for-early-medical-abortion-permanent-in-england/.

Royal College of Obstetricians and Gynaecologists. 2022b. "Women's Health Leaders Renew Calls for the UK Government to Decriminalise Abortion." Press release, August 8. https://www.rcog.org.uk/news/women-s-health-leaders-renew-calls-for-the-uk-government-to-decriminalise-abortion/.

Scottish Government. 2022. "Health and Social Care." *Early medical abortion at home.* https://www.gov.scot/news/early-medical-abortion-at-home-1/.

Sheldon, S. 1995. "The Law of Abortion and the Politics of Medicalisation." In *Law and Body Politics: Regulating the Female Body*, edited by Jo Bridgeman and Susan Millns. Dartmouth.

Sheldon, S. 1997. *Beyond Control: Medical Power and Abortion Law*. Pluto Press.

Sheldon, S. 2016. "The Decriminalisation of Abortion: An Argument for Modernisation." *Oxford Journal of Legal Studies* 36 (2): 334–365. https://doi.org/10.1093/ojls/gqv026.

Sheldon, S., and K. Wellings. 2020. *Decriminalising Abortion in the UK: What Would it Mean?* Policy Press.

Simms, M. 1985. "Legal Abortion in Great Britain." in *The Sexual Politics of Reproduction*, edited by Hilary Homas. Gower Publishers.

Taylor, E. A. 2017. "British Attitudes to Abortion." *NatCen*.

Todd-Gher, J., and P. K. Shah. 2020. "Abortion in the Context of COVID-19: A Human Rights Imperative." *Sexual and Reproductive Health Matters* 28 (1): 1758394. https://doi.org/10.1080/26410397.2020.1758394.

Tongue, Z. L. 2022. "Telemedical and Self-Managed Abortion: A Human Rights Imperative?" *European Journal of Health Law* 30 (2): 158–181. https://doi.org/10.1163/15718093-bja10092.

Undurraga, V. 2014. "Proportionality in the Constitutional Review of Abortion Law." In *Abortion Law in Transnational Perspective*, edited by R. J. Cook, J. N. Erdman, and B. M. Dickens. University of Pennsylvania Press. https://doi.org/10.9783/9780812209990.77.

Watson, K. 2018. "Why We Should Stop Using the Term 'Elective Abortion.'" *AMA Journal of Ethics* 20 (12): E1175–1180. https://doi.org/10.1001/amajethics.2018.1175.

Wenham, C., E. Coast, K. Footman, T. Leone, R. Nandagiri, and J. Strong. 2020. "Abortion and Covid-19: Why We Need to Support Women's Right to Abortion in Health Emergencies" (blog). *LSE British Politics and Policy*, May 13. https://blogs.lse.ac.uk/internationaldevelopment/2020/05/13/abortion-and-covid-19-why-we-need-to-support-womens-right-to-abortion-in-health-emergencies/.

WHO (World Health Organization). 2020. *Maintaining Essential Health Services: Operational Guidance for the COVID-19 Context; Interim Guidance*, June 1. https://www.who.int/publications/i/item/WHO-2019-nCoV-essential_health_services-2020.2.

WHO. 2022. *Abortion Care Guideline*, March 8. https://www.who.int/publications/i/item/9789240039483.

Yamin, A. E., and P. Bergallo. 2017. "Narratives of Essentialism and Exceptionalism: The Challenges and Possibilities of Using Human Rights to Improve Access to Safe Abortion." *Health and Human Rights Journal* 19 (1): 1–11.

Yanow, S., L. B. Pizzarossa, and K. Jelinska. 2021. "Self-Managed Abortion: Exploring Synergies Between Institutional Medical Systems and Autonomous Health Movements." *Contraception* 104 (3): 219–221. https://doi.org/10.1016/j.contraception.2021.06.006.

Zurbriggen, R., B. Keefe-Oates, and C. Gerdts. 2018. "Accompaniment of Second-Trimester Abortions: The Model of the Feminist Socorrista Network of Argentina." *Contraception* 97 (2): 108–115. https://doi.org/10.1016/j.contraception.2017.07.170.

Index

For the benefit of digital users, indexed terms that span two pages (e.g., 52–53) may, on occasion, appear on only one of those pages.

Tables are indicated by an italic *t*.

Abdulwahab, Ismail Mohamed 135–136 n.16
abortion care, *see* United Kingdom, abortion care
Agamben, Giorgio 37–38
AIDS, *see* HIV/AIDS
Alpha variant of COVID 124
American Convention on Human Rights 3
Anand, Janet Carter 190–191, 198
anonymization of health-related research data 286–289, 293, *see also* data protection in public health emergencies
antiviral medications 47
Arend, Stefan 206
Aristotle 37–38
Australia
  abortion care 306–307
  COVIDSafe app 257–258 n.6, 271–272 n.5
  outdoor activity restrictions
    lessons for future pandemics 84–85
    overview of 81, 84*t*
    proportionality assessment of 81–84
Austria, COVID responses 63–64, 170
autonomy concerns 58–59, 65–66, 207–208, 213, 215, 324

Balthasar, Andreas 193–194
Barnett, Michael L. 211
Bautista-González, Elysse 93–94
Beauchamp, Tom L. 4, 64–65
beneficence principle 107–108, 171–172, 175, 212, 215–216
border closures 21–22, 143–144, 146–147
burden of proof for pandemic responses 17, 36–37

California, nursing home policies 166–167
Canada, nursing home policies 169
care homes, *see* nursing homes
caring *versus* curing decisions 23–25
Chia Shi-Lu 144
children
  Australia, playground closures 81
  impact of COVID responses on 14, 36, 107–108, 231, 249–250
  Switzerland, marginalization of 249–250
  in UK long-stay hospital wards, *see* United Kingdom, infection control in pediatric wards
  see also school closures; sexual and gender minority (SGM) youth
Childress, James F.
  hypothetical proportionality assessment 13–14, 16
  on pandemic management 68–69
  on proportionality generally 4–5, 11, 17, 64–65, 108
  on public health ethics 210, 321, 328
Chile, resource allocation
  bioethical guidelines on 22–23
  COVID responses in Chile 21–22
  holistic approach 24–25
  introduction to study 20–21
  media discourse on 22
Cianciardo, Juan 97–98
community decision-making, *see* public participation in decision-making
compliance with COVID policies
  European survey on 46
  in Hong Kong SAR, *see* Hong Kong SAR, contact tracing and digital tracking
  in Italy 31–32, 39
  in Mexico 94–96
  in Singapore 143
  in United Kingdom 124
  US states, uncertainty over 16–17
contact tracing and testing
  in Australia 83
  data protection implications, *see* data protection in public health emergencies
  digital technologies for 269

in Hong Kong SAR, *see* Hong Kong SAR, contact tracing and digital tracking
in Israel, *see* Israel, contact tracing by security services
in Italy 29–30
in Mexico 91–92, 100
sexual and gender minority (SGM) youth and 113
in Switzerland 56, 243
in United Kingdom 123–124
Conte, Giuseppe 29–30
Convention Against Torture and Other Cruel, Inhuman or Degrading Treatment or Punishment (UN) 185–186, 197–198
Cook, Rebecca 305–306
COVID-19 pandemic
compliance with policies, *see* compliance with COVID policies
deaths linked to, *see* COVID-related deaths
early stage, uncertainty during, *see* uncertainty in COVID-19 pandemic
ECtHR jurisprudence relevant to, *see* European Court of Human Rights (ECtHR), proportionality analysis by
exceptionalism during 37–38, 189, 199
abortion exceptionalism, *see* United Kingdom, abortion care
healthcare resource shortages in, *see* healthcare resource shortages
late stage 49, 146–147, 159, 257, 262, 275
media discourse in, *see* media discourse in COVID-19 pandemic
responses, impacts of, *see* inequitable impacts of COVID responses; psychological impacts of COVID responses
responses, overview of 1–2, 100–101
responses, specific, *see* contact tracing and testing; face mask requirements; lockdown policies; social distancing policies; vaccination campaigns
States' policies, *see* names of particular States
treatments for severe infections 47
WHO declaration of 89–90, 122–123
COVID-related deaths
in Chile 21–22
comparative data 91*f*, 92*f*
in Mexico 91–93
in Switzerland 48*f*
in United States 92–93, 156–162, 176*f*, 178*f*
without loved ones present 132, 135–136, 198
Cox, Caitríona 33
cultural competence/humility 117
Cuomo, Andrew 12–13
curing *versus* caring decisions 23–25

Dahal, Sushma 91–92
data protection in public health emergencies
European Data Protection Board on 273–274
GDPR (EU General Data Protection Regulation) on
anonymization rules 286–289
sensitive data processing, research exceptions 289–290
two-step compatibility test 285–286
introduction to study 285–286
proportionality assessments of
balancing competing interests 294–295
data subjects' interests relevant to 292–293
generally 291
lessons for future pandemics 295–297
necessity test 290–291
researchers' interests relevant to 294
technical-organizational measures to safeguard 293–294
see also privacy, right to
Delta variant of COVID 49, 146–147
Diedericks, Lienke 37–39
digital measures in COVID-19 pandemic
in Hong Kong SAR, *see* Hong Kong SAR, contact tracing and digital tracking
in Israel, *see* Israel, contact tracing by security services
other examples 257–258, 269–272
United Kingdom, telemedicine for abortion care, *see* United Kingdom, abortion care
due process 5–6

early medical abortion, *see under* United Kingdom, abortion care
Eisenberg, Maria E. 111
elderly persons
in Mexico 100
nursing home residents, *see* nursing homes
Switzerland, marginalization of 249–250
enforcement of COVID policies, *see* compliance with COVID policies
epidemiological research, data sharing, *see* data protection in public health emergencies

Erdman, Joanna 305–306, 321
European Committee for the for the Prevention of Torture and Inhuman or Degrading Treatment or Punishment 197
European Court of Human Rights (ECtHR), proportionality analysis by
COVID-19 pandemic cases 231–235
deferential approach in public health cases 224–225
derogations in public health crises 229–231
intensity of review 226–229
introduction to study 222–223
proportionality review formula, critique of 223–229, 234
see also proportionality principle
European Data Protection Board 273–274
European Health Data Space initiative 296–297
exceptionalism *versus* proportionality
abortion exceptionalism, *see* United Kingdom, abortion care
in COVID-19 pandemic 37–38, 189, 190*t*, 199
'executive underreach' concept 96–97
expert opinions, *see* scientific expertise

face mask requirements
in Australia 81, 84*t*
ECtHR case law on 232
in Italy 35–36
in Switzerland 56, 243–245
in United Kingdom 35–36, 124
in US nursing homes 163–165, 164*t*
Faden, Ruth 66–67
federal government decision-making in COVID-19 pandemic
Switzerland, public views on 57, 62–63, 67–68
United States 15–16
Finland, nursing home policies 169
Foronda, Cynthia 117
France, COVID responses 63–64
freedom of assembly 245
freedom of movement 34–35, 36–38, 232
fundamental rights and proportionality
ECtHR's approach, *see* European Court of Human Rights (ECtHR), proportionality analysis by
freedom of assembly 245
freedom of movement 34–35, 36–38, 232
generally 2–4, 97–98, 102, 186–187, 196–199, 224–225
health, right to 100–101, 239–240
human dignity right 7–8
inhuman or degrading treatment prohibition 185–186, 197–200
Israeli approach 259–260
privacy, *see* privacy, right to
Swiss approach, *see* Swiss Federal Supreme Court's proportionality assessments
see also proportionality principle

GDPR (EU General Data Protection Regulation), *see under* data protection in public health emergencies
gender minority youth, *see* sexual and gender minority (SGM) youth
Georgieva, Irina 46
Germany, mobile vaccination teams in nursing homes
background 208–209
introduction to study 205
lack of studies on 206
operational methods 206–209, 213–214
proportionality assessment of
ethical and human rights concerns 207–208, 211–214
public health benefits 209–210, 211–212
risk-benefit analysis 215–217
Giubilini, Alberto 214
Grabowski, David C. 211
Great Britain, *see* United Kingdom
Guidance for Managing Ethical Issues in Infectious Disease Outbreaks (WHO, 2016) 5–6, 34–35

Halliday, Samantha 324
health, right to 100–101, 239–240
health, WHO definition of 66–67, 262–263
'health deviance' in Covid-19 pandemic 199
healthcare resource shortages
caring *versus* curing decisions 23–25
in Chile, *see* Chile, resource allocation
as ethical issue 20–21
heroic healthcare workers narrative and 33
PPE (personal protection equipment) 123–124
healthcare workers
cultural competence/humility of 117
displays of solidarity with 31
hero narrative applied to 33
in Mexico 93–94

in Philippines 142–143, 147–148
PPE use, effects on patients 137–138, 208, 212
in Singapore, *see* Singapore, travel bans for healthcare workers
in United Kingdom 123–124, 126–127, 130–131, 136–139, 303–304, 312–313
in US nursing homes 162
vaccinations for 233, 241–242, 245
Hermerén, Göran 267–268, 301
Hernández Trujillo, José Manuel 94–95
HIV/AIDS
human rights response to AIDS crisis 228
hypothetical screening intervention 13–14, 16
SGM youth, interventions for, *see* sexual and gender minority (SGM) youth
Holzer, Felicitas 102 n.9
Hong Kong SAR, contact tracing and digital tracking
conclusions of study 280–281
digital measures overview 269–272
introduction to study 267–269
public reassurances about 272–274
vaccine pass requirements, proportionality reviews 275–280
hospital infection control measures
UK pediatric wards, *see* United Kingdom, infection control in pediatric wards
in United Kingdom generally 123–124, 132
human dignity right 7–8
human rights and proportionality, *see* fundamental rights and proportionality

inaction concept 89, 96–104, *see also* Mexico, delayed COVID response
inequitable impacts of COVID responses
on children and parents 14, 36, 107–108, 231, 249–250
pediatric patients, *see* United Kingdom, infection control in pediatric wards
in Chile, *see* Chile, resource allocation
domestic abuse increases 312–313
on lower-income workers 10–11, 94–96, 107–108, 157, 231, 274, 280–281
on nursing home residents, *see* nursing homes
outdoor space, unequal access to 36
regional socioeconomic contexts affecting 20–21
on SGM youth, *see* sexual and gender minority (SGM) youth
solidarity principle to offset 39–40, 67–68
Switzerland, public views on 60–61, 66–68
see also psychological impacts of COVID responses
inhuman or degrading treatment prohibition 185–186, 197–200
International Covenant on Civil and Political Rights (ICCPR) 3, 100, 259, 277–278
International Covenant on Economic, Social and Cultural Rights (ICESCR) 3, 100, 259, 277–278, 280
Ireland, nursing home policies 170
Israel, contact tracing by security services
background 256–258
balancing of rights principle in Israel 259–260
introduction to study 255
judicial review findings on 260–262
privacy right in Israel 258–259
proportionality assessment of 262–264
Italy, lockdown policies
background 29–30
introduction to study 28–29
master narratives justifying 32–33, 37–40
outdoor exercise ban 31, 34, 36, 38
proportionality assessment of 34–37
public responses to 31–32, 34

Jamrozik, Euzebiusz 38
justice, procedural 6, *see also* public participation in decision-making; transparency
justice, social, *see* inequitable impacts of COVID responses

Kirk, Jessica 37–38
Kritzinger, Sylvia 63–64

Latin America
case studies, *see* Chile, resource allocation; Mexico, delayed COVID response
health inequalities in 20–21
LGBTQI+ youth, *see* sexual and gender minority (SGM) youth
lockdown policies
in Australia, *see* Australia, outdoor activity restrictions
border closures 21–22, 143–144, 146–147
in Chile 21–22
compliance with, *see* compliance with COVID policies
ECtHR case law on 232

lockdown policies (*Continued*)
inequitable impacts of, *see* inequitable impacts of COVID responses
in Italy, *see* Italy, lockdown policies
in nursing homes, *see* nursing homes
places of worship closures 10, 14, 233–234
quarantine after positive tests, *see* quarantine rules
school closures, *see* school closures
'state of exception' arguments applied to 37–38
in Switzerland, *see* Switzerland, containment measures
uncertainty over effectiveness 12
in United Kingdom 122–124, 127
abortion care by telemedicine, *see* United Kingdom, abortion care
in US nursing homes, *see* US nursing homes, isolation policies
in US states, *see* US states, physical distancing policies
see also social distancing policies
López-Gatell Ramírez, Hugo 88–90
Lowy, Ilana 37–38

Madrigal-Borloz, Victor 110
Maestri, Mattia ('Patient 1' in Italy) 29–30, 34
Maina, Joseph 37–38
mandatory vaccinations 4–5, 214, 228–229
Mann, Jonathan 263
Martakis, Kyriakos 210
Massachusetts, nursing home policies 167–168
McDonald, Matt 37–38
media discourse in COVID-19 pandemic
in Chile 22
in Italy 31–32, 34
master narratives of 32–33, 38–40
Melbourne, outdoor activity restrictions, *see* Australia, outdoor activity restrictions
mental health concerns, *see* psychological impacts of COVID responses
Meretoja, Hanna 32–33
Mexico, delayed COVID response
background 90
introduction to study 88–89
other deficiencies
confusing guidelines 94, 100
of contact tracing and testing efforts 100
failure to adopt fiscal measures 96
of vaccination scheme 93–94, 100
weak enforcement 94–96
overview of measures 89–90
proportionality assessment of
cost-benefit analysis 102–104
criteria for 90
employment precarity context 94–96, 101, 103–104
excessive deaths estimated 91*f*, 91–93
inaction and proportionality principle 89, 96–99, 103–104
rights impact analysis 100–102
uncertainty context 101–103
Meyer, Frank 206
Miller, Robin Lin 112
Montel, Lisa 100–101
Mureainik, Etienne 97

Ndiritu, Nelson 37–38
Netherlands, nursing home policies 170–171
Nistelrooij, Inge van 65–66
noncompliance with COVID policies, *see* compliance with COVID policies
nonmaleficence principle 64–65, 107–108, 171–172, 212, 215–216
normative uncertainty 13
Nuffield Council on Bioethics 187–188, 190–191
nursing homes
COVID responses overview 162, 184–185, 189–191
social isolation effects
fundamental rights implications 186–187, 196–199
international studies 169–171
lessons for future pandemics 199–200
in Switzerland, *see* Swiss nursing homes, isolation policies
in United Kingdom 132, 171
in United States, *see* US nursing homes, isolation policies
vaccination campaigns
in Germany, *see* Germany, mobile vaccination teams in nursing homes
in United States 159*f*, 159, 165

Obrador, Andrés Manuel López 88–90
Odone, Anna 209–210
Omicron variant of COVID 49, 146–147, 159, 257, 262, 275
omissions and proportionality principle 98–99, 103–104
Ottley, Emily 315

outdoor activity restrictions
in Australia, *see* Australia, outdoor activity restrictions
in Italy 31, 34, 36, 38

pandemics, proportionality assessments, *see* COVID-19 pandemic; public health emergencies, proportionality assessments
Parmet, Wendy 109
personal autonomy concerns 58–59, 65–66, 207–208, 213, 215, 324
Philippines, travel bans for healthcare workers 142–143, 147–148
physical distancing policies, *see* lockdown policies; social distancing policies
places of worship closures 10, 14, 233–234
positive duties of states 98
Powers, Madison 66–67
Pozen, David E. 96–97
PPE (personal protection equipment) shortages 123–124
precautionary principle
generally 17–18, 82, 102–103
Israeli context 261–262
Italian context 35–36
Swiss context 187–189, 190*t*, 196, 248
see also uncertainty in COVID-19 pandemic
Principles and Guidelines on Human Rights and Public Health Emergencies (2023) 3–4
privacy, right to
case studies, *see* Hong Kong SAR, contact tracing and digital tracking; Israel, contact tracing by security services
data protection, *see* data protection in public health emergencies
generally 108–109, 135, 187–188, 259
mandatory vaccinations and 228–229
of nursing home residents 190–191, 200, 211, 215
of sexual and gender minority (SGM) youth 114–115
procedural justice 5–6, *see also* public participation in decision-making; transparency
proportionality principle
adequacy requirement 97–98
application, consistency analysis 5, 14
application, risk-benefit analysis 4–5, 11–12, 64–65, 79–80, 82–83
beneficence and nonmaleficence principles 64–65, 107–108, 171–172, 175, 212, 215–216
constitutional law basis requirement 97–98
ECtHR's application of, *see* European Court of Human Rights (ECtHR), proportionality analysis by
generally 2–4, 186–187, 267–269, 301
'least infringement' requirement 34–35, 79–80, 81–82, 97–98
omissions and 98–99, 103–104
as procedural justice safeguard 5–6, *see also* public participation in decision-making; transparency
Swiss application of, *see* Swiss Federal Supreme Court's proportionality assessments
vulnerability of 199–200
see also fundamental rights and proportionality; public health emergencies, proportionality assessments
pseudonymization of health-related research data 286–289, 293, *see also* data protection in public health emergencies
psychological impacts of COVID responses
on children 12
on healthcare workers 33, 136–139, 145–146, 148–150
of Italian outdoor exercise ban 36
physical confinement effects 10–11
on sexual and gender minority (SGM) youth 113
social isolation effects 10, 84*t*, 168–171
see also inequitable impacts of COVID responses
public health emergencies, proportionality assessments
autonomy concerns 58–59, 65–66, 207–208, 213, 215, 324
bioethical concerns 4–6, 107–109, 187–188, 210, 216*f*, 259
burden of proof for 17, 36–37
Childress *et al.* on, *see* Childress, James F.
data protection, *see* data protection in public health emergencies
delayed responses (Mexico case study), *see* Mexico, delayed COVID response
of ECtHR, *see* European Court of Human Rights (ECtHR), proportionality analysis by
evidence collection for 79–81, 84–85

public health emergencies, proportionality assessments (*Continued*)
  case studies criticizing, *see* Australia, outdoor activity restrictions; Italy, lockdown policies
 exceptionalism *versus* proportionality 37–38, 189, 190*t*, 199
 nursing home case studies, *see* nursing homes
 precautionary principle alternative, *see* precautionary principle
 Principles and Guidelines on (2023) 3–4
 resource allocation decisions (Chile case study), *see* Chile, resource allocation
 for SGM youth, *see* sexual and gender minority (SGM) youth
 solidarity principle for 39–40, 67–68
 by Swiss Federal Supreme Court, *see* Swiss Federal Supreme Court's proportionality assessments
 by Swiss public, *see* Switzerland, containment measures
 uncertainty context, *see* uncertainty in COVID-19 pandemic
 WHO guidance on (2016) 5–6, 34–35
 see also proportionality principle
public participation in decision-making
 as procedural justice safeguard 5–6
 relational autonomy concept and 65–66
 sexual and gender minority (SGM) youth participation 116
 in Switzerland 44–46, 57, 62–63, 196, 249–250
 in United Kingdom 132, 140
 see also transparency

quarantine rules
 Hong Kong SAR, digital enforcement, *see* Hong Kong SAR, contact tracing and digital tracking
 human rights implications 109
 Italy, noncompliance with 31
 Mexico, noncompliance with 94–95
 for sexual and gender minority (SGM) youth 113
 see also lockdown policies

RDE (rule of double effect) 4
relational autonomy 65–66
religious worship, restrictions on 10, 14, 233–234
resource shortages, *see* healthcare resource shortages
right to health 100–101, 239–240
risk assessment challenges, *see* uncertainty in COVID-19 pandemic
Robinson, Lisa A. 174
Rubin, Olivier 101–103
rule of double effect (RDE) 4

Scheppele, Kim L. 96–97
Schmidt-Semisch, Henning 199
school closures
 in Chile 21–22
 in Italy 31, 36
 Swiss measures to prevent 242, 244
 in United Kingdom 124
 in US states 12, 14
 see also children
Schorb, Elisabeth 199
Schröder-Bäck, Peter 210
scientific expertise
 in Italy 30
 research, data protection rules for, *see* data protection in public health emergencies
 Swiss public opinion on 54, 58–59, 62–63, 68
 trust in 68–69
 US public opinion on 63–64
 see also uncertainty in COVID-19 pandemic
self-isolation rules, *see* quarantine rules
Sen, Amartya 65–66
Sendai Framework 65–66
sexual and gender minority (SGM) youth
 definitions and demographic estimates 109–111
 introduction to study 107–109
 proportionate public health measures for
  data collection and conceptualization 114–116
  feasibility, acceptability and utility needs 116–118
  general recommendations 118–119
 stigma, health disparities arising from 111–114, 119
Sheldon, Sally 327, 330
Simms, Madeleine 325–326
Simoni, Alessandro 32
Singapore, travel bans for healthcare workers
 COVID response overview 143–144
 introduction to study 142–143

policy announcement and reactions 144–147
proportionality assessment of 147–151
Siracusa Principles 3–4
Smet, Stijn 224–225
social distancing policies
compliance with, *see* compliance with COVID policies
inequitable impacts of, *see* inequitable impacts of COVID responses
in Mexico 94
Switzerland, perceived proportionality of 56
in United Kingdom 123–124, 132–134
in US nursing homes, *see* US nursing homes, isolation policies
in US states, *see* US states, physical distancing policies
see also face mask requirements; lockdown policies
social justice concerns, *see* inequitable impacts of COVID responses
Socorristas en Red (Argentine abortion support group) 327–328
solidarity principle 39–40, 67–68
Squire, Corinne 32–33
stigma, health disparities arising from 111–114, 119, 196, 292, 294, 303–304, 320, 323–324
Swiss Federal Supreme Court's proportionality assessments
appropriateness test 244–246
collision of rights during COVID-19 pandemic 239–240
conclusions of study 251–252
density of review 246–247
duty to protect justification 249–250
emergency context and 250–251
introduction to study 237
necessity test 243–244
proportionality under Swiss Constitution 45–46, 47, 238–239
public interest assessments 241–242
public opinion contrasted with 62–65, 70
suitability test 242–243
uncertainty context and 247–248
Swiss nursing homes, isolation policies
fundamental rights implications 186–187, 196–199
introduction to study 184–186
overview of measures 191–194
proportionality assessment of
delegations of decision-making responsibility 193–195
failure to consult residents or relatives 196
lessons for future pandemics 199–200
prolonged adherence to precautionary principle 196
questionable efficacy of visiting bans 194–195
theoretical basis 186–191
see also US nursing homes, isolation policies
Switzerland, containment measures
judicial review of, *see* Swiss Federal Supreme Court's proportionality assessments
legal basis 44–46
for nursing homes, *see* Swiss nursing homes, isolation policies
popular support in referendums 44–46
public perception of proportionality of
acceptance of pandemic seriousness 54–62
autonomy concerns 58–59, 65–66
criteria for assessment 59–62
data collection period 47–49
decision-making on measures 57–59, 62–63, 68–69
measures deemed proportionate 55–57, 62
participants 51–53, 69
proportionality concept 62–65, 70
quotes in original languages 71–75
rejection of pandemic seriousness 53–54, 62–64
research method 50–51
social justice concerns 60–61, 66–68
vaccination certificates 45, 48, 56, 68

Tan, Cheryl 148–149
telemedicine for abortion care, *see* United Kingdom, abortion care
teleworking 10–11
Texas, nursing home policies 167
Toebes, Brigit 108–109
torture prohibition 185–186, 197–200
track and test schemes, *see* contact tracing and testing
transgender young persons, *see* sexual and gender minority (SGM) youth
transparency
as procedural justice principle 5–6
right to health and 100–101

transparency (*Continued*)
Swiss containment measures and 45–46, 61, 68
trust related to 68–69, 273–274
WHO guidance on 34–35
see also public participation in decision-making
travel bans for healthcare workers
in the Philippines 142–143, 147–148
in Singapore, *see* Singapore, travel bans for healthcare workers
Trump, Donald 11

uncertainty in COVID-19 pandemic
generally 11–14, 228
Mexican decision-makers' responses 101–103
precautionary principle, *see* precautionary principle
Swiss Federal Supreme Court's responses 247–248
US state governors' responses, *see* US states, physical distancing policies
Undurraga, Veronica 328–329
United Kingdom
abortion care, *see* United Kingdom, abortion care
COVID response overview 35–36, 122–124
nursing home policies 132, 171
pediatric wards, infection control measures, *see* United Kingdom, infection control in pediatric wards
United Kingdom, abortion care
in COVID-19 pandemic 307–311, 314–315, 322–324
early medical abortion, drugs and regimens 302–303, 323
introductions to studies 300–302, 320–321
medicalization of abortion, proportionality assessment 325–326, 330
in Northern Ireland 304–305, 321–323
regulatory regime, proportionality assessment 303–307, 314, 322–323, 324–325, 328–329
in Scotland 302–303 n.4, 305, 309–311, 312 n.11, 322–324
self-managed abortion, proportionality assessment 326–328
by telemedicine, future prospects 311, 315, 329–331
United Kingdom, infection control in pediatric wards
background 124–125
broken ward communities, effects of 127–131
conclusions of study 139–140
overview of 125–126
parents, effects on 96–103
purposes of 126–127
ward staff, effects on 136–139
United States
COVID-related deaths in 92–93, 156–162, 176*f*, 178*f*
nursing home policies, *see* US nursing homes, isolation policies
scientific expertise, public perceptions of 63–64
SGM youth in, *see* sexual and gender minority (SGM) youth
state-level COVID policies, *see* US states, physical distancing policies
Universal Declaration of Human Rights 7–8, 98
US nursing homes, isolation policies
COVID-related deaths in nursing homes 157–162, 176*f*, 178*f*
effects of isolation on 168–169
COVID vulnerability of residents 156–157, 177*f*
federal-level policies over time 163–166
introduction to study 155
proportionality assessment of
ethical focus need 171–172
intangible values incorporation 174–175
quantitative analysis, challenges of 172–174
psychological and cognitive effects on residents 168–170
relatives, effects on 170–171
state-level policies 166–168
see also Swiss nursing homes, isolation policies
US states, physical distancing policies
introduction to study 10–11
in nursing homes 166–168
sources of uncertainty for governors
costs *versus* benefits 12–14
effectiveness of measures 12
federal government support 15–16
other states' support 15–16
public compliance 16–17
uncertainty management, lessons from case study 17–18

vaccination campaigns
alleged moral duty to be vaccinated 214
in Chile 22
in German nursing homes, *see* Germany, mobile vaccination teams in nursing homes
for healthcare workers 233, 241–242, 245
Hong Kong SAR, vaccine pass requirements 275–280
mandatory vaccinations 4–5, 214, 228–229
in Mexico 93–94
public health benefits 209–210, 211–212
risk-benefit analysis for 107–108, 215–217
in Singapore 146–147
Switzerland, vaccination certificates 45, 48, 56, 68
in United Kingdom 124
in US nursing homes 159*f*, 159, 165
Valfort, Marie-Anne 110
Velasco-Ibarra, Eugenio 89–90, 95–96
Vigezzi, Giacomo Pietro 209–210

working from home 10–11
World Health Organization (WHO)
on abortion care 302–303, 304–305, 328
COVID-19 declared as global pandemic by 89–90, 122–123
COVID response recommendations 100–101
Guidance for Managing Ethical Issues in Infectious Disease Outbreaks (2016) 5–6, 34–35
'health' definition 66–67, 262–263
on Omicron variant of COVID 49
pandemic preparedness recommendations (2005) 30
worship, restrictions on 10, 14, 233–234

young people, *see* children; sexual and gender minority (SGM) youth

www.ingramcontent.com/pod-product-compliance
Ingram Content Group UK Ltd.
Pitfield, Milton Keynes, MK11 3LW, UK
UKHW040920150926
475595UK00008B/186/J

9 780197 759349